CITIES OF THE SOUTH

.

CITIES OF THE SOUTH

Citizenship and Exclusion
in the Twenty-first Century

Edited by

Barbara Drieskens,
Franck Mermier
and Heiko Wimmen

SAQI

in association with

Heinrich Böll Foundation
Institut Français du Proche-Orient

ISBN: 978-0-86356-611-0

A full CIP record for this book is available from the British Library.
A full CIP record for this book is available from the Library of Congress.

Manufactured in Lebanon

SAQI

www.saqibooks.com

in association with

HEINRICH
BÖLL
FOUNDATION

www.boell-meo.org

and

www.ifporient.org

Contents

Cities and Globalisation – Challenges for Citizenship

The Heinrich Böll Foundation, a German political foundation affiliated with the Green Party, is concerned with civic education, the promotion of democracy and the peaceful resolution of conflicts. One of the key concepts guiding this work is the idea of 'active citizenship' – meaning an understanding of citizenship centred around and building upon the active participation of citizens in the shaping of society, not only by casting their ballots in elections, but through direct involvement in political processes and the public sphere on a constant, even daily basis. Such involvement can manifest itself in the formation of citizens' initiatives, by participating in NGOs or by influencing decisions through lobbying, media campaigns or direct political action. Quite often it sets out to challenge conventional wisdom, established procedures and the hegemony of powerful interest groups entrenched within institutions and administrations, insisting that the broader public has a right to know and a right to have a say. As the namesake of our foundation, the German novelist and Nobel laureate Heinrich Böll, once put it: 'Meddling is the only way to stay relevant.'

Today, such 'meddling' or active citizenship faces the challenges of intensified global integration on the political and economic level. As authority and decision-making are being moved away from national to regional or international levels and bodies, the chances of citizens to make their voices heard and to make a difference seem to be diminishing. How can mobilisation against certain economic policies hope to succeed if those policies are imposed by international agreements or bodies that are beyond the reach of public pressure, and not accountable in elections? How can a citizen initiative, say, hope to preserve the character of an urban neighbourhood if the headquarters of a multinational corporation or international agency opens next door, and real estate prices go through the roof?

The issue appears even more relevant in the metropolises of the Global South. Rather than opening up new horizons and opportunities, globalisation here seems likely to bring about the final collapse of the modernist narrative, which expects development and urbanisation to engender a process of rapid (if at times violent) homogenisation and inclusion, leading to political struggles over the meaning of membership, participation and rights that will eventually engender the emergence of the *citoyen*/citizen/*Staatsbürger*. Rather, the elites of the Global South appear to be bypassing the local and national arena on both the political and the economic level, and tend to retreat to (sub)urban enclaves insulated against active forms of citizenship by a mix of economic and security-related barriers. Rather than becoming strategic sites for the making of modern citizens, cities of the Global South may be seen as the most blatant manifestation of a New World Order built upon the exclusion of ever-larger population segments as 'surplus humanity'.[1]

On the other hand, globalisation also offers an opportunity to take 'meddling', or civil action, to global levels. Internationally organised consumer boycotts have more than once forced large corporations to amend environmentally hazardous practices. Defenders of human rights rely more and more on international campaigns. Linking up to an emerging global civil society and accessing global media have become crucial – and in many instances, the only – means for those attempting to resist marginalisation and exclusion to bypass the local structures of authoritarian power-wielders and safeguarding and restoring their citizenship and often basic human rights. While the campaigns themselves become de-territorialised, they still seem to need the urban space as a framework within which to develop the sense of community and common purpose necessary to engender a dynamics of action and a momentum for change, and as the stage to enact this momentum in a physical public sphere for it to become self-sustaining. In 2005, both the public movements in the Ukraine and in Lebanon succeeded largely because they were able to capture the national, and later the international, imagination by claiming physical urban space charged with historic significance and emotion.

Such examples show that despite accelerated global integration we are witnessing, public space and in particular urban space remain crucial as the physical places where citizens interact, but also as sites where globalisation and its symbols implant themselves and may be contested. How these spaces are shared or struggled over thus affects the degree to which citizens experience globalisation as a process that is accessible to them and that can enrich their lives and open new avenues of participation, rather than perceiving it as a one-way process bound to strip them of whatever agency and autonomy they used to have.

So far, research on the consequences of globalisation for concepts of national sovereignty, and with it the practices and principles of citizenship attached to the nation state, has largely focused on the Northern Hemisphere, and on cities such as New York, London or Tokyo. But globalisation, as the word itself indicates, does not stop at the outskirts of these cities. It also affects the lives of citizens in metropolises such as Cairo, Casablanca or Istanbul, and the effects on citizenship in these societies might be quite different, and even more profound. To gain a more comprehensive understanding, it seems necessary to go beyond the notion of only one model of global integration and to examine how the phenomenon unfolds in different geographical settings.

Setting out from these considerations, the Middle East Office of the Heinrich Böll Foundation and the Institut Français du Proche-Orient in Beirut have worked with each other for a period of nearly two years to bring together a group of young researchers to tackle these questions from a variety of disciplinary angles and for different geographical settings, initiating exchanges and dialogues on a South-South axis. Their findings were presented at a dedicated conference held in Beirut in December 2005, and during the Second World Conference of Middle Eastern Studies in Amman in June 2006. While the Middle East and North Africa took clear prominence in the contributions, due both to the professional and academic backgrounds of the organisers and the audiences at the public events, the results of this endeavour would seem relevant to other areas characterised by rapid urbanisation and uneven development that are not covered here, such as Sub-Saharan Africa or Southeast Asia, and will hopefully help broaden the debate over the effects of globalisation on citizenship beyond the conventional frame of reference focused on the industrialised North.

Kirsten Maas[2] and Heiko Wimmen

Notes

1. Davis, Mike, *Planet of Slums*, London, New York: 2006, p. 174.
2. Director, Heinrich Böll Foundation – Middle East Office, 2004–2006.

Towards New Cosmopolitisms

In the increasingly massive literature on the city and on fashionable notions such as citizenship and globalisation,[1] the present volume aims to enrich the debate by rooting reflections in particular urban experiences. We choose very different and contrasting examples of Southern experiences to underline how global processes are mainly expressed in a diversity of local responses. Despite their supposed generalising and homogenising effects, processes of globalisation produce in the first place differences. Rather than speaking of globalisation as a singular noun, we should pluralise it to refer to the different historical processes of globalisation and to the many contextual ways of understanding the concept. We look at 'Cities of the South', and even if we consider the notion of 'South' here in a geographic sense, its ideological connotation (South versus North, periphery versus centre, rich versus poor) is inevitable. Each space has its own 'South'; we talk about the slums of Mumbai, the *favelas* of Rio, the *dahiye* of Beirut. We are looking at the geographic South with particular attention to the places of exclusion as structural complement for the centre. This requires an anthropological attention with an eye for what remains invisible: multiple facets of globalisation remain to be explored, particularly in the cities of the South where the urban takes unprecedented forms due to its particular positioning in the hegemonic order of globalisation.

Our unit of analysis is 'the city' that is still too often applied as a universal concept with general characteristics that mask the multiple urban realities. In the context of the South, the city can be understood in different ways, and is reinvented in new and always singular ways. Case studies show the stringent effects of globalising processes on urban expansion and transformation, sharpening social distinctions and the disproportional division of resources, well-being and social rights.

The case studies in this book are taken from different countries with an emphasis on Middle Eastern cities, which shouldn't astonish the reader knowing that the encounter between the different contributors was set in Beirut. We could, however, reflect for a moment on some particularities of the Arab city. The ancient character of its urban society led to the accumulation of multiple strata of civilisation that crystallised in the Islamic era, giving it its salient features of which the association bazaar-mosque led to the construction of numerous theoretical models.[2] Contemporary Arab cities cannot be understood from the perspectives of culturalist models because their specificity – if it exists – cannot be reduced to religious or cultural factors and their common features are due more to the urban crisis that they share than to their belonging to a supposedly single cultural area. At the same time, it is very well possible that globalisation tends to produce new types of apparent homogeneity such as media spaces, consumption patterns, social and spatial segregation and new family patterns that produce urban but also regional identities. On the privileged scene of the city, globalisation seems to produce a new cultural pan-Arabism, springing from the dialectic between globalisation and regionalisation.

In 2007, for the first time in human history, the number of people living in cities will surpass the rural population. Ninety-five per cent of this increase will occur in cities located in poor countries. In twenty-five years, developing countries will comprise 4 billion inhabitants, about 80 per cent of the urban population of the world.[3] Saskia Sassen summarised the new paradigm of the place of the city in globalisation processes (which has become, nowadays, the new creed of globalisation studies):

> We see a re-scaling of the strategic territories that articulate the
> new system. With the partial unbundling or at least weakening of
> the national as a spatial unit come conditions for the ascendance
> of other spatial units and scales. Among these are the sub-national,
> notably cities and regions; cross-border regions encompassing
> two or more sub-national entities and supra-national entities, i.e.
> global digitised markets and free-trade blocs.[4]

The role of the nation-state in the process of globalisation is today a point of dissent between those who predict its dissolution and those who look at the creative ways states adapt to the new context. Still, it is quite generally agreed upon that cities form the nodes in the grid of globalisation and play an increasingly important role. Today, however, it is the category of the city itself that must be questioned, with its increase in size and density; its internal contradiction between suburbs and centre; and changes in its social, political and economic life. Alongside the rise of the so-called 'global cities', we observe the emergence of cities mirroring the globalised, in a melting pot of differentiated globalisations on their own scale and linking local fragmented identities to the national and the global. The urban remains, therefore, a significant unit of analysis to question social dimensions and contemporary transformations. An approach from the perspective of the city as a scene of movement and not as an enclosed world can help us avoid falling into the bias of an unquestioned paradigm of the city. While discussing contemporary African cities, Dominique Malaquais writes that scholars, urbanists and architects, in their discussions of the urban in Africa today, use concepts and representations of the city that mostly originate in Europe and North America more than a century ago.[5] He adds that these concepts are badly adapted to African realities today. We would like to broaden this idea to encompass all the cities of the South. It is mainly around notions such as place, borders, belonging and urban identity that a new reflection needs to be developed, grounded in concrete urban experiences to reformulate the category of city and its universal assumptions.

The notion of urbanity is often used to denote the socio-cultural identity of the inhabitants of the city or to refer to a type of social organisation proper to urban society – a perspective we've inherited from Simmel, the Chicago School, Goffman and de Certeau.[6] These authors use this notion to refer to the incessant movement of undifferentiated masses, with its heterogeneity that imposes an attitude of reserve and suspicion[7] and necessitates the adoption of the protective cover of anonymity inherent to the urban phenomenon and governing the social relations in public spaces.[8] In many studies on globalisation these traits are presented as characterising the 'global city', implying that globalisation enforces and exaggerates these tendencies. Indeed, Robin Cohen mentions that the inhabitants of global cities are confronted with 'the need to confront and oppose the anonymous, rational, meritocratic, progressive and universal elements of globalisation'.[9] This process has also produced cosmopolitan realities that are often constraining and inevitable, and that could appear as the dark side of globalisation (forced migrations, 'sweatshops', the trafficking of persons, the drug trade, etc).

In fact, cosmopolitanism cannot only be defined as 'a willingness to engage with the other and be restricted to dilettantes or connoisseurs'.[10] In fact cosmopolitanism is 'infinite ways of being' and cannot be confined to a single, positive definition.[11] Ulrich Beck argues that the process of 'cosmopolitisation' refers to latent forms of cosmopolitism, unconscious, passive, that are often the secondary consequences of world trade or global threats such as natural climate disasters, terrorism and financial crisis. He writes:

> ... my existence, my body, my own life become part of a different world, of culture, of religion, of foreign histories and global risks related to interdependence without my knowledge and my will.[12]

Alain Tarrius, with his concept of 'circulatory territories', reveals the appearance of new forms of cosmopolitism that imply the distancing of family ties simultaneously with learning to circulate between different normative worlds. These new forms of otherness, these identities that are strange more than different, are constructed and recognised at the dawn of the ability to belong here and there simultaneously, to contest and transform the laws of the reproduction of identity based upon family and local belongings.[13]

Who Inhabits the City?

The vocabulary of politics in European languages is strongly marked by the city and its forms of social relationships. From the Greek term *polis*, city, the term of *polites*, citizen, is derived. The Latin word *civitas*, denoting the city and referring to territorial belonging, is derived from the term *civis*, which refers more to relationships between the citizens.[14] While the notion of citizenship in Arabic was derived from the term *watan*, nation, terms referring to the notion of civil (as in civil society) or civility come from the term *madina*, city. James Holston and Arjun Appadurai remind us of the common dichotomy between the national and the global in relation to the issue of citizenship and national identity, and that cities remain 'especially privileged sites for considering the current renegotiations of citizenship'.[15] Cities have been considered the birth ground of European citizenship; can they play the same role in the countries of the South, caught up in globalising processes that tend to universalise the democratic ideal without much questioning and without adapting it to the context?

Balibar suggests that peripheral zones, where most cities of the South can be situated, are melting pots for the formation of citizenship in the democratic tradition because of the intensity of the struggle between secular and religious cultures and the sharpness of socio-economic differences.[16] Indeed:

> The confrontation with different forms of exclusion (social and
> therefore political since these two notions have never been really
> separated) always constitute the basis of citizenship and the
> periodical touchstone of its veracity.[17]

With the enormous growth and transformation of contemporary cities and
the accelerated urbanisation of whole societies, the urban context is more
and more marked by the dissociation of different forms of belonging: being
a citizen, belonging to the city and inhabiting the city are conditions that
cannot be assimilated.

New identities engendered by the urban experience become mobilising
forces for new claims to participation, inclusion and belonging. In his
chapter on Sofia and Alicante, Alain Tarrius shows in detail how new
forms of migration structure European cities, introducing new socio-spatial
morphologies. These morphologies born from 'circulatory territories' emerge
in parallel to other spaces created by the global flows of consumer society,
filtered by local agents. These agents of globalisation are not restricted to
urban elites who often adopt discourses of hybridism and *métissage* to their
own celebrations, but are also found among merchants, new Diasporas and
entrepreneurs operating in close proximity to or, on the contrary, completely
outside the state. New forms of mediation arise, limited and shaped by the
degree of openness and closure the state apparatus imposes on transnational
flows. To what extent do these modes of economic investment and forms
of mobility create new territorial and political belongings, which reshape
the notion of citizenship? Leïla Vignal analyses the emergence of a new
geography of consumption that combines the dynamics of globalisation and
state policies in Beirut, Damascus and Cairo. She pays particular attention
to the networks of globalised consumption and their territorialisation in
these metropolises. Diane Singerman, in her chapter on Cairo, focuses on
the new urban-based cosmopolitan geography and mobilisation related to
consumption and the increasing conflicts over public spaces.

Governing the City

On the political level the city can appear as a metonym of the relations
between the state and its subjects. This is even more pertinent in the context
of the countries of the South, where the mechanism delegating local power is
often oriented towards the maintenance of a high level of control rather than
towards the political representation of the populations. This phenomenon
has been enforced by a mode of political governance and administration

that remains remote from and is little representative of the social content of the city.

A recent dynamic has emerged with the affirmation of new sectors in civil society perceived as a third sector between the public and the merchant ones.[18] The right to the city becomes a claim shared by different and distinct actors from servants and immigrants to business elites.

> The concentration of (transnational) servants, for example, allows them a strategic position they could never gain in small towns. This 'presence', [as] Sassen suggests, translates into the possibility of laying claims on the city, and allows these actors to unbundle the conditions of their powerlessness and to develop a form of politics that not only gives them visibility but that also has the potential of challenging the global elites' project.[19]

Cities form the scene where national powers and international actors experiment with new forms of governing; new power relations are introduced, contested and reinforced. They offer a space for social and political mobilisation. Even if the processes involved surpass the urban territory, it still remains the symbolic base of political expression. It is the city that determines the expression and forms of crises.

Pierre Hamel, Henri Lustiger-Thaler and Margit Mayer argue that:

> ... it is impossible to speak about grassroots democracy, a defining characteristic of the progressive urban movement, without addressing the impact of globalisation, as both constraining or enabling phenomenon which connects the mundane of everyday life to discussions on the new forms of social and global citizenship detected in a locally inscribed practice.[20]

Processes of globalisation create new opportunities, but for how many cities and for whom within these cities? They generate an increasing fragmentation of urban spaces and societies. Large proportions of the urban population receive no benefits and even suffer the negative effects of these selective and excluding processes.

Under the influence of global discourses on 'good governance', the Moroccan government introduced several reforms reorganising the distribution of power between local authorities and national ones. Myriam Catusse shows us in her chapter how decentralisation doesn't necessarily lead to the deconcentration of power or to the increased political representation of the inhabitants of the city. The conflicts provoked by these reforms led, unexpectedly, also to the re-politicisation of the urban space.

With the example of Dubai, Marc Lavergne analyses the contents of citizenship in a city-state where citizens are the minority and where their status is linked with the social and political marginalisation of the overwhelming majority of the inhabitants and with their tribal affiliation and allegiance to the *emir*. In the case of Dubai, should we therefore speak of citizens or subjects? By referring to the paradox of Dubai, the author describes a particular urban model that characterises the Gulf states, notably with regard to its segregation patterns that are inscribed in the morphology of the city as much as in urban practices. Their relations with the outside, through the mediation of merchant networks or a mobility in search of entertainment and modern education, have contributed to the formation of a certain kind of cosmopolitanism as a factor of innovation which is, however, quite different from the kind that characterises, for example, Beirut. Beirut's cosmopolitanism stems from a Mediterranean urban order that was both colonial and Ottoman, and which connected the chain of port cities from Algiers to Alexandria.[21] In Beirut of the 1970s, as Melhem Chaoul explains in his chapter, leftist and nationalist demonstrations were organised according to a well-established ritual reflecting the vertical and hierarchical relation to the leader. These demonstrations had a very particular itinerary through the city, with strong symbolic connotations. After the killing of Prime Minister Rafik Hariri in February 2005, a new form of demonstration and political mobilisation seemed to develop. Do these new patterns reflect a potential for new power relations and new forms of political participation?

Spaces of Exclusion

Urban expansion and processes of globalisation not only have an impact on the urban morphology and on relations between centre and periphery, but also redefine social frontiers within the city. These are translated in spatial practices, introducing a multiplicity of implicit and permeable frontiers as well as clearly cut and intransigent borders that cross over and cut up urban space, confining spaces for the excluded – such as refugee camps, *favelas* or detention spaces – and defining exclusive spaces for the rich and powerful, such as gated communities and business districts.

If, in some cases, globalisation leads to the disconnection between the city and its hinterland as mentioned by Cohen,[22] there is often a complementary relationship between both despite the dichotomy and the extreme contrasts. The periphery does not only provide the cheap labour and necessary consumers for the globalised centre; it plays an active role as essential constituent of the city. Spaces such as slums, squats and camps are also spaces where urban models are constructed: Michel Agier, in his chapter, speaks of 'the invention of the city' in refugee camps that are precarious and provisional places, but over the course of time adopt an air of urbanity. There are also the zones of protection, detention centres and refugee camps; Engin Isin and Kim Rygiel argue that global cities are in need of such spaces that regulate global mobility.

Marginal spaces and spaces of exclusion play an active role in the production of the city through processes of transformation and inversion. Informal quarters are a typical example of the first process where informality always seems to also involve a process of formalisation. The *favelas* of Rio de Janeiro, studied by Mariana Cavalcanti, are simultaneously integrated into the city through the gradual transformation of temporary constructions into brick and through the legalisation of their status. On the other hand, these neighbourhoods remain outside and are even an inversion of the city, as territories of the drug trade and therefore stigmatised moral regions.

A new urban cosmopolitanism inscribes itself in these geographies of centrality and marginality, producing places within the city that are culturally marked and with their transnational connections, on the one hand are highly localised and on the other transcending locality.[23] The link between globalisation and new forms of cosmopolitism invites us to reconsider the definition of the urban and to introduce cosmopolitism as one of the characteristics that permit us to evaluate the degree of 'urbanity' of the cities. The specific cosmopolitism of each city becomes a universal characteristic of cities in general.

Imagining the City

The different forms of urbanisation and multiple ways of appropriating urban space provide competing ways of territorialising identity. Territory has become an interplay of relationships expressed through the organisation of powers, the development of feelings of belonging, legal or spontaneous forms of appropriation, practices and uses, representations and imaginaries.[24] These can be hegemonically expressed in urban planning, in the commodification of space, strategies of avoidance (Sharon Zukin speaks of 'cappuccino strategies'[25]) or, on the contrary, they can sneak in from below in informal quarters, slums or squats, reshaping the urban and constituting increasingly large parts of it especially in the cities of the South.[26]

Contemporary urban culture is characterised by a rough competition between cities selling their images. This process turns heritage into an asset for the marketing of cities, from which cities of the South are not exempt. Zukin argues that culture becomes a powerful means of controlling cities:

> As a source of images and memories, it symbolises 'who belongs' in specific places. As a set of architectural themes it plays a leading role in urban redevelopment strategies based on historic preservation or local 'heritage'.[27]

Heritage becomes an important tool to attract foreign investment and, as Ayşe Öncü shows in her chapter on Istanbul, a way to produce an identity that is supposed to represent an urban but also national ideal that responds to the global model of cosmopolitism. In this way the global feeds on the local by transforming it, and the local responses contribute to the diversification of the global without effectively challenging globalisation. Today the city is the privileged scene where invention of tradition serves the invention of cosmopolitanism more than the invention of the national or the local.

While the figure of the stranger is constitutive for the city and the city includes territories of otherness, processes of globalisation can produce deterritorialised spaces that do not function as public spaces of encounter. The exacerbated commodification of urban territory creates exclusive places of urban representation that are increasingly alienated from its inhabitants. Thus real estate speculation, economic stakes and struggles for domination are inscribed in the urban architecture of messages that are to be consumed and that define identities and customers.[28]

However, Vyjayanthi Rao, in her chapter, shows how one kind of space can transform in the other, and how spaces of exclusion such as squats and slums, which arose in the deadly shadows of textile mills, chemical factories, toxic dumps and in the margins of railroads and highways (to paraphrase Mike Davis[29]) become desirable spaces for speculation and investment. Rao shows, through analysis of the Mumbai phenomenology, the relationship between architectural forms, spatial imagination and social exclusion. Indeed:

> The problem is not only the access of certain groups to certain portions of the urban space, but also the way the occupation or the exclusion of quarters and buildings is manifested in space, of which the cultural identities are inscribed in the facades, the shop displays, the places of circulation.[30]

Public space in the city can be considered as the threshold between local spaces and practices on the one hand and increasing long-distance interconnectedness on the other. The degree of anonymity, accessibility and hospitability of the spaces of a city reflect on the emanation of the city as public sphere. This is an important criterion of the urban that differentiates between the cultural role of cities as vectors of cosmopolitanism. Mermier shows that Beirut has contributed to the constitution of a pan-Arabic public sphere through the development of the Lebanese publishing sector.

In the case of Beirut, its cosmopolitism survived even the departure of foreigners, as happened during the civil war 1975–90, and is not anymore the result of a co-presence of different communities but is translated in a plural identity of spaces and persons, of cultural models and lifestyles. Beirut is not bound by a well-established national identity. The symbolic frontiers of Lebanese society are as permeable as its national borders, leading to co-existing, non-consensual definitions of who is included and who is not.

The notion of citizenship has always been tied up with the nation and therefore includes the definitions of borders and modes of exclusion that characterise the nation-state. The idea of a cosmopolitan citizenship could be a different name for universalism and appears as a reaction to the imposed character and negative consequences of globalisation processes. It refers also to the plurality of identities and spatial belongings, and to the development of individuality that characterises the metropolis, according to Simmel.[31] This universal cosmopolitism is in the first place an expression of a way of relating to the world, 'the mundane condition of man'.[32] It should, however, be differentiated from the particular modes of being cosmopolitan in the different practices of urban heterogeneity. This alerts us to the tension that exists between a certain reductionist sociology, with its universal categories and the multiplicity of the anthropological, everyday experiences. We often have an idealised comprehension of cosmopolitanism in the encounter with the other, but the urban experiences of today teach us that the cosmopolitism of the city rests also on hierarchies and forms of exclusion intrinsically related to mobility. Despite its uncertain definition, cosmopolitism could offer an intellectual tool to think about the articulation between the individual, the plurality of social worlds and the new paradigm of the city as it arises from the cities of the South.

Barbara Drieskens and Franck Mermier

Bibliography

Bacqué, Marie-Hélène, Blance, Maurice, Hamel, Pierre and Sintomer, Yves, 'Editorial', in *Espaces et Sociétés, Ville, action "citoyenne" et débat public*, 123/4, 2005, p. 10.

Balibar, Etienne, *Nous, citoyens d'Europe? Les frontières, l'Etat, le peuple*, Paris: La Découverte, 2001.

Beck, Ulrich, *Qu'est-ce que le cosmopolitisme?*, Paris: Aubier, 2006.

Benveniste, Emile, 'Deux modèles linguistiques de la cité', in *Echanges et communications, Mélanges offerts à Claude Lévi-Strauss*, vol. 1, The Hague: Mouton, 1970.

Cohen, Robin, *Global Diasporas. An Introduction*, Seattle: University of Washington Press, 1997.

Davis, Mike, 'Planet of Slums', in *New Left Review*, 26, 2004, pp. 5–34.

Gérard, Valérie, 'Etre citoyen du monde', in *Tumultes (Citoyennetés cosmopolitiques)*, 24, May 2005, pp. 13–25.

Grafmeyer, Yves and Joseph, Isaac, 'Présentation. La ville laboratoire et le milieu urbain', in Yves Grafmeyer and Isaac Joseph, eds, *L'école de Chicago. Naissance de l'écologie urbaine*, Paris: Aubier, 1984, pp. 5–52.

Hamel, Pierre, Lustiger-Thaler, Henri and Mayer, Margit, 'Introduction', in Pierre Hamel, Henri Lustiger-Thaler and Margit Mayer, eds, *Urban Movements in a Globalizing World*, London and New York: Routledge, 2000, pp 1–22.

Hannerz, Ulf, *Transnational Connections*, London and New York: Routledge, 1996.

Holston, James, ed., *Cities and Citizenship*, Durham: Duke University Press 1999.

Holston, James and Appadurai, Arjun, 'Introduction: Cities and Citizenship', in James Holston, ed., *Cities and Citizenship*, Durham and London: Duke University Press 1999, pp. 1–18.

Ilbert, Robert, 1991, 'De Beyrouth à Alger. La fin d'un ordre urbain', in *Vingtième siècle*, 32, pp. 15–24.

Isin, Engin, ed., *Democracy, Citizenship and the Global City*, London: Routledge, 2000.

Mondada, Lorenza, *Décrire la ville. La construction des savoirs urbains dans l'interaction et dans le texte*, Paris: Anthropos, 2000.

Pétonnet, Colette, 'L'anonymat ou la pellicule protectrice', in *Le Temps de la Réflexion (La ville inquiète)*, 1986, pp. 247–61.

Roncayolo, Marcel, 'La ville est toujours la ville de quelqu'un', in *De la ville et du citadin*, Marseille: Editions Parenthèses, 2003, pp. 52–73.

Sassen, Saskia, 'Locating Cities on Global Circuits', in *Environment and Urbanization*, vol. 14, 2002, pp. 13–30.

—— 'Whose City is It? Globalization and the Formation of New Claims', in

James Holston, ed., *Cities and Citizenship*, Durham and London: Duke University Press, 1999, pp. 177–94.

Simmel, Georg, 'Métropoles et mentalité', in Yves Grafmeyer et Isaac Joseph, eds, *L'école de Chicago. Naissance de l'écologie urbaine*, Paris: Aubier, 1984, pp. 61–77.

Tarrius, Alain, *Les nouveaux cosmopolitismes. Mobilités, identités, territoires*, La Tour d'Aigues: Editions de l'Aube, 2000.

Wirth, Eugene, 'Villes islamiques, villes arabes, villes orientales? Une problématique face au changement', in Abdelwahab Boudhiba and Dominique Chevallier, eds, *La ville arabe dans l'Islam*, Tunis-Paris: CERES-CNRS, 1982, pp. 193–225.

Zukin, Sharon, *The Cultures of Cities*, Oxford: Blackwell, 1995.

Notes

1. See, for example, Isin, ed., *Democracy, Citizenship and the Global City*; Holston, ed., *Cities and Citizenship*; and Hamel, Lustiger-Thaler and Mayer, eds, *Urban Movements in a Globalizing World*.
2. Taking distance from Orientalist models such as the 'Islamic city' and its corollary the 'Arab city' led to the construction of other models like the notion of 'oriental City', introduced by the geographer Eugene Wirth (Wirth, 'Villes islamiques, villes arabes, villes orientales? Une problématique face au changement'), or to attempts at historic categorisation with the notion of 'urban order' proposed by Robert Ilbert (Ilbert, 'De Beyrouth à Alger. La fin d'un ordre urbain').
3. Davis, 'Planet of Slums', p. 4.
4. Sassen, 'Locating Cities on Global Circuits', in *Environment and Urbanization*, vol. 14, No. 21, 2002, p. 13.
5. Malaquais Dominique, 2006, Flux et imaginaires, http://www.etudes-africaines.cnrs.fr/communications/malaquais2.pdf.
6. Grafmeyer and Joseph, 'Présentation: La ville laboratoire et le milieu urbain', p.42.
7. Simmel, 'Métropoles et mentalité'.
8. Pétonnet, 'L'anonymat ou la pellicule protectrice'.
9. Cohen, *Global Diasporas: An Introduction*.
10. Hannerz, *Transnational Connections*, p. 103.
11. Sheldon Pollock, Homi K. Bhabha, Carol A. Breckenridge and Dipesh Chakrabarty, 'Cosmopolitanisms', *Public Culture*, 12 (3), 2000, pp. 577–89.
12. Beck, *Qu'est-ce que le cosmopolitisme?*, p. 42.
13. Tarrius, *Les nouveaux cosmopolitismes*, p. 243.
14. Benveniste, 'Deux modèles linguistiques de la cité'.
15. Holston and Appadurai, 'Introduction: Cities and Citizenship', pp. 2–3.
16. Balibar, p. 16.
17. Ibid., p. 125.
18. Bacqué, Blance, Hamel and Sintomer, 'Editorial'.
19. Hamel, Lustiger-Thaler and Mayer; 'Introduction', p. 788.
20. Ibid., p. 4.
21. Ilbert, 'De Beyrouth à Alger. La fin d'un ordre urbain'.

22. Cohen, *Global Diasporas*, p. 167.
23. Sassen, 'Whose City is It? Globalization and the Formation of New Claims'.
24. Roncayolo, 'La ville est toujours la ville de quelqu'un', p 55.
25. Zukin, *The Cultures of Cities*, p. 28.
26. Davis, 'Planet of Slums', p. 13.
27. Zukin, *The Cultures of Cities*, p. 1.
28. This is how Mondada summarises the approach of Sharon Zukin. See Mondada, *Décrire la ville*, p. 35–8.
29. Davis, 'Planet of Slums', p. 16.
30. Mondada, *Décrire la ville*, p. 35–8.
31. Simmel, 'Métropoles et mentalité'.
32. Gérard, 'Etre citoyen du monde' p. 13.

JEAN-FRANÇOIS BAYART

The Paradigm of the City

To speak of the city as a 'new frontier' of globalisation is to refer, naturally, to Joel Garreau's work, *Edge City*,[1] as well as to all literature concerning the 'global village', particularly the work of Saskia Sassen.[2] However, this contemporary debate should not make us forget that the rapport between the city and globalisation, as well as the rapport between the city and citizenship, are old, even ancient, considerations. Etymologically, in French the notion of citizen, *citoyen*, stems from that of the city dweller, *citadin*. Its evolution is based on and informed by cities, more precisely cities that relied on trade with 'world-economies' (according to Fernand Braudel) regardless of the popularity of an ethos of autarky in certain cities such as Athens, Rome or Palmyra.[3] The notion of citizenship also blended in with the expansion of a universalist religion, Christianity, of which the ecclesiastical institutions – seminaries, funeral rites, and cultural practices – contributed to the emergence of new spaces and a new concept of urbanity.[4] It then was able to develop alongside market development and capitalist expansion, which saw the city-states, merchant and port cities and industrial metropolises become the primary vectors of this expansion.

The first task here, then, is to specify the historical dimensions of the relationship between contemporary globalisation and the city and citizenship without lapsing into generalisations. From this point of view, the period under consideration stretches from the end of the eighteenth century to the present, contrary to the short time span preferred by international relations and global studies theorists when they emphasise the radical ruptures caused by the collapse of the Soviet Union (1989–91), the beginnings of the neo-liberal hegemony (1980) and following the end of the Second World War. In reality, the nineteenth century set the foundation for contemporary globalisation with the beginning of the synergy between the global expansion of capital and the system of nation-states to which we are still very much tied, despite popular discourse on the 'retreat' or the 'failure' of the state.[5]

The city has always been the fulcrum of this capitalist and nationalist globalisation, but it was a historically unique city – in a certain sense, an urban 'event'. The Industrial Revolution meant a massive rural exodus and the birth of the large metropolis, along with its sprawling suburbs, which we still inhabit today despite their various structural incarnations. A few among these suburban areas grafted themselves onto older parts of the city and caused their walls to shake and shift, often in the literal sense when it was a question of fortified European cities. The Old Continent, in fact, does not hold a monopoly over such urban mutations. A few of the large industrial cities in Asia, Latin America and the Middle East also have ancient histories. Elsewhere, the nineteenth-century mutations led to the *ex nihilo* creation of megacities according to political, military, mining, or industrial designs.

Such was the case in many parts of sub-Saharan Africa, as well as in many important cities across North America. In fact, the large migrations of the nineteenth and twentieth centuries are inextricably linked to urban development, despite the 'Wild West' mythology: San Francisco was at the heart of California's Gold Rush, with its massive Chinese immigrant population from southern China. The capitalist expansion of that time created world-cities, uniquely cosmopolitan, such as San Francisco and Panama City. It also led to the 'globalisation' of old cities, imperial or national capitals such as London, Paris, Vienna and Istanbul. Finally, the prodigious transformation, technological as well as cultural, provoked by the Industrial Revolution cannot be dissociated from the city, which became the source of ideas and innovation and places of social and cultural distinction. The arts, music, pop culture, social science and the material culture of capitalism are all urban creations. Perhaps this is self-evident, but it is important to articulate the point here because this wasn't always the case. The desert and the countryside were, in certain eras (especially for Christianity), centres of knowledge and of intellectual and artistic innovation.

The globalised city is not anathema to the countryside. The city remains attached to the countryside through rural migration, supply lines, leisure activities, family visits, election campaigns and the political mobilisation of notables and processes of 'merchandise authentification'.[6] The relationship between Nature and Village has for two centuries been a part of cultural, political, and social legitimisation among city dwellers, always the first to think that 'the earth does not lie' but that rural people are 'country bumpkins'. The city itself has the potential to become more rural, what geographers and sociologists call 'rurbanisation', an example of which is Kinshasa during the 1980s, when that city was poised for economic collapse. The countryside, in turn, knows urbanisation through the spread and growth of agglomerations, known as urban 'generalisation', which sees the city becoming in some way 'generic' and shaping regions, countries and sub-continents following the example of Paris Ile-de-France, the Netherlands, the coastal areas in West Africa, the East Coast of the US and China.[7]

The relationship between this urban 'event' of the last two centuries and the definition of citizenship is evident, as well as complex. In brief, we could say that citizenship has been characterised since the nineteenth century as both 'national' and 'popular'. These two characteristics are urban: The nation is seated in the capital and thinks through mass media, located and produced in cities that are at the centre of its attention. This, too, after all, is not univocal. Maoism attempted, at certain periods, to dissociate citizenship from the city by sending intellectuals and the Red Guard to re-education camps in rural areas. The Khmer Rouge, in 1975, emptied Phnom Penh and the main cities of Cambodia of their inhabitants in order for the 'new people' to be educated by the 'ancient people' of the countryside, the ones whom they liberated from imperialism and from the Lon Nol dictatorship. It is important here to recognise that the relationship between the city and citizenship, as cities are globalised, is plurivocal and ambiguous. Thus, in countries like the US, Argentina and South Africa, cities, rural exodus and international migrations were the matrices of democratic but also authoritarian citizenship – which included historical experiences of racial segregation as well as multiculturalism or militancy in favour of civil rights.

In a generic way, the great ideologies of the past two centuries – socialism, communism, fascism, national socialism and democratic liberalism – were political responses or political expressions of the industrial and urban revolutions of the nineteenth century and of their global expansion within the nation-state. Similarly, the last significant revolution of the masses in the twentieth century was at first urban, or at least fuelled by a massive rural exodus (Iran). This lead to the institutionalisation of an Islamic republic based on an urban ethos and lifestyle, that of the being-in-society (*adam-e edjtemâ'i*) capable of harmonising private life and participation in the public sphere.[8] Once again, the intertwining of the 'urban' and the 'citizen' appears in all its ambivalence. The Islamic republic is certainly not entirely democratic, but at least it draws half of its legitimacy from elections held at regular intervals, with an uncertain outcome, as was proved by the successive victories of two outsiders in the presidential elections of 1997 and 2005. It makes use of coercion, but allows for political and social participation on the part of women unrivalled in the rest of the Middle East.

In other words, the city is no doubt a necessary, but not sufficient, condition of democratic citizenship. What Julien Gracq calls its 'form' is an underlying element of this differentiation between public and private spheres that constitutes public freedom and the 'public use of reason'. But it is not always true that 'city air is free air' as Hegel wrote. Therefore we need to refine our analysis of the combination of globalisation, urbanity and citizenship.

The Territoriality of the Global City

Contrary to some international relations theories or a certain postmodern anthropology, the globalised city is not just a matter of immaterial flux. It remains a territorial reality.

Migrations have left their marks on the urban space of industrial cities in a much more systematic way than suggested by concentrated ethnic neighbourhoods or arrays of ethnic restaurants. The Filipino housekeepers in Rome, for example, are found in 'pockets of gathering' to exchange information and food, at the risk of inciting the ire of neighbours or the authorities – particularly at the EUR Fermi subway station, at the Mancini bus stop and around Termini station, until police harassment pushes them under a flyover, along the Tiber, into a barracks abandoned by Albanian refugees.[9]

In Tokyo, Ueno Park, ideally situated on subway towards the Narita airport, was a preferred refuge for Iranian immigrants squatting one of its alleys. The police finally brought 'good order' in the park, but it continues to be a convenient rendezvous spot, at the foot of the Saigo Takamori statue, at the exit of the JR station. 'It is dangerous to pass through here at night,' one can read written in Persian on the underground wall leading to this station. Vendors from Tehran suspiciously selling fraudulent phone cards (among other things) operate in the streets of the Shibuya district, where they are immediately recognisable once pointed out. This small world also has its habits in cafés, Turkish restaurants and pizzerias in Roppongi, where the owners or managers are Iranian, adopting a fat-necked *javânmard* ('good man') comportment bordering on caricature.[10]

More remarkably, the Congolese of Paris have opened about sixty clandestine bars, called *nganda*, often in squatted buildings. People go to the *nganda* late at night to drink, eat, do 'bizness' (illicit activity), get high, dance and partake in ostentatious consumption.[11] A few hundred kilometres north, in the multi-ethnic and multi-religious Bijlmer neighbourhood in Amsterdam, Ghanaian Christians have covertly set up cult places in the parking lots of big buildings.[12]

These phenomena are examples of a kind of popular, transnational territoriality, where spatial lines configure the states and urban metropolises in the shadow of the 'new geography of centrality',[13] no less territorial, which the most recent globalisation period gave rise to. In Manhattan, the 'pockets' into which West African street vendors are gathered (Lexington Ave and 42nd St, Times Square, Canal St) are tightly intertwined with the territorialisation of important places of 'Internet galaxy' finance and of multilateral governance.[14] The spatial anchoring of transnationalism from 'the South' is neither a simple juxtaposition nor the residue of a previous world, anachronistic and condemned to disappear. The 'new geography of centrality' encourages immigration, including (and perhaps above all) clandestine, because a greater production capability of the capital requires abundant and cheap labour, especially in the textile industry and other lowly qualified tertiary activities.[15] On the other side, informal or criminal transnational commerce relies on the urban fabric of the industrial world. At the heart of big cities, certain neighbourhoods have specialised in 'off the books' businesses, and in the production of goods for this market. Examples include 125th St in New York (right up until the destruction of the African Market in October 1994); the neighbourhoods of Sentier and Château-Rouge and a few streets of the 11th *arrondissement* in Paris; the neighbourhoods of Belsunce in Marseille, Yenikapı and Laleli in Istanbul; or the Galerie Ixelles in Brussels – places that are 'glocal' as much as they are transnational, by virtue of the cooperation among networks of foreign and domestic merchants.

The 'new economy' and the Internet have their preferred territories of which Silicon Valley became the symbol. On a global scale, the irrefutable centre of this 'new economy' is the US, thanks to its broadband capacity and the number of domain names registered there. Trailing far behind the US, most cities in Western Europe and in South Korea are 'wired', although Japan is curiously an exception to this group. On a national scale, the territoriality of the Web is also visibly to the benefit of a few big cities, or more specifically a few neighbourhoods: South of Market ('SoMa') in San Francisco; Silicon Alley in Lower Manhattan (especially before the attacks of 11 September 2001) and Midtown East in New York; Santa Monica, the Ventura Freeway Corridor and the San Gabriel Valley in Los Angeles. Thus, in January 2000, five cities in the world, where 1 per cent of the population lives, accounted for 20.4 per cent of Internet domains, and the fifty main cities in the world in which 4 per cent of its population lives accounted for 48.2 per cent of domain names.[16]

The territorialisation of the globalising process engenders a definitive transformation of the city, as opposed to its predicted disappearance at the dawn of the virtual age and of telework.[17] Its precedents were due to the accelerated urbanisation of the nineteenth century that led to the rise of new 'global' cities, some of which enjoyed only ephemeral glory such as San Francisco, Panama City, Manaus, Singapore, Hong Kong, Shanghai, Baku. Today we see 'metropolitan regions' emerging, becoming the nodal points for linking global networks such as the Internet, telecommunications, capital and transportation: the Bay Area of San Francisco; the zone that stretches from Ventura to Orange County in southern California and has now crossed the Mexican border; the various conurbations of the East Coast of the US; Greater London; the Paris Ile-de-France region; the 'Blue Banana' of the Rhine Valley and its trans-alpine extension; the Tokyo-Yokohama-Nagoya axis that the Shinkansen draws towards the south to Osaka, Kobe and Kyoto; the enormous agglomeration of Hong Kong and of the Pearl River delta in southern China; the megacities of countries that we hope to be 'emerging'.[18] Through suffering and a massive 'social energy',[19] sordid life practices are invented to which globalisation's detractors, despite their best efforts, fail to do justice in their critiques.

Yes, the 'limit-city', even the 'city of the outside' – Edge City[20] – is clearly the 'new frontier' of globalisation, the place where essential social relationships are forged, relationships constituting the city's historical regime of 'domination' and 'subjectivity'. From an economic, sociological and demographic perspective, this is a profoundly new reality. It is no less doubtful that these social relations are in the process of expanding their hold throughout the world, according to reticular processes, although the inadequate but often-used term 'network' does not suffice to reflect the extent and the complexity of this new transformation.

From these initial observations we can draw two provisional conclusions: On the one hand, the concept of the city retains all of its pertinence provided that it refers to historical situations and includes the transformations of the 'form of the city'. On the other, the concrete analysis of urban activities, the urban 'art of doing' or of Michel de Certeau's 'making use' of the city[21] must substitute the meta-discourses on the 'Global City' in terms of 'Panic City'.

The Historicity of the City

The city in the throes of globalisation does not indicate an 'end of history' any more than it does an 'end of territories'. The city is a product of history, and each one is endowed with a unique historicity that should be considered on a case-by-case basis, and where possible in terms of a historical *terroir*,[22] according to the methodology of the historical sociology of politics. Neighbourhoods, streets and buildings sometimes have a singular past that constitutes a group of 'diachronic interactions', of 'legacies' or of 'antecedent conditions'.[23] But it is the more general effect of historicity that participates more precisely to 200 years of globalisation. The contemporary city is the fruit of colonial interaction. This is evident for the majority of large cities in the 'South' of which a few, as mentioned before, were created during the colonial era and whose architecture and city planning carry the mark of the colonising power. But this is also true for the metropolises in the 'North', even if this is less known.

Colonisation fostered the advent of an original urban civilisation, one that invented its own material culture in terms of clothing, diet, personal hygiene, leisure, artistic creation and political mobilisation. The *fait social total* of the colonial or para-colonial city in Africa and in Asia was interwoven with social changes in Europe, America and even Japan. The simultaneous spread of imperial dishes and beverages – such as rice dishes, curries, couscous, ginger ale and tea as well as beer, whiskey, Portuguese red wine, tomato sauce, bouillon cubes or canned sardines – in the colonies and metropolises illustrates this form of 'mutual interaction', just as England's expansion at the heart of the European state system since the Middle Ages led to the incorporation of Bordeaux wines, port, Madeira and Marsala into the diet of its upper classes and fed their collective perception of being distinguished.

Similarly, the working-class cities and the 'garden cities' or 'new cities' that surround the historical centres of the Old Continent since the Second World War are throwbacks to a colonial era, straight-lined urban planning model, which channelled the rural exodus of the natives and diminished the risk of epidemics in particular areas. For example, hygienists and progressives (who placed themselves within the broad utopian tradition of the nineteenth century) along with French urban reformers conceived and theorised their projects, taking into account both the requirements of the Industrial Revolution in France as well as the demands of colonial conquest. Their careers met with people like Augagneur, the mayor of Lyon before being named Governor General of Madagascar in 1905; Lanessan,

Governor General of Tonkin from 1891–94; and above all Lyautey, Resident General of Morocco from 1912–25. In Lyon, the work of Tony Garnier, who benefited from the support of Herriot, Augagneur's successor, became the reference and was copied throughout many Moroccan cities by his counterpart of the Villa Medicis, Henri Prost, to whom Lyautey conferred the urban planning of this new protectorate. In this domain, as in others, the presiding general deployed a neo-conservative method of authoritarian government, centralised, rational, and 'enlightened', whose message was directed at both the counter-example of Algeria's colonisation and at the decadent parliamentary system of the metropolis.

Prost, a real dandy, promoted a quasi-aristocratic 'culture of the self' which sought to criticise bureaucratic mediocrity and fascinated part of the public opinion and the French administration. He opposed himself to the military engineers from the polytechnical school and the School for Bridges and Highways and established a form of urbanism based on the Social Museum, created in 1884 as a real 'community of experts' of French imperial and republican modernity. In 1931, the Conference on Urbanism in the Colonies hailed Prost as the greatest urbanist of modern times, and at the same time recommended the adoption of a 'territorial planning and extension' project that would also allow for the respect and coexistence of the various 'races' and their cultural practices.[24] In those years, Algiers had become the centre of impassioned urban debates because of its unbridled growth and contesting the neo-Moorish style prevalent since the turn of the century. Prost took part, along with Le Corbusier, who had his own vision to radically redesign the city. Even though Le Corbusier's projects were rejected, his disciples were active at the heart of the urbanism group of the Algiers region, established the day after the start of the Second World War. It was one of their rivals, Fernand Pouillon, who was appointed to construct three cities destined for Muslim populations: Diar es-Saada, Diar el-Maçoul and Climat de France in Bab el-Oued.[25]

Often very polemical, this development of the colonial city – which from its very beginnings inspired the invention of the industrial city between Saône and Rhône – was echoed throughout France in the form of upper-class residences or *grands ensembles* during the postwar reconstruction of the country, the baby boom, the exodus from the countryside, the massive influx of immigrant workers and *pieds-noirs* refugees and the 'Glorious Thirty' of economic growth. One could speak of the 'assassination of Paris'.[26] The assassins had ascended the ranks in Indochina, south of the Sahara and North Africa, notably Paul Delouvrier, the father of the 'new cities' who was appointed first representative in the Algerian government, in charge of the Constantine Plan, from 1958–61, before being named District General of the region of Paris upon his return, and then Regional Prefect of Paris in 1966. The city dweller and the contemporary suburbanite, who have long thought themselves separated from colonial politics, are nonetheless the inheritors of the colonial city, of which the riots in the French suburbs in 2005 were clear reminders.

City and Subjectivity

In this era of globalisation, the city remains the principal mode of subjectivity, which is to say of the 'production of modes of existence or lifestyles',[27] and more precisely the city remains the central place for the emergence of new 'techniques of the body'[28] inherent in the material culture of mass consumption. It is the site, *par excellence*, of achieving commercial desire, or rather the site where desire, exploitation and violence overlap in a way that Marx, long before Freud, summarised in the following formula: 'I rob you, giving you pleasure.'[29]

Thus, at the turn of the millennium, fashion glamour, in the style made popular by rap artists from the Los Angeles suburbs, heightens the senses of the consumer without its outrageousness or vulgarity causing offence.[30] Distribution experts have deliberately played this card for the last twenty years and have focused on the 're-enchantment of commercial gestures and spaces' via 'fun shopping' and 'retailtainment'. 'Shopping' must, in their perspective, be a source of hedonistic and playful gratification. According to two researchers at the Ecole Superieur de Commerce in Paris:

> By appealing to an additional sense besides those that are usually solicited by cosmetics, we increase the probability of purchase and, by taking the client into such an original universe, we allow them to live an experience that make higher prices more acceptable.[31]

Conversely, 'the success of discount and hard discount stores stems from a theatricality of ... disenchantment'.[32] Confronted by this 'lumpenconcurrence' and the challenge of e-commerce, shopping centres transform into 'spaces of conviviality and desire' where signs convey to their clients – beg your pardon, their 'visitors' – an 'unforgettable life experience', and where the act of selling (and buying) is raised to the level of an 'art of living' that includes restaurants, hair salons, spas or day care facilities for children.[33] Malls such as the Fashion Centre at Pentagon City, in Washington, DC;

the Mall of America in Bloomington, Minnesota; the West Edmonton Mall in Alberta; the Dubai Mall in the UAE; or more modest venues such as the Carré Sénart in Paris are all famous examples, and they benefit from their incredible popularity. The West Edmonton Mall is the number-one tourist site in Canada, before Niagara Falls. The large computer and electronics mall, Surcouf, on Avenue Daumesnil in Paris, is the fourth-most popular tourist site in France. The sales in London and, increasingly, in Paris are a strong attraction in European leisure, whereas the Dubai Shopping Festival attracts approximately 2.8 million visitors per year and include parades, fireworks, lotteries and promotions.[34] More commonly, consumers partake in 'fun shopping' on a weekly or even daily basis, going to the large malls, setting up meetings or 'zoning' like Muscovite 'mall rats'.[35] Gradually, the shopping centre transforms into a 'new urban space'; it is 'one of the few places where real social diversity still exists,' says Jean-Michel Silberstein, the managing director for the Centre National des Centres Commerciaux. This is echoed by sociologist Samuel Bordreuil:

> It is a space that unites groups of people belonging to at least three generations, with a breadth that we don't find in other urban areas, or sought out by urbanites. There is a notable presence of 'seniors', but also of children who feel much less 'displaced' at the mall then at any other urban place.

An extension or perhaps a substitute for the city, the shopping centre now proposes – aside from administrative or public services, such as gas and electric agencies or the post office – promotions, artistic activities or performances.[36] Finally, hedonism becomes the motivation or the main pretext for visiting a store. It is the place where we stage ourselves *vis-à-vis* ourselves and the other, where we are initiated as adolescents in the world of merchandise, strolling through the department stores with our friends, where we tend to our bodies in 'beauty spaces'.

It is probably in the areas of Omotesando, Roppongi, Aoyama, and Shibuya in Tokyo, that the spectacle of consumerism is both most refined and most playful. The big designer labels have all opened boutiques there and hired renowned architects, designers, and artists to craft their spaces. Examples include Jun Aoki for Louis Vuitton in Omotesando and Roppongi Hills; Jacques Herzog and Pierre de Meuron for the Prada 'epicentre' in Aoyama; Ettore Sottsass, Ron Arad, Toyo Ito, Andrea Branzi, Sol LeWitt, Louise Bourgeois and Takeshi Murakami for the planning and design of Planet 66, the 'city within the city' that magnate Minoturu Mori built in Roppongi Hills.[37] These sites, with their sophisticated, minimalist decor, are created as homes for and embodiments of the 'selling ceremony', an expression coined by Yves Carcelle, the president of Louis Vuitton.[38] It describes this new retail environment aimed at women clients with rich and impeccable taste, who enjoy being catered to by highly personalised, exceptional service personnel. The presentation of the pieces, the gestures of the personnel, the packages, are incredibly stylish; the services after sale are staggering – Hermès uses seven craftspeople to this purpose – and the offers more and more personalised.[39]

The Saturday afternoon tour of the chic boutiques of Omotesando and Roppongi Hills is a regular activity for teenagers or young couples. It is an occasion for often-exuberant creativity that defies the canon of Western elegance and takes on the form of a true pop culture movement, or at least a middle-class movement, like we see in the very hip area of Shibuya. The young women nicknamed the 'Shibuyettes' have created a sort of transnational 'street fashion' modelled on the *kawaii* style ('cute', childlike) that is aesthetically stunning and provocative, and is now all the rage across Asia; its fashion temple is the 109 Building, not far from the JR station.

Yet the pleasure derived from the act of buying, possibly even erotic, excludes neither frustration, nor theft and its repression. 'When a patrol car comes upon a first-generation North African kid decked out in Ralph Lauren and sporting Weston shoes, that patrolman is entitled to have his doubts,' said a police officer in one of the densely populated suburbs of Toulouse, home of a thriving parallel economy in the resale of stolen goods and where youth riots erupt every now and again.[40] The shopping centres, the 'garrison-entrepôt'[41] of industrial societies, are under heavy surveillance, contracted out to private security companies (or, in some countries, to criminal gangs) according to the logic of 'outsourcing'. They are, in this regard, one of the social institutions that global 'governmentality' relies upon, somewhere between pleasure and coercion. They are also fragments of the public space where social groups assess themselves in terms of symbolic and sometimes physical violence: sites where one can hate as much as one is socialised.[42]

This *stricto sensu* subjectivation falls back on the mediation of merchandise, and the globalising city provides useful resources to do this both on the symbolic and material level. In Turkey, the confrontation between secular and Islamic democrats does not transcend the material culture and its political economy – rather, it espouses the forms and becomes entangled with them. Yael Navaro-Yashin goes as far as to say that 'the secular and Islamist identities in modern Turkey are manufactured products', although they are naturally not experienced as such, but rather as quasi-primordial identities.[43]

In fact, the Islamic-democratic party of Tayyip Erdoğan, the AKP, and the business groups close to it, grouped under the Independent Industrialists' and Businessmen's Association (MUSIAD), are among the inheritors (and beneficiaries) of the liberalisation period presided over by Turgut Özal during the 1980s. He was close to the brotherhood of the Naqshbandi. It is thus a 'green capitalism', with its yuppies, that is directly integrated into industrial globalisation and lies at the basis of the conservative and Islamic liberalism of the government for which the AKP today carries the electoral torch.

One of its exclusive productions is women's Islamic clothing, with its various components from the silk *pardösüs*, the overcoat that students wear, to the various scarves such as the *türban*. Thus the Islamic veil, the 'covered' and 'Muslim' woman (wearing the headscarf or *tesettür*), stems from the importance of merchandise. They give rise to effects of fashion (*moda*), no matter what the pious merchants say. They are presented at fashion shows; they constitute a market; they have their own commercial brands; and they are commercialised in the informal market in the Topkapı neighbourhood, in Istanbul, where modesty confronts the arrogance of the shopping malls that multiplied in number in the 1980s.

But they are also for sale in the large Tekbir store in the Fatih neighbourhood, where the television screens show the latest designer collections. Tekbir was one of the first stores to make Islamic apparel fashionable. Under the deceptive appearance of Islamic fundamentalism, this phenomenon is not far from globalisation. On one hand, certain articles of Muslim clothing are imported and sold for their style and quality. The foreign textile industry is at the service of the faith and constitution of the Islamic 'moral subject', with its apparently neo-Ottoman, 'life-style'. On the other hand, Turkish businesses export *türban* and *pardösüs* to Western Europe, the Middle East and Asia, either traded in formally registered exchanges or in the flourishing suitcase business in the station-markets in the Yenikapi and Laleli neighbourhoods of Istanbul.

At the other end of the political spectrum, the Özalian overture has equally boosted the rise in power of certain companies such as Mudo, Yargıcı and Zeki Triko, which offer their clientele the finest goods of 'modernity' and of 'civilisation' in explicit neo-Kemalist terms and in a polemic response to Islamic fashion. The 'fetishism' that continues to celebrate Atatürk and increases even with the presence of the Muslim movement across the political landscape has its own set of accessories (busts, photos, pins) that allow secular people to clearly mark their difference and their resistance.[44] But despite these explicitly political emblems, the essential is their adherence to mass consumption that was first available to them, and all other Turks, via shopping malls. For in these commercial spaces, such as Galleria, Akmerkez, Capitol, Bauhaus and Carrefour, on the European and Asian banks of Istanbul, 'people make the experience of civilisation', according to the newspaper *Hürriyet*,[45] – that of a 'lifestyle' that promotes a national identity through the appropriation of foreign codes (dress, food, architecture, etc).

This has always been one of the paradoxes of Kemalism. In order to politically invent a national (Turkish and Anatolian) popular culture and challenge the multicultural cosmopolitanism of Constantinople, Kemalism turned itself towards the universal engineering of 'Westernisation'. In particular, it turned towards the transnational and trans-ideological architecture of the Modern Movement, whose annual International Congress of Modern Architecture has diffused its precepts since 1928. The 'New Architecture' was received in Ankara as the advent of the 'future city' in its Manichean battle against the 'city of the past', Istanbul, and as an expression of the 'new truth' that was spreading throughout the world. It saw itself, without question, at the service of 'civilising commutation' (*inkılap*) and of 'revolution' (*devrim*) driven by the state, and as the instrument of the 'internal colonisation' (*iç kolonizasyon*) of Anatolia. In its 'model villages' the peasants had to learn 'how to sleep in beds, how to use tables and chairs'.

The 'New Architecture', however, did not hide the interest it had in French or Italian colonial urbanism in North Africa. In the cities, cubic houses and apartments meant residents were thrown into the new republican, familial and hygienic 'lifestlyle'. The endeavour quickly hit its economic limits and the architecture became less 'new' than 'national' by the end of the 1930s, in part because of the fading utopian and revolutionary spirit.[46]

Turkey's entry into the world of global mass consumption, beginning in the 1980s, has changed the terms of the question. Its relation to merchandise has in some ways democratised, no matter what the financial difficulties are for the majority of households and the heavy price paid for recurrent inflation. For women, shopping mall visits have been a mode of social participation in the public space as well as a renegotiation at the heart of the family of their economic power.[47] The mass market is now shared, thanks to concerted pressure, whereas in the first decades of the Republic the majority of the population was excluded from the commercial sphere. The urban struggles of subjectivity represent an 'intensely national conversation'[48] that feeds on Turkey's integration into the globalising process and on the contradictory appropriation of the material culture of capitalism.

In a more general way, this material culture has become enmeshed with 'techniques of the body' – these, too, being essentially urban practices, which have tended to impose themselves on the whole of society; or, at least, they have become a measure of social distinction. Ways of eating, walking, loving and leisure, have all come out of a mass urban material culture. To highlight but one example, one does not move the same way with 'city' shoes as one does with clogs or boots. Urbanisation is similar to a corporal and driving evolution that carries its set of benefits, but also its drawbacks (myopia, backaches, obesity). Thus, this corporal and driving metamorphosis constitutes in some way the incarnation of citizenship. They are political techniques of the body unique to the city. The best example of this is the demonstration, the civic march in a public space for the purpose of venting professional or political grievances, but which participates on a more fundamental level in the ritual formation of the city itself.[49] Examples include rows of marching workers; revolutionary processions, reaching a previously unheard of height in the fall of 1978 in Tehran; the anti-globalisation protests during the G8 summits; flash mobs; even the site-specific exercise of 'bio-power' during Gay Pride parades. Peasant revolts testify, paradoxically, to the uniquely urban nature of this form of political action. They march in the cities, not in the fields. It is the same with another political technique of the body, that of the suicide bomber who detonates him/herself on roads or in public places. Nonetheless, it is the daily experience of city life that is the condition for the civic experience in terms of what it permits (or forbids, according to racial and social segregation), 'the public use of reason' and the 'social movement' – the term 'movement' taken in the literal sense of the term.

City in Waiting

The consideration of the material and bodily practices of the political subject within globalising cities brings us to a final paradoxical observation. Contrary to popular belief, contemporary urban centre is not only all about 'speed', 'urgency', 'high-speed Internet'. The 'compression of time and space' that characterises globalisation, if we follow David Harvey, is offset by stockpiling, relegation and delay. Moreover, the city implants a bodily technique specific to this purpose – the waiting line or queue. The city has systematised the queue the world over. In Hong Kong, for example, it was not the rule to wait patiently in line in order to be served in banks, restaurants or anywhere else up until the mid-1970s. The same went for loading and unloading zones for ferries, taxis and other forms of transportation. McDonald's introduced the queue, and its regular customers now snub the poorly groomed continental visitors who try to push their way to the counter.[50]

We have often jeered at the thought of Soviet-style queues, but perhaps they were a fundamental avant-garde socialist contribution to globalisation? We do not cease to place ourselves in lines, and we do this in an increasing number of places and on an increasing number of occasions, to reap the benefits of our commercial society: in restaurants for self-service or before the *maître d'hôtel* seats us; at airports for check-in, baggage claim, boarding, using the bathroom and disembarking; at the cinema (certain Parisian cinemas having invented the double-queue, one for purchasing tickets, the other for entrance into the theatre); at the Sainte-Geneviève library, Panthéon or the Centre Georges-Pompidou library; in the hope that free spots will open up in front of museums hosting particular exhibitions; at the doors of a large store on the first day of a sale; on the sidewalks of consulates or prefectures to obtain visas or day passes; at the supermarket checkout. The queue has become so present in our daily lives that we don't even notice it any more.

From the point of view of the 'micro-physical power', the queue is in some way the entryway to globalisation. Yet it is not at the margins of the process, but rather at its heart, an integral constituent. We form lines in the poshest places in New York, or in the early morning in the Faubourg Saint-Honoré, in front of the UK consulate, a stone's throw from the Elysée. We do this weekly at Carrefour or at Leclerc to buy our essentials. We do it when we need to use a form of transport that has mastered the 'compression of time and space', the airplane. Even Mohammed Atta had to wait in line to buy his box cutters and board one of the planes that would destroy the World Trade Center. The liminal experience of waiting produces subjectivation. This is confirmed by anthropological research, among other fields, and highlighted in Eliane de Latour's movie *Bronx Barbès* (2000), which explores the ghettos of the Ivory Coast's largest cities.[51] The cross-race ethos, at the outset globalised in its imagined dimension, of the 'warrior' and his reputation, cultivated by the 'old men' and their 'sonny boys' in their desire to be well-styled, at once separates itself from the localised ('ethnic') lifestyle of the village, asserts its universality and claims the right to respect, which money, clothes and paternity bring. From this perspective, the term 'ghetto' should not lead to confusion. The ghetto is not a hidden dungeon where its 'ghettomen' stagnate. It is a place of gathering for the young people who flank the public space and remain narrowly inserted into it. It is, for example, located close to an intersection or a marketplace. It is visible and recognised for what it is, even though a part of its activities are invisible and illegal. It is in permanent interaction with its immediate environment, and also opens onto the world that nicknames, fashion and the odyssey of emigration allow to appropriate:

> At first glance, the street presents an image of liberty, of universality, of invention. It captures the most recent cultural vibrations of the planet. It presents itself as a chance for a new, seemingly unconstrained life, linked to celebration and to pleasure, to a reconstituted utopian solidarity vying for domination, to escape its lot.[52]

The ghetto experience is liminal in the sense that it sheds the meaning of its former skin by giving it a new name, a new look and a new understanding, that of the 'sciences' (implied in the art of stealing). It begins with an old technique, an initiation tier, a colonial tier and a *Houphouëtiste*[53] tier, of correction. A 'ghettoman' explains:

> A young boy, upon his arrival, is beaten with sticks and kicked so as to turn him into an animal. You can see something that is very difficult to do, you will send him off, he will leave by himself, and he will return with what you asked of him.[54]

If all goes well, it will lead to the constitution of a different 'moral subject':

> As a kid, when I returned from a robbery with my money – I could sometimes return with 2 or 3 million – there were 'big brothers' who would rob me. They would take everything, absolutely everything. They gave me nothing. After, when I found the courage, they no longer robbed me. When you try to rob me, I point my gun at you; you act like an idiot, and I'll make your feet dance. This is how I lived. After that, they respected me. They couldn't do anything to me anymore. Ah, then I became strong! At that moment, I became a boy![55]

The ghetto experience is also liminal, because it is experienced temporally. The global 'types' who are venerated are not only fighters, sports stars, or mythical gangsters, but also the bosses, the self-made men: 'I want to be a businessman, manage buildings, societies, taxis, and have lots of money.'[56] Deep down, these 'warriors' have soft hearts:

> I dream of having a luxurious lifestyle, and to be able to do things for my mother because my father has passed away and I have only my mother left. She's in Mali. I dream of the time she has left, even if it's a small house, I will get it for her so that she can rest there. I think of all this, of my children's future, my little brothers and my little sisters.[57]

They even have a romantic side with their 'go' or 'love', whom they take pains to distinguish from their 'woman on the side', whom they do not love – this even if their loved one was won over by rape, possibly even gang-rape:

> I take you by force because I love you. I cannot waste my time dating you, no, I take you by force and then after making love, I take you and I sit you down and say to you 'Ah, little sister, excuse me, the truth, I am a fan of yours' [...] I rape her alone or not. We guys, we raped a girl with seven of us, afterwards the girl became my girlfriend. Ah, yes, that's love![58]

Except when we hold on to an eschatology of globalisation, the world's renaissance through urban expectations cannot be taken for granted, even though the underprivileged have historically been the prime focus of subjectivation. We recall that, for Michel Foucault, this notion designates notably 'the operation by which individuals or communities constitute themselves as subjects, within the margins of constituted knowledge and established power, giving way to new forms of knowledge and power'.

> This is why subjectivity comes in tiers, perpetually unhinged, in a sort of fold, whether folding in or folding over [...] In many social formations, it is not the masters, but the social outcasts who constitute the focus of subjectivation [...] The subject is born through moans as much as he is through exaltation.[59]

Thus, those who were freed in Roman antiquity, or the slaves or fugitives in the Yoruban cities of the nineteenth century, were the preferred 'bringers' of the Christian way of life.[60] But we must be careful not to go from Charybdis to Scylla, to the stigmatisation of the new 'dangerous classes' harboured in the suburbs and clandestinely immigrating, if we believe the 'securo-crats' of all sovereignty colours, in their naive sublimation of the de-territorialised 'multitude' desirous of, and subversive to, the 'Empire'.[61]

This is all the more so because the relationship between citizenship and the globalising city is often mediated by violence. Delinquency is a social phenomenon of the masses in the majority of Latin American and African cities, and it is noticeable in many metropolitan areas in North America and Europe. Riots are an urban mode of political action that we find both in the industrialised world – North America, Great Britain and France – and in Latin America, Africa, the Middle East and Asia. Finally, civil war has torn apart countless capital cities in the last thirty years: Beirut, Sarajevo, Mogadishu, Brazzaville, Freetown and Kigali all fell victim to conflict, bombing, ethnic cleansing, and the bloody discrimination of roadblocks. A final paradox emerges when we see that these urban forms of political violence remain often prisoner to old tensions that have run through the notion of citizenship since Antiquity. It is the unavoidable and intractable reality of the urban condition, especially when this condition is 'globalised' – the tension between those who claim to be native and those who are called non-native, all designated as victims of massacres, pogroms, pillages and expulsion.

So, upon initial analysis, this is what the theme of our conference evoked for a political theorist who has never made the city a subject of study, properly speaking, but who has attempted a historical sociology of globalisation. No doubt our work will provide food for thought and will allow us to explore these and other avenues further.

Bibliography

Adelkhah, Fariba, *Etre moderne en Iran*, Paris: Karthala, 1998.

Badot, Olivier and Dupuis, Marc, 'Le réenchantement de la distribution', www. lesechos.fr/cgi-bin/btnimpr.pl, 2003.

Bayart, Jean-François, *L'Etat en Afrique. La politique du ventre*, Paris: Fayard, 1989.

——*Le Gouvernement du monde. Une critique politique de la globalisation*, Paris: Fayard, 2004.

Bozdogan, Sibel, *Modernism and Nation Building. Turkish Architectural Culture in the Early Republic*, Seattle: University of Washington Press, 2001.

——*La Turquie kemaliste. The Atatürk Era. A New Turkey and a New Generation*, Istanbul: Ray Sigorta, 1998.

Brown, Peter, *Le Culte des saints. Son essor et sa fonction dans la chrétienté latine*, Paris: Les Editions du Cerf, 1996.

Castells, Manuel, *L'Ere de l'information. 1: La Société en réseaux*, Paris: Fayard, new edn, 2001.

——*La Galaxie Internet*, Paris: Fayard, 2002.

de Certeau, Michel, *L'Invention du quotidien.1: Arts de faire*, Paris: UGE, 1980.

Chevalier, Louis, *L'Assassinat de Paris*, Paris: Calmann-Lévy, 1977.

Deleuze, Gilles, *Pourparlers – 1972–1990*, Paris: Editions de Minuit, 1990.

Durakbasa, Ayse and Cindoglu, Dilek, 'Encounters at the Counter: Gender and the Shopping Experience', in Deniz Kandiyoti and Ayse Saktanber, eds, *Fragments of Culture. The Everyday of Modern Turkey*, London: I. B. Tauris, 2002, pp. 73–89.

Garreau, Joel, *Edge City: Life on the New Frontier*, New York: Doubleday, 1991.

ter Haar, Gerrie, *Halfway to Paradise: African Christians in Europe*, Cardiff: Cardiff Academic Press, 1998.

Hardt, Michael and Negri, *Empire*, Paris: Exils Editeur, 2000.

Horne, Janet R., 'In pursuit of Greater France: visions of empire among Musée social reformers, 1894–1931', in Julia Clancy-Smith and Frances Gouda, eds, *Domesticating the Empire. Race, Gender, and Family Life in French and Dutch Colonialism*, Charlottesville: University Press of Virginia, 1998, pp. 21–42.

Kalberg, Stephen, *La Sociologie historique comparative de Max Weber*, Paris: La Découverte, 2002.

de Latour, Eliane, 'Du ghetto au voyage clandestin: la métaphore héroïque', in *Autrepart*, 19, 2001, pp. 155–76.

——Héros du retour, in *Critique internationale*, 19, April 2003, pp. 171–89.

——Métaphores familiales dans les ghettos de Côte d'Ivoire, in *Autrepart*, 18, 2001, pp. 151–67.

Le Pape, Marc, *L'Energie sociale à Abidjan. Economie politique de la ville en Afrique noire, 1930–1995*, Paris: Karthala, 1997.

MacGaffey, Janet and Bazenguissa-Ganga, Rémy, *Congo-Paris. Transnational Traders on the Margins of the Law*, Oxford: James Currey, 2000.

Marx, Karl, *La Première critique de l'économie politique. Les Manuscrits de 1844*, Paris: UGE, 1972.

Mauss, Marcel, *Sociologie et anthropologie* (1950), Paris: PUF, 1980.

Mermoz, Mélanie, 'Un nouvel espace urbain', in *Alternatives économiques*, 205, July–August 2002, pp. 52–5.

Mongin, Olivier, *La Condition urbaine,* Paris: Editions du Seuil, 2006.

Navaro-Yashin, Yael, *Faces of the State. Secularism and Public Life in Turkey*, Princeton: Princeton University Press, 2002.

Parrenas, Rhacel Salazar, *Servants of Globalisation. Women, Migration and Domestic Work*, Stanford: Stanford University Press, 2001.

Peel, John David Yeadson, *Religious Encounter and the Making of the Yoruba*, Bloomington: Indiana University Press, 2000.

Rabinow, Paul, *French Modern. Norms and Forms of the Social Environment*, Chicago: The University of Chicago Press, 1989.

Roitman, Janet, 'The garrison-entrepôt', in *Cahiers d'études africaines*, 150–2, XXXVIII (2–4), 1998, pp. 297–329.

—— 'La garrison-entrepôt : une manière de gouverner dans le bassin du lac Tchad', in *Critique internationale*, 19, April 2003, pp. 93–115.

Sassen, Saskia, *Globalisation and its Discontents: Essays on the New Mobility of People and Money*, New York: The New Press, 1998.

Stoller, Paul, *Money Has No Smell. The Africanisation of New York*, Chicago: Chicago University Press, 2002.

Trexler, Richard C., *Public Life in Renaissance Florence*, Ithaca: Cornell University Press, 1980.

Vacher, Hélène, ed., *Villes coloniales aux XIXᵉ–XXᵉ siècles. D'un sujet d'action à un objet d'histoire (Algérie, Maroc, Libye et Iran). Essais et guide bibliographique*, Paris: Maisonneuve et Larose, 2005.

Veyne, Paul, *La Société romaine*, Paris: Editions du Seuil, 1991.

——*L'Elégie érotique romaine. L'amour, la poésie et l'Occident*, Paris: Editions du Seuil, 1983.

——*L'Empire gréco-romain*, Paris: Editions du Seuil, 2005.

Warnier, Jean-Pierre, ed., *Le Paradoxe de la marchandise authentique. Imaginaire et consommation de masse*, Paris: L'Harmattan, 1994.

Warnier, Jean-Pierre and Rosselin C., eds, *Authentifier la marchandise. Anthropologie critique de la quête d'authenticité*, Paris: L'Harmattan, 1996.

Watson, James L., 'Introduction: transnationalism, localization, and fast foods in East Asia', in James L. Watson, ed., *Golden Arches East: McDonald's in East Asia,* Stanford: Stanford University Press, 1997, pp. 28–9.

White, Jenny B., *Islamist Mobilization in Turkey: A Study in Vernacular Politics*, Seattle: University of Washington Press, 2002.

Notes

1. Garreau, *Edge City: Life on the New Frontier.*
2. Sassen, *Globalisation and its Discontents.*
3. Veyne, *L'Empire gréco-romain*, chs. 5–6.
4. Brown, *Le Culte des saints.*
5. Bayart, *Le Gouvernement du monde*, ch. 1.
6. Warnier and Rosselin, *Authentifier la marchandise* and Warnier, *Le Paradoxe de la marchandise authentique.*
7. Mongin, *La Condition urbaine.*
8. Adelkhah, *Etre moderne en Iran.*
9. Parrenas, *Servants of Globalisation*, pp. 206 and following.

10. Source: observations by Fariba Adelkhah in Tokyo (March–April 2003). About the figure of the *javânmard* see Adelkhah, *Etre moderne en Iran*, ch. 2.

11. MacGaffey and Bazenguissa-Ganga, *Congo-Paris*, pp. 142 and following.

12. ter Haar, *Halfway to Paradise*, p. 40.

13. Sassen, *Globalisation and its Discontents*.

14. Stoller, *Money Has No Smell*.

15. Ibid. and Sassen, *Globalisation and its Discontents*.

16. Castells, *La Galaxie Internet*, ch. 8; see also the cartography of Matthew Zook (www.zooknic.com).

17. Castells ibid.

18. Castells, *L'Ere de l'information. 1: La Société en réseaux*, p. 502.

19. Le Pape, *L'Energie sociale à Abidjan*.

20. Garreau, *Edge City: Life on the New Frontier*.

21. de Certeau, *L'Invention du quotidien. 1: Arts de faire*, pp. 180 and following.

22. Bayart, *L'Etat en Afrique. La politique du ventre*.

23. Here we mostly follow Kalberg, *La Sociologie historique comparative de Max Weber*, in particular pp. 206–48. The author notes that Weber proposes no systematic account for these two concepts that regularly occur in his texts.

24. Rabinow, *French Modern. Norms and Forms of the Social Environment*, *passim* (notably ch. 9); Horne, 'In pursuit of Greater France: visions of empire among Musée social reformers, 1894–1931'; Vacher, ed., *Villes coloniales aux XIXᵉ–XXᵉ siècles*.

25. Exposition 'Alger, paysage urbain et architectures', Paris, Cité de l'architecture et du patrimoine, 2003; de Roux, E., 'Comment s'est bâtie Alger la Blanche', *Le Monde*, 19 August 2003, p. 20.

26. Chevalier, *L'Assassinat de Paris*.

27. Deleuze, *Pourparlers – 1972–1990*, p. 156.

28. Mauss, *Sociologie et anthropologie*, pp. 368–9, 384.

29. Marx, *La Première critique de l'économie politique*, p. 170.

30. See, for example, 'Style 5: Glamour spécial mode été 2001', supplement of *Libération*, 10 March 2001.

31. Badot and Dupuis, 'Le réenchantement de la distribution', p. 1.

32. Ibid., p. 2.

33. Account of professionals reported by Grosjean, B., 'Les centres commerciaux misent sur le rayon plaisir', *Libération*, 28 August 2002, pp. 2–4.

34. Ibid.; Badot and Dupuis, 'Le réenchantement de la distribution'; Biassette, G., 'Le "mall" de Washington, condensé du rêve américain', *La Croix-L'Evénement*, 3 September 2003, p. 28; Lutaud, L., 'Dubaï se rêve comme La Mecque mondiale des soldes', *Le Figaro Entreprises*, 20 January 2003, pp. 18–19; 'In this world, shopping can be an art', *International Herald Tribune*, 12 December 2002, p. 18.

35. Tavernise, S., 'In Moscow "mall rats" signs of improving times', *International Herald Tribune*, 6 February 2003, p. 2; M.-P. Subtil, 'Les Moscovites découvrent les hypermarchés', *Le Monde*, 15–16 December 2002, p. 12.

36. Mermoz, Mélanie, 'Un nouvel espace urbain'.

37. Interview with Jun Aoki, *Axis* [Tokyo], 102, March–April 2003, pp. 58–63; *The Japan Architect*, 48, winter 2003, pp. 30–3; 'Miuccia Prada, retour à Tokyo', *Le Figaro*, 3 July 2003, p. 17.

38. Alessandrini, M., 'Roppongi Hills, la cité globale', *Le Nouvel Observateur*, 25 September 2003, p. 42.

39. Sources: interviews and personal observations, Tokyo, April 2003; Forestier, N., 'Les petites marques du luxe commencent à souffrir sur le marché japonais', *Le Figaro-Economie*, 8 October 2003, p. IX.

40. Laval, G., 'Frimes bizness: à la Reynerie, à Toulouse, une minorité vit de la fauche', *Libération*, 26 January 1999, p. 14.

41. Roitman, 'La garnison-entrepôt: une manière de gouverner dans le bassin du lac Tchad' and 'The garrison *entrepôt*'. The analogy is evident in the extremely high-security shopping malls of South Africa.

42. Jean-Michel Silberstein quoted in Mermoz, p. 53.

43. Navaro-Yashin, *Faces of the State*, p. 79, in his chapter with the explicit title: 'The market for identities: buying and selling secularity and Islam'.

44. Ibid., pp. 85 and following.

45. Ibid., p. 91.

46. Bozdogan, *Modernism and Nation Building*, notably pp. 101, 174, 193 and following. See also edns 1–49 of *La Turquie kémaliste*, published between 1933–48, from which certain parts are published in *La Turquie kemaliste. The Atatürk Era. A New Turkey and a New Generation*, also cited.

47. Durakbasa and Cindoglu, 'Encounters at the counter: gender and the shopping experience'.

48. White, *Islamist Mobilization in Turkey*, p. 53.

49. Trexler, *Public Life in Renaissance Florence*.

50. Watson, 'Introduction: transnationalism, localization, and fast foods in East Asia'.

51. de Latour, 'Métaphores sociales dans les ghettos de Côte d'Ivoire', p. 151–67; 'Du ghetto au voyage clandestin: la métaphore héroïque'; and 'Héros du retour'. The words in italic are in *nushi*, the street language of the Ivory Coast.

52. de Latour, 'Métaphores sociales dans les ghettos de Côte d'Ivoire', p. 153.

53. Félix Houphouët-Boigny was president of Ivory Coast for over thirty years until his death in 1993. The term refers both to the clientelist system based on the raising and redistribution of taxes installed by the president and to the political movement that regroups different opponents of the regime of president Bédié.

54. Ibid., p. 156.

55. Ibid.

56. de Latour, 'Du ghetto au voyage clandestin: la métaphore héroïque', p. 173.

57. de Latour, 'Métaphores sociales dans les ghettos de Côte d'Ivoire', p. 152.

58. Ibid, p. 164.

59. Gilles Deleuze commenting on the work of Michel Foucault, in *Pourparlers – 1972– 1990*, pp. 206–7.

60. Veyne, *La Société romaine*, ch. 1 and *L'Elégie érotique romaine*, p. 90; Peel, *Religious Encounter and the Making of the Yoruba*, pp. 241 and following.

61. Hardt and Negri, *Empire*.

PART ONE

Cities in Motion

ALAIN TARRIUS

Europe without Borders: Migration Networks, Transnational Territories and Informal Activities

In the last twenty years, new forms of migration have become increasingly apparent around the Mediterranean basin. Since the mid-1980s these seem to be characterised by the international 'pendular' movements of thousands of Moroccans and Algerians, mostly small-scale entrepreneurs who transport goods from Western Europe back to their native cities and villages. This is how we have come to identify, during surveys conducted in 1985 and 1986, a high-volume commercial system in Belsunce, Marseille's central historic neighbourhood. This commercial area welcomes approximately 700,000 buyers from North Africa each year. Throughout the years this commerce has become internationalised and now supplies carpets, electronic appliances, audiovisual equipment, automotive spare parts, etc to commercial 'runners' who make door-to-door deliveries for clients who cannot obtain visas to travel to Marseille.[1] This has caused a massive transformation for thousands of 'small migrants', often unemployed or in financially precarious situations, who could earn a relatively good living from their 'competence of circulation'. In 1995, we counted 42,000 vehicles making two return trips per month from the South of France to Morocco via Alicante and Algeciras, or towards Algeria via Alicante and Oran. Approximately 160,000, mostly Moroccans, situated near the Spanish border and up near Toulon and Valence, lived off of these revenues.

Since 2001,[2] our attention and investigations have focused on 'circular' migrants rather than 'pendular' migrants. These are mostly Afghans and Caucasians who embark on international rotations of ten to sixteen months via Iran, the UAE, Syria, Istanbul, the coast of Bulgaria, the Black Sea, Odessa and Georgia, and then return home. They transport electronics from Dubai, jewels and clothing from Syria and leather jackets from Istanbul to Sofia. They work piecemeal jobs during their rotation. Contrary to the aforementioned Moroccans and Algerians, they don't live in the countries they travel through.

Nevertheless, this articulated difference between mobile and stationary living does not erase the strong similarities between these two migratory tendencies. In essence both migratory groups, while they renounce their localised dependencies on large-, medium-, and small-scale enterprise, now place themselves at the service of large globalised companies and, given the highly competitive conditions and prohibitive logistics of official trade agreements, circulate products among populations otherwise deprived of them.

This 'shift in dependency' influences the positions of these tens of thousands of new migrants in terms of the politics of integration of the nation-states they cross. There is a considerable lack of integration; an economic complementation with one's home region; the ability to adapt to a variety of cultural contexts; and the institution of 'circular territories'[3] mapped out by the transient movement of the various migrant networks. This has created means and modes of communicating with local societies different from those proposed by the historical segmentation of national political borders.

It is this point that we would like to examine carefully in this chapter by showing how, to the east and west of the Mediterranean basin, European cities are increasingly structured by the presence of foreigners belonging to these new migratory systems. They present social-spatial morphologies that vary greatly from the usual forms of poverty in these areas. These new forms could perhaps be best described as 'post-migratory'. Issues of spatial and social mobility, historically reserved for population movements within one nation, can be extended, permitting us to recognise the nature and production of these new waves of foreigners to a far greater degree than systems of either emigration or immigration, which no longer seem to make sense. 'How does one enter the city and step out of it?' Robert Ezra Park already asked, to which we add, 'independent of the territorial level or the distance one comes from?' How does one become part of a neighbourhood, along with all the others who make up these cosmopolitan worlds based on transient populations? These are the questions that have guided our investigations. In particular, we will discuss Sofia, the capital of Bulgaria, and Alicante, port city of the Spanish Levant.

Sofia: When Gentrification 'After Socialism' Does Not Depend on the Emergence of a 'Middle Class'

The research conducted in Sofia was time-consuming, and not only because we were in the midst of witnessing an ex-socialist city transitioning to capitalism, where property transfers were one of the essential markers of the accrued pauperisation of the population while the other marker was the emergence of a wealthy class. It was also because at that particular time, the urban transformations were indications of a double linkage to the vast outside world: linking to the Middle East through its long-standing migrant populations, and linking to Western European nations through their powerful mafias. Three populations witness to contemporary urban transformations reveal here, in particular, the transition towards capitalism: past and present Middle Eastern migrants, Gypsies and poverty-stricken populations and finally, business communities who draw their newfound riches from this urban renovation and various other rackets.

Sofia's population has just recently surpassed 1.3 million inhabitants. This city is situated 500 m above sea level, at the foot of a mythic mountain, Vitocha. Its centre comprises a zone of 'socialist' architecture built in the 1950s on the Stalinist model, streets lined with individual houses and buildings built between 1900–10, a few houses from the eighteenth century scattered here and there, Austro-Hungarian architecture and endless concentric stretches of buildings, ranging between four and six stories, built in the 1970s and 1980s.

From popular fraternity to the takeover of commercial sectors: the Syrians of Sofia

Bulgaria prior to 1991 had allied itself with a 'brother people' in the Middle East: the Republic of Syria. Bulgaria's prominent education system admitted engineering students as well as other students in highly specialised disciplines. These students came primarily from either politically powerful families or wealthy merchant families who were allied with the political elite – essentially *bazaaris*.

The bourgeois business class of Damascus preferred to send its children to Sofia rather than to far-distant places like Moscow, not because the training was superior but because Sofia's proximity, via Istanbul, made it easier to supply merchandise that was otherwise absent from the Bulgarian market and in demand. A Syrian clothing merchant from Aleppo took us on a visiting tour to his fellow countrymen in the centre of Sofia, around the former socialist party headquarters, made up of expansive esplanades and massive buildings undergoing 'global gentrification' (such as a former party palace transforming into a Hilton hotel). The accounts that each man shared with me of his migratory path towards settling down point to a unique model:

> Before 1991, we stayed five or six years in Bulgaria, partly because of our studies and partly because we could continue the clothing and jewellery commerce between Damascus and Sofia which was set up in the mid-1970s. We weren't really established yet, but everyone knew they could buy from Syrian students. After 1991, several hundred of us became naturalised Bulgarians, and several hundred others were granted permanent residency status;[4] so we then set up chain stores from Damascus or from Aleppo. We also began selling electronics, in addition to jewellery and clothing, in collaboration with the Iranians and Afghanis.
>
> For the last five years, our central neighbourhood has been increasingly populated by Egyptians, Palestinians and Tunisians, who start up low-cost restaurants and food shops. We are very appreciated by the Bulgarians who frequent, more and more, our neighbourhood. We aren't subject to racism, because we don't encroach on the professions of Bulgarians, and they do good business with us in the downtown commercial centre.

We studied the Middle Eastern migrations in Bulgaria.[5] Since 1997, after the great crisis that led to the exodus and expulsion of hundreds of thousands of Turkish-speaking Bulgarians back to Turkey, a transnational migratory pattern was established between Afghanistan and the border of the Black Sea via Iran, the UAE (especially Dubai), Syria, Turkey and Bulgaria. The return routes generally begin at the Bulgarian port city of Burgas towards Georgia, via Odessa in the Ukraine. Through Azerbaijan, these migrants return to the cities and villages they left twelve to eighteen months earlier.

We are in the midst of one of these transnational migration patterns that have developed since the 1990s. These migrants, almost exclusively men, work here and there over the course of their journey, and many of them act as 'carriers' or smugglers for merchants in Dubai or Syria. From the Emirates, the latest electronics – MP3 players, microcomputers – are smuggled. The Afghan or Iranian 'runners' involved in this trafficking usually act on command from Syrian merchants in Sofia. The merchandise is tax-free and bypasses any import quota restrictions; the Syrians in Dubai set the selling price for their goods, on average at 65 per cent below the price in Western Europe.

The resale value of these goods in Sofia nets them profits anywhere between 40 to 60 per cent, which represents a net gain of about €3,000 for the smuggler and €2,000 for the destination merchant on a shipment worth about €20,000. From Damascus to Aleppo, gold jewellery is always transported; bought at 30 per cent cheaper than its resale price in Bulgaria, the financial gain on this exchange is shared: An Afghan 'runner' could reasonably hope to earn €4,500 after one trip. In Istanbul, leather garments sewn or labelled in the Afghan sweatshop district near the *Outogar* (the large departure station for Balkans-bound buses) are stuffed into trailers. A hundred or so leather jackets resold at about €60 each will fetch about €1,500 for the smugglers. The money earned by working odd jobs along the smuggling routes covers the costs of being on the road and allows these men to send small sums of money home to their families.

Finally, after unloading in Sofia, Syrian merchants either sell the goods on the spot or circulate them en route to Serbia. Unsold merchandise from previous shipments is transported, via a maritime route along the Black Sea beginning at Burgas or Varna, to Constanza in Romania and Odessa in Ukraine, and finally to Georgia. This 'return complement' brings in about €4,000. In a one-year circuit, these Afghans and Iranians can count on earning approximately €12, 000.

Four weeks of riding buses from Istanbul to Varna or Sofia throughout the month of June allowed us to estimate the flux of Afghans at 6,000 people.[6] Buses are chartered in Istanbul destined for Sofia, or merchants wait for smugglers in Burgas, the port city near the Turkish border. The revival of a pre-socialist local practice in Bulgaria was brought to our attention: the *gourbet*. Inhabitants from various villages gather together in order to go off to work in neighbouring Balkan countries (in such jobs as seasonal fruit picking or construction). It seems as though these groups buy merchandise from the Syrian retailers so as to resell the goods along their regional routes.

The Bulgarian Syrians are thus at the heart of a vast international transfer of merchandise. These new transnational migrants, who are increasingly numerous, acquire and develop the competence to circulate, which conforms to the practices of 'wild', ultra-liberal, economic globalisation. It is their role to reach any and every customer they possibly can, no matter how remote or small the market, and provide them with merchandise that, due to national political problems affecting local politics, would otherwise be unavailable to them. At first glance, it seems clearly paradoxical that these forms of contraband, currently very much in fashion in the pre-capitalist world, are contributing to this massive capitalist expansion.

The increasing density of 'Arab' populations (as Bulgarian demographers call them) in the heart of Sofia is thus not a classic phenomenon of the appearance of poor ethnic neighbourhoods in a city under expansion. The 34,000 Arabs, half-legal and half-illegal, who were registered in a census conducted by the NGO International Centre for Minority Studies and Intercultural Relations in Sofia, were generally wealthier than their Bulgarian counterparts. They represented the dynamic emergence of Middle Eastern business savvy, a vast 'South' from Cairo to Islamabad.

On the question of any visible signs of this wealth, the Syrian merchant I spoke with at length said that today the role of his people was to strengthen their position in the city with discretion. When the level of street business was well-established, it was good to generalise the efforts to renovate the older buildings that make up their residential neighbourhood, as opposed to the ill-conceived and gaudy renovations underway in other parts of Sofia. He said:

> We should not be lumped in with the local mafia population, who parade their wealth about and provoke a deep aversion on the part of their fellow Bulgarians. For now, the mafia still has a certain cachet, but once Europe or the people of Bulgaria, depending on the possible political scenarios, decide to get rid of them, we will be sufficiently established to finally be able to be ourselves: sincere Bulgarian citizens, opening up economic possibilities and political perspectives (undreamed of given the current situation) with a Middle East historically allied in good times and estranged in times of conflict and misery.

This analysis was similarly offered by a number of Syrians, Afghans, Lebanese and Palestinians who spoke to us. This point of view has also appeared regularly in Bulgarian newspapers over the course of the last five years. Political debates about the legitimacy of adhering to the European community feed off the debate between the 'alliance of the South' versus the 'oppression by the North'.

A conspicuous gentrification: The nouveau-riche *must be mafia*

When we asked about the presence of rich populations in Sofia likely to participate in urban development, our Bulgarian research colleagues unanimously responded that this group represents about 15 per cent of the capital's population, and that more than half of this 15 per cent earn their incomes through mafia practices. We have therefore tried to learn who exactly these people are. This percentage is, in fact, derived from the population of residential areas of Sofia that have undergone large-scale renovations since 1996. These are often very ostentatious, such as one palace that looks like a fortified castle, as well as the nickname for the surrounding houses of 'Beverly Hills', built in the hilly neighbourhoods from Dragalevtsi to Vladaya, south of Sofia, in the foothills of Vitocha, towards neighbouring Macedonia. This particular neighbourhood is built on the very spot where, ages ago, the villas of the *nomenklatura* stood. In fact, we should deduct from this population the ancient owners who support themselves by renting out parts of their villas, their new renters the small business owners[7]; the service personnel in the large villas; the new professionals who purchased modest houses; and the artisans (especially builders) who build themselves their own modest homes. Then that 15 per cent figure would be much closer to 5 per cent.

Middle Eastern populations are conspicuously absent from these neighbourhoods, where two types of local rehabilitation are carried out. First is the renovation of old villas, ranging from simply painting façades and replacing windows and doors to more comprehensive renovations managed by architecture firms. Second is the construction of new villas, surrounded by high fences, camera surveillance and patrolmen dressed in black with black hats, who signal to passers-by to stay away before reaching for their walkie-talkies in the event of non-compliance. Muzzled dogs on leashes are usually visible.

Following a quick visit to a few sites with Svetla (see endnote #7), hurried along by the shouts of ever-present guards, I returned alone, dressed in a suit, to one of these neighbourhoods, which looked to me to have achieved the heights of Hollywood-style bad taste. The hotel-palace in the form of a six-storied fortified castle, flanked by turrets and festooned by multicoloured crenels, sat atop a cluster of six other fenced-in villas, an aquatic sport complex 'Swachgames', body-building rooms and a medical centre featuring, in English on a giant exterior sign, the physicians' names, areas of specialisation and professional affiliations with American, English and Swiss addresses. (I noticed a Parisian address for the nephrology society, which I could not locate once I returned to France.)

During this visit, I managed to enter into the hall of the hotel-castle and asked for a room. I was told there were no vacancies, yet there were no cars in the parking lot, all the room keys hung from a display case and all the curtains in the rooms were drawn. Then I limped my way towards the medical practice, having learned from the large sign that an osteopath from a London academy was on staff. The receptionist informed me that the practice was a 'private international foundation' and that consultations were by appointment only. When I pleaded that it was an emergency, she suggested that I call an ambulance to take me to a hospital in Sofia. I walked along the 'Swachgames', resonating with the delighted shrieks of swimmers, and walked into one of the fenced-in areas that bordered on seven large villas. Two elderly people, uniformed in grey, gestured to me to be on my way.

Just then a car pulled up and two black-clad guards inside laughingly said, 'It's enough for today,' and politely asked me to get in the back seat. They drove me back to the small place in Dragalevtsi where Svetla was waiting for me at a tiny café with three other people, maintenance workers for the 'establishments' I had just tried to visit. Each one told me the hotel never had any guests, just as the medical facility never had any doctors, but that the stream of large, black, four-wheel drive BMWs, Mercedes, and Porsches was incessant, with guards always sitting behind those tinted windows. It would be hard to find a better setting for a B-movie.

My interlocutors attributed the secretiveness of these *nouveau riches* to the fact that no one knows the origins of their fortunes, lest there be expropriations for multiple families in Sofia. They also pointed out that these people, despite themselves, were drawing thousands of visitors to their gated neighbourhood, who want to see 'the spectacle' from the main road. These visitors are instant consumers, and the small cafés like the one Svetla runs were popping up everywhere. By three in the afternoon that Saturday, several hundred people were getting off the #64 and #98 buses, giving the place the air of a fancy fair.

People spoke up to denounce these abuses of wealth, and some went on excursions up to the gates of the hotel-palace before being thoroughly insulted by the guards standing behind a pack of dogs. On occasion a luxury car would drive by with turned-up windows, slowing down as it neared the irate crowd. It happened even that a passenger showed his head and spat in the direction of the crowd. The former members of the *nomenklatura* or their children served sandwiches and candy prepared at home and wrapped in newspaper while heightening, in their daily anger, the level of collective indignation. The words exchanged among these people, who claimed their neighbours as witnesses, were indignant: 'Look at where we are now! This is the promise of liberty!'

'It's worse than before,' said others, drawing the response from ex-apparatchiks, 'Never have we spit at the people.' These were among the key phrases exchanged on this spot of 'the spectacle of gentrification', phrases often heard in other parts of Sofia.

Gentrification and pauperisation linked to the emergence of the nouveau riches

The allusion made by Svetla's three friends and by a university colleague to the plundering of apartments by the mafia certainly corresponded to reality. Beginning in 1993, and particularly in the southern neighbourhoods near Touka where people switch from the #14 tramway to the #64 and #98 buses en route to Dragalevtsi, credit agencies began opening up on the ground floors of apartment buildings built in the 1970s and 1980s, where the apartments belonged to mid-level bureaucrats who often stayed on working at severely reduced salaries of €80–€120 per month.

These credit agencies advertised formulas for 'long-term cumulative credit', meaning credit notes allowing people to buy, whether necessary or not, food, clothing, appliances and electronics. At the end of two or three years, a bill would be presented to families who, unable to pay it, were then evicted from their homes, left with barely enough to allow them to live in the old, dilapidated apartments downtown. Once everyone in a building had been swindled and evicted, the building's renovation would follow, then drawing in slightly richer families (incomes vary between €250–€400 per month) able to quickly adapt to European integration. These families are then targeted with 'rent-to-own' contracts, directly guaranteed by the managers of the credit agencies in the ground floor offices, who then move on to another building.

In the last two years, real estate prices have increased fivefold under the concerted influence of the above-mentioned practices and of the arrival of English investors, who create little renovation ghettos in a few neighbourhoods in Sofia and even in rural villages, dismantling the traditional farming practices. Currently, Bulgarian banks do not lend money for these kinds of purchases.

Small convenience businesses such as cafés, hair salons, etc that are not tied to their credit-agency predecessors set up shop on the ground floors, and their owners await their promotion to 'middle class' status, adopting in advance its supposed corresponding tendencies. The problem, however, is that this population is badly weakened by the stagnation of its purchasing power compared with the increases in real estate value. The vast majority of these renters borrow money from the mafia real estate agents, having signed contracts that include debt readjustment clauses based on increases in property value. In short, the 'gentrification of the poor' feeds that of the rich.

These property manipulations aren't the only wealth-generation strategies of the mafia. Bulgaria is a prized route for Afghan and Turkish heroin trafficking (it's often the same Afghan morphine base, which is then altered in Turkey). Some Afghan 'runners' don't take the detours through the Gulf States in order to stick to the traffic of legal goods. They pass directly through northern Iran, Azerbaijan or Turkey first, then through Georgia and the Black Sea, and end up in Bulgaria via Istanbul or Burgas. The Turkish-speaking people in southern Bulgaria, more or less assisted by the Muslim Roma, take over from the Afghans to pass into Macedonia and then into the 'stateless' region in the 'greater Albania', west of Kosovo. From here they reach Montenegro, where they load up illicit drugs in small ports along the Adriatic Sea destined for Italy.

The Roma involved in this type of commerce are actually few in number. Many more, as is the case in other parts of Europe, consume the low-quality heroin that they carry with them, which has incited NGOs such as Médecins du Monde to intervene.

Two Roma communities have been in Sofia for over thirty years. One community to the west along Alexandrov Avenue, consists of some small houses, and the nostalgic inhabitants show us the brooms and uniforms they used to wear over fifteen years ago, when each family was assigned duties for the upkeep of the streets. The other community, to the east near the train station, is made up of buildings now in a state of squalor. Disease and misery have quickly degraded the very look of this population. Children wear torn rags; beg in the streets; mothers sit in circles on the damp floors of the courtyards; rusted cars are about, and piles of garbage sit in the lobbies of buildings and in the windowsills.

In the city as in the countryside, the Roma's economic organisation, based on cooperatives in which they worked in a variety of jobs, has collapsed since the regime change. Even if some exceptional, richer places bear witness of the implication of some inhabitants in illicit trafficking, the misery in these neighbourhoods is generalised. In Podgorica, Montenegro, where we observed the trucks arriving from Bulgaria that facilitate the drug trafficking in these 'stateless' zones, we didn't see a single Roma driver or guide. However, the trucks belonging to companies managed by Bulgarians were seen in the gentrified hillsides of Dragalevtsi. Here, as in the rest of Europe, the Roma act as the trees that hide the forests.

In brief, the unchecked accumulation of wealth among a tiny group, with its outrageous gentrification projects, and the attempts at the gentrification through building renovations of a weak and manipulated population, has given way to the abandonment of the poorest people and led to increasing stigma and xenophobia towards them.

The lot of the common people

We have just examined the situation of about 20 per cent of the population in Sofia. Salaries of the other 80 per cent, when there is work to be had (the unemployment rate is over 27 per cent), rarely surpasses €100 per month. A trip to the large outdoor markets and street vendors allowed us to take note of the prices of the most common food products. Onions, tomatoes and fruit sell for €0.40–€0.60 per kg; a litre of wine also costs €0.40–€0.60; turnips and potatoes sell for €0.30; dried beans, for €0.80. Smoked salted pork sells for €2.50–€3 per kg; fresh pork, for €2–2.50 per kg. Lower-quality cuts of beef sell for €5 per kg; dried fish sells for €3 per kg and fresh fish, for €6 per kg. Fruits and vegetables are bought individually – one mandarin here, three potatoes there.

Rent in buildings erected during the 1970s and 1980s, which cover most of the city reconstructed in the aftermath of the Second World War, varies depending on size: €60 for a two-room apartment, €80 for a three-room apartment. Social assistance doesn't amount to very much, perhaps €20 per child. After brief calculation, we find that it is impossible for a family to live in Sofia these days. Families gather into a single small apartment; others simply leave the city and move to villages, and everyone maintains strong relationships with their rural family or friends.

The heaps of jams, preserves, vegetables, and cured meats are impressive. Kitchen ceilings are strewn with dozens of cuts of meat for drying. Every family that can rent out a bed in a room of their apartment will crowd in with others somewhere else. In a central square between the Ministry of International Economic Affairs and a large Serbian Orthodox church, we counted 127 homeless people one Friday afternoon. What appeared to be a demonstration or a gathering of people vying perhaps for distribution of food or clothing, in fact, didn't follow this logic. A priest at the entrance of the Orthodox church told me that here people don't fear the police:

> In the event that the police vans arrive to pick them up and take them out to the suburbs, they all come into my church where they can't be touched.

Many people today feel nostalgic for the socialist era, and this feeling is not only shared among low-income earners but also among professional teachers (per month, a university assistant earns €150; a professor, €350; a schoolteacher, €180). The sight of the streets, considering the meagre means of shoppers, becomes dismal as soon as one walks beyond the few avenues around the immediate centre. There are very few businesses, and they offer outdated or obsolete products. On the other hand, the Arab quarter is frequented by anyone looking for new, good-quality products, which confers upon this area a kind of 'reverse gentrification' status.

So goes the 'transition towards capitalism', the tireless ideological theme of demand created by the ability to wait just a little bit longer. Approximately 45 per cent of the urban population suffers in abject poverty; 20 per cent live miserably; 15 per cent are foreigners building their own prosperity; 12 per cent live a 'dignified' existence on salaries ranging from €400–800 per month; and about 8 per cent flaunt their unimaginable wealth.

Alicante: Rehabilitation and Gentrification in a 'Globalised' City

Alicante, comparable to the large port of neighbouring Valencia 170 km north, has historically played the role of Spain's open port on the Mediterranean, specifically for Madrid. Valencia's port specialised more in large movements of merchandise, and drew much more development for the city once industries set up along its waterfront in the nineteenth century. The trade in agricultural products during the twentieth century grew even more, without supplanting the role of industry. The port at Alicante, however, was (and still is) reserved for travellers; goods produced in Madrid are offered in the local boutiques near the piers to merchants touring the Mediterranean in order to buy or order goods in bulk.

Although both cities are in the Catalan region, Valencia and Alicante vary historically in terms of their contrasting populations, the former being a densely populated working-class city, the latter mostly a commercial trade city, with populations from Spanish or foreign descent. Valencia had a total population of 777,000 inhabitants in 2000 and 747,000 in 2005, and Alicante had a population of 275,000 and 267,000 respectively. However, whereas Valencia is a compact city separated from its port, Alicante is a low-lying city giving directly onto its port. It is at the heart of a conurbation of cities: Benidorm, 40 km north; Santa Pola, 17 km south; and Elche and Crevillente, 22 km and 27 km west, respectively. The exchanges between these cities are constant and high in volume, to the extent that the true size of Alicante's service and commercial activities extends to over 450,000 inhabitants. Its loss of 8,000 inhabitants between 2000–05 was largely compensated by a population increase in these other cities.

Territorial zones and specific populations in Alicante

Even though a boulevard divides the highly populated residential zones from the municipal city, the waterfront and the 'Santa Barbara' Moorish castle are what moulded the socio-urban morphologies in Alicante. The hilly area stretching from the Moorish castle to the port is a labyrinth of small streets and stairways connecting these two sites. Alicante's 'old village' is called the *casc antic*, a common designation for historic city centres in Spain, and is made up of small whitewashed houses with blue doors and tiled balconies woven among small Mediterranean gardens (with fig and pomegranate trees, bougainvillaea, citrus trees, grape vines).

Until the 1960s, the area north of the port was entirely reserved for commercial fishermen and craftsmen, and these mariners all lived in the *casc antic* houses. The unity between this neighbourhood, the old port, and the population began to change in the 1970s, when the English bought up 85 per cent of the fishermen's houses and docked their pleasure boats in the old port. In the 1980s the municipal government created a massive real estate and luxury hotels project in the northern part. Bars, seafood restaurants and nightclubs all appeared along the renovated jetties, separated from the *casc antic* by a housing development from the 1930s which houses a variety of administrations and shields the English homeowners from late-night noises emanating from the port. This urban port 'enclave' is largely open at the maritime section of the conurbation.

A large casino was recently added to the southern part of the old port (a tunnel under the harbour joins the two quays). This tourist area, is packed every night, between 5 PM and 4 AM, with luxury boats from Benidorm, Santa Pola and other small seaside ports. The residential square-metre values are now exorbitant compared with values in other parts of Alicante. In July 2005, a house in the *casc antic* measuring about 90 sq. m with a garden measuring 20 sq. m was sold for €1,300,000, whereas at a distance of 300 m from this house, in the old city, slightly larger houses in excellent condition are selling for €108,000 or €140,000. We met a modest Spanish family descended from a long line of fisherman a few days before they finalised the sale of their house. They spoke to us about their hatred of these new arrivals:

> Everywhere in Spain, we're being forced to move away from the

old ports and neighbourhoods along the sea [...] We cannot live with those English anymore; they imitate us, but it's all superficial [...] Now if you go out and walk past an Englishwoman wearing a *mantilla*, you don't want to wear yours anymore, not even for the Christianos y Moros festival. And everything is like this, you feel completely ridiculous in everything you do, what you eat, what you look at, what you say [...] We are one of the last families who remained, and we're now moving out to the other side of the Rambla Núñez, 800 m from here, in Spain. And these people pay so much, so much.

There is clearly an unbearable feeling for these people of becoming 'exotic'. The newcomers also create their own specific culture, and symbolically attach themselves to the traditional cultures along the sea as well as to the rich international populations extending from Almería to Cadaqués along the Mediterranean coast. This part of Alicante, somewhat extracted from the city, is in conurbation with all the other distinctive areas along the European coast of the Mediterranean. The people who visit the casino and register their pleasure boats are the 'jet set' class, including Saudis, UAE residents, Russians and other excessively rich people from poor countries. They have all established themselves along the north docks of Alicante's port, introduced in a way by the small English population in the *casc antic*. Gentrification is happening here, certainly, and ethnic diversity, but in no case is there any ethnic mixing with the rest of the city. The *casc antic* has become a centre for many Northern people who can now work for their companies online from the Spanish coast or else divide their time between home and Spain.

Next to the *casc antic*, along the marina towards the south, lies the old maritime 'lower city', which up until the early 1980s housed a cluster of hotels modelled on the waterfront hotel district of Cannes, Nice and other French Riviera cities. A beautiful tree-lined walkway, *l'Esplanada d'España*, separates it from the quays. These hotels, now supplanted by the ones built on the north pier, expose their greyish façades and are home to a number of cheap ground-floor restaurants. Behind these buildings, about 300 m inland, lies the strange city of the 'five-and-dime stores and boarding houses'. This is where dozens of Algerian and Moroccan businesses sprang up in the 1990s, and where anyone coming from these countries could inexpensively rent a place. North Africans still live here in cheap renting places and work in the restaurant, hotel, or retail business in this same lower city. This area has no relationship with the poor North African populations at the outskirts of the city or in certain dilapidated downtown areas. In fact, the Moroccan and

Algerian business associations pooled the resources of its members in order to purchase and renovate a number of buildings in this area, and no one who lives here is unemployed. The various businessmen and local city officials consider it a neighbourhood 'success story'.

This neighbourhood in Alicante is also open to conurbation and internationalisation: Crevillente, a city of over 30,000 inhabitants to the west of Alicante and Elche, is a stop along the highway that spans the Mediterranean between Italy, Marseille and Morocco and boasts over fifty rug and electronics businesses. This is where, each day, thousands of migrant 'runners' load their vehicles with this merchandise en route to Morocco and Algeria. Furthermore, thousands of Algerians and Moroccans, arriving from Spain and other parts of Europe, board ferries at the large dock east of the nearby port, the veritable maritime border between Oran and Melilla. This small neighbourhood in Alicante, with its incessant flow of migrant merchants based in European countries, rivals its richer neighbour the *casc antic* in terms of the quantity and frequency of human and commercial traffic.

Yet the different groups living in these two neighbourhoods are not very inclined to interact with one another. A few rundown apartment buildings house extremely poor people, either in collective cohabitation or squatting. Here, as in many other European cities, despite the level of tolerance exhibited by the authorities *vis-à-vis* North African merchants and business owners, the stigma of 'Arab' is often still mixed in with the stigma of being poor. However, these North Africans maintain a special relationship with another specific population in Alicante: The *pieds-noirs* repatriated from Algeria at the beginning of the 1960s. We can thus observe within the city's central areas a juxtaposition of two worlds and of two parts of the city, apart from the agglomeration of Alicante.

In the North African commercial district, the municipality undertook the renovation of streets, sidewalks and building façades, perhaps to avoid alienating their rich neighbours in the *casc antic* and the north docks or perhaps to go along with the North African commercial dynamism by making a few improvements. An urban policymaker told us that, when a new foreign population emerges in Alicante, the tradition has been to assist it in settling in as best it can, in the interest of the city's merchants and craftsmen. It is, however, hard to match these claims with the treatment of the Gypsies, confined to miserable housing in a northern neighbourhood of the city. Also, the treatment of poor Moroccans, who have recently arrived in port towns in the south to work in the agricultural and service sectors, reminds us that the local idea of a cosmopolitan Alicante has its limitations.

In fact, it rather seems as though these two 'success stories' of neighbourhood rehabilitation, along with the population change, were permitted to the extent that bourgeois families from Alicante had a vested interest in this change. The renovation and city planning of both the north quay and the *casc antic* satisfied, through the real estate ventures of the chamber of commerce and industry, the heads of the port companies that had been deteriorating since the 1960s. As for the implantation of the North African commercial centre in the old 'lower' city, it was accompanied by the *pieds-noirs* who, since the 1960s, were developing the maritime trafficking of people and had acquired, during the last pro-Franco period, an important influence on the local bourgeoisie.

The *pieds-noirs* were probably, during the pro-Franco period, the first migration that attempted a renewal of port-related activity. Over 30,000 of them passed through Alicante, and 12,000 among them stayed. It was a 'return' of a population that had beem expatriated since the beginning of the twentieth century. Most often these people had lost all connection with their Spanish roots. Attached to the idea of a 'French Algeria', the option to exile themselves in this Spanish region so close to Oran around 'civil' OAS leaders like Joseph Ortiz seemed to them to be a better temporary solution than resettlement in France. The municipality and the state conceded to them a sliver of the seaside public domain, beyond the Postiguet beach, below the Moorish castle, north of the port. There they built a large collection of apartment buildings on the sea, and thousands moved in.

The *pieds-noirs* did not wait long to invest in port-related activities. Some among them used their experience managing international navigation companies in Algeria to invest in Mediterranean commercial navigation and in passenger and mid-sized cargo transportation. A number of Jews were among them, and took up contact with the recently settled Moroccan Jews in the city. Once the Moroccans appeared in Crevillente in the 1990s and, at the same time, the Algerians from France left Marseille for Alicante in order to be closer to Oran and Algiers, these *pieds-noir* entrepreneurs saw an opportunity to take up passenger shuttling to North Africa. The Alicante-Oran route was organised on a daily basis, and the route to Melilla was introduced with success. This is when space was bought in the lower city and ceded to the Algerians and Moroccans for their commercial activities, consisting of loading up the individual vehicles of the 'runners'. Thus the *pieds-noirs*, considered a not-so-foreign population, appear to reinforce the truly foreign population mentioned above and yet forged no links with other foreign populations. A theme of 'otherness' marks the urban expropriations along the sea, and orients them towards distant lands.

In 1998, the European Community decided to endow Alicante with a European Institute of Standardisation (EIS), built along the route between Santa Pola and the airport. This institution boasts over 2,000 salaried employees, of which half are engineers and senior executives. A luxury real estate venture was developed immediately next to the institution's campus. Here, however, it seems as though this new population is diverging from the standard process of settling into Alicante. There was no question of tailoring a new territory taken away from the local native population; the ethnic diversity of the newcomers did not lend itself to this procedure, and these new families mostly choose to live in the south and to the west of the conurbation, creating a sort of iridescent cosmopolitanism in a variety of central neighbourhoods in Alicante, Elche and on the coast towards Santa Pola.

A French family – the husband an engineer, the wife a translator, and their two children ages seven and ten – invited me into their home at the entrance to Santa Pola. They explained their choice for living there quite simply: clean sandy beaches within walking distance (unlike the hardly accessible beaches of Postiguet in Alicante); the EIS, where they both work every day; the neighbouring airport; roads and highways allowing for easy access to Elche to the northwest and Murcia to the south; and rents that are, on average, 30 per cent lower than the bourgeois neighbourhoods in Alicante. With these many advantages, it is easy to foresee the development of an international hub in the southern part of Alicante and beyond in the coming years. In time, the whole of the maritime coast within the conurbation will come to experience the same changes as Alicante.

The majority of the population of Alicante making up the 'Spanish city' rarely claims to be descended from the 'original families' or Catalans (we are to the extreme south of the historically, politically and linguistically influential Catalan area), and is more often than not from Madrid or Albacete. For them, the neighbourhoods and populations we've just discussed are distant: 'port people' sums up this strangeness. The young people frequent a few of the nightclubs in the north quay district, but prefer to go to the ones in Santa Pola where the entrance fees are less costly. On the other hand, the large public covered or open markets, the numerous small businesses and the artisans, but more importantly the doctors, lawyers and other professionals are located in this urban zone. The place is called the 'Spanish city', built in part during the 1920s and in part during the 1950s, west of the *casc antic* and of the old lower city. Near the industrial port, to the south, are clusters of faded public housing projects, between three and five stories high. This is where the workers and employees of the industrial port live, along with a number of lower-ranking employees of the businesses and companies in the 'Spanish city'.

The value of real estate does not seem to be affected by the gentrification of the foreigners' neighbourhoods. The average price of the square footage is approximately €1,400, similar to that of the larger, more homogeneous cities such as Murcia or Valencia. The population of the 'Spanish city' has dropped considerably in the last five years, going from 205,000 to 197,000 inhabitants. This has helped to maintain reasonable real estate prices as well as to encourage a private initiative to increase the surface of living space, because 'neither the wealthy nor poor foreigners' from the port-side neighbourhoods are interested in these local offers.

The 'exotic tour' of the area, according to the residents of the 'Spanish city', has a couple of stops along the way. It begins in the south with the EIS, moving on to the old lower city where a stop is made to allow people to buy inexpensive jewellery and to eat inexpensive food. Then follows a stroll along the *l'Esplanada d'España* up to the north docks, where people can admire the yachts and other luxury boats or go for a walk through the streets of the 'English city', the ex-*casc antic*. From here they can observe once again, from the *Corniche*, the *pieds-noirs*' quarter. This tour takes up an entire afternoon and is a weekly tradition for thousands of Alicante residents, aside from the seasonal dips in the sea south of the port towards Santa Pola, avoiding the beach just below the EIS.

The reciprocal to these behaviours does not exist. People do not go from the foreigner neighbourhoods into the 'Spanish city', except perhaps to go to a specific store or to the large indoor market.

Managing 'circulating cosmopolitanism'

The municipal authorities and their political opponents are developing a theory consistent with urban management. All the foreigners in Alicante, coming from near like the North Africans or far like the Europeans and others, must live soundly with the local population. The foreigners in Alicante are highly mobile and have a higher-maintenance lifestyle compared with the local population, necessitating a physical separation. The municipal authorities must work towards allowing access to foreign areas by creating pedestrian space, parks, quays, parking facilities – basically everything that can contribute to the pleasure of this famous 'tour' by the inhabitants of the 'Spanish city'.

The Arabs are confined within a specialised area, the lower city, with roads leading to the sea and to the highway, responding to the mission to concentrate all of the poverty of the city into a specific area, while all the 'native' populations are segregated in the Spanish city. ('We can see the north docks, but cannot touch it. It's like visiting the zoo, except we don't have to pay an entry fee,' says one young Alicante native from the Spanish city.) In answer to the question whether these two types of segregation will not eventually lead to the development of a voyeuristic relationship, the answers reveal the politics of urban development. Says a city planning official:

> In the first instance, the segregation of the rich and poor populations is to maintain civic peace. Secondly, setting up the transient population along the seaport ensures that the noises emanating from this area at any time of the day or night do not affect the rest of the city. The traffic flow is such that it allows easy access to, and exit from, these areas without stopping in the 'Spanish city', where the non-tourist infrastructure – educational, sport and cultural – is developed. Finally, the articulation of Alicante to the world can no longer materialise itself, as in the past, by a few new houses built among the existing homes, but gives rise to 'neighbourhood-worlds'.

Having discussed in numerous and various ways the theories of 'sustainable development', 'governance' and 'ethnic diversity', our guide told us: 'Ethnic diversity exists here more than in other places, but on a different scale.' The mission of the public authorities is, according to him, 'to oversee the proper dispensation of private funds from and for the foreign populations for services directed at them, and to improve traffic-related planning'.

You Mentioned Borders?

Our investigations allowed us to identify Sofia and Alicante as relatively unique models, the most pronounced examples, we would say, of the transformation of cities through recent migratory movements. It should be noted that these two cities are in 'border' positions in the traditional spatial concept in 'circulatory territories', which mark vast criminalised areas avoided or traversed nonstop by the 'runners' without exercising their commercial competencies.

For Alicante, it is Andalusia as the region that specialises in the traffic of people – illegal migrants for agriculture, women for prostitution – as well as cigarettes, synthetic drugs, the range of European products sold in the markets of Casablanca and cannabis destined for Germany and the Netherlands. For Sofia, it is the vast, stateless region north of Macedonia, west of Kosovo and south of Montenegro, which some designate as the lost territory of 'greater Albania'.[8] Here, in a total absence of services (schools, telephone, transportation, postal services, electricity), agricultural properties were devoted to raising cattle and to housing thousands of 'defeated' people from the wars in the Caucasus, the Middle East and the Balkans, all waiting for hostilities to resume over Albanian and Muslim identity.

The Afghan and Caucasian migrants who provision the Syrians of Sofia do not go through here, and the drugs from Afghanistan that are shipped in massive quantities to these highly criminalised areas en route to Italy are trafficked by local societies. Thus it is in these zones that the borders between dominant, isolated and even antagonistic models of underground economies that are of import on both an international and local level become fluid and porous, and allow circulating individuals the freedom to move from one to the other.[9]

Yes, the debate over Europe's control over its Turkish and Moroccan borders appears to be *passé*, outdated. However the debate about the 'rise of the Souths', about the inevitably porous nature of European borders, is always of relevance.

Notes

1. My research in Marseille lasted from 1984–94 and led to the publication of *Arabes de France dans l'économie mondiale souterraine,* La Tour d'Aigues: Editions de l'Aube, 1995, re-edited in 2000 under the title *Economies souterraines. Un comptoir commercial maghrébin à Marseille*. From 1995–2000 I did research on the movement of Moroccans and Algerians in the South of France and Spain towards Morocco: *La mondialisation par le bas*, Paris: Balland, 2002. Since 1995, local teams in Marseille have continued the observation of the Belsunce neighbourhood (Michel Péraldi, etc). Other research on poor and rich ethnic populations has permitted me to refine the notion of 'circular territory' in its methodology and theoretical frame. See, notably, *Anthropologie du mouvement*, Paris: Paradigmes, 1989 and *Les Fourmis d'Europe*, Paris: l'Harmattan, 1992.
2. Research was conducted within the framework of a study conducted with Lamia Missaoui for the Plan Urbanisme, Construction et Architecture on 'gentrification' and social mixture in cities such as Sofia, Trieste and Alicante (research report November 2005). Our perspective exceeded the limits of the cities in order to understand the impact of new forms of migration and their international networks.

We have, therefore, focused on the articulation of the mobility of foreigners and their sedentarisation in different quarters of the cities under observation and other cities where the same migratory networks passed through. It was through immersion among these Afghan and Caucasian populations, during their trajectories on buses and trucks, that we built relationships favourable for our research. We worked as deliverymen's assistants in May and June 2004, delivering packages between Istanbul, Burgas and Varna over seven weeks. The encounters with transportation professionals and migrants permitted us afterwards to move among the 'stateless' zones close to Albania.

3. I proposed this notion since 1986 and elaborated it in *Les nouveaux cosmopolitismes*, La Tour d'Aigues: Editions de l'Aube, 2000.

4. Statistics are imprecise: the census of 1992 indicates 5,438 'Arabs' in Bulgaria, counted as part of the 'Muslim population' that constituted 14 per cent of the population (with the Turkish-speaking Bulgarians and the Pomaks). The census from 2001 indicates 3,000 Syrians of different status, who created over 1,000 enterprises (businesses, bazaars and artisanal workshops) in Sofia. An IMO study in 1994 indicates 1,780 Syrians, 1,780 Iraqis, 390 Iranians and 129 Afghans with permanent or long-term resident status.

5. This study was conducted with the assistance of researchers from l'Institut d'Etudes Anatoliennes d'Istanbul (IFEA) – CNRS and MAE. The data was sufficient to understand urban transformations in Sofia, but was only a starting point for greater research on Balkan migrations.

6. In the total absence of any other data, it was possible to conduct this study thanks to Jean-François Pérouse, a researcher at IFEA who put us in contact with someone working in maritime transportation who was of Russian origin and had worked in the port of Algiers for ten years before *perestroika*.

7. In my research I was assisted by Svetla, a forty-five-year-old Bulgarian and the daughter of an ambassador, who did her secondary and higher education in France and Switzerland and obtained her PhD in chemistry in Bulgaria. When her father fell into disgrace in 1991, she was reduced to selling sandwiches in a shop in Dragalevtsi, where her family tries to preserve their house by renting out two floors.

8. The Albanian-speaking regions extend, in fact, until Romania.

9. We also conducted research, on the author's account, on these phenomena of permutations and overlapping migration logics and the normative references that identify them, along the 'big transversal' from Turkey and the Caucasus to Portugal.

LEÏLA VIGNAL

The Emergence of a Consumer Society in the Middle East

Evidence from Cairo, Damascus and Beirut

Since the 1990s, Middle Eastern urban societies have seen the emergence of a consumer society. This article discusses the main features of this process, the links it has with globalisation and the impacts it has on cities, which can be seen as constituting the 'new frontier' of globalisation.[1] I shall specifically build my remarks upon the evidence I collected in Beirut, Damascus and Cairo, with a strong emphasis on the last, obviously the biggest and the most economically diversified city of the three.

The 1990s were a turning point in the Middle East, and especially in Lebanon, Syria and Egypt, regarding the development of branded goods and international brands. Economic liberalisation and greater openness to economic globalisation have enhanced investments – domestic, Arab and foreign – which, to a large extent, target the consumer goods sector (food and non-food products). Furthermore, since the removal, in January 2005, of the main trade barriers between Arab countries, the goods produced in the countries of the region cross borders (relatively) easily, creating the first inter-Arab free trade zone (GAFTA: Greater Arab Free Trade Area).

Multinational and Arab corporations play an important role in this process. They are among the key investors in the sector of consumer goods, and have a strong impact on its evolution: they introduce new standards, new legal environments, new distribution networks, new marketing practices. They are part of the emergence of a new industrial base, which is mainly metropolitan, as well as of the reshaping of a new geography of consumption that affects mainly the urban landscape of metropolitan areas. In that sense, the emergence of a consumer society is one of the key factors of the metropolitan shift that is underway in the metropolises of the Middle East.

Before entering the description of this new consumer society, it has to be remembered that it has emerged in countries where the average level of living is low: in 2005, the annual GNP per capita was about US $3,813 PPP[2] in Egypt, while in Syria and Lebanon this figure stood at $3,585 and $5,480 respectively.[3] Furthermore, the economic and social disparities within the three societies are significant. Hence, only a relatively small proportion of society can potentially take part in these emerging patterns of consumption in each locale. The development of the consumer society is, then, in no way comparable to what it has been in developed countries, where the democratisation of consumption has accompanied the extension of the paid work force.

I shall focus on two aspects of the new places, forms and networks of globalised consumption in these three metropolises of the non-oil countries of the Middle East, the networks of 'globalised consumption' and the emergence of a mass market.

Networks of 'Globalised Consumption'

The 1990s witnessed the beginning of a dramatic reshaping of the retail networks in Lebanon as well as in Egypt and Syria. Although the independent private family shop is still the dominant model of retailing in these three countries, new types of retailing points have appeared:

- *Retail chains*, mainly of foreign origin. These foreign chains are mainly implemented by local or Arab corporations through licence affiliations;
- *Super- and hypermarkets*, which have been developing since the end of the 1990s. All the hypermarkets and most of the supermarkets operate under licence;
- *Shopping malls*, which include the former sales formats (i.e. retail chains and super/hypermarkets).

The 1990s as a turning point

Let's take an example in each category as an illustration of the turning point of the 1990s:

Retail chains The majority of the retail chain sector is locally operated and owned, despite the foreign brands it displays. The latter are present in the Middle East through licence agreements between local entrepreneurs and foreign investors, or through direct investment by foreign companies in industrial plots. Three examples of the takeoff that occurred in the retail chain sector can be observed, with an accelerating curve until today:

In Egypt (see Figure One), the development of fast-food restaurants took off in the 1990s, with three chains and seventeen fast-food joints in 1990, five chains and eighty-eight restaurants in 1996 and nine chains and 227 restaurants in 2005.

Figure One: Development and localisation of foreign fast-food chains in Egypt[4]

Fast-food	Opening of the first restaurant	Total of restaurants in Egypt		Part of restaurants (in %)	
		in 1996	in 2005	in Cairo	in Alexandria
KFC	1976	24	72	64	14
Wimpy's	1976	18	3	100	0
Pizza Hut	1989	15	48	65	13
Baskin Robins	1994	16	26	58	23
Mc Donald's	1994	15	50 (2003)	-	-
Hardees	2001	0	15	87	7
Cinnabon	2003	0	6	83	17
Saint Cinnamon	2003	0	4	75	25
Costa Coffee	2004	0	3	67	23

Similar results are seen in Beirut (see Figure Two), where the 1990s mark the eve of a new urban landscape in which the fast food restaurants play an important part.

**Figure Two: Chronology of the implementation
of foreign fast-food chains in Beirut[5]**

Year	Fast-food Brand
1992	KFC, Hardee's, Baskin Robins
1993	Pizza Hut
1996	Starbucks
1997	McDonald's
1999	Burger King, Subways
2000	Lina's
2004	Chez Paul

In Damascus (see Figure Three), the same general trend exists, but for the garment sector only, as there are no foreign fast-food chains in Syria. In the garment sector, the development of textile industries working under licence mainly producing for the local market began in the 1990s as well.

**Figure Three: Chronology of the implementation
of casual clothing in Syria[6]**

Opening of the first shop	Brand
1991	Adidas
1994	Benetton, Maglificio MG, Loïs
1996	Naf-Naf
1997	Kickers, Ted Lapidus
1998	Pierre Balmain
2000	Stefanel
Between 1998 and 2003	Azzaro, Best Mountain, Absorba

Super- and hypermarkets The spread of the super- and hypermarkets follows the same pace: the implementation of these new retail surfaces started in Egypt as well as in Lebanon at the end of the 1990s. There are no proper super- and hypermarkets in Syria to this day. The hypermarkets, which are all operated under licence, had to wait until the first years of the new century to enter these countries: Carrefour, a French chain, opened its first two hypermarkets in Egypt in 2003 and 2004, in Alexandria and in Cairo.

A third, located in Cairo, opened in 2005 and a fourth one, also in Cairo, is scheduled to open in 2008. Its licence, which belongs to the Emirati Majid al-Futtaim Group of Companies based in Dubai, covers the whole Middle East. The group has already announced plans to open a hypermarket in Dbayeh, a northern suburb of Beirut. Géant Casino, another French chain whose licence belongs to the Lebanese corporation ADMIC, opened its first hypermarket in Dora, another northern suburb of Beirut, in 2004.

Shopping malls Shopping malls are also an innovation of the 1990s. The first mall opened in Cairo in 1989, but there were as many as twenty-six in 2006. The same trend affects Beirut, as specialised agencies announce that Beirut will add 275,000 sq. m of retail surface between 2003 and 2010. Although Beirut and Cairo do not lead the regional race in this matter, as shown in Figure Four, they are growing, if one takes into account their starting point. Damascus is at the very end of this curve, with only two small malls, opened in 2002 and 2005.

Domination of the metropolis

These new retailers are mainly located in the major metropolitan areas. For instance, we see in Figure One that two-thirds of Egyptian fast-food restaurants are located in Greater Cairo. The figures are even more striking for shopping malls and super-/hypermarkets, which are solely situated in Cairo with the exception of a combined mall/Carrefour hypermarket in Alexandria.

This is not a big surprise. So far, metropolises are the biggest markets, yield the highest revenues and provide a favourable urban mix of both density and diversity; but what is more striking is that in the Middle East metropolitan locations do not leave much room to others.

A narrow potential market

This very narrow geography of consumption reflects the market targeted by the investors. In Egypt, some accounts estimate a customer base of about six to eight million urban dwellers,[8] others calculate approximately 20 per cent of the total population (in a population of seventy million, this would account for fourteen million people).[9] Narrow in size, this market is also narrow in its geography, encompassing the metropolis and maybe, at a later stage, the main secondary cities.

Figure Four: Percentage of shopping malls' retail surface in the Middle East (as projected for 2005)[7]

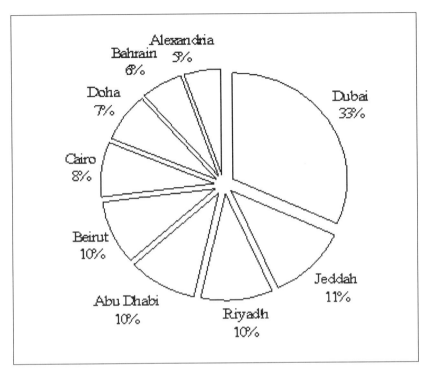

The concentration in the metropolises is perhaps a temporary situation: for obvious economic reasons, investors tend to secure their investments by going where the customers are, i.e. to the big cities, waiting for the market to develop. Nevertheless, for the time being, we can witness no change in the trend towards concentration of the new retailing points in the metropolitan areas, and later in the wealthiest areas of the secondary cities and some tourist spots. Metropolises are considered strategic locations.

Reshaping the geography of metropolitan centralities: the emergence of 'globalised' neighbourhoods

These new retailing formats have contributed to the construction of new intra-urban centralities, and to the collapse of established ones. Of course, by 'centralities', I don't mean necessarily the geographical centres of the city, but areas that concentrate attributes of centrality. To be or not to be located in those centralities is part of a new strategic marketing approach to the city.

From this point of view, the example of Cairo is very clear.[10] There, the emergence of 'globalised neighbourhoods', as we could call them, corresponds to the emergence of areas that concentrate the highest number and diversity of foreign-brand shops and fast-food chains. These neighbourhoods follow a northeast/southwest geographical axis, from the neighbourhood of Heliopolis and Madinat Nasr in the northwest to Mohandessin and Dokki on the west bank of the Nile, and through the *Corniche* of Bulaq and Downtown on the east bank. Regarding the shopping malls, twenty-one out of twenty-six are located on the east bank, especially in the areas of Madinat Nasr/Heliopolis, and near the river (*Corniche* of Bulaq, Downtown).

Three new secondary axes have been developing since the 2000s: one in the southwest part of the agglomeration, towards both the Pyramids in Giza and the new settlement and industrial city of Sixth of October; two in the southeast part of Cairo: one towards Katameyya in the continuation of Ma'adi and one along the Suez road. This strategic approach of the metropolis and the shaping of 'globalised neigbourhoods' follow different logics, which we can summarise as follows:

Key logics

The logic of the market. The proximity to the markets is, in sound economic logic, a key element of a commercial strategy. As the markets targeted by those new retailing formats are middle- and upper-class, they are implemented in the wealthy neighbourhoods (Giza, Zamalek, Mohandessin, Dokki, Heliopolis, Madinat Nasr) as well as in the business areas (Heliopolis, Mohandessin) and the tourist spots (the banks of the Nile and the Pyramids).

The foreign partnership logic. Whatever form it takes (be it direct investment, joint venture, licence/franchise agreement), the foreign partnership impacts the commercial geography, as standards are to be met in the choice of location of the shops or restaurants. These are to be central and highly visible. This obeys, to a large extent, a logic related to the internationalisation of the franchise system. In doing so, the foreign-brand shops are taking part in the process of qualitative change within the cities.

The logic of the souk. The concentration of different kinds of shops in certain areas constitutes in itself an attractive case for other shops to set foot in the same district. When they reach a certain critical mass, centralities are sort of 'self-generating': they attract more and more new elements. If, for some

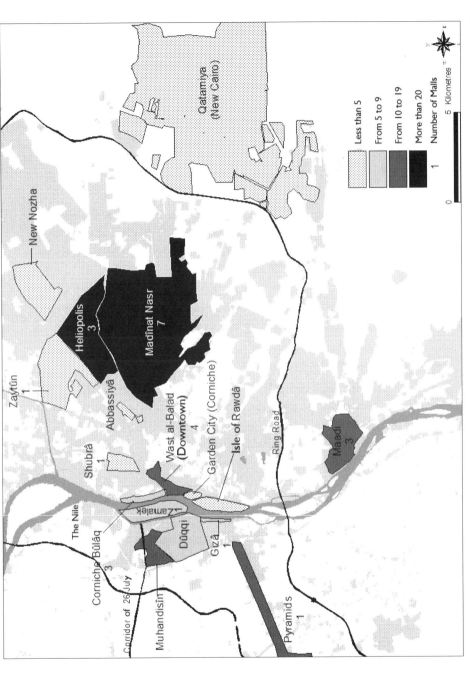

The Neighbourhoods of Global Consumption in Cairo: Localisation of the Main Shopping Malls and of the International Brands of Fast Foods and Ready-made Garments

Legend:
- Less than 5
- From 5 to 9
- From 10 to 19
- More than 20

Number of Malls
- 1

0   5   Kilometres

Labels on map:
- Qatamiya (New Cairo)
- New Nozha
- Heliopolis 3
- Madīnat Nasr 7
- Zaytūn 1
- Abbassiyā
- Shubrā 1
- Wast al-Balad (Downtown) 4
- Garden City (Corniche)
- Isle of Rawdā
- Ring Road
- Maadi 3
- The Nile
- Būlāq
- Zamalek
- Dūqqi
- Gīza
- Corniche 3
- Corridor of 26 July
- Muhandisīn
- Pyramids 1

scholars, this logic of concentration is the contemporary translation of the logic of the *souk*,[11] it is also driven by an international trend of concentration of franchise shops that takes place in all the cities of the world. What exists in Cairo is also true in Beirut, where one could find on Verdun Street alone, in 2000, fifty foreign-brand shops, or in Damascus, for instance, in the commercial area of Shaalan, where one finds established shops of the entire Syrian-licence garment industry.

The polarisation effect. The foreign-brand retailing system is one of chain retailing. Chains allow the simultaneous occupation of different points in the city, as well as in national territory or, for some of them, in the whole of the Middle East. This ubiquity enhances access to goods, but it is also used as a marketing tool in a new comprehensive marketing strategy: if they own several licences, some corporations open shops or restaurants of all their brands in the same location, creating a polarisation effect in one spot meant to attract customers. The Kuwaiti group Americana, for instance, implements its Pizza Hut, KFC and Hardee's restaurants next to each other.

Globalised versus non-globalised neighbourhoods?

Shopping malls and new retail formats are, as seen earlier, conveniently located in the new central places of the cities and in wealthy neighbourhoods – which include the new outskirts of the metropolis. Theoretically, their accessibility is optimal due to their location. Meanwhile, in terms of real accessibility, they are virtually off-limits for people who do not own a car. In Greater Beirut, more than two-thirds of families own a car (60 per cent of families for the governorate of Beirut and 81.2 per cent of families of the governorate of Mont-Liban[12]), but in Damascus, in 2004, only 112,400 cars were registered in a population of 2.8 million.[13] Hence the emergence of globalised neighbourhoods questions the emergence of a consumer society as an inclusive or an exclusive one, both spatially and economically.

The Emergence of a Mass Market:
the Example of Daily Consumption Products

A second important evolution since the 1990s is the diffusion of brand products, especially of global brands. This is particularly striking in the field of daily consumption products – what is called, in marketing jargon, the FMCG (Fast-Moving Consumer Goods): mainly food, to which I would add household products. As relatively low-cost products, they are part of a mass-production economy and aim, potentially, to reach the whole population and the whole territory.

An underdeveloped brand market

The Middle Eastern markets are not yet dominated by brands. They are on the verge of becoming so, but for the time being they are still characterised by non-branded and informal consumption. In Egypt, for instance, only 16 per cent of cheese sold is branded, while the figure is only 5 per cent in Syria.[14] The prospect of development for the agrofood industry is therefore huge. The same demonstration could be made in other sectors of the FMCG industry.

Towards a potential universal market

These goods are more accessible to the wider populations than the goods displayed in the 'globalised areas' I have just described. First, they are more accessible economically: the FMCG are focused on daily needs and offer common types of products (milk, cheese, snacks, preserves, washing powder, etc) that are not among the most expensive ones. Furthermore, to gain markets in countries with a low *per capita* income, the goods are often adapted. For instance, a corporation like Nestlé, which also targets the uppermost fringe of consumer groups with low purchasing power (so-called 'C'-customers according to marketing classifications), has developed special packaging to reach these clients: small packages with small quantities, available for small money. The cost of the packaging for such small quantities does not allow for significant profit margins on the individual sale, but economic gain is expected to be achieved on the overall scale.[15]

Second, they are more accessible in spatial terms for a large proportion of these consumers, since they are displayed in the grocery down the street. Availability at your doorstep, at your local store – which is still, in Egypt, Lebanon and Syria, the first provider of daily goods[16] – is a key factor for generalised consumption. The brands are therefore pursuing a policy of universal presence, in every shop, every place where a potential market exists.

The impact of multinational corporations

Multinational corporations are increasingly key actors in the diffusion and construction of a mass consumption market. First, they are the ones that, more and more, produce branded goods in the Middle East, alongside imports: they implement factories through direct investment, joint ventures or by buying national industries. With the launch of GAFTA, they have assumed a big share in intra-regional trade; now the shelves of Syrian grocery stores are full of shampoos and preserves produced in the new industrial zones of Sixth of October or Tenth of Ramadan, located in the once-desert outskirts of Cairo.

Second, they are developing new practices and networks of distribution, with the progressive introduction of international requirements: better management of orders and deliveries, better reactivity, more reliability in deliveries, better control of the whole distribution process, increased transparency of prices. The implementation of super- and hypermarkets will soon add further requirements to the distribution sector; as powerful actors in retailing, they set their own rules in order to fit distribution to their needs.

Third, new marketing strategies, which are developed in specialised departments of major corporations, are succeeding in increasing brand awareness throughout the region. Classic mass advertising through main media channels still exists, but a whole new world of direct advertising is developing, for instance promotional campaigns, distribution of samples, outdoor billboards, even shelf presentation in the shops, are the new media for proximity and mass diffusion at the very local level. Unlike the retailers that we saw previously, located in the globalised neighbourhoods, the key dynamic of the spread of brands seems here to be the search for ubiquity, maximum awareness and impact on the largest parts of the population.

Towards the Emergence of a Consumer Society

From this description, the emergence of a consumer society could appear to be a two-pronged process: on one hand, there is the emergence of globalised commercial areas in the metropolis, targeting the wealthier and better-connected population; on the other hand, there is the unfolding of mass-market consumption, which targets a wider market.

This perception, while appealing at first glance, would be nonetheless too schematic, for two reasons. First, retailers in 'globalised neighbourhoods', shops, shopping malls, fast-food outlets, are not solely known, seen and used by the wealthy population, which they aim first and foremost to cater for. As the Egyptian sociologist Mona Abaza has brilliantly demonstrated in her work on Cairo,[17] the majority of the users of these shopping malls are in fact *promeneurs* who are not buying anything. They belong to the not-wealthy-enough population, but they do come to the mall for many other reasons

– most importantly, to be in a unique and all-too-rare type of semi-public space. As a commercial place, the mall is then diverted from its first *raison-d'être*, especially by women and young people.

As a social object, this diversion illustrates the fact that objects are defined by the use people make of them and not only by the intentions of their creators.[18] As a spatial object, it shows that mobility is a key element of any geography. This mobility allows those new globalised places to be part of the mental urban representations and references of populations living far from them, even far from the metropolis. Globalisation is not, if ever, the condition of a little elite.

Second, even if brands are designed for universal recognition, their diffusion is still limited by hard-to-change economic factors, as it takes place in low-income societies; by cultural factors, one of them being low brand awareness; by distribution factors (the main brand-retailing points are located in cities); and by industrial factors, as the new industry does not yet have the capacity to cater for the whole population.

More essentially, three concluding remarks should be made in relation to the question of cities and citizenship. First, the emerging consumer society is massively urban. Metropolises, as places linking diversity and density – this powerful definition of urbanity has been proposed by the French geographer Jacques Lévy[19] – are strategic places for globalisation. But it would be wrong to conclude that globalisation does not spread beyond their material infrastructures. Conversely, it would be wrong to ignore that the existence of those infrastructures creates attraction, leading to further forms of concentration and polarisation to the benefit of the metropolises.

Second, obviously the emergence of new places for consumption and the diffusion of brands are extremely visible in contemporary landscapes, and therefore contribute to the definition of new forms of social and spatial segregation – segregation that indeed exists, as has been shown. At the same time, every society builds its own territory: the new geographies of consumption that emerge are, in each city, deeply rooted in its own history. Globalisation, here analysed through the consumption side, could then be seen more as a revealing than a creating process, or as only one of several factors that shape societies as well as their territories. In that sense too, globalisation is a 'partial' condition.[20]

Finally, if an object is defined by how it is used, then people are actors, even when and where they consume.[21] It could then be argued that individuals may benefit from expansion of the consumer society, in their roles as citizens, if for instance (as mentioned in the case of shopping malls in the Middle East) new spaces are opened up where young people and women can experiment with new modes of social participation. The same could be said about consumption of global goods, more accessible to more people and not only to the wealthiest. Democratisation of the market does not lead to democratisation of the society, but could we not think about it as a process that empowers, in a certain field, people who were previously excluded?

Bibliography

Abaza, Mona, 'Egyptianizing the American Dream: Nasr City's Shopping Malls, Public Order, and the Privatized Military', in Diane Singerman and Paul Amar, eds, *Cairo Hegemonic: State, Justice, and Urban Social Control in the New Globalized Middle East*, Cairo: American University of Cairo Press, 2007, pp. 193–220.

—— 'Emerging Life-Styles and Consumer Culture in Egypt, in *I quaderni di Merifor, Egitto Oggi, a cura di Elisabetta Bartuli*, 2001, pp. 119–134.

—— 'Shopping malls, consumer culture and the reshaping of public space in Egypt', in *Theory, Culture & Society*, vol. 18(5), 2001, pp. 97–122.

Bakhros, Walid, *Les nouvelles centralités commerciales de l'agglomération beyrouthine: mémoire de DESS d'urbanisme*, Balamand: Institut d'urbanisme de l'Académie Libanaise pour les Beaux-Arts, 1999, unpublished.

Bayart, Jean-François, *Le gouvernement du monde: une critique politique de la globalisation*, Paris: Fayard, 2004.

de Certeau, Michel, *L'Invention du quotidien. Tome I: Arts de faire*, Paris: Gallimard, 1990.

Didiot, Béatrice and Cordellier, Serge, *L'Etat du monde 2005: annuaire économique et géopolitique mondial*, Paris: La Découverte, 2004.

Ghorra-Gobin, Cynthia, 'L'émergence de centres commerciaux dans la ville: une version américaine et moderne des souks?', in *Annales de Géographie de l'Université St-Joseph*, Beyrouth, 1986, pp. 141–58.

Lévy, Jacques, *Le tournant géographique: Penser l'espace pour penser le monde*, Paris: Belin, 1999.

Pages, Delphine and Vignal, Leïla, 'Formes et espaces de la mondialisation en Égypte: Une lecture spatiale des changements récents', in *Revue géographique de Lyon*, vol. 73(3), 1998, pp. 247–58.

Raymond, André, 'Espaces publics et espaces privés dans les villes arabes traditionnelles', in *Maghreb-Machrek* 123, 1989, pp. 194–202.

Vignal, Leïla, 'La "nouveelle consommation" et les transformations des paysages urbains à la lumière de l'ouverture économique': L'example de Damas', in

Sylvia Chiffoleau, ed., *Revue des Mondes Musulmans et de la Méditerranée* (REMMM, 115–116), 2006 pp. 21–41.

Notes

1. Jean-François Bayart, lecture presented at the conference *Cities and Globalisation: Challenges for Citizenship,* Beirut, 9–11 December 2005.
2. PPP = Purchasing Power Parity.
3. 'Tables statistiques' in *L'Etat du Monde 2005.*
4. Leïla Vignal, 2005; compiled from Internet resources; Kompass Egypt 2005; interviews; newspapers.
5. Ibid.
6. Leïla Vignal, interviews, 2005.
7. See *Retail International*, Vol. 2(2), autumn 2003.
8. Mission économique du Caire, *Le secteur des produits laitiers en Egypte*, May 2005.
9. Abaza, 'Egyptianizing the American Dream'.
10. A developed analysis of this process in Damascus is available in Vignal, 'Les nouveaux types de consommation à Damas'.
11. Ghorra-Gobin, 'L'émergence de centres commerciaux dans la ville'.
12. The figure for other governorates is 50 per cent. Source: *Lebanon Facts & Figures 1999*, Bank Audi, Beirut.
13. The figure for the whole country is 206,130. Source: Statistical Abstract, 2004, Damascus.
14. Interview: Bel, Syria; interview: Americana, Cairo.
15. Interview: Nestlé, Cairo; interview: Nestlé, Syria.
16. Euromonitor International, 'Retailing in Egypt', September 2004, London.
17. Abaza, 'Shopping Malls, Consumer Culture and the Reshaping of Public Space in Egypt'.
18. de Certeau, *L'Invention du quotidien.*
19. Levy, *Le tournant géographique.*
20. Bayart, *Le gouvernement du monde.*
21. Ibid. de Certeau, *L'Invention du quotidien.*

DIANE SINGERMAN

Cairo Cosmopolitan: Citizenship, Urban Space, Publics and Inequality

Recently, an interdisciplinary collection of international scholars collaborated to produce a volume on politics, culture and urban space in Cairo. As the co-editors of this project, Paul Amar and I have been struck by the commonality of several themes reiterated in its chapters, which range from an analysis of emergent Nubian identity to restoration efforts in Fatimid Cairo and *Belle-Epoque* Cairo, film spectatorship in downtown cinemas, contests over public space at the Giza Zoo and control of the media and popular culture. The richness of this material allows us to understand how complicated and nuanced the normative project of citizenship in Cairo has become, within the context of globalisation, the spatial economy of Egypt and renewed political activism in Egypt. In this chapter, I unapologetically mine the depths of this two-volume project that has just produced *Cairo Cosmopolitan: Politics, Culture and Urban Space in the New Globalized Middle East* and will soon produce *Cairo Hegemonic: State, Justice and Urban Social Control in the New Globalized Middle East*.[1]

Our research has been intentionally grounded spatially in neighbourhoods, markets, shops, malls, squares, villages, towns and historic areas, where one can see the physical and material manifestation of national, regional and global flows and disjunctures. I want to begin with a general discussion of the new spatial economy of Cairo, which was both planned and unplanned. From this general understanding of how Cairo as a megalopolis has changed significantly, we can then proceed to a discussion of what Leïla Vignal and Eric Denis have called the 'privatizing of public space'[2] or, to use Yasser Elsheshtawy's term, the 'quartering of urban space.'[3]

These moves to transform valuable public space to further private ends is typically legitimated by various discourses of exclusion and danger, supposedly emanating from crime, pollution, terrorism, Islamism or the anarchic and backward 'demographic masses' in Cairo, to use El Shakry's term.[4] After this discussion, I will segue into the ways in which contests over public space and public resources and a view of the majority of Cairenes as 'the Internal Other' have implications for the critical question of national identity and the ways in which various sub-national identities and constituencies have, or do not have, a 'sense of belonging' to the nation and concomitant quest for citizenship.[5]

The chapter concludes with a discussion of the growing political mobilisation from below that is placing more demands for justice, representation and the rule of law on the Egyptian regime. This tentative and costly mobilisation is shaped by struggles over public space, Egyptian heritage, identity and cultural production. The neo-liberal project of the state encourages consumption in malls, gated communities, coastal tourist villages and coffeeshops, even as it has reduced educational, health, housing or transportation services for those who cannot afford the cosmopolitan world. Economic and cultural forces seem to produce a type of delocalised consumption, where spaces, foods, residential communities and even politics are targeted towards foreigners, tourists and the upper-class cosmopolitan elite. If private property has become more entrenched within some sectors of the economy, and globalisation has facilitated some types of political mobilisation, the political rights and responsibilities of citizenship are still strongly curtailed by the current regime's quest to maintain power – displayed by the state's use of violence during the 2005 parliamentary elections and political demonstrations in 2005 and 2006. At the same time, activists are exploiting political opportunities and creatively filling the political space of authoritarianism with legitimate demands from a broader cross-section of society than in the past. It would be folly to be too optimistic about the inroads these protestors can make, but it is important to recognise their innovative strategies and campaigns as they emerge.

New Cartographies of Redistribution in Cairo:
The City Expands into the Desert

Historicising the Egyptian state's planning projects is critical to understanding how the state and its domestic and international political allies have envisioned Egypt's future. Although we have titled our volume *Cairo Cosmopolitan*, which largely focuses on the megacity, El Shakry argues that one has to see Cairo's changing spatial footprint as a result of policies both to the urban and the rural, and she discerns a noticeable continuity between the Nasser and Sadat eras. Both strategies for statist development generally neglected urban areas, though for very different reasons:

> [Under Nasser] social planners imagined Cairo as a revolutionary planning hub, in which rural space was privileged, and targeted for improvement, in the reconstitution of space. Nationalist discourse, and social reformers, posited the city as the quintessential site of the modern (the seat of rational state planning and the development of modern forms of power), and the rural as the site of national identity (with the peasantry as representative of the demographic masses).[6]

During the Sadat era, by contrast, 'urban population density began to be radically targeted, as state technocrats and urban planners proposed the development of desert and satellite cities as a solution for the decentralization of Cairo' (although under Nasser, new cities were also built in rural areas, and workers' cities were constructed in urban areas).[7] Following Sadat's announcement of the *Infitah* (Open Door Policy), the concept of the Greater Cairo region introduced in 1974 spurred the development of desert cities 'built away from that "narrow green strip of land", in order to depopulate Cairo, decentralize it, and stop the continuing loss of arable land due to housing construction'.[8] (Plans to decentralise Cairo faltered, however, since the capital is just as dominant in the Egyptian political, economic and cultural fields as it always has been).[9] Legal, bureaucratic and financial support for these new cities and towns followed, providing tax incentives and cheaper, expansive land for industry, manufacturing, joint ventures and franchise operations.

In particular, 'Law No. 59 of 1979, codifying the new settlement policy, inaugurated the creation of eighteen new cities in Egypt, including relatively freestanding new towns (e.g. Sadat City, Tenth of Ramadan) and satellite cities (e.g. Sixth of October, Fifteenth of May); and created a favourable economic environment for private-sector investment and the use of foreign expertise.'[10] Throughout the 1980s, these plans continued to pursue 'the containment and maintenance of an optimum size for Cairo (a sealing off) and the development of self-sufficient new communities (new settlements and satellite cities), with the "residual population" of Cairo expected to be absorbed into the "new settlements" (a funneling out)'.[11] This conceptualising of the products of demographic growth as 'residual populations' conveys the Egyptian state's problematic view towards new households seeking scarce affordable housing, particularly newlywed households, the implications of which will be described further below.

These new initiatives to launch desert cities and new settlements have only been partially successful as economic ventures.[12] As the Sadat era privileged economic development, '... the urban density of Cairo (especially of the popular classes) was demonised' because 'social planners perceived urban density as consuming economic growth'.[13] Accompanying this reinforced strategy of attracting economic and residential investment outside the inner urban core of Cairo was a familiar-sounding discourse that blamed the problems of Egypt – its backwardness, disorder, instability and insatiable demands – on the 'demographic masses'. Yet in the *Infitah* era, the demographic masses no longer signified the rural peasantry but suggested, in the popular imagination and in the media, the urban poor or popular classes. The demonisation of the urban poor is a very important component of the ideology of growth and development of the Sadat and post-*Infitah* era, supported financially and politically by the new alliance with American and European financial and political interests.

Denis explains that a 'security risk discourse', a product of the neo-liberal order, propels elites to abandon the city and opt for life in neo-Orientalist or *Belle-Epoque* gated communities with 'elected' mayors, luxurious golf courses (despite the scarcity of water resources) and two-car garages. At the same time, they feel like great Egyptian nationalists when they move to these communities, as advertisements and state rhetoric identify them as 'pioneers' reclaiming the desert and making it 'productive'. Denis argues:

> To be sold, the gated communities brandish and actualize the universal myth of the great city where one can lose oneself in privatized domestic bliss. Promoters exploit more and more the stigmatization of 'the street', spread by the media on a global scale, and finally of the Arab metropolis as a terrorist risk factory that is necessarily Islamic. Far from being rejected, the Islamist peril is exploited by the Egyptian authorities to legitimize political deliberalization, while it promotes a particular landscape of economic restructuring. The current regime redirects and displaces the urgency of law and the immediate interests of Egypt's elites through the affirmation of market and security systems, of which the gated communities are a prominent feature.[14]

Later he adds the following, describing elite cosmopolitan life and the way it reinforces a discourse of exclusion and 'othering':

At the centre of this new way of life are Egypt's elites, themselves connecting together the archipelago of micro-city communities that they administer as if they were so many experimental accomplishments of a private democracy to come. The gated communities, like a spatial plan, authorize the elites who live there to continue the forced march for economic, oligopolistic liberalization, without redistribution, while protecting themselves from the ill effects of its pollution and its risks. In the same way, these elites rejoin the transmetropolitan club of the worldwide archipelago of walled enclaves. The potential guilty anxieties relative to the suffering of ordinary city dwellers are, then, masked by global rejection of the city, according to an anti-urban discourse that incorporates and naturalizes pollution, identifying it with poverty, criminality, and violent protests against the regime. In this elite perspective, Cairo has become a complex of unsustainable nuisances against which nothing more can be done, except to escape or to protect oneself.[15]

While the colonial metaphor of the 'unwashed masses' demanded the reform of the 'traditional', backward, poor, illiterate or unhealthy peasants before the Nasserist revolution in 1952, this more urban fear is clearly overlaid and thus made more politically useful in the post-colonial world by linking the popular classes with the political threat from the Islamist movement in Egypt. Spatially, this new urban threat resides in the *'ashwa'iyat*, or spontaneous, random, informal, peri-urban areas of Greater Cairo that now house more than half the city's residents, having satisfied 80 per cent of housing needs for the last twenty years. The informal sector is not only the source of most residential construction in Cairo, but has produced 40 per cent of the non-agricultural jobs.[16]

As various Islamist groups began operating and organising in areas such as Imbaba, Ain Shams or al-Zawiyya al-Hamra, the bureaucracy, state and media 'discovered' the phenomenon of informal housing areas despite the fact that millions of lower- and middle-class people had been living there for some time. As they engaged in battles with radical Islamist groups, the regime began to pay attention to the neighborhoods where activists lived and from which they recruited sympathisers. Many of these areas had been agricultural fields until the 1970s and 1980s, and the government did not provide services to the thousands of new residents as they bought land illegally, built their houses while ignoring government construction and zoning regulations and gradually devised ways to integrate their newly-residential neighbourhoods to the rest of metropolitan Cairo through largely private sector transportation links.

As Denis and Vignal argue so persuasively in *Cairo Cosmopolitan*, the state indirectly subsidised private sector efforts to build desert communities, gated communities and new settlements away from extant urban areas through the provision of subsidised infrastructure by state or military institutions, cheap bank loans from the public sector and selling desert land held by major public stakeholders such as public insurance companies, Egyptian State Railways, the Ministries of Housing and New Communities, Defence, Agriculture and Land Reclamation and religious endowments.[17] In contrast, lower-income individuals and families gradually built privately financed apartments or family compounds in the peri-urban, lower-class residential areas on formerly marginal or agricultural lands (Manshiet al-Nasr, Ain Shams, Bulaq al-Dakrur, al-Zawiyya al-Hamra, etc). The growth of informal-sector residential areas is as much part of the neo-liberal order in Egypt as the creation of luxury gated communities and desert economic zones.

Whether through its direct policies of turning away from building affordable rental housing and building new towns and luxury gated communities in the desert, or through its indirect policies of ignoring its own regulations regarding construction, development, zoning and planning, the government clearly tolerated the huge expansion of informal housing areas. Turning a blind eye allowed for the minimum satisfaction of housing needs of the poor and lower middle class at the lowest possible cost to the state, ultimately ensuring a low-wage labour force.

In the 1990s in particular, as Islamist movements and the state engaged in violent confrontations and the former attacked government officials, the police and national political figures, the *'ashwa'iyat* came to be defined as a deviant phenomenon in Egyptian public discourse, and by association, the residents of those areas as deviants. Defining five to seven million Cairenes who live in informal housing areas as deviants then allowed the government to legitimate political repression and surgical 'removals' of the worst of these 'cancerous' areas, as a former Minister of Local Administration in the early 1990s (who was also an oncologist and former head of the Cancer Institute) was fond of labelling the *'ashwa'iyat*.[18] He suggested that in treating cancer one does not destroy the whole body but acts selectively to remove dangerous and potentially damaging tissue. Benign cancers can be treated by excision, by cutting away the diseased, infected tissue.

The policy corollary is the programme euphemistically called 'removals', where housing is bulldozed or residents are forced to move into areas even further away from the city centre. The Egyptian government has pursued this 'removal' policy (notice the passive voice; the subject, or the one who does the removing, is left out), although local resistance has stopped some of them.[19] Other communities are kept in the dark for years, fearing the rumoured government 'removals' that dissuades these residents with insecure housing from investing in improvements to their homes, communities and businesses, as Petra Kuppinger has noted in communities in Giza.[20]

Cancer can also be cured through radiation and chemotherapy, i.e. the destruction of living cancerous cells to save healthy cells, and this can be seen in the strategy of destroying the evil, malignant criminal elements in informal housing areas (terrorists) while 'upgrading' the healthy elements by investing in a civilising mission of schools, youth centres, government-controlled mosques and religious charities, gardens, and also 'upgrading' physical capital by constructing roads, electrical grids, sewers, public transportation and markets to improve the health and welfare of these areas and their accessibility to state agencies, particularly the security services.[21] 'Upgrading' projects began in the mid-1980s, often financed by various international agencies and governments, and received far more resources and attention from the highest levels of government following violent confrontations between the government and Islamists, particularly after the siege of Imbaba in 1992. In this confrontation approximately 16,000 security agents surrounded and occupied several neighbourhoods in Imbaba, in response to the increasing presence and boldness of the Islamic Group (*al-Gama' al-Islamiya*) in the area.[22]

In a fairly insidious process reflected in most of the print media, residents of informal housing areas and Islamists are constructed as the backward, dangerous, uncivilised 'Internal Other':

> A single look at the streets and alleys of Imbaba – the scene of the events – causes nausea, as if their inhabitants weren't like other humans, or as if they were a category on its own.[23]

Almost all of their political efforts and mobilisation are criminalised, and their agency is denied in this discourse, evacuating their history in the process and denying them any legitimacy. In a very common pattern of argument, one journalist suggested that informal housing areas were remnants of the past, where no 'modern' services existed, and thus it was not surprising that the 'backward' and 'irrational' Islamic Group should thrive there:

> Al-Mounira is *'ashwa'iya* from start to finish. In al-Mounira there are no schools, health clinics, social clubs and youth centre, or buses. It is a life belonging to past ages. Hence, why should it not be invaded by extremist fundamentalists?[24]

This criminalisation of politics encourages the cycles of violence, repression and frustration that unfortunately continue to dominate Egypt today. The public discourse of the modern Egyptian state echoes in very unsettling ways the civilising mission of the colonial powers, which argued that the colonial bureaucratic and military administration would bring modernity, progress and order to backward civilisations. Islamists, as the internal 'Other', are typically portrayed as irrational, 'backward' thugs, terrorists, troublemakers and agitators, and the poverty and frustration common in informal housing areas is blamed for producing these thugs. Once the 'environment' of the informal housing area is recognised as the source of terrorism, the residents themselves also become culpable.

If cities have historically given rise to citizens and demands for membership in a community with political rights – where they have the right, not the privilege, to pursue freedom through the practice of political representation – then the phenomenon of the spontaneous, informal communities that are the *'ashwa'iyat* may present even more impediments for the growth of citizenship rights in Egypt, because the logic of modernist assumptions diminishes the subjecthood of residents from these communities.[25] Labelling these vast areas of the Cairo megacity *'ashwa'iyat* (which connotes that they are 'spontaneous' eruptions or randomly settled) contrasts with the idea that they were planned, regulated and organised rationally as 'normal' neighbourhoods like the satellite or desert cities. The point here is that as random, irrational settlements they are stigmatised and fall on the side of that which is not modern, and thus that which is disordered.

Zygmunt Bauman argues that '… Order and chaos are modern twins'.[26] This strict dichotomy, which fears disorder and ambivalence because it eschews the classificatory scheme of modernism, is embodied in the relationship of the Egyptian state to these residents. As mentioned, the state and international development agencies may have tried to upgrade *'ashwa'iyat* and modernise the areas via lights, accessible boulevards, police stations, parks or clubs, but as a disorderly 'demographic mass' (to return to El Shakry's term), the residents are not worthy of representation and inclusion in the body politic. The disorder they produce is supposed to be contained and neutralised, but as irrational actors they are not invited into subjecthood, nor does the government allow them the rights of political representation, public discourse, freedom and civil rights. In other words, their powerlessness is naturalised.

Far from the world of *'ashwa'iyat*, the Egyptian state tries to criminalise more middle-class and elite political actors as well, by crushing NGOs and using anti-terror laws and emergency law provisions against them whether they are leftists, liberals, Nasserists or leaders of human rights or women's rights organisations. If the pervasive restrictions against their political activity do not work, media puppets slander them; the security forces threaten their families; or the government brands them as traitors and foreign agents of Israel and/or the US.[27]

When the state defines politics as 'criminal' or 'traitorous', government agencies can then equate political participation with a strong threat, which can then explain and excuse the overwhelming use of force when even small numbers of demonstrators courageously protest in Cairo. The various complex and interwoven security apparatuses of the Egyptian state typically marshal thousands of security personnel when protests are planned and use violence and sexual and verbal harassment to dissuade others from overcoming their fear and participating. There remain vast constraints on civil liberties and political rights in Egypt, although there is some hopeful evidence that a wider cross-section of Egyptian political parties, the Muslim Brotherhood and civil society have been 'irrationally' taking larger political risks and continuing to demonstrate in Egypt.[28]

The dehumanisation of vast segments of the urban population of Egypt who live in informal housing areas or engage in Islamist activism also allows the government security forces to legitimise their brutal violence to themselves as they deny these residents their humanity. In the extreme, as Frank Chalk and Kurt Jonassohn argue, a genocide starts when its organisers promote a campaign that redefines the victim group as worthless 'outside the web of mutual obligations, a threat to the people, immoral sinners, and/ or subhuman'.[29] While genocides are still rare, and not about to occur in Egypt, they are preceded by long brutal skirmishes or small massacres and political discourses that equate political dissent with irrationality, illegality and treason.

New Hierarchies of Access in Cairo Cosmopolitan

If political exclusion is so common and citizenship rights so weak, it is not surprising that notions of the Egyptian 'public' are also weak, and several chapters in *Cairo Cosmopolitan* describe frail notions of the public from a spatial and political dimension. The privatising exclusivity of the new development model popular in Egypt challenges the very definition of the 'public' today and who has the right, and access to, public goods and services. Denis argues that the Egyptian state has been offering up its public patrimony, 'opening vast expanses of territory to be divided up amongst a handful of private developers, while stimulating the flow of capital through the sale of land'.[30]

The phenomenon of gated communities is a form of fixing worth, investing the unshared gains flowing directly from the liberalisation and privatisation process and then fixing them in a new global/local hierarchy and landscape. These constructions are inscribed in stone and real estate, from wealth extracted from the public heritage and from public lands in a context of inflation, certainly reduced in relation to the 1980s but characterised by a strong monetary devaluation.[31]

Who will purchase the hundreds of thousands of flats that are being built in the desert in new gated communities, when the middle and upper classes of Cairo are still quite small? Denis suggests that Greater Cairo includes approximately 315,000 families who are upper-middle-class or upper-class, representing the wealthiest 10 per cent of the population.[32] But he also notes that 320 companies have acquired land and announced projects that, potentially, would construct 600,000 residences (which equals the number of residences constructed in the Cairo region, for all segments of the population, between 1986 and 1996)![33] The entire upper strata of Egypt would have to purchase two apartments each to meet the supply of this new wave of construction. Perhaps Egyptian developers imagine they can attract foreigners from the Arab world and Europe, but it is unlikely that Egypt can compete with the boom in luxury housing construction in Dubai, Beirut (at least before the summer of 2006) or other regional capitals.[34] The Egyptian economic crisis in 2000 was an answer to these seemingly unsustainable new real estate developments, when banks faced liquidity crises and the real estate bubble burst as property prices collapsed and prominent businessmen suffered humiliating, widely publicised financial losses and occasional corruption investigations.[35]

The unsettling but incredibly enlightening analysis by Vignal and Denis in *Cairo Cosmopolitan* provides another case study for Anna Tsing's arguments about the 'performative dramas of financial conjuring' in our globalised world.[36] Writing about the Asian financial crisis, she explores the huge Bre-X mining scandal from 1994–7 at the end of the Suharto era in Indonesia. International investors, primarily Canadians, invested feverishly in a gold rush in a remote area that was ultimately found to be a scam. Various multinationals and factions of the Suharto clan and the Indonesian military were implicated in the bizarre episode before it went up in smoke. Some investors did very well, flipping their shares as the stock rose wildly on the Toronto Stock Exchange, while others lost their shirts. The entire episode, Tsing and others argue, ultimately contributed to the Asian financial crisis (1997) and the end of the Suharto era (May 1998).

What is particularly instructive for the case study of overbuilt luxury gated communities in the deserts around Cairo is Tsing's understanding of how 'nation-making' projects of 'franchise cronyism' finance capital become linked with 'greedy elite dreams of an authoritarian nation-state supported by foreign funds and enterprises'.[37] In the forests of Indonesian Borneo, a small obscure Canadian mining company teamed up with expatriate geologists to strike a claim to a Klondike-like gold vein, securing the Indonesian military to enforce the foreign multinational's rights to the gold over the local customary rights of the forest inhabitants. She argues that Canadians were so quick to invest in this scheme because it was familiar to them and reinforced their frontier culture and quest for 'discovery' (after Canadian environmental regulations had blocked domestic mining exploration) in which 'the rights of previous rural residents could be wiped out entirely to create a Wild West scene of rapid and lawless resource extraction: quick profits, quick exits'.[38]

Her notion of the role of financial conjuring in the global economy brings back the imaginary to free-trade discourse. Tsing writes:

> A distinctive feature of this frontier regionality is its magical vision; it asks participants to see a landscape that doesn't exist, at least not yet. It must continually erase old residents' rights to create its wild and empty spaces where *discovering* resources, not stealing them, is possible.[39]

She discusses the importance of scale here, or the 'spatial dimensionality necessary for a particular kind of view'[40] in the sense that 'finance capital is a program for global hegemony; franchise cronyism is one particular nation-making project; [and] frontier culture is an articulation of a region'.[41]

In Egypt, the voices of those who might have had customary rights to the desert land that has been appropriated for new developments around Cairo are never heard, nor do we hear much about how various public agencies attained the 'rights' to public lands or the authority to sell them to the highest bidder or their cronies. What Egyptian developers have done with their exhortations to reclaim the desert, as Bre-X did in Indonesia, is to create *drama*, because, as Tsing points out, 'the importance of drama guarantees that it is very difficult to discern companies that have long-term production potential from those that are merely good at being on stage'.[42] Denis and Walter Armbrust have both researched the visual presentations of glossy, glamorous advertising campaigns in TV, films and the print media that have been launched by developers to 'conjure' up more people to invest in and reside in these luxurious, gated communities.[43]

Many questions remain before we can understand the foreign, local and parastatal investment and involvement in these schemes, as well as to answer the elusive question about who continues to reap profits even as so many of these developments lie empty and unfinished. Tsing's analysis reminds us about the critical importance of 'contingent processes that bring globalist, nationalist, and regionalist projects' into being, as well as the 'cultural specificity and the fragility of capitalist and globalist success stories'.[44]

Moving beyond questions about land speculation and investment conjuring in the desert, another theme that is explored in many contributions in *Cairo Cosmopolitan* is the way in which Egypt's public patrimony is being eroded in its inner urban core. Public places and entire neighbourhoods and their historic monuments are being remade or poorly renovated to attract international tourists and their visions of Islamic, traditional or Fatimid Cairo. Elsheshtawy, in our volume, examines the fate of a public square between Sultan Hasan Madrassa (a fourteenth-century religious school) and the Al-Rifa'i mosque (nineteenth century), which was initially converted to pedestrian use in 1984 and became popular with local residents as there were few public spaces in the older, densely populated, mixed-use neighbourhoods of Cairo. Yet by 2003, the government had fenced in and closed the gates to the square, since it viewed local residents as a 'threat' to be contained and removed so that tourists would be able to enjoy a sanitised space (i.e. one without Egyptians) that could serve their gaze and imagination. The case of this public square between two great monuments of Islamic Cairo demonstrates how tourist sites in the contemporary era display 'Egyptianness' only according to a carefully crafted script. As Elsheshtawy notes, the Sultan Hasan Madrassa (school and mosque complex) is now a 'stage for tourists to take pictures ... an open-air museum isolated from the rest of Cairo and geared towards the global trade of tourism'.[45]

Metaphorically, whether governments decide to convert formerly open pedestrian malls into tourist spaces, or private developers backed by government-subsidised loans and land sales build gated communities isolated from the urban centre, global trends in cities seem to be characterised by efforts to 'wall some in and keep others out'.[46] Those that the government tries to keep out typically represent the popular classes or rural residents who visit Cairo *en masse*. For example, due to the increased Islamist challenge to the government and political violence as well as to huge anti-American and anti-war protests around al-Azhar in 2003, the Cairo city police and the national government even closed off public squares to hugely popular Sufi festivals such as the *mulid* of Hussein.[47] While this effort was successful during the beginning of the *mulid*, by the end of the festival the public had retaken the square and the police and official authorities looked the other way.

City officials in many global cities are encouraging this 'quartering of urban space' to reap the awards from tourists and investors, yet this leaves sharper divisions between rich and poor that are not only economic in nature but shape political relations between citizens and the state.[48] Kuppinger, for example, describes the unsettling disparity between a village just adjacent to the Pyramids in Giza that does not have basic access to water and utilities, and the vast international and national investment in the Pyramids Plateau and surrounding museums and luxury hotels. As she argues:

> With the reorganization of global capitalism, and specifically the extension of the global tourism industry, sites like the Giza Pyramids increasingly eluded merely local control and came to cater to global politics and financial interests. Rationales of tourism became central for spatial policies and decisions. Subsequently, such spaces become economically and culturally removed from their territories and displaced into global realms.[49]

The Pyramids are the quintessential symbol of Egyptian national heritage, and claim to be the iconic wonder of world civilisation. Yet, more and more, the Pyramids and other popular tourist sites have become commodified as part of the global tourist economy and wholly dependent upon it. Does the Egyptian state invest in water for the lower-class urban quarters of Giza or does it try to raise $350 million dollars for the Grand Egyptian Museum that will not only house a massive number of Egyptian artifacts in a complex of over 200 acres, but will be one of the largest museums built in the world?[50] In the international tourist economy, as Elsheshtawy explains, cities themselves become 'brands', and mega-museums, world heritage sites or neo-Orientalist green spaces like the recently-built al-Azhar Park are but attempts to keep 'market share'.[51] While international funding often supports these mega-museums and new 'green spaces', the publics that are being targeted are external to the body politic and the domestic public has little influence over how its tax dollars and public monies are spent. This trend might be termed 'delocalised consumption' since tourists are the target audience.

In Egypt, the issue of 'local control' and the strategic objectives of urban planning are fundamentally influenced by a political system, which is heavily centralised and authoritarian. As Caroline Williams argues, the Egyptian state proposed 'relocating' thousands of textile merchants from al-Moski, a central area in historic Cairo, to enhance its appeal to tourists. Yet many foreign and Egyptian critics pointed out that even tourists might not want to come to admire a phantom village, and as of 2006 al-Moski was still a commercial textile market.[52] The wholesale vegetable and fruit traders of Rawd al-Farag were not as lucky as their counterparts in al-Moski; government bulldozers destroyed their large market in 1994 because they had refused to move to a new 'modern' market seven times the size of the old one, located on the outskirts of Cairo 20 km from the city centre. Two years of legal appeals and protests from the market's leaders and workers were initially successful in delaying the closure of the market, but in June 1994, as leaders and government representatives were supposedly negotiating again to delay closure, violence broke out and 1,000 troops ringed the market before bulldozers finally succeeded in levelling it.[53]

What options do the residents or merchants of El-Tayibin in Giza and Fatimid Cairo, or public-sector housing residents in Zawiyya al-Hamra or al-Rifa'i Square, have to protest government policy or investment strategies? How can the merchants in *Wust al-balad*, downtown Cairo, which was built in the late nineteenth and early twentieth centuries, compete with the proliferation of vast malls in the exurbs of Cairo? Can Egypt's elected representatives in the weak and ineffectual Egyptian Parliament protest government policy? Are they and the leaders of communities even brought into the decision-making process as the government and its allies draw up plans for new tourist museums, distant 'modernised' markets and new ring roads linking desert gated communities and satellite cities to central Cairo?

Cosmopolitan Belonging or Exclusionary Circuits?

Cairo Cosmopolitan is infused with new and rearranged hierarchies of exclusion, and it is the hierarchy and exclusion implicit within a move towards the cosmopolitan that is quite problematic. Vignal and Denis suggest that Egypt, a country of 'weak or modest technological capacities, of course owes its integration into the archipelago of great metropolises to its abundant and cheap manual labor', where all sectors of the economy function 'on the basis of minimal salaries for work, and maximum subsidies for elite speculation'.[54] While manufacturers, often linked to international companies and government supporters (or at least crony capitalists), benefit from the tax breaks and cheaper rents in the vast new satellite cities such as Sixth of October or Tenth of Ramadan, workers commute long distances on minibuses – making it more difficult for women to gain these private sector jobs.

The hierarchy explicit in cosmopolitanism and a neo-liberal order is manifested in many realms of Cairean life. When young men emigrate to finance the typically substantial costs of marriage in Egypt, they may spend years saving for and preparing their new marital abode. As Farha Ghannam shows in *Cairo Cosmopolitan,* jobs in the Gulf for lower-income men are often the sole route to savings and their imagined dreams of prosperity; yet even if they succeed in finding employment in oil-producing countries, once they return to Egypt their desire for more income and new consumer goods remains shaped by the ideas, money and products brought from these countries. Ghannam raises a critically important point about the multiplicity of global influences in Cairo, and 'directs our attention to other emerging hierarchies and power relationships that regulate interactions between cities *other* than New York, Los Angeles, and London' (emphasis added).[55] In the Arab world, '[c]lass in particular has been significant in regulating ... travel plans, work in Kuwait, and transnational connections. While upper-class Egyptians travel to and from the US and Europe (for education, vacation, and treatment) with ease, cities such as Paris and New York are largely off limits to young men ...'.

Furthermore, while some members of a family may enrich themselves by working in Libya or Kuwait, others are not able to secure visas or positions abroad and thus 'new forms of inequality [are] produced by global processes within the same city, the same neighbourhood, and even the same family'. The migrants' access to wealth and promised prosperity comes without citizenship, as Ghannam argues, and ironically 'the club of Gulf exclusion for migrants, reinforces longing and belonging back in Cairo', facilitated most recently by an explosion in international communications.[56]

In various ways, Cairo is marked by a 'high degree of segmentation in the spheres of both production and consumption'.[57] Armbrust points out a seismic shift in the economic and political centre of gravity in Cairo. Cairo is 'globalised' for all of its citizens, but what this means is less a democratisation of cosmopolitanism than the hardening of a new hierarchy of access to certain kinds of activities. In his research on popular culture, films and film spectatorship, he finds:

> [The] rituals of movie-going, dominated in downtown Cairo for a few brief decades by downwardly mobile middle-class male youth, are gradually being set aside for a more fortunate class defined by their access to Gulf or European economic standards. The fate of the downtown movie audience therefore is a microcosm for broader processes that marginalize everyone restricted to the national public sphere.[58]

As the poverty line has risen in the 1990s, de Koning points to a new bourgeoisie and a relatively affluent professional upper middle class that 'finds work in a small, yet significant internationally oriented top segment of the labour market' where 'wages tend to be three to five times higher than those paid in similar occupations in the "less modern" sectors of the formal economy, including the large public sector and civil service'.[59]

Egypt's demography is shaped by a youth bulge and the largest cohort of adolescents (ten to nineteen years old) in its history. Many young people are left on the lower rung of this cosmopolitan hierarchy as post-*Infitah* economic policies leave them among the most unemployed in the nation. Youth unemployment in 1998 was triple the total unemployment in Egypt.[60] Armbrust argues that after male youth took over the movie theatres in the late 1980s, the downtown film district had lost favour in the eyes of cultural gatekeepers:

> Elites willfully mischaracterised these young men as a barbarian invasion of lower-class 'tradesmen', thereby obfuscating a phenomenon that was, in reality, connected to a broad downgrading of middle-class fortunes in the post-Nasser era. As open market economies inexorably became the only policy choice on offer, promises made in an earlier era of social advancement through education began to ring hollow. The life-stage of 'student' began to look like a prison sentence as it elongated into eternity while marriage – traditionally the boundary between childhood and adulthood – receded into the distance.[61]

To conclude this section by returning again to the wonderful work of Vignal and Denis, the picture looks rather bleak:

> The metropolis that has taken shape in this context of export-

oriented logics and accrued dependence of Egypt on the US has spatially concretized the increasing gap between an impoverished urban population and the tenants of the new, privatized productive city. The support structure for the urban poor is less and less secure, owing to the gradual retreat of state support for basic food products (bread, notably) and to inflation. Meanwhile, the more prosperous tenants of the newly reordered city enjoy exclusive semi-public spaces, such as shopping malls, or completely private gated communities. The face of poverty has changed with the passage from a society of shortages to a society of consumerism, *without a redistribution of revenue that would enable either the growth or survival of the middle class.* Cairo is tending towards decline, in accordance with a double standard: on the one hand, the popular majority focus on survival, while on the other hand, a thin layer of city dwellers consume on a world-class scale, affording a lifestyle that is increasingly similar to those in other international cities.[62] (Emphasis added.)

Yet, the picture is not only bleak. Young women from the middle and upper classes may be finding more places to drink coffee and socialise with men. Couples and families can now shop at new, air-conditioned malls or stroll around downtown Cairo using pedestrian malls while appreciating the restored stock market and the diverse heritages of Egypt. Families can visit the gardens of the al-Azhar Park and the café just beyond Darb al-Ahmar while appreciating the beautiful gardens and manicured open space.

Other constituencies in Egypt are trying to reshape Egypt's national identity into a more inclusive, heterogeneous one that would recognise their own 'imagined communities' and ethnic and regional identities. For example, Catherine Miller notes how Upper Egyptians (*Sa'idis*) are redefining their sense of *'asabiya* (solidarity) based on a common lineage to celebrate their regional origin in the southern part of the country, which is not only the poorest and least developed, but typically lampooned by Cairenes as populated by 'backward', stupid, stubborn people.[63] No matter how wealthy or politically powerful Upper Egyptians become, they are nevertheless collectively identified with poor, unskilled migrants and with the stigmatised perception of the *'ashwa'iyat* as the locus of extremism, crime and poverty. Yet the regional identity that Upper Egyptians are embracing and promoting in their quest for political and communal leadership is itself also influenced by their experience of migration, since the Gulf urban model value in Saudi Arabia or Kuwait values the 'tribe' as one of the most authentic and legitimate types of social organisation, and uses a 'tribal rhetoric' that privileges blood origin and genealogy to challenge Egypt's modernist discourse, which ignores ethnicity and difference.[64]

Egypt's strong centralist and nationalist identity, promoted by Nasserism, has prohibited public expression and political expression of any kind of communalism, either based on religion (the Copts, for example), region (Upper Egypt) or ethnicity (non-Arab Nubians). Yet Nubian intellectuals and activists, Upper Egyptians, lower-class Cairenes and even members of Sufi brotherhoods struggle to assert themselves. They fight to have dark-skinned Egyptians and Nubians represented in the visual media (or veiled women, for that matter); to revive the Nubian languages of Kanzi and Fadicca; or to promote an Upper Egyptian identity (honour, solidarity, respect for elders, kinship unity, piety and respect for religious duties) as an antidote to the more Westernised Cairene elite.[65] As Nicholas Puig tells us, musicians who play live music at weddings and *mulids* from the *Souk al-Musiqiyin* (the musicians' market) have become 'stigmatized by the rest of Cairo inhabitants as a group of outsiders with very low social status' since the 'urban focal-point of cosmopolitan Arab music and dance performance has relocated across the Nile to the river-side hotels as well as to the cabarets of Pyramids Road with an audience made up mostly of Gulf and Saudi Arabs'.[66] Yet some musicians, such as the popular singer Sha'ban 'Abd al-Rahim, manage to break through the barriers and compose hit songs that celebrate popular culture, sometimes articulating controversial political positions as well, and fuelling new political protest.

Conclusion

Some of the new forces and contests briefly examined above hopefully explain the context for renewed political activism and cosmopolitan claims-making in Egypt. After the public demonstrations of 2005 and 2006 and the emergence of the Egyptian Movement for Change (*Kifaya*, or 'Enough!'), cooperation has increased between some political groups in Egypt such as the Muslim Brotherhood, leftist secular forces and some professional syndicates such as the Journalists' and Lawyers' Syndicate and the Club of Judges, the traditionally independent and outspoken association of the Egyptian judiciary. Domestic and foreign pressure persuaded President Hosni Mubarak to propose a national referendum to amend the constitution to allow competition in the presidential election, and for the first time since the pre-Second World War liberal age, political parties and individuals did contest the September 2005 elections.[67] The Muslim Brotherhood gained 20 per cent of the vote in the parliamentary elections, despite cascading attempts from the government to limit their success at the polls after it became obvious in the three stages of the elections that the Muslim Brotherhood was doing well – despite being banned as a political party (candidates affiliated with the Brotherhood ran as independents). Secular, leftist and nationalist forces are far behind the Muslim Brotherhood in fundraising, or in developing a popular ideological platform, new leadership cadres and a national network of activists, and thus did poorly in the parliamentary elections. Cairo's residents are acting more like citizens and increasing their claims-making on their government, while using new tactics for mobilising support, publicising their campaigns, producing new, particularly younger leadership and enhancing solidarity and coalition-building.

Perhaps the increased facility of communications and ease of disseminating information through cell phones, the Internet and the mass media has made political organising somewhat easier. Clearly, the US has placed some pressure on Mubarak (however suspect its policies may be to Egyptians) to minimise state violence towards demonstrators and to hold more competitive elections; although, after Hamas won the Palestinian elections in February 2006, the US campaign for democratisation suddenly reversed course as it refused to recognise the results of the Palestinian election, orchestrating a shameful boycott and isolation of Hamas (and the Quartet powers largely supported this action). After the Hamas election and the US's clearly weakened commitment to democracy in the region, one could argue that Egyptian security forces reverted to using more direct violence against even small numbers of demonstrators who rallied in support of the Club of Judges and their continued resistance to government manipulation of election law and election monitoring in May 2006.

Nevertheless, the presence of cameras, the international media or NGO campaign monitors, or Internet postings of photos of government violence, or the sexual molestation of demonstrators, have not stopped security forces from using their usual repertoire of thugs and intimidation. The regime, through its military and financial alliances, still seems quite strong and well-supported nationally and internationally. Yet, disaffected young people are predominant among the population in Egypt, and more of the 'demographic masses' in both the countryside and cities seem to be willing to join the fray in claiming their rights. There is still great fear of active political engagement because people are well aware of the risks, observing that even wealthy cosmopolitan elites are hung out to dry if they cross the government, suddenly charged with corruption or labelled as traitors.

Others might argue that as global financial flows become more critical to

Egypt, it does not really matter whether or not Egyptians gain a greater share of political representation and political rights, because Egyptian national sovereignty has been diminished by globalisation itself. Egyptians are no longer setting the terms for the flow of information, finances, migrants, technology or war-making. In this sense, as Cairo becomes increasingly culturally porous, economically interdependent and politically induced into more universalist economic and legal orders (such as international, bilateral and regional conventions on trade, investment, intellectual property rights, human rights law, international technology standards, etc), it loses its weight in the community of nations.

The final connection between *Cairo Cosmopolitan* and questions about citizenship and cities necessitates reconsidering the normative debates and historical struggles surrounding citizenship. As Gershon Shafir explains:

> Both citizen and human rights institutionalize the ethical and political principle of formal equality by depoliticizing and decommodifying access to rights and resources. Rights lie outside of or above partisan or state politics and, in Dworkin's terms, are recognizable by their ability 'to trump' even appeals to collective goods.[68] At the same time, they were conceived of and evolved within certain parameters: *granting citizenship was intended to ameliorate economic inequality, namely to enhance social solidarity among selected individuals in the face of continued inequality –* not to equalize social and economic conditions ...[69] (Emphasis added.)

Throughout Cairo (which, as mentioned, is increasingly porous to global and regional flows of labour, capital, advertising and universalist legal and economic codes), inequality remains a controversial political issue. If liberalism proposed citizenship as a salve to political inequality, one wonders if nationalism or Islam will continue to provide enough solidarity to maintain the Egyptian state's domination? In the post-colonial, post-Oslo world, where Egypt has signed a peace treaty with Israel and long ago gained independence from Britain, will the Egyptian government still be able to maintain its rule and legitimacy through its 'cold peace' with Israel, ambivalent, instrumental embrace of the Palestinian cause, manipulation of religious nationalism, anti-globalisation sentiments or anti-Americanism? Or will the Egyptian state need to embrace or enhance citizenship rights as a solution to inequality, as it grows and deepens? The developmentalist and nationalist era during the Nasser years provided a sense of solidarity to the nation and a mission, however controversial and contested, yet since then the mantra of economic growth has probably decreased social solidarity; many feel vulnerable to economic changes, and Islamists have associated growth and consumerism with Westernisation or corruption.

One of the motivations behind the demonstrations in 2005 and 2006 was certainly protest at the erosion of social rights in Egypt, along with increased poverty and unemployment, which many blame on the neo-liberal project. The rights discourse articulated by demonstrators included economic rights as much as political rights. While the neo-liberal discourse promotes economic growth as a solution to economic inequality, it remains silent on the need for political equality. As Mona al-Ghobashy suggests:

> The younger representatives of Egypt's ruling class may be technologically savvy, US-educated and American-accented, and properly deferential to private sector dominance and the 'laws of the market', but when it comes to institutionalising binding consultation of citizens or protecting citizens from arbitrary state power, their silence is palpable.[70]

Moreover, if the 'demographic masses' are blamed by the state for 'consuming' economic growth, as El Shakry argues, this perception promotes the idea that the poor or the lower middle class are wasting the fruits of the neo-liberal project.[71] In the end, we are back to asking the question:

> Whose Cairo? ... Which Cairo do we talk about and in whose name? ... There is Cairo, the city of migrant workers; Cairo, the city of informals, who occupy much of its space; Cairo, the city of unique urban pockets whose residents feel that they live elsewhere; Cairo, the city of gated communities and exclusive urban malls that transport their visitors to another world; and Cairo, the city of expatriates and experts who spend lifetimes trying to figure it out.[72]

Egyptians are struggling, in the face of great risks and asymmetrical power, to claim their rights, to ensure justice, legality, participation and representation, while maintaining their cultural, ethnic, regional, and religious identities. In that sense, Cairo is becoming more cosmopolitan. Fanny Colonna describes how young people in the city of Isma'iliya have created regional TV stations, weakening the capital-city monopoly on print and visual media in Egypt, in order to represent and investigate local problems and the place of their cities and villages in the national discourse and imaginary – yet they only operate with a fraction of the resources of their colleagues in Cairo.[73]

If the Egyptian government, supported by a militarised security state and international allies, continues to tolerate and promote political and economic exclusion, the political opposition will face a very tough road; yet there is more room for optimism today as a new generation of organisations, however small, strives to work in coalitions, agreeing on a simple framework for change: 'Enough.'

Bibliography

AlSayyad, Nezar, 'Whose Cairo?', in Diane Singerman and Paul Amar, eds, *Cairo Cosmopolitan: Politics, Culture, and Urban Space in the New Globalized Middle East*, Cairo: American University in Cairo Press, 2006, pp. 539–42.

Armbrust, Walter, *Anywhere But Here: Music and the New Conventions of Location in Egyptian Visual Culture*, paper presented at the Middle East Studies Association Annual Meeting, Washington, DC: 2005.

—— 'When the Lights Go Down in Cairo: Cinema as Global Crossroads and Space of Playful Resistance', in Diane Singerman and Paul Amar, eds, *Cairo Cosmopolitan: Politics, Culture, and Urban Space in the New Globalized Middle East*, Cairo: American University in Cairo Press, 2006, pp. 415–43.

Bauman, Zygmunt, *Modernity and Ambivalence*, Cambridge: Polity Press, 1999.

Chalk, Frank and Jonassohn, Kurt, *The History and Sociology of Genocide*, New Haven, CT: Yale University Press, 1990.

Colonna, Fanny, 'A Round Trip to Isma'iliya: Cairo's Media Exiles, Television Innovation, and Provincial Citizenship', in Diane Singerman and Paul Amar, eds, *Cairo Cosmopolitan: Politics, Culture, and Urban Space in the New Globalized Middle East*, Cairo: American University in Cairo Press, 2006, pp. 445–542.

De Koning, Anouk, 'Café Latte and Caesar Salad: Cosmopolitan Belonging in Cairo's Up-market Coffee Shops', in Diane Singerman and Paul Amar, eds, *Cairo Cosmopolitan: Politics, Culture, and Urban Space in the New Globalized Middle East*, Cairo: American University in Cairo Press, 2006, pp. 221–33.

Denis, Eric, 'Cairo as Neo-Liberal Capital? From Walled City to Gated Communities', in Diane Singerman and Paul Amar, eds, *Cairo Cosmopolitan: Politics, Culture, and Urban Space in the New Globalized Middle East*, Cairo: American University in Cairo Press, 2006, pp. 47–71.

—— 'From European to American Models of Urban Planning: Partition, Suburbs, and the Spatialization of Poverty and Islamism', paper presented at the Middle East Studies Association Annual Meeting (Thematic

Conversation: Contemporary Research on Cairo, Roundtable on 'Space, Urban Planning, Globalisation and Development'), Washington, DC: 1999.

—— 'La mise en scène des 'Ashwa'iyyat. Premier acte: Imbaba, Décembre 1992', in *Egypte/Monde Arabe*, 20(4), 1994, pp. 117–32.

Denis, Eric and Séjourné, Marion, 'ISIS Information System for Informal settlements', Unpublished draft report for the Urban Research Participatory Urban Management Program, Ministry of Planning, Gesellschaft für Technische Zusammenarbeit (GTZ) and Observatoire urbain du Caire Contemporain (OUCC), 2002.

Dorman, W. Judson, 'Authoritarianism and Sustainability in Cairo: What Failed Urban Development Projects Tell Us about Egyptian Politics', in Roger Zetter and Rodney White, eds, *Planning in Cities: Sustainability and Growth in the Developing World*, London: ITDG Publishing, 2002, pp. 146–66.

—— 'Of Demolitions & Donors: The Problematics of State Intervention in Informal Cairo', in Diane Singerman and Paul Amar, eds, *Cairo Hegemonic: State, Justice, and Urban Social Control in the New Globalized Middle East*, Cairo: American University in Cairo Press, 2007.

Dworkin, Ronald M., *Taking Rights Seriously*, Cambridge, MA: Harvard University Press, 1977.

Elsheshtawy, Yasser, 'From Dubai to Cairo: Competing Global Cities, Models, and Shifting Centers for Influence', in Diane Singerman and Paul Amar, eds, *Cairo Cosmopolitan: Politics, Culture, and Urban Space in the New Globalized Middle East*, Cairo: American University of Cairo Press, 2006, p. 235–50.

—— 'Redrawing Boundaries: Dubai, the Emergence of a Global City', in Yasser Elsheshtawy, ed., *Planning the Middle East City: An Urban Kaleidoscope in a Globalizing World*, New York: Routledge, 2004, pp. 169–99.

—— 'Urban Transformations: Social Control at al-Rifa'i Mosque and Sultan Hasan Square', in Diane Singerman and Paul Amar, eds, *Cairo Cosmopolitan: Politics, Culture, and Urban Space in the New Globalized Middle East,* Cairo: American University in Cairo Press, 2006, pp. 295–312.

Gertel, Joerg 'Civilizing Cairo's Market-Spaces: Powerful Merchants Battle the Economic Narratives of Experts', in Diane Singerman and Paul Amar, eds, *Cairo Hegemonic: State, Justice, and Urban Social Control in the New Globalized Middle East*, Cairo: American University in Cairo Press, 2007.

Ghannam, Farha, 'Keeping Him Connected: Globalization and the Production of Locality in Cairo', in Diane Singerman and Paul Amar, eds, *Cairo Cosmopolitan: Politics, Culture, and Urban Space in the New Globalized Middle East*, Cairo: American University in Cairo Press, 2006, pp. 251–66.

Al Ghobashy, Mona, 'Egypt Looks Ahead to Portentous Year, *Middle East Report Online,* http://www.merip.org/mero/mero020205.html, 2 February 2005.

Hegab, Salah-Eddin Mohammed, 'New Towns Policy', in *The Agha Khan Award for Architecture. The Expanding Metropolis: Coping with the Urban Growth of Cairo*, Cambridge, MA: Agha Khan Program for Islamic Architecture/ MIT Press, 1985, pp. 171–5.

El Kadi, Galila, 'Trente ans de planification urbaine au Caire', in *Revue Tiers Monde* 31 (121), 1990, pp. 185–207.

Kuppinger, Petra, 'Pyramids and Alleys: Global Dynamics and Local Strategies in Giza', in Diane Singerman and Paul Amar, eds, *Cairo Cosmopolitan: Politics, Culture, and Urban Space in the New Globalized Middle East*, Cairo: American University in Cairo Press, 2006, pp. 313–44.

Madoeuf, Anna, 'Mulids of Cairo: Sufi Guilds, Popular Celebrations, and the "Roller-Coaster Landscape" of the Resignified City', in Diane Singerman and Paul Amar, eds, *Cairo Cosmopolitan: Politics, Culture, and Urban Space in the New Globalized Middle East*, Cairo: American University in Cairo Press, 2006, pp. 465–87.

Miller, Catherine, 'Upper Egyptian Regional-Based Communities in Cairo: Traditional or Modern Forms of Urbanization?', in Diane Singerman and Paul Amar, eds, *Cairo Cosmopolitan: Politics, Culture, and Urban Space in the New Globalized Middle East*, Cairo: American University in Cairo Press, 2006, pp. 375–97.

Ministry of Planning, *The Five Year Plan: 1978–1980*, Cairo: Ministry of Planning, 1978.

Omar, Nabil, 'Imbaba's Empire of Terrorism', in *al-Ahram*, 8 December 1998, p. 3.

Puig, Nicolas. 'Egypt's Pop-Music Clashes and the "World-Crossing". Destinies of Muhammed 'Ali Clashes', in Diane Singerman and Paul Amar, eds, *Cairo Cosmopolitan: Politics, Culture, and Urban Space in the New Globalized Middle East*, Cairo: American University in Cairo Press, 2006, pp. 513–36.

Sarat, Austin and Kearns, Thomas R., eds, *Human Rights: Concepts, Concepts, Contingencies*, Ann Arbor: The University of Michigan Press, 2001.

Sassen, Saskia, *The Global City*, Princeton, NJ: Princeton University Press, 2001.

Shafir, Gershon, 'Citizenship and Human Rights in an Era of Globalization', in Alison Brysk and Gershon Shafir, eds, *People Out of Place: Globalization, Human Rights, and the Citizenship Gap*, New York: Taylor and Francis, 2004, pp. 11–25.

El Shakry, Omnia, 'Cairo as Capital of Socialist Revolution?', in Diane Singerman and Paul Amar, eds, *Cairo Cosmopolitan: Politics, Culture, and Urban Space in the New Globalized Middle East*, Cairo: American University in Cairo Press, 2006, pp. 73–98.

Shryock, Andrew, *Nationalism and the Genealogical Imagination: Oral History and Textual Authority in Tribal Jordan*, Berkeley: University of California Press, 1997.

Singerman, Diane, *Avenues of Participation: Family, Politics, and Networks in Urban Quarters of Cairo*, Princeton: Princeton University Press, 1995.

—— 'The Construction of a Political Spectacle: The Siege of Imbaba or Egypt's Internal "Other"', prepared for the Conference Series on 'Political Structures and Logics of Action in the Face of Economic Liberalization: Distributive and Normative Processes in the Arab Countries of the Mediterranean, organised by CEDEJ/Freie Universität Berlin at the Center for the Study of Developing Countries at Cairo University, 1997.

—— 'Islamist Movements and the Siege of Imbaba: Neighborhoods as the Uncivilized, Deviant "Other"', in Diane Singerman and Paul Amar, eds, *Cairo Hegemonic: State, Justice, and Urban Social Control in the New Globalized Middle East*, Cairo: American University in Cairo Press, 2007.

Singerman, Diane and Amar, Paul, eds, *Cairo Cosmopolitan: Politics, Culture, and Urban Space in the New Globalized Middle East*, Cairo: American University in Cairo Press, 2006.

Singerman, Diane and Ibrahim, Barbara, 'The Cost of Marriage in Egypt: A Hidden Variable in the New Arab Demography and Poverty Research', in Nick Hopkins, ed., *Cairo Papers in the Social Sciences, Special Edition on 'The New Arab Family'*, 24 (Spring), pp. 80–116.

Smith, Elizabeth, 'Place, Class and Race in the Barabra Café: Nubians in Egyptian Media', in *Cairo Cosmopolitan: Politics, Culture, and Urban Space in the New Globalized Middle East*, Cairo: American University in Cairo Press, 2006, pp. 399–413.

El Tawila, Saher and Zeinab Khadr, 'Patterns of Marriage and Family Formation among Youth in Egypt', National Population Council, Center for Information and Computer Systems, Faculty of Economics and Political Science at Cairo University, 2004.

Tsing, Anna, 'Inside the Economy of Appearances', in Arjun Appadurai, ed., *Globalization*, Durham, NC: Duke University Press, 2001, pp. 155–88.

UN-Habitat, *Cities in a Globalizing World: Global Report on Human Settlements*, London: Earthscan Publications, 2001.

Vignal, Leïla and Denis, Eric, 'Cairo as Regional/Global Economic Capital?', in Diane Singerman and Paul Amar, eds, *Cairo Cosmopolitan: Politics, Culture, and Urban Space in the New Globalized Middle East*, Cairo: American University in Cairo Press, 2006, pp. 99–151.

Williams, Caroline, 'Reconstructing Islamic Cairo: Forces at Work', in Diane Singerman and Paul Amar, eds, *Cairo Cosmopolitan: Politics, Culture, and Urban Space in the New Globalized Middle East*, Cairo: American University in Cairo Press, 2006, pp. 269–94.

Yousef, Tarik, 'Youth in the Middle East and North Africa: Demography, Employment, and Conflict', in Blair A. Ruble, Joseph S. Tulchin, Diana H. Varat with Lisa M. Hanley, eds, *Youth Explosion in Developing World Cities:*

Approaches to Reducing Poverty and Conflict in an Urban Age, Washington DC: Woodrow Wilson International Center for Scholars, 2003, pp. 9–24.

Notes

1. Singerman and Amar, eds, *Cairo Cosmopolitan*. As mentioned in the text, many of the insights in this chapter were developed through the contributions of my co-editor Paul Amar, particularly in co-writing the introduction, 'Contesting Myths, Critiquing Cosmopolitanism, and Creating the Cairo School of Urban Studies' in *Cairo Cosmopolitan*, pp. 3–42.
2. Vignal and Denis, 'Cairo as Regional/Global Economic Capital?'.
3. Elsheshtawy, 'From Dubai to Cairo'.
4. El Shakry, 'Cairo as Capital of Socialist Revolution?'.
5. Our volumes discuss Cairo's growing cosmopolitanism while trying to avoid the universalist, homogeneous and voluntaristic association of the term. Rather, we have emphasised the sense of cosmopolitanism, which exhibits new hierarchies of access – whether to consumption, to services or even to production, as Vignal and Denis suggest in *Cairo Cosmopolitan*. However, here I will not discuss further our particular sense of cosmopolitanism and other debates on the relevance and normative implications of the term, for the purposes of brevity (see *Cairo Cosmopolitan*).
6. El Shakry, 'Cairo as Capital of Socialist Revolution?', p. 75.
7. Ibid., p. 86.
8. Hegab, 'New Towns Policy', as quoted in El Shakry, p. 88.
9. Vignal and Denis, 'Cairo as Regional/Global Economic Capital'.
10. El Kadi, 'Trente ans de planification urbaine au Caire', as quoted in El Shakry, p. 88.
11. El Shakry, 'Cairo as Capital of Socialist Revolution?', p. 89.
12. Vignal and Denis, 'Cairo as Regional/Global Economic Capital', pp. 140–1.
13. El Shakry, 'Cairo as Capital of Socialist Revolution?', p. 94.
14. Denis, 'Cairo as Neo-Liberal Capital?', p. 49.
15. Ibid., p. 50. See also Teresa Caldeira, *City of Walls: Crime, Segregation and Citizenship in São Paolo*, Berkeley: University of California Press, 2000.
16. Denis and Séjourné, *ISIS Information System for Informal settlements*; Vignal and Denis, *Cairo Cosmopolitan*; Singerman, *Avenues of Participation*.
17. Denis, 'Cairo as Neo-Liberal Capital?', p. 24.
18. I am indebted to W. Judson Dorman for this information.
19. Dorman, 'Of Demolitions & Donors'.
20. Kuppinger, 'Pyramids and Alleys'.
21. Dorman, 'Authoritarianism and Sustainability in Cairo'; Dorman, 'Of Demolitions & Donors'.
22. Denis, 'La mise en scène des 'Ashwaiyyat'; Singerman, 'Islamist Movements and the Siege of Imbaba'.
23. *Akhir Sa'a*, December 16, 1992; quoted in Denis, 'La Mise En Scène des 'Ashwaiyyat', p. 124.
24. Omar, 'Imbaba's Empire of Terrorism'.
25. Shafir, 'Citizenship and Human Rights in an Era of Globalization'.
26. Bauman, *Modernity and Ambivalence*.
27. Note the allegations of recent presidential candidate Ayman Nour, who described how the Egyptian government tried to blackmail him with tapes of his bedroom

pillow talk with his wife; see 'Egypt: A Test Case for Democracy', CNN, http://edition.cnn.com/TRANSCRIPTS/0511/20/cp.01.html, 20 November 2005.

28. Al Ghobashy, 'Egypt Looks Ahead to Portentous Year'.
29. Chalk and Jonassohn, *The History and Sociology of Genocide*, p. 28.
30. Denis, 'Cairo as Neo-Liberal Capital', p. 58.
31. Ibid., p. 61.
32. Ibid., p. 52.
33. Ibid., p. 71.
34. Elsheshtawy, 'Redrawing Boundaries', pp 169–99.
35. Denis, 'Cairo as Neo-Liberal Capital', p. 68.
36. Tsing, 'Inside the Economy of Appearances', p. 161.
37. Ibid., p. 162.
38. Ibid.
39. Ibid., p. 175.
40. Ibid., p. 161.
41. Ibid., p. 162.
42. Ibid., p. 169.
43. Armbrust, 'When the Lights Go Down in Cairo'; Denis, 'From European to American Models of Urban Planning'.
44. Tsing, 'Inside the Economy of Appearances', pp. 187–8.
45. Elsheshtawy, 'Urban Transformations', p. 309.
46. UN-Habitat, 'Cities in a Globalizing World'; Elsheshtawy, 'Redrawing Boundaries'.
47. Madoeuf, 'Mulids of Cairo'.
48. Sassen, *The Global City*; Elsheshtawy, 'Urban Transformations'.
49. Kuppinger, 'Pyramids and Alleys', p. 314.
50. Ibid.; Williams, 'Reconstructing Islamic Cairo'.
51. Elsheshtawy, 'Urban Transformations', pp. 310–11.
52. Williams, 'Reconstructing Islamic Cairo', pp. 284–5.
53. Gertel, 'Civilizing Cairo's Market-Spaces'.
54. Vignal and Denis, 'Cairo as Regional/Global Economic Capital?', p. 147.
55. Ghannam, 'Keeping Him Connected', p. 253.
56. Ibid.
57. de Koning, 'Café Latte and Caesar Salad', p. 224.
58. Armbrust, 'When the Lights Go Down in Cairo', p. 416.
59. de Koning, 'Café Latte and Caesar Salad', p. 224.
60. Yousef, 'Youth in the Middle East and North Africa', p. 14.
61. Armbrust, 'When the Lights Go Down in Cairo', p. 415. Marriage has receded into the distance because the groom's side contributes approximately 75 per cent of marriage costs, which was found in a 1999 survey to approximate LE 20,194 (approximately $5,957 in 1997). This exceeds GNP *per capita* by four and a half times. In another comparison, the costs of a single marriage were eleven times average annual household expenditures *per capita* (Singerman and Ibrahim, 'The Cost of Marriage in Egypt', p. 92). The age of marriage for Egyptian men has become increasingly delayed and '…thirty-seven per cent of males and eighteen per cent of females are likely candidates to face late marriage beyond the age of 30' (El Tawila and Khadr, 'Patterns of Marriage and Family Formation among Youth in Egypt', p. xii).
62. Vignal and Denis, 'Cairo as Regional/Global Economic Capital?', p. 111.
63. Miller, 'Upper Egyptian Regional-Based Communities in Cairo', 1842.
64. Shryock, *Nationalism and the Genealogical Imagination*.

65. Miller, 'Upper Egyptian Regional-Based Communities in Cairo'; Smith, 'Place, Class and Race in the Barabra Café'.

66. Puig, 'Egypt's Pop-Music Clashes and the "World-Crossing"', p. 521.

67. Ayman Nour, the leader of al-Ghad (the Tomorrow Party) was stripped of his parliamentary immunity and imprisoned for supposed offences in establishing al-Ghad in late 2004. Nevertheless, despite these charges, he won 7 per cent of the electoral vote (second only to Mubarak) – although he was returned to jail at the end of 2005 and sentenced to five years in jail. Some appeals are still pending.

68. Dworkin, *Taking Rights Seriously*, p. xi; Sarat and Kearns, eds, *Human Rights: Concepts, Concepts, Contingencies*, p. 9.

69. Shafir, 'Citizenship and Human Rights in an Era of Globalization'.

70. Al Ghobashy, 'Egypt Looks Ahead to Portentous Year'; see http://www.merip.org/mero/mero020205.html, 2 February 2005.

71. El Shakry, 'Cairo as Capital of Socialist Revolution?', pp. 73–98.

72. Al Sayyad, 'Whose Cairo?', p. 539.

73. Colonna, 'A Round Trip to Isma'iliya'.

PART TWO

Governing the City

Myriam Catusse with Raffaele Cattedra[1]
and M'hammed Idrissi-Janati[2]

Decentralisation and Its Paradoxes in Morocco[3]

Recent institutional and political reforms in Moroccan local government offer interesting sites to investigate the possible articulations between urbanism and the exercise of citizenship in the age of globalisation. By analysing them we can question the nature of power relations and competing forms of legitimacy within the city. The new Communal Charter adopted in October 2002 provides a series of reforms both deeply grounded in Moroccan urban history – and its political stakes in the nation – and greatly inspired by contemporary norms of 'good governance'.[4]

In the introductory part of this chapter I shall present the national and ideological context in which the new reforms of decentralisation are introduced. This will clarify the main issues at stake in the idea of decentralisation in Morocco. I shall show how the new local charter is inscribed in a long history of political relations between the centre and city governance. The elements of change introduced by this law do not alter the weight of control from the central power. I shall then compare two authoritative local figures (the Mayor and the *Wali*) and discuss their evolution in order to question the political resources procured by technical competencies (with the support of the King) and by elective legitimacy. In the last part we'll see through the analysis of the last elections, nevertheless, that the cities in the context of globalisation remain the stage where the political struggle between representation and technical competence is still played out.

First, let us examine the context in which the new law was adopted and put into practice. 'Reform of the Moroccan state' has been inscribed in the public agenda since the World Bank published reports in October 1995 blaming the Kingdom's economic strategy, and its systems of education and administration. It specifically targeted administrative structures. This document, and the declaration of the King following its publication,[5] marked the starting point of a series of reforms.[6]

In terms of administration, a national programme on governance was developed beginning in 1996 under the coordination of the Minister of Economic Planning with support from the United Nations Development Programme (UNDP).[7] The formation in April 1998 of a government headed by the socialist party leader Abderrahmane Youssoufi accelerated the programme's dynamic. Private and public decentralisation, evoked in a general manner, were the main themes of the seventh national colloquium on local communities in 1998. According to reformers and officials, these are explicitly inscribed in a plan of democratisation.[8] They are also promoted by donors who encourage decentralisation reforms in Morocco. In November 2001, the United States Agency for International Development financed its own diagnostic study on the 'local capacity for good governance'. Also that same year, the French government implemented a '*Programme d'appui à la decentralisation au Maroc*'.

This chapter will show that the 'decentralisation' at stake in these reforms is less concerned with local elected authorities than with local institutions whose power is derived from the national government, increasing the competition between two kinds of local institution. Power is transferred to local representatives of the central power more than to local voters. In Moroccan institutional history, which is largely influenced by the French tradition, the representatives of the central power are called '*déconcentrées*' and the elected authorities '*décentralisées*': 'Decentralisation' refers here to the transfer of competencies – and resources – to local *elected* authority, while '*deconcentration*' is the term used to refer to administrative decentralisation, the transfer of competencies within a single state administration from its national level to its local level. This is key to understanding the logics and paradoxes of the contemporary reform of city governance in Morocco, especially as regards its outcomes on citizenship.

No Moroccan city can claim to participate in any major way in the control and management of the global economy, to go back to the quasi-canonical definition of the 'global city' proposed by Saskia Sassen.[9] The closest you can get to this definition is the large coastal strip that stretches over 250 km around Casablanca. With 20 per cent of the population, the city's economic and financial centre (its Central Business District [CBD]) houses the activities of the 'high' service sector.[10] The city was affected both positively and negatively by the reorientation of Morocco's political economy, especially with regard to structural adjustment programmes put into place in 1983 and the country's integration into a free-market economy with the European Union and with the US (initiated by partnership accords signed in 1996 and 2004, respectively). This has accelerated Morocco's economic integration in the 'global market'.

Different Moroccan cities partake in a globalisation process that has mostly taken two forms. First, we note the major transformations the urban fabric is undergoing because of economic changes, most notably via the privatisation process, European offshoring and the opening up of economic borders and customs. This has specifically affected the Moroccan labour market, the professional activities of city dwellers and the regulations concerning them (e.g. the number of citizens without work and the increase in social welfare).[11] This has also contributed to the increase in urban population and to the extension of *bidonvilles* (shantytowns) on the periphery of big towns.

Second, Moroccan cities do not escape the wave of reforms carried out more or less on a global scale, and in the scheme of international development agencies working towards 'better urban governance'. This leitmotif is sufficiently broad to adapt to a variety of measures covering a range of directives that are often inconsistent and give rise to multiple and contradictory discourses. The city is designated as a target for reform without clearly defining its areas. 'The city' is supposed to show coherence, or at least a degree of autonomy. Development agencies regularly refer to four attributes to define the territory of the 'ideal' and 'globalised', if not 'global', city: 'competitiveness' in the global market; 'liveability and decent quality of life' for the poor; 'good governance'; and 'bankability'.[12] Behind the technical and economic jargon, however, lies the political question of power and its sharing. In this sense, it is the definition of citizenship (and the ability of the city's inhabitants to take part in its politics) as much as the conditions of its exercise in an urban context that is questioned in relation to local leadership and decentralisation. In their actions, the reformers most often privilege security and economic 'efficiency' over other concerns and invoke a developmentalist paradigm that showed its limits long ago ('market now, democracy later').

The reforms of the local government were implemented in this context. The Moroccan Parliament ratified a new Communal Charter on 3 October 2002. This text, which replaced the one from 1976, apparently put the local communities – notably at the municipal level – at the centre of a vast plan for territorial administration while the municipalities have for decades been relegated to the margins of both administration and 'urban development'.

In reality, however, the liberalisation of the domestic economy associated with the rapid growth of city slums has 'economised' the urban question. The imperative to decentralise economic policies and to encourage private investment was reinforced, and this deprived municipalities of many competencies. 'Controlling and developing'[13] still remain the main leitmotifs of Moroccan urban policies.

If we cannot deny the strategic importance of cities in the making of modern citizens, it remains so that the urban framework produces social cleavages and forms of modern domination that we propose to examine through the prism of the transformation of local governance in Morocco. The recent forms of 'decentralisation' in Morocco pose questions to models of citizenship that are constructed or deconstructed in these urban spaces under conditions of profound change. The modalities and conditions of participation in public life are inscribed in a triple process. First, 'municipalisation', within the scope of the new Communal Charter, answers more to decisions 'from above' than to grievances 'from below'. Second, the city defined by municipalisation is more the 'urbs' (the territorial perimeter) than the *civita* (the political model). Finally, municipalisation introduces changes of scale. The repositioning of the political centre determines and constrains the 'municipalisation' of the city, and the public representation of city dwellers. They are caught in a game of power among the authorities.

Decentralisation? The Rationales of Local Public Action Reform

Announcing the emergence of an urban government model centred around the 'uniqueness' of the city, the new Communal Charter – both strongly supported by the King and ex-opposition political parties such as the Union of Socialist Popular Forces (USFP) – shows a reformist will. At the outset, it substantially transforms the landscape of the City Councils by fusing the Municipalities of the fourteen urban agglomerations of more than 500,000 inhabitants across the country. To understand what is at stake with the adoption of the new law, we need to look at it within the history of decentralisation in Morocco.

Up until 2002, 'Moroccan-style' decentralisation, in the strict sense of transferring power to local elected assemblies, has been divided into four principal levels:

1. The Local Council (urban or rural, the distinction set by law);
2. The Urban Community, in certain agglomerations that

federate the activities of multiple urban Municipalities;

3. The Prefecture or Provincial Assembly, with limited jurisdiction;
4. The Regional Council, which only attained local community status in 1996.

The jurisdictions of these institutions are variable, and authorities sent by the national government limit their respective constituencies, causing overlap, redundancy or conflict. *Caïds*, *Pachas*, Governors and *Walis* are appointed by the King to represent the central administration at different levels. Their 'jurisdiction' is rarely defined with any precision, but as representatives of the King (and as officials from the Minister of the Interior) they concentrate more powers and resources than the elected authorities. Extreme confusion exists among the multiple jurisdictions that plot, share and trace the contours of the urban political and administrative landscape. Far from appearing like a simple accident in the institutional history of Morocco, this state of uncertainty reflects a mode of government founded in large part on imprecise and shifting laws of an arbitrary nature. It is an important tool in the security control of the state.[14]

It is difficult to obtain precise and up-to-date maps reflecting recent changes, and maps of the various administrative perimeters are often lacking. Local officials sometimes appear to be ignorant of the precise definition of their jurisdictions. This reflects a tradition of censorship and the withholding of information, especially when it's a matter of seeing, in images, the relationship between territory and politics – and even more so on an urban scale.

Table 1: Local communities in Morocco in 2002,
before the reform of the Communal Charter[15]

Local Communities	Legislative Branch	Executive Branch
Regions (16)	Regional council is indirectly elected by way of the electoral college	The *Wali*, governor of the Province or Prefecture of the administrative centre of the region, appointed by a *dahir*[16]
Provinces (45) or Prefectures (26)	Provincial or Prefectorial assembly elected by indirect, universal suffrage based on councillors' college and the professional colleges	Governor of the Province or Prefecture, appointed by the King

Local Communities	Legislative Branch	Executive Branch
Urban Communities (14)	The Urban Community council includes the presidents of the urban Municipalities in the agglomeration, and their vice-presidents, members by right	The *Wali*, also in charge of overseeing its budget
Local Councils (249 Municipalities and 1,298 rural Local Councils)	City Council elected by direct universal suffrage	President of the Local Council, elected by the City Councils

As a supra-municipal community comprising presidents and vice-presidents of the urban Municipalities making up 'the city', the Urban Community was, before the introduction of this Communal Charter, responsible for coordinating transversal infrastructure projects such as highways, electricity, sanitation and sewage systems, trash collection, slaughterhouse management, etc. This formula was mostly used throughout the 1990s when, for security reasons, the agglomerations were divided into several Municipalities. Between 1992 and 2003, there were fourteen Urban Communities in Morocco: Casablanca (grouping together 27 Municipalities), Rabat (5), Sale (5), Fès (5), Marrakech (5), Meknès (6), Skhirate/Temara (2), Tangier (3), Oujda (4), Safi (3), Tétouan (2), Agadir (4), Taza (2), Kenitra (3).

Depending on the places, the contexts and their principal players, the Urban Communities acquired, over the course of the 1990s, a variable degree of influence and importance in the governance of cities. For political reasons, the Urban Communities of Rabat and Casablanca were sites of intense political competition. But their jurisdiction concerning community and public services were heavily shaken in the last few years. With the generalisation of the concession of public utilities to private companies, they were partly stripped of their functions.

The Communal Charter of 2002 thus eliminates the Urban Community Council from the institutional architecture. It abandons the formula of cities divided into various Municipalities and reinstalls a system of a unified administration by 'fusing' the Municipalities. In the case of towns of more than 500,000 people, this is done through the introduction of elected *arrondissement*[17] councils.

From twenty-nine urban Municipalities in 2002, the agglomeration of Casablanca forms only one unique Municipality in 2003, with only one President for the City Council and with sixteen *arrondissemement* councils with limited jurisdiction. It now has only 131 City Councillors compared to 1,147 in the previous configuration.

The new Charter redistributes (at the margins, of course) the resources and capabilities of the various local political institutions, especially in urban areas. This alters a threefold movement that has, up until this point, characterised the *raison d'être* of Moroccan 'decentralisation'. First, since 1976 the institutional reforms concerning the local government have tended towards fragmentation and the multiplication of actors, institutions and urban territories. Following the violent riots of June 1981, the number of Prefectures in Casablanca grew from one to five, which duplicated and divided the municipal inter-urban institutions.

These Prefectures cut up the territory and interfere with the jurisdiction of the Municipalities both spatially and in terms of responsibilities and political decisions. This division of Casablanca was also accompanied by other plans for the territorial control of the state, such as the completion of an urban highway that had the effect of practically slicing the metropolis in two and isolating the working-class neighbourhoods and the extensions of the southern periphery. From 1977 to 2002, we can thus count seven different territorial configurations in Casablanca.

Table 2: Twenty-five years of urban apportioning in Casablanca (1976–2002)[18]

Years	Wilaya of greater Casablanca	Urban Community	Prefectures	Municipalities	Rural Local Council	Total Local Councils	Region of greater Casablanca	Total number of administrative units
1976–81	–	1		5				6
1981–5	1	1	5	5				12
1985–90	1	1	6	17	6+ 1°	23		31 + AUC
1990–2	1	1	7	16	6	22		31 + AUC
1992–7	1	1	7	27+ 1*	7	35	1	44 + AUC
1997–2002	1	1	9	29	6	35	1	47 + AUC + IRU

Added to this segmentation of the cities' administrative structures, there were many organisations – be they public or private, individual or collective, professional or development associations – intervening on an *ad hoc* basis in diverse areas of the cities. Nevertheless, the increase of actors involved in urban governance didn't lead to a dispersion of power, but rather to the centralisation of decision-making. Almost all major decisions affecting urbanism during the last few decades were made at the Palace. Two actors directly dependent on the Minister of the Interior, the urban agencies and the *Wilaya*, became more powerful in the 1990s for the former and more recently for the latter, reinforcing the central power.[19]

Consequently, the Municipalities developed a strict dependence on the Ministry of the Interior and, under its authority, the General Direction of the Local Communities (GDLC). This is the second major tendency that characterises the evolution of urban government in Morocco, at least up until the adoption of the new Communal Charter. The same year that the Communal Charter of 1976 was promulgated, Driss Basri arrived at the head of the Ministry of the Interior. During his twenty years' tenure, he established the political-administrative network that defined the Kingdom's territorial administration. As Minister of the Interior between 1976 and 1999, he extended the influence of his ministry and created a web of complex formal and informal networks. The GDLC maintained a double supervision of the City Councils, both budgetary and technical as well as juridical. This strongly hindered the participatory and democratic potential of the elected Municipalities.

The local tax system, which mainly dealt with the regulation of licences, urban taxes and the redistribution of VAT (property tax) fees, depended essentially on the central government's redistribution of resources. This deprived the City Councils of any margin of autonomy. The lack of financial autonomy gave the local governments little space to negotiate the distribution of power in the Moroccan government. Rather than attempting a *coup de force*, the Local Councils preferred to draft their proposals and to plead their case with the Minister or his local representatives. This was possible whenever the Local Council's board had the jurisdiction, political will and logistical ability to do so. Geographical proximity and political support were often an advantage enjoyed, for example, in the case of Rabat, but this task was clearly more arduous for the more modest and remote City Councils.

Local collectivities were also politically marginalised by the way elections were organised. Local and national elections took place under the supervision of the GDLC. Election campaigns and ballots were moments of mobilisation and designation 'from below' by members of City Councils as well as ways to control political and civil societies.[20] The means of control are plural and complex, having evolved throughout the seven local campaigns that Morocco has undergone since independence, incorporating physical and symbolic violence as well as political and economic pressure and cartographic manipulation. The result was that the candidates in the election seemed as much (if not more) dependent on their allies, well positioned within the leadership of the local communities, as on the choice of the voters.

Another dynamic intersecting that of decentralisation, and which contributes to the multiplication of political actors in the city, could be qualified as 'privatisation of the city'. On one hand there are the non-public actors in the metamorphosis of urban configurations, which might include land or architectural operations or perhaps the indirect effects of economic activities. Urban space thus resembles a commercial space to be 'administered', 'managed' or 'profited from'. On the other hand, there are non-public or non-institutional actors who find themselves invested with responsibilities of 'public services' through the delegation of administrative duties or within the frameworks of local associations.

Entire areas of jurisdiction dealing with urban issues are transferred from the Municipalities to national or international private groups. Since the move towards privatisation in 1991, big international companies such as Lyonnaise des Eaux, the Bouygues group and its Moroccan subsidiary company Bymaro or, more recently, Vivendi in Rabat, Tangier and Tétouan, have invested in urban utilities (here, water supply).[21] Their intervention rationales were based on their own action plans and their private interests, and do not necessarily contradict public politics in terms of development and urbanism. Nevertheless, because they are not formally integrated into the larger urban project, their actions could incite conflict over the occupation and use of space.

Their interventions draw new boundaries within the city without necessarily taking into consideration the distinctions between the 'legal city' and the 'illegal city' or the legal status of space, and without any concern for egalitarianism. The city dweller, barely the citizen, is first and foremost perceived as a 'client', a 'consumer', a beneficiary or a voluntary member of associative action. In essence, the negotiations, discussions and agreements relating to these contracts take place not only in a non-public manner, but also without any real association with local elected officials. Until their disappearance, the Urban Communities were, *de jure*, in charge of these kind of utilities, but they did not have, *de facto*, great latitude to interfere in the terms of the contracts, which were most of the time studied by the Ministry of the Interior, the GDLC and the director of state-owned or private concession companies and negotiated directly at the Palace.

Nevertheless, in the case of the concession of the state-controlled corporation for electricity and water supply, the REDAL at Rabat-Salé, the elected City Councillors protested successfully against the first agreement signed with a Luso-Spanish consortium, in the name of the defence of citizens' interests.[22] Furthermore, Lamia Zaki shows that in the shantytowns of Casablanca, the elected officials intervened *a posteriori* in order to act as mediators between the Lydec society (the Lyonnaise des Eaux subsidiary for electricity and water supply) and residents refusing to pay their electricity bill.[23]

In terms of 'privatising' the city, it is important to mention the more and more visible intervention of local associations that are less present in the urban decision-making process than in the various forms of the implementation of public action.[24] The particular dynamism of neighbourhood associations participates in new forms of spatial appropriation.[25] These associations are characterised by a great heterogeneity, among cities, among neighbourhoods and sometimes at the heart of a single large neighbourhood. The quest for an urban identity seems to be, in all cases, at the centre of the aspirations around which newly arrived individuals organise themselves. Despite its youth and constraints, this urban local association movement was able to attain some successes. But it also suffered from a number of problems that limited its added value. The first kind of limit is the ambiguous attitude of the public powers *vis-à-vis* these neighbourhood associations. They are perceived as a means of compensating for the disengagement of state-controlled power, and their place in the local government remains unpredictable, often rendering their actions transient. Added to this factor is the poverty of the material and human means at their disposal. Most of them assume a temporary character; few succeed in equipping themselves with permanent structures. Finally, the omnipresence of the state has not disappeared in popular representations. In the public imagination, the spaces outside people's homes are of the public order and are therefore the responsibility of public representatives, thus of the Local Councils.

From the security imperatives of the 1980s to the development imperatives of the 1990s and 2000s, the role of the Municipalities remains extremely minor. The Palace stays central in the initiation and control of urban policies. In this context, the adoption of the new Communal Charter is more part of a broader course of reorganisation of the administrative structures in Morocco from above than a response to the grievances of local democracy.

Local Leadership in Transformation?

We have seen how the new Communal Charter was implemented in the context of a longer history of decentralisation that, in fact, gave little autonomy to local actors. I shall now show how its implementation intervenes in the exercise of local leadership.

The invention of the 'Mayor': a new actor in the city?

The new Communal Charter contributed to the reshaping of the urban political game, and thus to the relations between city dwellers and their 'representatives'. Certain clues seem to point at a reinforcement of power at the heart of the Municipality, and most of all in the hands of the president of its City Council.

On one hand, the jurisdictions that the Communal Charter of 1976 assigned to the old Urban Communities of the fourteen cities are now transferred to the level of the new City Council. Thus, if the *arrondissements* of 2003 lose in power to the detriment of the new 'Municipality', the latter wins in power in relation to the former jurisdictions of the Urban Communities. On the other hand, the Charter reduces the importance of the supervision of the Ministry of the Interior of the City Council only marginally, as it modifies neither the principle nor the system. The preliminary control of legality is thus reduced to matters determined by the law. The delay period in which the Minister of the Interior has to sign for payment is also fixed. The text of the Charter provides a reinforcement of the jurisdictional control of the acts of the authorities that supervise (such as control of the regional banking courts created by a new law on the control of public finances). Parallel to this, general inspectors of the territorial administration have been formed at Kenitra in order to 'control' the governors' actions. But no mission has yet been conferred upon the first promotion.

In this context of political and technical reinforcement of the municipal jurisdictions, for the first time journalists called the president of the City Council 'Mayor' when they were commenting on the elections of September 2003, as though a new function had appeared in the urban government. The new Communal Charter extended the prerogatives of the president of the City Council. Article 7 of the 1976 Charter allowed the forced resignation of the president based on a two-thirds vote of the council members, and led to the dismissal of many presidents between 1999 and 2001; but it was abolished by the 2002 Charter. What's more, in the new Charter the cessation of the president's function automatically leads to the cessation of the board of the City Council. As a supplementary privilege, the 'president of the Local Council becomes not only the executive authority of the Municipality, but receives, by law, from His Majesty the King a *dahir* that provides him with His Majesty's high recommendations'.[26] This is not without importance in Morocco, and adds to the legitimacy of the ballot the legitimacy of the royal seal.

The powers of Mayors in terms of police administration are from now on defined. Several political parties demand since long that the requisitioning of the public forces becomes obligatory when the president demands for it, but this demand remains dead letter. Many elected presidents and their councillors feel, therefore, powerless for lack of access to the police. They rely on the good will of the Prefecture for the execution of decisions.

The apparent reinforcement of the powers of Mayors went with a reformulation of the status of elected officials.[27] First, the plurality of offices is banned. Second, elected officials must from now on prove they have a level of instruction equal to that of the end of primary schooling. This is a response to criticisms that the locally elected representatives have been subject to for a decade, accused of incompetence, corruption or poor public finance administration.[28]

Besides the dispositions the new Charter introduced, the power of the Mayors became very limited due to the conditions of their election in 2003. The 2002 Local Charter introduces a new kind of ballot system: in towns of more than 25,000 inhabitants, proportional representation was adopted, replacing the previous 'first-past-the-post' system. In constituencies of less than 25,000 inhabitants, the first-past-the-post system was maintained.

Paradoxically, the local elections of 2003 highlighted the feeble political and territorial legitimacy of the newly elected officials. The rate of abstention continues to rise. Official participation was 75 per cent in the 1997 elections, and dropped to 50 per cent in 2003. In the big cities, the rate of participation did not surpass 47 per cent. In the largest agglomerations, the concrete organisation of the election of Mayors was controversial. A series of scandals during the elections immediately compromised their legitimacy. Due to both the ballot system and the number of parties in the running (twenty-six), there was an extreme dispersion of votes. This explains why the designation of the president of the City Council among the councillors led to secret negotiations, treason and various alliances between the leaders and the parties aiming for the presidency in the large agglomerations. Because of this game, in the big cities, many candidates without popular support ended up being elected.[29]

It remains to be seen to which extent these new legislative and political rules of the game will play a role in the municipalisation of the city. The main indications point towards a situation of dependence of the Local Councils *vis-à-vis* the central administration. Nevertheless, because of the symbolic and political weight that Municipalities hold by virtue of being the representatives of the city and not of the 'parties of the city', we could imagine a new configuration of power relations in which the president of the City Council plays a more important role.

The advent of the 'Techno-Wali': relocation of the control of the central government and new models of leadership

Parallel to this fragile emergence of the 'Mayor' in the 2000s, another figure imposed itself on the politics of the city – with a technocratic legitimacy, not a representative one. Over the past decade, the regional *Walis* started to speak on behalf of the city and assumed the main decision-making on all matters of urban administration and/or policies. *Walis* are regional governors appointed by the King. Even if they hold important executive powers at the local level and are appointed by the King, they claim to be politically neutral, an idea strengthened by the media. This contributes to the 'depoliticisation' of the local political arena.

Up until the mid-1990s, the institution of the *Wilaya* slowly developed without real legal existence, coordinating the various activities of the urban authorities. The King referred to them for the first time in 1981 when, after urban riots, he pointed out that the '*Wali*', as governor of the main Prefecture of the region of Casablanca, had to coordinate the action of the various Prefectures and Provinces of the region. Alongside this *de facto* creation of the first *Wilaya*, it was decided to increase the number of Prefectures in this town. The creation of the *Wilaya* was generalised in all the regions between 1983 and 1997, a fact that was strongly related to security measures and political control of urban population. For instance, after violent riots in December 1990, the cities of Fès, Marrakech and Meknès were divided into many Prefectures and endowed with a supra-prefectorial structure (*the Wilaya*) in charge of coordination. Beyond the coordinating function, the *Walis* intervene mostly in terms of security and especially in serious situations such as after popular uprisings, as guarantors of the public order at the local level, representatives of the Ministry of Interior in the service of whom they are all recruited.

Despite the gradual generalisation of the '*Wali*' title, Moroccan law remained, for more than twenty years, silent about both the status and the power of the *Walis*. They only legally existed because of a ministerial decree of 1983 granting them power as governors, a decree kept 'secret' and unpublished in the *Bulletin officiel*. This decree attributes three missions to the *Wali*: 'maintaining public order'; 'urbanism'; and 'economic and social development'.

An important step, when it comes to city governments, was taken with the institutionalisation process of the *Walis* in the early 2000s, still without legal codification. In January 2002, the regional *Wali* found himself endowed with particular prerogatives in a royal letter about the 'decentralised management of investment'.[30] This letter conferred upon them important and new functions: they were put in charge of the decentralised management of investment and of 'economic and social development'. In particular, the letter ordained the creation, under their supervision, of Regional Investment Centres (RIC), which centralise services for economic operators (Moroccan or foreign) interested in local investment.

Politically, the role of the *Walis* has been clearly affirmed in the last few years. The royal letter followed the departure of former Minister of the Interior Driss Basri, in September 1999, and the nomination of new governors. This brought a new generation to the head of the *Wilaya* whom the media called 'Super-*Wali*' or 'Techno-*Wali*'. On 27 July 2001, seven out of nine *Walis* appointed were, for the first time, from outside the Ministry of the Interior. They were graduates of the best French schools, engineers and often heads of important public or private offices in the Kingdom, some of which had participated in the privatisation programme.

The day after their nomination, newspaper headlines speculated about the mark these *Walis* would be leaving: 'A "dream team" of *Walis* to shake up the administration'; '*Walis*' new look'; '*Walis*-management'; 'Private bosses for the public'. The accent in these expectations and collective representations was on the *Walis*' ability to manage the city according to the 'rules of private management'.[31] Keeping in mind the social origins of most of them, they could not rightly have been considered outsiders. Nevertheless, like the new Minister of the Interior Driss Jettou, they embodied a new generation of political men, close to the Palace and also often in business, promoting a certain 'technocratisation' of the policies and politics of the city.

This apparent reversal of the Palace's priorities, through the reform of the *Wilaya*, showed its limits in the local election of 2003. The elections were considered arduous for the authorities as well as the Palace. The 'Islamist' Party of Justice and Development (PJD) displayed its ambitions, after its remarkable scores in the 2002 legislative elections. Its leaders emphasised their local and urban electoral base.[32] At that time, the so-called 'Techno-

Walis' were relieved of their duties and replaced, except in Marrakech, by individuals from the Ministry of the Interior.

In general, since 2002, the prerogatives of the *Walis* have increased in the cities, combining security and economic imperatives. These economic and security functions reduce the possibilities for the intervention of several ministers at the city level through the delegation of ministerial powers, and reinforce the territorialisation of the central state.

Even though the *Walis* do not have much power in legal terms, the question is whether they will cede some of their decision-making powers to the 'Mayors'. This Manichean alignment of the fates of the *Wali* and the Mayor these last few years in Morocco suggests conflicts of authority and jurisdiction between these political actors in the city. Far from announcing the end of politics, this has contributed to a reinvention or reorientation of the modes of political action.

Reinvestment of the Local Arena? The Election Strategies of the PJD

Here I shall show, through an examination of the attitude of the PJD over the course of the last electoral consultations, how the technical argument can go together with representative legitimisation and cannot simply be considered a 'resurgence of the democratic temptation (...) in the face of the inability of the political class to fully carry out its role'.[33] The PJD has adopted a strategy of conquest of national power (the party remains loyal to the monarchy) through the conquest of local powers. In this way the false alternative between a representative legitimacy and a technological legitimacy is broken.

The results of the local elections in 2003, as the Minister of Interior presented them on a national scale, are misleading if we do not pay attention to what happened at the level of the city. In terms of candidacies, the PJD was absent from 82 per cent of the electoral districts. Therefore, if it appeared in eleventh position on the national level, it revealed itself to be the second electoral force of the Kingdom in medium-sized cities.

After the bomb attacks in Casablanca on 16 May 2003, the PJD adopted a low profile. Despite the protest of the party's base, its leaders chose to concentrate its presence in only 18 per cent of possible electoral districts and in only half the *arrondissements* in the cities with more than 500,000 inhabitants, where they could effectively expect important victories. None of the main party representatives ran in the elections. In general terms, they only supported 34.8 per cent of the candidates. This strategy of auto-limitation paradoxically reinforced the PJD's representative legitimacy.

It made use of some impressive local victories in the districts where it ran as examples to prove its putative electoral force and efficient and tangible territorial inscription in the city.

The party's attitude was interesting in many other ways too, especially because its leaders as well as its local candidates (re)politicised the urban arena and the Municipality. They emphasised a political project based on proximity, associated with urbanity and contributed to the rehabilitation of the Municipal councils. They therefore inscribed themselves in a legal pattern that uses structures of representation, neglected by other partisan groups, to impose themselves on the political field.

In developing a theory of urban territorial representation, the PJD turned the local administration into a politicised arena. The elites and militants of the party pretended to establish the Municipality anew at its 'right' value and criticised and condemned what they considered as a 'misuse' of representative institutions.[34] The party's elected officials or candidates emphasised, furthermore, their own capacity to control their territory, notably through organising protests. Finally, the leaders of the party presented their final candidates as spokesmen in terms of 'trustees', trustworthy representatives, autonomous in their judgements because of their abilities and expertise and not influenced by pressures from above or below.

In addition, in order to conquer the Municipality, these leaders relied on a strategy emphasising their capacity to produce information and to master technical projects. Expertise, or at least knowledge or technical savvy, became a weapon or resource in political competition. In this way the discussion was situated in the 'technical' domain to avoid a political conflict, but at the same time the technical confrontation took a decidedly more political turn. The party asserted that it prepared a diagnostic for each city where it had elected representatives and where its deputies in Parliament fought particularly hard for the reform of the Communal Charter as a priority matter. Its leaders disqualified their political opponents, locally elected officials or decentralised authorities by questioning their abilities. Commenting on the new text of the law, a municipal councillor from the PJD in Fès affirmed:

> The text demands that the president of the Municipality have a certain level of education. But this isn't convincing, because what is asked for is simply an elementary school certificate! The expectation would have to be raised to a bachelor's degree or higher. Among the obstacles [to community politics] is the ignorance of elected officials. It's a big obstacle.[35]

Their 'technocratic' or 'technical' partners sometimes shared this feeling. The governor of the urban agency[36] in Fès affirmed, on the eve of the adoption of the new Communal Charter:

> For city planning, there too, the Municipalities have an essential role to play. They deliver the building authorisations. But in practice, we do all the work, and they receive the payment. They are the ones who spend the taxes. We are a public services organisation. We sell public services: ideas and documents. But for free.[37]

He insisted that his skills, and those of his colleagues, were just the opposite:

> There is a bit of everything: architects, engineers ... but mostly architects ... It's a big advantage, the weight of competence, when you speak. It's not like those who let other people do the talking.

This competition among the urban political actors, whose jurisdictions are blurred and mixed, illustrates the importance of asserting their abilities, or contesting the validity of others' abilities. The PJD governor cited above is an economics professor, and defies the 'Techno-*Walis*' in this field:

> The *Walis* have a lot of other things going on. The logic of development must come from investment. Its agents are not made for this, though. They should concentrate on security issues. There's a new vision: the 'manager' ... But it's just for show: Who's going to handle the files?

The PJD is far from being the only political group to be interested in urban affairs. The parties from the 'national movement' (mainly USFP and Istiqlal) have since long claimed to be representatives of the cities' inhabitants, and to have competence in governance. Furthermore, many candidates and local officials are strongly anchored in the territoriality of their action. What was remarkable about these last elections is the strategy ostensibly displayed by the PJD, leading to a reconsideration of the political arena in big Moroccan cities. This was clearly different from the schema of a local political arena emptied of its politics and solely in the hands of technicians. The idea that the PJD produced a modernisation of the modes of urban governance is expressed in an exemplary article in the French-speaking magazine *Jeune Afrique l'Intelligent* about the PJD mayor of Meknès:

> The administrative structure of Meknès has been rationalised. The four Municipalities were grouped into one, which has improved its efficiency by simplifying procedures. And already the residents are benefiting: The creation of one office that deals with building permits ('a first!') has added to the drastic reduction of the delays for permits from 'several weeks to sometime less than 24 hours'. This certainly plays its role in the real estate boom that the city is experiencing ... In all domains, the Belkora team has adopted a 'quality measure' that conforms to the ISO 9001 [*sic*] adopting management indicators and personnel training ...[38]

Conclusion

Contemporary transformations of urban leadership in Morocco can lead to two avenues that certainly merit further thought and investigation. First, we need to underline the extreme fragmentation of legitimate territories in the city. There are constituencies for campaign elections; there are the territories of the Prefecture and of the *Wilaya* that extend in theory far beyond that of the Municipality; there is the field of far more localised associations such as the domains of the companies providing electricity or water, trash collection or reliable transportation. This complexity of territories interferes with the exercise of citizenship. The city is, on one hand, a space for mobilisation and protest, where power is fought for, but the struggles for power also play out on the level of policymaking, as shown in this analysis of the processes of municipalisation.

Second, in Moroccan cities, the relations between political actor and public action are undergoing a transformation. The decentralisation process and the inherent institutional and political rationales affect, on one hand, the strategies adopted by groups and individuals exercising or claiming power and, on the other, the tools and rationales for public action. The weight of the centralisation and the lack of public resources limit political competition and the extent of public action.

The 'technocratisation' of the local elite is part of a long and well-studied history of the domestication and diffusing of dissent, to use an expression by Mohammed Tozy.[39] This tends to partially neutralise the political game by weakening the elected officials and diminishing the scope of representative legitimacy. Nevertheless, local leadership cannot be totally removed from urban representation. We saw this with the appointments and the dismissals of the 'Techno-*Walis*' and with the electoral success of the PJD. This forces us to reconsider the link between politics and policies and to question the relation between what happens on a local scale and what happens on a national scale. The weight of centralist history in the deployment of local Moroccan communities remains a determining factor in terms of the relationship between citizenship and urbanity, but the political arena of the globalised city cannot be considered emptied of *politics* and solely in the hands of *policy*makers.

Bibliography

Allain-El-Mansouri, Béatrice, 'La Délégation du service privé de la gestion de l'eau potable au Maroc: le cas de Rabat-Salé. La quête de la bonne gouvernance', in Claude de Miras, ed., *Intégration à la ville et services urbains au Maroc. Apport du programme PRUD à l'analyse de l'urbanisation au Maroc: Gouvernance, services collectifs et compétences urbaines*, Rabat: INAU/IRD, 2005, pp. 163–90.

——*L'Eau et la ville au Maroc. Rabat-Salé et sa périphérie*, Paris: L'Harmattan, 2001.

Ameur, Mohamed, 'Les Associations de quartier, nouveaux acteurs en milieu urbain marocain', in Pierre Signoles, G. El Kadi and Rashid Sidi Boumedine, eds, *L'Urbain dans le monde arabe. Politiques, instruments et acteurs*, Paris: CNRS éditions, 1999.

Bennani-Chraïbi, Mounia, 'Actes de vote et d'abstention à Casablanca', in Mounia Bennani-Chraïbi, Myriam Catusse and Jean-Claude Santucci, eds, *Scènes et coulisses de l'élection au Maroc. Les législatives 2002*, Paris: Karthala, 2004, pp. 163–85.

——'Mobilisations électorales à Derb Soltan et à Hay Hassani (Casablanca)', in Mounia Bennani-Chraïbi, Myriam Catusse and Jean-Claude Santucci, eds, *Scènes et coulisses de l'élection au Maroc. Les législatives 2002*, Paris: Karthala, 2004, pp. 105–61.

——'Représenter et mobiliser dans l'élection legislative au Maroc. Introduction', in Mounia Bennani-Chraïbi, Myriam Catusse and Jean-Claude Santucci, eds, *Scènes et coulisses des élections au Maroc. Les législatives de 2002*, Paris: Karthala, 2004, pp. 20–3.

Cattedra, Raffaele, *La Mosquée et la Cité. La reconversion symbolique du projet urbain à Casablanca (Maroc)*, doctoral dissertation, University of Tours, 2001.

Cattedra, Raffaele, Catusse, Myriam and Idrissi-Janati, M'hammed, 'Changer d'échelles de gouvernance? Réflexions autour de la promulgation de la

Charte communale de 2002 au Maroc', in *Actes du colloque Terrains et échelons de la gouvernance. Expériences en France et au Maghreb*, Montpellier: GESTER, forthcoming.

Catusse, Myriam, 'Les coups de force de la représentation', in Mounia Bennani-Chraïbi, Myriam Catusse and Jean-Claude Santucci, eds, *Scènes et coulisses de l'élection au Maroc. Les législatives 2002*, Paris: Karthala, 2004, pp. 69–104.

——'Le local en questions. Débat de recherche', in *Année du Maghreb 2003*, Aix-en-Provence: CNRS éditions, 2005, pp. 205–33.

——'La réinvention du social dans le Maroc ajusté', in *REMMM*, no. 105–106, 2005, pp. 221–46.

Catusse, Myriam, Cattedra, Raffaele and Idrissi-Janati, M'hammed, 'Municipaliser les villes? Le gouvernement des villes marocaines à l'épreuve du politique et du territoire', in Claude de Miras, ed., *Intégration à la ville et services urbains au Maroc. Apport du programme PRUD à l'analyse de l'urbanisation au Maroc: Gouvernance, services collectifs et compétences urbaines*, Rabat: INAU/IRD, 2005, pp. 313–61.

Haoues-Jouve, Sinda, *Vingt ans de politique d'assainissement à Casablanca: enjeux, acteurs et limites. 1976–1997*, unpublished doctoral dissertation, Institut Français d'Urbanisme (Champs-sur-Marne), Université de Paris VIII, 1999.

Idrissi-Janati, M'hammed, 'Des citadins "ordinaires" face à un projet urbain de percée routière dans la médina de Fès', in Isabelle Berry and Agnes Deboulet, eds, *Les compétences des citadins dans le Monde arabe. Penser, faire, et transformer la ville*, Paris: Karthala, 2000, pp. 289–311.

Kaioua, Abdelkader, *Casablanca. L'industrie et la ville*, Tours: URBAMA (Fascicule de Recherches no. 31), 1996.

El Maoula El Iraki, Aziz, *Des Notables du Makhzen à l'épreuve de la gouvernance. Elites locales, gestion urbaine et développement au Maroc*, Paris: L'Harmattan, 2002.

Mecherfi, Amal, 'Autonomie et développement local dans la nouvelle charte communale', in *La Nouvelle Charte communale, vers une collectivité locale citoyenne*, Rabat: Editions de la REMALD, no. 44, 2003, pp. 11–20.

de Miras, Claude, ed., *Intégration à la ville et services urbains au Maroc. Apport du programme PRUD à l'analyse de l'urbanisation au Maroc: Gouvernance, services collectifs et compétences urbaines*, Rabat: INAU/IRD, 2005.

Naciri, Mohammed, 'Les politiques urbaines: instruments de pouvoir ou outils de développement?', in France Métral et al., eds, *Politiques urbaines dans le Monde arabe*, Lyon: Maison de l'Orient, 1985, pp. 14–22.

——'Territoire: contrôler ou développer, le dilemme du pouvoir depuis un siècle', in *Maghreb-Machrek*, no. 164, 1999.

Rachik, Abderrahmane, *Ville et pouvoirs au Maroc*, Casablanca: Afrique Orient, 1995.

REMALD (Revue Marocaine d'Administration Locale et de Développement),

La nouvelle Charte communale et la nouvelle organisation des préfectures et provinces, Rabat: Collection textes et documents, no. 72, 2003.

Sassen, Saskia, *The Global City: New York, London, Tokyo*, New Jersey: Princeton University Press, 1991.

Signoles, Aude, 'Réforme de l'Etat et transformation de l'action publique', in Elizabeth Picard, ed., *La Politique dans le monde arabe*, Paris: Armand Colin, 2006, pp. 239–61.

Signoles, Pierre, El Kadi, G. and Sidi Boumedine, Rashid, eds, *L'Urbain dans le monde arabe. Politiques, instruments et acteurs*, Paris: CNRS éditions, 1999, p. 19–55.

Veguilla del Moral, Victoria, 'Le "pourquoi" d'une mobilisation "exceptionnelle": Dakhla', in Mounia Bennani-Chraïbi, Myriam Catusse and Jean-Claude Santucci, eds, *Scènes et coulisses des élections au Maroc. Les législatives 2002*, Paris: Karthala, 2004, pp. 235–63.

Zaki, Lamia, 'Deux candidats en campagne: formes de propagande et répertoires de légitimation politique au bidonville', in Mounia Bennani-Chraïbi, Myriam Catusse and Jean-Claude Santucci, eds, *Scènes et coulisses des élections au Maroc. Les législatives 2002*, Paris: Karthala, 2004, pp. 187–243.

—— *Pratiques politiques au bidonville, Casablanca (2000–2005)*, doctoral dissertation, Institut d'Etudes Politiques, Paris, 2005.

Notes

1. Université Paul Valéry, Montpellier.
2. ENS, Fès.
3. This chapter is based on the Moroccan part of larger research conducted between 2000 and 2003: Emile Lebris, ed., 'Les Municipalités dans le champ politique local. Effets des modèles exportés de décentralisation dans la gestion des villes en Afrique et au Moyen Orient', report for GEMDEV-ISTED/Program PRUD, February 2004. For a summary, see: http://www.isted.com/programmes/prud/syntheses/Atelier_D/Emile_Le-Bris.pdf. For a summary of the Moroccan part, see Catusse, Cattedra and Idrissi-Janati, 'Municipaliser les villes?'
4. See UN-Habitat, 'La Campagne Globale pour la bonne gouvernance': www.unchs.org/govern/frintro.doc.
5. See the speech by the King Hassan II at the opening of the Parliament's Fall Session in 1995. Discours et interviews de Sa Majesté le roi Hassan II, mars 1995–mars 1996, Rabat, Minister of Communication, 1996.
6. For a description of the various initiatives see Khalil Ben Osmane, 'La Réforme administrative otage de la réforme de l'Etat', in *La Nouvelle Gouvernance au Maroc, Administration du Maroc, Bulletin scientifique annuel de l'observatoire marocain de l'Administration publique*, no. 4, pp. 11–20.
7. The program is titled 'Programme National de Gouvernance et de Renforcement Institutionnel' (National program for governance and institutional reinforcement). See PNUD, *Etude sur la Reforme de l'Administration en Relation avec le Processus de Décentralisation et de Déconcentration*, PNUD/Ministère de la Prévision économique

et du plan du Maroc, Direction de la Programmation. 'Programme National de Gouvernance et de Renforcement Institutionnel', 2002.

8. The website of the official Maghreb Arab Press proposes a paper about decentralisation confirming the explicit democratic goal of the project. See 'La Décentralisation, Bilan et perspective' at www.map.co/ma.

9. According to Sassen's approach, the 'global city', a new type of metropolis, the command centre of international capitalism, was born in a double paradoxical dynamic: over-diversification in manufacturing all over the world and the centralisation of globalised coordination, forecasting and management; see Sassen, *The Global City*.

10. Kaioua, *Casablanca*.

11. Catusse, 'La réinvention du social dans le Maroc ajusté'.

12. Concerning the urban policies of the World Bank and its focus on the decentralisation of urban management, see Annick Osmont, *La Banque mondiale et les villes; du développement à l'ajustement*, Paris: 1995 ; for a sharp analysis on the 'good urban governance' rhetoric, see Patrick Haeringer, 'Les mots d'Istanbul', in *Vivre autrement, 6ᵉ Série: Istanbul 96*, juin 1996, p. 3.

13. Naciri, 'Territoire: contrôler ou développer'.

14. Rachik, *Ville et pouvoirs au Maroc*.

15. Source: Catusse, Cattedra and Idrissi-Janati, 'Municipaliser les villes?', p. 355.

16. A *dahir* is a royal act. It can be legislative or administrative, and has the force of law.

17. The *arrondissements* are administrative subdivisions of great cities comparable to French cities like Paris, Lyons or Marseille.

18. Source: Cattedra, *La Mosquée et la Cité*.

19. For a description of the genesis of the Urban Agency of Casablanca, see Rahal Moujib, *L'Agence urbaine de Casablanca*, Casablanca: Afrique Orient, 1989; for an analysis of the roles of the Urban Agencies in city planning and in the political control of the town, see Rachik, *Ville et pouvoirs au Maroc*.

20. For a political history of elections in Morocco, see Mounia Bennani Chraïbi, 'Représenter et mobiliser dans l'élection legislative au Maroc' in Bennani-Chraïbi, Catusse and Santucci, *Scènes et coulisses des élections*, pp. 15–53. In the same book, Lamia Zaki, Victoria Veguilla and Mounia Bennani-Chraïbi analyse micro-electoral mobilisations in neighbourhoods of Casablanca or in Dakhla in the south of Morocco. They show how politics from 'below' are the fruit of interactions between local strategies by various social actors and political constraints from the centre that exercise strong means of control on candidates and voters.

21. Regarding the privatisation of water supply in Casablanca and Rabat, see Haoues-Jouve, *Vingt ans de politique d'assainissement à Casablanca*; Allain-El-Mansouri, *L'Eau et la ville au Maroc*; and Claude de Miras and Julien Le Tellier, 'Le Modèle marocain d'accès à l'eau potable et à l'assainissement. Casablanca et Tangier-Tétouan', in de Miras, *Intégration à la ville et services urbains au Maroc*, pp. 163–90 and pp. 219–54.

22. Allain-Mansouri, 'La Délégation du service privé de la gestion de l'eau potable au Maroc', pp. 163–90.

23. See Chapter IV of Zaki, *Pratiques politiques au bidonville*.

24. See the analysis of Aude Signoles on the reshaping of public action in the domain of urban policies (in the Arab world): 'The public authorities use distinct actions *vis-à-vis* these two private actors: Less formalised partnerships for associations and contracts of delegation for enterprises.' The author emphasises, however, that in certain cases, such as ecology in Lebanon, the relationships between the

associations and urban policies tend to institutionalise. Signoles, 'Réforme de l'Etat et transformation de l'action publique', p. 247.

25. On the development of neighbourhood associations in the city of Fès, see Mohamed Ameur and Abdelaziz Filali Belhaj, *Développement urbain et dynamiques associatives: rôle des amicales dans la gestion des quartiers urbains*, Rabat: Centre d'études et de communication de l'Agence nationale de lutte contre l'habitat insalubre, PGU-Maroc, 1997 ; and Ameur, 'Les Associations de quartier, nouveaux acteurs en milieu urbain marocain', p. 339–54.

26. Law 78–00, art. 30.

27. Mecherfi, 'Autonomie et développement local dans la nouvelle charte communale'.

28. On the dismissals of many local councillors in 2000 see, for instance, Myriam Catusse, 'Affaires, scandales et urnes de verre à Casablanca. Les ambiguïtés de la démocratie locale à l'ère de la bonne gouvernance', in *Annuaire de l'Afrique du Nord*, CNRS éditions, 2000–2001, vol. XXXVIV, pp. 279–306.

29. Catusse, 'Les coups de force de la représentation'.

30. See the Royal Letter to the Prime Minister on Investment Management Devolution, 9 January 2002, www.maroc.ma.

31. According to one of these 'Techno-*Walis*', Driss Benhima, *Wali* of Casablanca (2001–3): 'Dans le monde actuel, le cadre de définition de la gestion publique est celui de l'entreprise'. See Driss Benhima, 'Mes ambitions pour Casablanca', in *Maroc Hebdo International*, no. 490, 14–20/12.2001. For a Mayor's point of view, see also 'Gouvernance de la ville: l'élu manager s'exprime', in *Labyrinthes*, no. 10, August/ September 2004, pp. 34–5.

32. On the strategy of the PDJ leaders during the 2003 electoral campaign, see Catusse, 'Les coups de force de la representation'.

33. Mohammed Tozy, a specialist on Islamist mobilisation in Morocco, interview, *La Vie Economique*, July 2001.

34. For a description of the various discourses about the local arena, see Catusse, 'Les coups de force de la représentation'.

35. Interview, 9 November 2002.

36. The urban agency is a technical institution created in the 1980s, responsible for the production and application of urban planning projects.

37. Interview, 10 November 2002.

38. Jacques Bertoin, 'Meknès, la vitrine du PJD se lézarde', *Jeune Afrique l'Intelligent*, 22 June 2005.

39. See Mohammed Tozy, 'Les enjeux de pouvoir dans les "champs politiques désamorcés au Maroc"', Michel Camau, ed., *Changements politiques au Maghreb*, Paris: 1991.

MARC LAVERGNE

Global City, Tribal Citizenship: Dubai's Paradox

Dubai tries, quite successfully, to promote itself as the archetypal 'global city'. This oil emirate on the southeastern shore of the Arabian Gulf indeed attracts a continuous flow of visitors and customers from the entire world, while the overwhelming majority of its inhabitants are foreign residents. These range from the top executives of foreign companies, and civil servants who make the city function under the control of the local *emir*'s family and its close local and foreign associates, to the huge masses of cheap labour originating mainly from South and Southwest Asia. Altogether, foreign inhabitants are estimated to represent over 95 per cent of Dubai's total population. Stated differently, the local population, usually referred to by the Arabic term *watani* ('nationals'), is a tiny minority in its own country. Obviously, one would expect that the clear demarcation between citizens and non-citizens should settle the question of who has a say in the city's public affairs; but the situation is more complex, as neither the local population on one side nor the aliens on the other enjoy a similar and equal official or non-official status and share of wealth and power. These discrepancies play an important role, as the notion of citizenship appears more multifaceted than it looks at first sight.

The question raised by the extreme case of Dubai has to be looked at not only as a kaleidoscope or combination of immensely diverse social and legal conditions, but in a more dynamic sense, as offering a good opportunity to clarify the question of the relationship between globalisation and citizenship. It is widely considered that the process of globalisation could lead to a weakening of the situation of urban dwellers who enjoy, in most cases, theoretically, the status of citizens. The functioning of large and increasingly heterogeneous urban fabrics might render the relationship between rulers and ruled more complex than the face-to-face of traditional government, and induce a widening variety of status and participation in running the public affairs of the city.

In order to assess the real state of the notion of citizenship in Dubai, one has to consider its double meaning:

Civil rights universally upheld as fundamental human rights granted to anyone, and which include the right to state protection; participation in social life; religion and customs; and economic rights that may be granted under specified conditions and restrictions, such as the right to own real estate and property, to establish oneself on a more or less permanent and secure basis, to open, own and run a business, etc.

Civic and political rights, only granted by citizenship *stricto sensu*. These may entitle the individual to take part in the city's public affairs, to vote and elect or be elected as a representative to local or national consultative or deliberative councils or assemblies, or even to executive bodies like the local government, be it a municipality or a federal state. It should be noted here that Dubai is not only a town, but also strenuously and to a large extent successfully attempts to assert itself as a quasi-state. It maintains a large degree of autonomy within the Federation of the United Arab Emirates, which it reluctantly joined on the eve of independence from the United Kingdom in 1971. So the question here is not only that of citizenship within the framework of a city, but also within a larger body, which could include the question of a nation-building process with its cultural and ethnic dimension.

Globalisation is advocated by its idealistic supporters as bound to lead to the vanishing of national identities: the diversity of statuses should eventually melt in a comprehensive 'world citizenship' uniting all 'colours' into one Global Village.[1] But while free trade and the mobility of goods are strongly enhanced by the World Trade Organisation rules that provide for a global market of goods and services, the mobility of human beings is strictly limited to the needs of manpower in industrialised or wealthy countries, and of tourism from those same well-off societies to specific spots in poor countries.

Be it in industrialised countries or in the oil states of the Gulf, the inflow and stay of manpower is severely controlled by state authorities, and these workers' official status is kept as precarious and as low as possible so as to keep at their lowest the economic conditions of this foreign labour, in a context of fierce competition between wage levels from one country to another. In the case of Dubai, another factor that explains the denial of any form of citizenship to the huge majority of its dwellers is the demographic gap between the local population and the quantity of foreign labour needed to pursue the economic ambitions of the city's ruling elite. So far from being a 'melting pot', Dubai remains a patchwork of human groups ruled by a strict if unofficial social and spatial segregation, where human beings interact solely in the prospect of creating and sharing profit and wealth – albeit on an extremely unbalanced footing.

Citizenship may also entail another meaning, that of one's feeling familiar with a place to the point of feeling a sense of belonging to it, being part of its human spectrum, being part of what gives it life – whether by living and working in it or just enjoying it, walking its streets, interacting with other people who share the same feeling. There is the root of citizenship, a feeling of concern about the city's daily life and growth, concern for the decisions taken about its future. This feeling is by no means dependent on the legal status of the individual; on the contrary, world metropolises have often had their destinies influenced by newcomers devoid of any official say in a municipality's decisions. In most cases, though, contrary to Dubai, several layers of migrants have stratified over long periods of time, the first ones acquiring the legitimacy to play a political and civic role, enlarging their circles over time to those who followed, as in the case of New York and other North American cities.

What Dubai Needs to Become a Global City

Typically, the first question that comes to mind in this context would be: what does it mean to be global? I, however, would like to first tackle the question: what is it to be a city? The difference between city and town is well-known to geographers. The town is merely a human gathering place of urban characters, while the city tends to consist of a more political concept as far as its own government is concerned, and also the dominant role it might play in the surrounding area or through its long-range networks. Over time, the city has acquired an additional meaning (probably inspired by the City of London), which implies that its function is a focal point for economy and finance.

Hence the question is: is it possible to conceive of globalisation without democracy, or without any kind of participation by workers in the shaping of their life environment? More specifically, is not globalisation an obstacle to democracy, or *vice versa*? Is Dubai's thriving growth not due, at least in part, to the absence of democracy? In that case, is it not showing the way for successful globalisation, which would imply the negation or suppression of civic and political rights in favour of economic competitiveness?

The first aspect to consider is that Dubai, from its inception, has been considered by its rulers as an economic tool before anything else. Hence the term 'Dubai enterprise' attached to it from the time of the late Sheikh Rashid bin Saeed (reigned 1958–90), one of a long line of *emirs* of Dubai who made its ambition come true. Before it was considered a city, Dubai was seen as a profit-making business rather than as a cradle for a local or imported society.

If most towns owe their existence to the fulfilling of economic needs, it is often the result of a spontaneous aggregation of individuals and groups who develop the skills and interactions needed by the surrounding environment and increasingly, by the needs of the town's life itself. In the case of Dubai, the beginning of the fortune came through free trade, imposed by colonial powers during the previous globalisation phase. Far from the myth of 'merchant adventurers' it promotes to invent a historical depth and an autonomous leadership comparable to that of Oman or Kuwait, the city was 'born' on the eve of the twentieth century as a support to British imperial projects (when the merchants of Lingeh, on the Persian shore of the Gulf, were attracted by the opportunity to escape the taxes that were about to be imposed on them). This first success was at the expense of the attempt by a still-independent state, Persia, to escape being subjugated by a world colonial power.[2]

One century later, after having been, successively, a trading centre for Gulf pearls, a smuggling gate for gold bound for the Indian market and for various goods headed for Pakistan and Central Asia, Dubai has turned into a regional supermarket and a gateway to vast and populous surrounding economies – first of all Iran and the neighbouring GCC countries. Its appeal extends even to increasingly remote markets of Africa and Central Asia, as a provider of goods and services to war-torn or bankrupt economies. The consumer goods that are sold to those clients are mainly cheap and basic, manufactured in the countries of the Far East and Southeast Asia.

With its well-known Free Zones, at the airport as well as in Jebel Ali, Dubai started to manufacture some of these imported goods itself using its assets, which combine modern infrastructure, efficient services and administration, cheap energy and labour and low taxes. But it remains basically a regional and transcontinental hub, with its airport and ports in the town and in Jebel Ali further south connected with the whole world, serving a wide array of surrounding harbours that are less well-equipped and well-run. The know-how of the Dubai Port Authority is so recognised, and its profits are so large, that it obtained the concession for several regional ports. In March 2006, it acquired the portfolio of the old banner of the British Empire, the Peninsular and Oriental, Steam Navigation Company, for nearly four billion dollars, making Dubai Ports the world's third largest port operator.

Dubai's development strategy, still based on the local, scarce oil resources but more and more on those lent to it by Abu Dhabi, the senior member of the UAE, goes further. It aims to establish a solid and diversified industrial base, with the blessing and the participation of the world's larger transnational companies. Therefore its rulers have well understood the necessity to go into more and more sophisticated activities. After the launching of an Internet City at the end of the 1990s comes the achievement of the Dubai Stock Exchange and the opening of universities based on the American model and curriculum (American University of Dubai, Dubai University College).

By offering these high-level facilities and an attractive environment for business, up to a standard that fascinates visitors and observers from all over the world with audacious achievements in urbanism and architecture, and by emphasising the development of a tourist industry, Dubai aims to attract foreigners and to entertain the most demanding residents. Golf courts are now a common sight, and the last 'must' of Dubai is the newly inaugurated Ski Dome. Far from being a waste of money, these world-class sports and cultural events serve to advertise Dubai as a booming enterprise and promising investment.

What Assessment Can Be Drawn from This Endeavour?

No doubt, Dubai's success story is impressive and, leaving aside all favourable factors such as the ready availability of oil money that makes the most eccentric projects feasible, one must recognise that all pessimistic predictions have been contradicted by facts. The vision and determination of the city's rulers are to be credited for this unabated growth. Dubai has been able to keep pace ahead of all competitors, through all obstacles and setbacks such as slumps in oil prices or economic crises like that which hit the emerging markets of Southeast Asia in 1998, not to mention the turmoil caused by wars and embargos around Iraq since the early 1980s.

Dubai enterprise has a manager; in each generation someone leads the way with new ideas and new plans to adapt to new challenges and get the best out of Dubai's assets in the prevailing conditions. It is the ruler or someone close to him by blood ties, like one of his brothers. However, the ideas are either inspired or converted into reality by a small group of advisers who are still mainly foreigners, although Dubai has started to produce its own young technocrats. These sons of the high-ranking families are educated at the best Western business schools and gain experience by completing their training in places like Singapore. The old business community, mostly of Persian origin, that created precious local and overseas links during one century of legal and illegal trade, also still plays a major role.

An objective observer cannot help but pinpoint some weaknesses that do not fit as well with the present enthusiastic atmosphere of hyperbolic laudation inspired by the giant, successful projects launched and blessed, one after the other in Dubai.

First, Dubai had to overcome some setbacks and relative failures: industrialisation plans have not met with the expected success, especially in Jebel Ali, which has remained, for most of its activity, limited to the packaging of imported goods. Dubai is now reviewing its plans, having realised that importing additional unskilled labour would only widen the demographic gap between foreigners and nationals for a rather insignificant benefit in terms of financial gain, technology transfer or access to new markets and partners.

More significant is the half-success met by the Internet City: the dream of building a new Silicon Valley, using brains drained from India and Western capital, has lacked what was crucial for Silicon Valley's creativity: a mix of individual freedom and the contesting of established rules and values, if not public order, plus a fertile terrain for intellectual and philosophical exchange, and the addition of money, technology and material comfort. In addition, the concentration of various specialisations in communication and information in one place is no longer considered a necessity. So behind Dubai's 'Internet City' label is not much more to be found than a gathering of major world component manufacturers in the computer industry in search of the incentives and facilities offered under this umbrella.

All told, Dubai still remains a rentier as well as a post-rentier economy, and its Gross Internal Product remains sensitive to the oil price curb. This shows that it has not yet acquired full independence from this basic resource; at least, that the confidence of foreign investors is still based to a large extent on the extraction of oil or on the support and guarantee given by Abu Dhabi to Dubai's extravagances.

Second, Dubai's attractiveness relies on the deficiencies of its customers, or rather, on its position as an island of stability in the midst of a troubled world. It benefited, for instance, from the Iraq-Iran war first, then from the violation of the UN embargo against Iraq, and has always managed to keep profitable commercial relations with Iran as well as with Iraq. Its economy is thus dependent on the difficulties and tragedies faced by the surrounding countries of Asia and Africa at large. Its growth is linked to regional instability, which makes it itself unstable, while other competitors may emerge following the recipes of its model. For instance, new maritime hubs like Salalah on the coast of Dhofar in Oman have recently started to divert part of the traffic from Jebel Ali; Salalah lies directly on the Indian Ocean, in a better position to provide a feeder service for transcontinental cargo.

One must not forget that Dubai also owes much of its attractiveness to its role as a laundering machine for dirty money from around the world. Some light was shed on this aspect after 11 September 2001, when the hunt for al-Qa'ida led to investigations concerning the movements of funds through Dubai's banking system.[3] But Dubai is not only a haven for terrorists or gangs like the Russian mafia that invests in the gigantic and flashy projects of The Palm Islands and the like; it is also a safe place for 'respectable' transnational companies to escape taxes in their home countries.

At the end of the day, the ruling elite has indeed some power of decision and the financial means to achieve its plans, however ambitious and sometimes unrealistic as they might seem. It shows an amazing ability to seize opportunities, anticipate the demand of customers and consumers as well as that of international companies at the world level and to feel new tendencies and respond to them without any psychological or cultural inhibitions.

But one can come to the conclusion that Dubai can hardly be considered a global city: it lacks decision and command functions of its own, as it depends much on the will of potential investors to choose this place instead of others, and it lacks internal substance and weight, be it demographic, social or even cultural. In that respect, Dubai presents a completely different case than that of Shanghai, with its huge hinterland, or even Hong Kong and Singapore, and is not part of the world network of leading cities.

The question still remains whether, like Palmyra or Petra in their time, Dubai does not enjoy an illusion of autonomy as it only benefits from the temporary interest of foreign powers, being at the heart of a strategic region for the world's economy and for overall domination by Western powers. Its own strategic choices in terms of development are kept under close scrutiny – first of all by Abu Dhabi, its senior partner and competitor, which has become, thanks to its immense wealth, the banker of Dubai; and on a higher level, from the US, which is in the final analysis the tutor of Dubai. Dubai is not, therefore, to be confused with city-states like Petra, Venice or the Flemish or Hanseatic cities of the past.

If a will appears to fill the gap, what kind of a society, what institutional and legal structures would have to be set in place to sustain the current project? In a word, what kind of city is to be shaped? This is now to be seen through a screening of the present human framework of the town.

A Tribal Society in a Rentier Situation

The original population settled on the shore of the Khor Dubai in 1833. It was a branch of the Bani Yas confederation that split from the main group centred on Abu Dhabi and the Liwa oases. The tribespeople made a living from the dates of their palm trees, from camel herding and sea fishing during the summer season. Like any Bedouin society, it was a hierarchical but fluid and, so to say, 'democratic' group, where power over the tribe was shaky, often shifting between major families. Each family head had the option of quitting the group to join another one, in case of disagreement over policy implemented by the ruler of the day.

The power structure was stabilised by the intervention of the British agents that vested one family as their close allies in the area, to counter the influence of the Qawasim, strongly entrenched in neighbouring Sharjah and in Ras al-Khaimah, their maritime stronghold farther north. What was to become the Al-Maktoum family in the 1930s was reinforced by arms and diplomatic support, and by the turn of the twentieth century, by the adjunction of a merchant community that transferred itself from the Arab emirates on the northern shore of the Gulf.

Its rule was strengthened even more by the discovery of oil, the royalties of which, in the hands of the ruler, frees him from the need to win over internal support and gives him the means to integrate all the citizens into his dependency through the distribution, at his discretion, of parts of the rent in the shape of the *kafala* ('sponsorship'), import licences, grants and subsidies.

Bedouins and merchants form the bulk of the local population who enjoy Emirati citizenship; they only represent 4 per cent of an entire population of roughly 1.22 million inhabitants, i.e. 50,000 people. Considered that half of these are females (who do not count as far as citizenship in terms of political participation is concerned) and children, one can estimate the total population of adult males, or potential citizens, at around 15,000. This tiny community is not well-known to outsiders, as it tries not to be drowned by the influx of foreigners, and tends to limit its contacts with foreigners to the requirements of administration and business, keeping social life as discreet as possible.

One can just guess that this society is as diverse as others in the neighbouring countries of the Gulf. It is divided among clans and families that have an unequal status in the traditional society, from prominent and wealthy families to former domestic slaves. So, behind the apparent uniformity due to the affluent oil rent, they do not all enjoy the same prestige and say in the community's affairs. The primacy given to lineage and blood ascendancy should also limit the say of the immigrated merchant community that was granted citizenship by the rulers, be it of Persian or Hadrami[4] origin.

The privileges attached to 'citizenship' and their limits

So-called Dubai citizens are granted a number of rights, some of which are similar to those granted to all citizens of the UAE, such as nationality or the right to be protected by the authorities – meaning, in practice, protection against claims resulting from conflicts with foreigners, be it a car accident or a business dispute. Some others are particular to each emirate, like the allowances paid to every family for housing, schooling its children or opening a business; all seven emirates are welfare states, but their generosity depends much on their oil revenue or on the subsidies received by the ruler of the Federation, that is to say from Abu Dhabi's budget.

Every ruler is expected to distribute some of the oil revenue for the welfare of its people, either directly or indirectly (by granting formal jobs in the public administration or access to the 'tutorage' of the foreigners living in the country through the system of *kafala* ['sponsorship']). On the other hand, the bulk of the local population cannot be said to be benefiting from civic rights. To turn a famous saying appropriately, 'no taxation, no representation'; the nationals of Dubai could be termed more properly 'subjects' than citizens. As long as oil and/or money flow, no official legislative or consultative councils have been set up through an electoral system.

The powerful and influential upper circles

Thus real power and say in public affairs is restricted to close of circles of influence around the person of the ruler. The personalities of successive rulers are surprisingly strong. Several of them have had true vision, seeing far ahead of local conditions at the time. But this gives the impression that

Dubai's success story is tied to one man's ambition, which, if true, would weaken the prospect of sustainability that it tries to create.

The new ruler, Sheikh Mohammed bin Rashid, is definitely the key promoter of the new steps in which Dubai is engaging, and has been in charge of economic development for a long time already, as Crown Prince next to his less-involved brother Maktoum; but his heir apparent is known for suffering addiction that would render him unable to properly oversee the emirate's affairs. If the government remains a family business, the education needed to run a more and more complex 'enterprise' opens the way for young technocrats, who serve as advisers to the new prince's cabinet. This meritocracy, promoting an ideology of liberalisation and globalisation, competes with elder tenants of power and influence who are more wary, through their networks, of the cultural and social dimension in which the whole process takes place.

These inner centres of power should not obscure the fact that the decision-makers of Dubai's fortune are in large part foreigners settled there or based abroad, in the major Western metropolises: these are the heads or representatives of transnational corporations, who make strategic choices in favour of or against any site in the world. The decision to establish the Internet City or an industrial Free Zone would be meaningless if those firms did not decide to transfer a part of their activities to these sites, and there is fierce competition over attracting those corporations' regional offices, manufacturing or, even better, research and development centres. While these decision-makers are, of course, not citizens, their actual weight and influence are much more significant than that of most of the local actors.

Finally, Dubai is now constrained by the need to live up to and abide by its own image, in order to keep attracting investors and building confidence. The heavy machinery is on its rails, and cannot be stopped, except at a price of a brutal economic slump that could trigger a chain reaction affecting both Dubai's citizens and the rest of the world. Dubai's image of modernity and success is that of triumphant world capitalism, and it is relayed by public opinion, customers and visitors who are influenced by the media and influence it in turn, themselves targeted by the constant activity of the offices of the Dubai Marketing and Investment Board scattered around the world.

The birth of a complex civil society

If Dubai's society has up to now been denied access to civic or political rights, one can still observe a recent tendency to the rising up of a civil society that, apart from the power circles, dares to let its voice be heard.

If an implicit social contract exists between the ruling class and the nationals, based on a not-too-unequal sharing of oil revenue, no such consensus has ever been established about the model and the speedy path of development imposed from the top. Ordinary citizens have started to feel anxious about the demographic imbalance between themselves and Dubai's migrants, and feel threatened in their survival as a distinct group, financially privileged but suffering from a loss of identity.

The generation gap is immense and cannot be filled, as the youngest (as in all Gulf countries) are educated by foreigners, be it at home or at school, and as dominant social values tend to be replaced by those of the migrants. Sheer socialisation, the condition of the strengthening of family and financial bonds, is rendered more difficult by drowning in the mass of foreigners. Thus associations have been founded that question the logic of importing more and more manpower, with the aim of increasing a GDP *per capita* that is already among the highest in the world. This resistance reaches the ruler's palace through traditional channels and through the family or tribal links that knit this tiny society together. So if formal representation of the population has not yet taken place, it doesn't mean the population's concerns are not taken into account.

A few years ago, along with the Internet City project, the emirate launched amidst much publicity the concept of 'e-government', which, it pretended, would enable it to satisfy the administrative needs of its inhabitants and allow everybody access to the ruling apparatus to express their views, suggestions, etc. Aimed at undercutting possible demands for greater participation in Dubai's affairs, under the guise of a fashionable and technically sophisticated Internet system meant to promote, at the same time, the openness and the modernity of the emirate's government, it soon proved to be just a technical device to simplify administrative procedures.

More seriously, there is a clear awareness in Washington and among the ruling Gulf elite of the risks of trying to build up a globalised economy without establishing a strong social base, risks that could take the form of social upheavals like the so-called 'Islamic fundamentalism'. In line with this, then-Heir Apparent General Sheikh Mohammed Al Maktoum, Minister of Defence of the UAE, spoke out about the need to open the society and 'normalise' its functioning in order to ensure its sustainability. One approach considered was to organise elections and establish a parliament, a move clearly bound to reinforce the loyalty of the rank and file of Emirati citizens to the system. However, it appears that this would have been a rather artificial exercise, organised top-down, and that one of its central aims would be to help close the ranks of nationals in the face of the growing demand by other dwellers to participate in public affairs. It remains to be seen how this novelty will be put in application, and whether this will be sufficient to give Dubai's citizenship some substance.

The foreigners, the social diversity behind a unique status

The foreigners do not benefit of any of the advantages granted to the citizens, and are not included in the political reform prospects. The common feature of their situation is instead an absolute precariousness, as they can, whatever their origin or professional or social position, be expelled from the country at any moment and for any reason. They are fully subject to the goodwill of their sponsor, who is either an individual or a local private or public institution. The state's protection granted to them is very limited; as mentioned earlier, in the case of a dispute with a national, local authorities systematically side against them.

This precariousness certainly is an advantage for the easy control of the flow of manpower according to the needs of the economy. Indeed, the number of foreign workers varies in line with oil prices, although an unknown number of workers stay illegally in the country, generally after the end of their official contract.[5] It is a double-edged sword, at least concerning the professionals, businessmen and highly qualified experts whose loyalty and long-term involvement in Dubai's development projects would be an asset. They benefit, in fact, from a large amount of tolerance and permissiveness, which goes together with a tight control of public and private behaviour by the discreet but efficient security forces. Their status resembles to some extent that of foreigners under the regime of Capitulations in the Ottoman Empire, where European consulates were conceded a judiciary and protective role for them and their local dependents and allies.

However, it is far from being enough to feel safe and instil in those foreigners a trust in their host country. The lesson of the invasion of Kuwait has not been lost. Palestinians, who had settled there as early as 1948 and helped build the first oil emirate, and who had lived there for several generations with the feeling of having found a second home, were mercilessly expelled as soon as the allied armies re-conquered Kuwait; they were accused of having supported and collaborated with the Iraqi occupants.

The foreigners' length of stay in Dubai is generally much shorter; however, it would be in Dubai's rulers' interests to not forget the loss of attractiveness and dynamism suffered by Kuwait after expelling an active workforce, together with their savings,[6] to say nothing of the image of ruthlessness and ingratitude displayed on that occasion. Aware of that obstacle to the development of the economy, Dubai's authorities decided to open the real estate market to foreigners in order to retain part of the expatriates' revenue and to ensure their deeper involvement in the future of the emirate. This step cannot be but a first one, as it raises the question of the residency status of those owners and then of their participation in city affairs as owners with legitimate financial interests in urban projects. It therefore might exacerbate the fears of ordinary citizens, who will feel their privileges endangered by these newcomers. A new intermediary status between citizen and foreigner might have to be invented to fit with this new situation.

On the other side of the spectrum, Dubai's boom rests on the toil of an army of modern slaves, contract workers imported from the villages of the Indian subcontinent and Southeast Asia.[7] Those who execute the unskilled work in the building, manufacturing or service sectors are not only deprived of any protection, but are, more often than not, denied basic human rights. Their passports are retained upon arrival; they are subject to the goodwill of their employer; and their housing, transportation and working conditions are often inhumane. They are usually not taken into account as part of the resident population, since they do not participate in consumption, leisure or other aspects of social life, working day and night and being accommodated in squalid camps on the outskirts of the town.

Nevertheless, a new phenomenon is the concern shown for their plight by some segments of the urban population. Some cases are raised in the reader's mail of newspapers like the English-language *Khaleej Times*, whose readers are mainly foreign, and who engage in heated debates about priorities and actions to be taken to correct the misconduct of companies and the neglect of the state regarding abuses. In some cases the authorities even take action, as when Dubai's police force the payment of wages in arrears. This shows that foreigners can have their voices heard, even if not through official channels, and that the authorities must take into account their opinions, first to maintain the smooth functioning of the system and second for Dubai's dependency on international public opinion – which might be shocked or moved by TV reporting on the dark side of Dubai's 'miracle'.

This example shows that Dubai's foreign population is not silent, and wants to have a say in public affairs and influence in running the affairs of the city. How and to what extent might this be achieved? For as much as can be observed, the foreigners would have no intention of settling definitively and severing links with their homelands; they would merely demand more flexibility in terms of residence and more participation in the local affairs of the city.

The question is whether such a move could be deemed acceptable by the local population and its rulers, and whether it would be in line with the defined strategy for Dubai's future growth, which aims at endowing it with the features and the role of a leading global city. The case of Dubai could help to reach an understanding of what the concept of 'citizenship' would entail for a foreign population barred from the political rights theoretically associated with it. Could the sense of belonging that results from residing in a place for a prolonged period of time, moreso when accompanied by the development of material or financial interests, conceivably entitle an involvement in the city's affairs without threatening the original population's and rulers' rights and privileges? I shall attempt to render these options more concretely through questioning Dubai's shaping and daily life, how a feeling of etymological 'citizenship' might emerge among the foreign population independently from the official status enjoyed by its inhabitants.

Urban Life and Social Structures: fragmentation or 'melting pot'

At first sight, Dubai seems to present a strong duality: on one side, the narrow and bustling commercial streets of Deira and Bur Dubai, on both sides of the Creek; on the other, the straight, majestic alignment of office towers along Sheikh Zayed Road. Or, the private sand beaches and nightclubs on the shore of Jumeirah, as opposed to the Shi'i mosque and Hindu temple of the Old *Souk*.

What is the functional link, if any, between these two civilisations, these two urban concepts set side by side? How is the identity of Dubai shared between these two worlds, and how do the inhabitants move from one to the other (if they do)? Is there an urban mosaic in Dubai, with an Indian town and an Arab town, for instance, like so many Chinatowns or Little Italys? Or is it, in that respect, what might be called a 'world city'? Some historical background may help to arrive at an answer.

A short but telling history

Present Dubai is no more than fifty years old – that is, the buildings dating from the 1970s are considered old, and indeed often look old and rundown, due to the poor quality of the building material used at the time and to the humid and salty air of the summer season. Only a few buildings are older (Sheikh Saeed Al Maktoum's House, the Dubai Museum, old merchant houses with their wind towers, some mosques). They are now recognised as historical heritage sites and are being restored as part of the process of gentrifying the old city centre, to be turned into trendy art galleries and cultural centres run by Westerners. But the backyards of Deira, behind the rehabilitated main streets of Al Ras or Al Buteen, are still home to the crowds of poor Pakistani and Indian migrants who work in the nearby shops.

From that starting point, Dubai has extended in concentric circles. The 1970s and 1980s were the start of the boom, and the network of road infrastructure and housing quarters was drawn then. Since 1990, extension has been mostly towards the south and the Jebel Ali port and Free Zones. The most impressive developments have been along the seashore, and now even offshore: the Burj Al Arab, one of the only 'six-star' hotels in the world, with its characteristic shape of a sail peaking at 321 m above sea level, is now already a classic. New projects are reaching new dimensions, such as the artificial Palm islands and the development project 'The World' on the future 'Dubai waterfront', aiming to be the most exclusive group of private leisure resorts in the world.

To what self-image does this new city relate? What image do Dubai's promoters want to project of the place, with their sometimes rather childish and simplistic representations, confusing Disneyland with the real world? For our purposes, the question is indeed whether Dubai chooses to become a global icon that has meaning for all possible clients, or whether it feels like being faithful to its roots, with the emphasis given, in architectural forms, to sails and palms? In any case, this new Dubai might well turn its back more and more on its past and on its Arab-Islamic identity, whatever the precise meaning of that would be.

It has been argued for some time that Dubai's duality has in fact been integrated into a single economic project, and that the wooden *dhows* that load their smuggled shipments of tyres and fridges to be transported to the northern shore of the Gulf were but the predecessors of the import-export companies housed in the modern CBDs at the crossroads of the six-lane highways, that one of the strengths of Dubai has always been its ability to connect traditional and modern economic ways using both high-tech and unskilled labour, at the service of backward and deprived economies.

A new orientation?

This new orientation, with its emphasis on a futuristic urban look and on 'high-tech' activities appears to widen the gap between the two sides of Dubai. If successful, this path might change the ethno-social features of the city, distancing it from its Arab-Islamic roots but also from the 'flavour' of the Indian subcontinent, turning it into a 'tasteless', generic 'Monaco of the Gulf'. Doubtlessly, one aim of this new orientation is also to reduce the need for imported manpower and thus to solve the question of citizenship, by turning Dubai into a destination that is only visited by an exclusive cosmopolitan 'jet-set society' and putting restrictions on the import of labour to a level necessary to provide services for the high-tech industries and the high-end services that the city hopes to attract.

While this may serve to lead Dubai to the apex of the globalisation process, it would still not be sufficient to make it into a global city, for the reasons already given. But there is another element that differentiates Dubai from the 'globalised cities' model: the passing from a centralised authority to the concept of governance, the participation of the city's inhabitants in its management as well as the privatisation of public services.

Up to now, the Municipality of Dubai, a powerful body, is in charge of all public services pertaining to the city's daily functioning. Due to its oil revenue, Dubai has not felt the need to concede its public services to private bodies, and the municipality ensures efficient service and at the same time allows the authorities to keep a close watch on the public and private spheres.

A human patchwork where each community has its landmarks

Each community or, to put it better, each social or ethnic group, uses a Dubai of its own. For instance, everyone involved in or around modern business of all kinds works in the same buildings, frequents the same clubs, lives in the same compounds and sends their children to the same schools. The middle class remains closer to its national origins, following a strategy of social promotion back home: on the British model, the Indians have their own schools, clubs, shops and restaurants, newspapers and TV channels, etc, but with little or no mixing between Keralese and Gujaratis, for instance, nor between different social classes or religion-based castes, in order to preserve the homeland segregation and distinctions. Newcomers like the Uzbek community are organised differently: they come to Dubai mainly for shopping, as many Africans do; hence their networks are built around hotels, translators and forwarding agents, air and cargo transport companies. With the tremendous growth of the city, it is more and more difficult for any inhabitant to have an overall view of it, so it seems only logical for people to remain within their own familiar places and networks. The fact that moving around the city is only practical by car, due to the heat as well as to the increasing distances and to the predominant North American lifestyle, makes the chances for interaction ever scarcer.

Is socio-spatial fragmentation compatible with an urban sense of belonging?

Dubai's human mosaic is not composed of separate clusters; even if some quarters, as discussed earlier, are more prone to sheltering social groups than others, there are no ethnic neighbourhoods. The socio-ethnic networks are scattered, with gathering points like religious buildings, clubs and schools often far away from each other. A level of interaction is thus secured, and, if inhabitants are not familiar with the whole city, everyone knows and frequents more than one place, especially the middle and upper classes who shuttle daily between home, school or place of work, then club or leisure activity. This provides a sense of being at home; not the original home, but an *ersatz* home, where life is often easier and more comfortable (even if nostalgia is always present) and where everyone has their own landmarks and memories, with time passing.

One might even suggest that foreigners feel more at home than the nationals, especially those who, like the Bedouins, are of nomadic origin. Even after two generations, they may not feel at ease in the city, which was created primarily by others for others. They have never been consulted on the urban design in general or even on their homes, which are designed for them by foreign architects and designers often after a blend of Indian and Egyptian tastes. Of course, the city belongs to them, but they don't feel they belong to it, even more so as they don't account for more than a twentieth of the population[8].

Living in compounds where they are mixed with the foreigners of the same level of income, they don't have any separate schools or clubs, and even in the professional sphere, they must deal with a majority of foreign colleagues. So in order to meet as a society of its own, as in the 'good old days' of poverty and deprivation, they must retreat out of town, for instance, during the summer months, to their farms in the desert, where they find renewed opportunities to socialise. They may even enjoy the time spent in their residences abroad more, where they can live among themselves while avoiding the crowd of their home city[9].

In short, precariousness is not only the lot of the foreigners; the nationals share that feeling of anxiety, and tend to withdraw or to find personal equilibrium in a foreign country. Modernisation and opening up have had their cost. Mental health problems take their toll among the youth, and wealth and related idleness have exacted another price, with the spreading of social deviances like drug addiction. Islamism can find fertile terrain in such a situation, as in Saudi Arabia, where the expectations of youth are met with a rising rate of unemployment.

To conclude, the basics of globalisation and the seeds of citizenship exist in Dubai, but the incautious connection of both could amount to collective social suicide for Dubai's national population. The choice is therefore an impossible one, and while the momentum of Dubai's race for progress will continue unabated, it may encounter growing dissent from local youth that will, more and more, strongly express demands for full citizenship in the sense of participation in the political arena, while the foreigners will content themselves with legal recognition of their existence and of their rights to live and express themselves freely in their daily life and business.

Bibliography

Abdullah, Muhammad Morsy, *United Arab Emirates. A Modern History*, London and New York: Croom Helm and Barnes & Noble, 1978.

Ghareeb, Edward and Ibrahim El-Abed, *Perspectives on the United Arab Emirates*, London: Trident Press, 1997.

Gunaratna, Rohan, *Al-Qaida – Au cœur du premier réseau terroriste mondial*, Paris: Autrement, 2001.

Heard-Bey, Frauke, *Les Emirats Arabes Unis*, Paris: Karthala, 1999.

Joffé, George, 'Concepts of Sovereignty in the Gulf Region', in Richard Schofield, *Territorial Foundations of the Gulf States*, London: UCL Press, 1996.

McLuhan, H. Marshall, *The Gutenberg Galaxy: The Making of Typographic Man*, Toronto: University of Toronto Press, 1962.

Peterson, John E., *The Arab Gulf States. Steps Towards Political Participation*, *Washington Papers* no. 131, New York: Praeger, 1988.

Rush Alan de Lacy, *Ruling Families of Arabia: United Arab Emirates*, London: Archive Editions, 1991.

Walker, Julian 'Practical problems of boundary delimitations in Arabia: the case of the United Arab Emirates', in Richard Schofield, *Territorial Foundations of the Gulf States*, London: UCL Press, 1996.

Notes

1. McLuhan, *The Gutenberg Galaxy*.
2. See Frauke Heard-Bey, *Les Emirats Arabes Unis*, Paris: 1999; also Joffé, 'Concepts of Sovereignty in the Gulf Region'.
3. See Rohan Gunaratna, *Al-Qaida – Au cœur du premier réseau terroriste mondial*, Paris: 2002.
4. Hadramis are a merchant community originating in the Hadramaut (South Yemen), granted nationality at an early stage.
5. Local authorities turn a blind eye to the illegal migrants who help keep salaries low, until a temporary economic slump signals the start of a new wave of mass hunts and expulsions.
6. That provided a welcome temporary boom to the Jordanian economy in the following years.
7. A new trend is the import of Chinese workers, who are deemed to be more docile and even cheaper than Indian, Pakistani, Thai or Korean manpower.
8. One can add that Dubai's lifestyle is not easily reconciled with Bedouin values and traditions of discretion, which is evident when compared to Abu Dhabi. With no difference as far as the amount of wealth or natural conditions are concerned, the atmosphere of Abu Dhabi is much more rigid and restricted than that of the more cosmopolitan Dubai.
9. In their favourite homesteads of London, Paris or on the French Riviera, and more and more since 11 September, back in the heights of Lebanon or Morocco, they can find both privacy as well as the anonymity of a foreign metropolis.

MELHEM CHAOUL

Demonstrations in Beirut

Urban Space and Societal Expression[1]

In Lebanon's contemporary history, the city of Beirut has been a privileged space for expression, communication and assertion of Lebanese society addressing itself to a range of audiences.[2] Of these modes of expression, one most frequently used is the demonstration; protesting has become one of the most popular means through which groups and political parties lay their claims, position themselves, defend themselves and above all show their strength. Demonstrating means to claim rights to the city, and to use – for only a brief time – the public space for something other than what it was designed for.

Recently, the currents and forces of 'change', modernising tendencies, reformers and dreamers have benefited from a favourable context. They have succeeded in influencing the course of events, in occupying the streets, the urban space (the *polis*), and in creating a pole of attraction for the whole of the territory. Above all, they have been able to introduce and maintain a new configuration of political practices in Beirut's urban space. To understand what created this new configuration of political practices in Lebanon, especially in terms of protesting, we must first try to revisit the traditional demonstration practices in Lebanon's contemporary history.

Staging a Demonstration in Beirut of the 1970s

Over the course of the 1960s and 1970s, protesting in Beirut – to voice social grievances as much as to voice national and patriotic causes – was foremost a collective political act that possessed an identity with reference to an organisation. It was linked to the rituals and political practices of the 'left' and its affiliated organisations that went, up until the end of the war, under the label of 'national and progressive parties and forces'. Of course, this does not imply that other political groups weren't aware of or didn't undertake this form of political expression. The focus of this research, however, is principally based on the hypothesis that this vast political movement was the basis of, and in a sense put into place, the ritual of what we can call the Beirut demonstrations of the 1970s whether 'national' (*kawmi* or *muzahara kawmiyya* or *wataniyya*) or 'demanding' (*muzahara matlabiyya*).[3] I consider this ritual and these forms of participation in the life of the city to have been conditioned by a political culture and a value system that favoured the following practices.

First of all, there was a prevailing centrality and strong personalisation of leadership. In general, political practice in Lebanon is strongly centralised, both at the government level due to a lack of participation and agreement, and at the level of political formations usually dominated by one decision-maker. The leader of that formation tends to be an uncontested individual and figurehead who sometimes takes on the air of a charismatic leader. This situation favours the verticality of the partisan formation at the heart of which the members or militants, as individuals or groups, are attracted to the leader. In return, the decisions and directives always emanate from above and are carefully, almost religiously, carried out by a submitted base.

Thus the staging of Beirut demonstrations in the 1970s conformed to a ritual that had become routine and repetitive, and was orchestrated by the decision-makers of parties and forces said to be 'nationalist and progressive' or by the trade unions, professional associations, and student unions. The entire protest was typically prepared in advance: directives, slogans, protest route, final destination and, most importantly, the ranking order of participants and formations were pre-established. The hierarchy of those on the front lines and those at the back, and the way in which participants were divided into distinct blocs, made the importance and size of each group visible and acknowledged (the assigned journalist was alerted to the location of a particular group so that its size was noted in the public record). We can almost speak of a 'semi-military' procession due to the verticality that governed the top-down relations.

A second characteristic of the political culture of that time was the obsession with unity, which was also reflected in the pattern of the demonstrations. Currents, organisations and multiple parties constituted a coalition of 'national and progressive parties and forces' and functioned as a federation. The obsession with unity and with the fusion of formations and groups into unique structures produced a discourse and a political practice glorifying unity and the absence of differences. This led to interminable discussions resulting in unachievable 'common programmes' full of contradictory elements imposed by the various coalitions, threatening disruption of solidarity with other groups. In effect, the dream of political action was to arrive at coalition groups governed by one leader, for which there would only be one spokesperson, where only one political programme would be applied in order to achieve but one goal. The corollary to this situation would become the concealment of differences and contradictions.

The 1970s demonstrations reflected this paradox of obsession with unity and the reality of differences. This reality was occulted and negatively experienced. From a distance (zoomed out), the protest looked like an enormous human wave undulating in the streets of the city. From up close (zoomed in), spaces were eventually distinguished; the demarcations among the various organisations, their specificities and their differences became clear. During this time, Jacques Berque compared the classic Arab poem, the *kasida*, to a Bedouin desert camp where each *bayt* is autonomous, yet participates in the group in a manner of apparent homogeneity. But when seen up close, we catch sight of the clear and specific separation of each familial entity. The protest of the 1970s structured itself in some way as a Bedouin caravan in a dialectic of apparent homogeneity and actual multiplicity.

The third characteristic of the political climate of the 1970s was one-way communication. It is important to note that political activity unfolded in a rather controlled media environment. Audio-visual information was, at the time, 'official', which in reality meant strong state control. Only the written press represented the private sector and public opinion. The result was that formations and political groups communicated almost exclusively with their own public and partisans. Militants, being politically stratified, only communicated with those who told them what they wanted to hear. The media voiced a series of monologues, refusing the idea of debate and exchange.

During the demonstrations, chanted slogans and relentlessly repeated claims followed a pre-mediated text. A specialised militant (*hattif*), whose function was acknowledged among his followers, chanted in a rhythm and cadence designed to incite the crowd, who would then repeat his words. The goal was to convey the message to onlookers standing in the streets and sidewalks, in doorways and on balconies and roofs. The atmosphere was intended to be solemn so as to reflect the seriousness of the cause, and to show that the militants and their associated parties were not there to have fun. When it was a student demonstration, it was important above all not to give the impression that they had granted themselves a day off to skip classes, but rather to protest in order to better work and study.

A fourth characteristic was the 'hardliner' discourse. This dominant discourse revolved around the theme of total confrontation with the aim of 'breaking the adversary's bones' (*ma'rakat kasr adm*), meaning to have all demands met, to liberate all territories and to completely eliminate the adversary. This discourse glorified 'total victory' and would accept nothing short of the fulfilment of 'all demands'; it sacralised certain themes and practices which became 'untouchable', constituted 'red lines' and unremittingly played on polarisation. In the end, however, this discourse showed its limits during negotiations, when the time came for 'mutual concessions'.

Finally, a fifth characteristic of the political culture of the 1970s was the highly defined space for action in the city. The national and progressive parties and forces had a class relationship with the city's neighbourhoods. They considered their political and social base to be the 'popular masses', the most disfavoured social groups, which they represented and in whose name they fought. These 'popular masses' were essentially located in the southwestern neighbourhoods of Beirut. Their living areas, following a south-north direction, reached the city centre, touching on the south side of Riad al-Solh Square.

There was also a symbolic date that gave its name to a symbolic place. The date is 23 April 1969 when a protest in support of the Palestinian resistance gathered in front of the Barbir Hospital and Makassed College at the intersection of Saeb Salam Boulevard (it was, at that time, Mazraa Boulevard) and Ouzaï Street, and was violently repressed, causing death and injury.

This crossroads, which had nothing in the way of a 'square' in the urban sense, was baptised by the 'national and progressive parties and forces' as '23 April Square' and became the starting point and gathering area for protests, at least until 1975. From there, the route was completely sketched out: The masses walk up Basta Street, which stretches up to the edge of Riad al-Solh Square, spill onto Riad al-Solh Street and then attempt to reach Place de l'Etoile, the seat of Parliament, either via Maurice Barres Street or by Maarad Street. When security directives were to prevent the arrival of the protesters at the Parliament, demonstrations would not reach the end of Basta Street, and it was near the Basta Tahta Mosque that confrontations with the security forces took place.

The 'people of Beirut' lived in neighbourhoods on both sides of the demonstration route. This is where the clientele of the organising parties and political forces were recruited. On the right of the line lie Ras al-Nabeh and Amiliyyé; then the demonstrations crossed Mazraa to arrive at Basta Fawka, Basta Tahta and Bachoura. On the left are Borj Abi Haydar, Moussaytbé and Zoukak al-Blatt.

One could argue that the demonstration route in its global configuration along south-north coordinates, across the lower-middle-class neighbourhoods and the more underprivileged areas to the south, reproduced within the city the global scheme of social mobility that characterised the Lebanese social fabric of the time. The demonstrations allegorically represented the movement of groups asking for integration into the city, groups essentially coming from the south and southeast who pushed to be recognised by the natives and public powers as members of the city.

It might be possible to formally compare the vertical structure of those demonstrations and the one organised by Hezbollah on 8 March 2005. Indeed, this demonstration showed all the characteristics mentioned above, but with one important difference: a different social content. It was not about claiming the city towards which one felt marginalised, but rather to confirm, thirty years later, that the city is already under the control of its southern suburbs.

The 14 March 2005 Protest: A Rupture?

To what degree did the 14 March 2005 demonstration constitute a break with the demonstrations of the 1970s? It seemed that on 14 March we could observe new practices, new rituals of 'public action', completely counter to the spirit of the previous century. Contrary to the vertical structure of traditional political movements and the leadership's one-way rapport with its 'base', the spirit of 14 March initiated the society into networks, horizontal connections, egalitarian relations and the mobilisation of individuals. The centre of Beirut was no longer the *destination* for the throngs of people in peripheral neighbourhoods, but rather a *gathering place* for clusters of people from all over the country. Participants came with different kinds of transportation, some provided by organisations, but were mostly organised in small groups according to their own means. Mobilisation was achieved through the maximum use of the most advanced technologies: cell phones, sms messaging, email, etc. Most importantly, the participants came of their own volition and through personal networks.

It is important to note that the leadership became secondary, subsidiary and ornamental. There were people making speeches, but no one was listening; no one was looking up to the speaker. What was important was the exchange among the people in the crowd. No more 'orders' and 'prefabricated slogans' were heard. It became a place of disordered words and spontaneous slogans.

The spirit of 14 March also opposed a unifying tendency and instead proposed a strategy for the management of plurality, which emanates from a high level of democratic practice and places itself in opposition to pre-established ideas and practices. This is why the political programme became a creative daily act, a project under construction, never achieved, always put into question. The most active members of the 14 March movement who became *de facto* leaders were proposing daily objectives, practices (tents, night watches, the debates that naturally followed), initiatives that were tested and either adopted or abandoned.

We also observed festive practices that broke with the everyday of traditional politics by introducing music, caricatures, humour, uplifting words and even performances between politics and entertainment. Above all, the spirit of 14 March replaced the politics at the centre of the city (figuratively and practically) and handed over the public space to its real owners, the citizens, reminding the Lebanese that what we call the 'political class' is neither an extra-social caste nor a race of nobles born to govern, but simply a group of 'representatives' whom the citizens have entrusted to manage (and manage well) the public sphere and the common interest.

Militancy, Protest and Urban Space in the Age of Globalisation

Carmen Abou Jaoudé, in one of her articles in the special issue of *L'Orient-Express* dedicated to the late Samir Kassir[4], concluded:

> The human wave that assembled at Martyrs' Square on February 21, 2005 and stretched the length of the road that runs along the downtown right up to the location of the explosion, surprised more than one person. A popular movement formed spontaneously, and was neither guided by political currents nor the political parties. It became an independence movement. Even the most brilliant analysts couldn't predict an upsurge of this size. The *Intifada* of independence was born.[5]

Thus this political movement is characterised by spontaneity and by the lack of a framework. How is this expressed in the actors' speech? First of all there is the city, the scene of the movement. Testimonials show that the main participants were people from the city, who work there all day long, who meet in cafés and restaurants; the main circle of actors in the movement of 14 March 2005 – students, journalists, academics, young businesspeople – belonged to the social fabric of Beirut and, starting from this epicentre, the demonstration drew in the whole of the territory. This group succeeded in creating, in the centre of Beirut, in a Martyrs' Square baptised anew as Liberty Place, a space for dialogue, communication and exchange. Further testimonials confirm this tendency:[6]

A young student: 'The *Intifada* allowed us, for the first time, to express ourselves freely, while up until now we have been subject to persecution and arrest by the regime and its apparatus because of our opinions.'

M. K., twenty-four-year-old teacher: 'The most important gain for the supporters of liberty was to have gathered together youth from all backgrounds who had overcome their confessional, political and regional differences to work towards a set of common goals: sovereignty, independence and the liberation of Lebanon.'

S. G., twenty-six-year-old lawyer: 'For the first time we were seen and heard. This central positioning allowed for media access and maximised the reach of the movement. The TV stations and all the media reported on our movement and our actions.'

The disappearance of the traditional 'professional agitator' – a militant trained by a particular political party – is a revelatory sign of the new era inaugurated by the 14 March movement. A previously unknown political actor in the Arab world made its appearance: the volunteer militant, acting of his or her own volition, without any particular political training, coming from any one of a number of backgrounds. Even if the 'student' and 'engaged intellectual' types were still dominant, we also find people from various professions, business owners, women, and, on occasion, mid- and top-level executives who 'came out just to have a look', as well as upper-class people who seemed a bit lost in the dissenting crowd.

There were a good number of communication experts within the core group of decision-makers who guided the daily action of the militants and of the 'Liberty Camp'. With their participation emerged a new type of participant in collective action. We have an account of how the 'Liberty Camp' was established: 'A group of friends (about thirty) organise themselves into discussion and coordination groups ... The group expands and it soon meets up with other people who bring to it their ideas.'

Meanwhile Samir Kassir, surrounded by journalist friends as well as advertising experts Eli Khoury of Saatchi and Saatchi and Nora Jumblatt, who was particularly active during this entire period, got to work on the *Intifada*'s image and its main goals. In the same group we also find Asma Andraos, the head of a specialised event planning firm,[7] and Shirine Abdallah, in charge of communication for *an-Nahar*, who was adopted as 'Mother of the Camp'.

The appearance of such unlikely personalities onto the political scene challenged the standard public perception of the Lebanese political actor. These new actors emerged thanks to the logic and spirit of a movement that, at its inception, went beyond parties and organisations. This shift allowed political action to become more dynamic and attractive, particularly to youth and women. This explains why the two masthead figures of this movement and its initiatives were representatives of this new ideal type of militant-actor in the information age: Samir Kassir and Asma Andraos. Perhaps the common denominator between these two personalities can be found in their link with the communications industry and their shared conception of the world founded on multiplicity, competency, aptitude and belonging.

In terms of content, and in relation to the goals to be achieved, two words were often repeated in the discourse among young actors: 'Dream' and 'reality', or even more so, the dream despite the reality.

S. N.: 'In the Camp, we shared the same objectives concerning the Syrian retreat and the truth of the Hariri assassination. We were also unified by a rejection of the prevailing political situation and a desire for change, particularly in terms of the political class.'

S. N.: '14 March was for change. Young people insisted their voices be heard. But the current political class ... is not in favour of change. The camp allowed for the realisation of a common dream and the hope of realising dreams to come. We must benefit from the *Intifada*'s gains together. A bond of understanding would have to be found, despite the deceptions linked to electoral alliances. A common goal must be found.'

S. G.: 'The 14 March movement was above all to effect change. The partisan herd mentality prevents change. Many people remain dependent on their political parties.'

N. D., twenty-year-old student: 'With the launch of the *Intifada*, my parents, who are of the war generation, were pessimistic. I told them I didn't want to share in their pessimism. I believed in the future. Now, I'm beginning to think like them. I feel as though I'm not represented, and that we're the only ones speaking out. We have been pushed aside. I don't know if we can still change things anymore [a feeling exacerbated by the legislative elections].'

The young people expressing themselves here did so one year after 14 March 2005. It is clear that they have two ambivalent sentiments: On one hand, they believed they had the chance to achieve something and that they were doing it, and on the other hand there were 'negative' forces working to obstruct change and progress.

Provisional Conclusion:
For a Preliminary Typology of the Lebanese Demonstrations

Between the advent of 1975 and the March 2005 movement, we find two types of demonstration: the *conquest demonstration* or *campaign* and the *assembly demonstration* or *friendly gathering*. The first is so-called because it symbolises a process by which the actors express their intent to 'play' at conquering something that seems inaccessible, or is difficult to access in real life. The demonstrations that were sparked at the southwest periphery of the capital towards the centre of power downtown mimicked in some way the desire of engaged actors to become whole citizens within the city and to participate within the decision-making political institutions. They took on the appearance of a campaign, of a political assault.

Similar demonstrations took place over the course of 2005, organised by Hezbollah in the direction of the US embassy, located outside the capital in the northern suburbs of Beirut. The demonstration had the appearance of a symbolic assault on a target representing a hostile and despised power. The gathering of 14 March, on the other hand, does not symbolise a conquering process but expresses a movement of attraction, of convergence, of goodwill. The crowd arrived from the four corners of Lebanon, belonging to all social groups, and found themselves, at the end of their journey, all together, unified.

Maybe we can conclude that the meaning and function of demonstrations in general and of Beirut's demonstrations in particular is that of a societal ceremony with a sacred connotation. It seems indeed clear that the demonstration presents itself as a reproduction of society, regenerating it on a smaller scale.

Demonstrations seem tributary to the identity of the organiser or the initiator. When this represents a central political body or power or a mass organisation, the demonstration becomes an organised, repetitive and boring exercise. But when groups from civil society decide to protest, it becomes a popular and political ceremony. For the latter – and the case of the 14

March movement is a stunning example – the demonstration becomes a foundational act, a ritual to install new social relationships among the whole of society. The ritual produces a magical effect that consecrates the vision of the political dream.

The act that initially determined the whole movement was laden with sacred emotion. Demonstrations, in general, carry an affective meaning related to death.[8] The assassination of Rafik Hariri was both perceived and experienced as a death sentence, a sacrifice that could work towards the creation of a new society. Another powerful moment on 14 March was the 'sermon' by the journalist Gebran Tueni (himself assassinated in December 2005). This 'sermon' was meant to mark a regeneration of Lebanese sociality as well as to act as a solemn declaration renewing the national pact (social in the Rousseauian sense) of the Lebanese community.[9] Here the demonstration reached its culmination, reproducing not only the social ties but also the utopia that legitimises them.

By way of a conclusion I propose the following questions for consideration: To what extent does demonstrating, as a tool for expression and political socialisation, currently remain an adequate form of collective political action in the city of Beirut? At the moment, Beirut is a Greater Beirut made up of the old administrative city and its large suburb, a series of neighbourhoods and settlements that are no longer hindered by the necessity of integrating into the city space. Over the course of the last few decades, clusters of urban or semi-urban spaces have been built around municipal Beirut, which guarantees basic services to its residents. Individuals are primarily interested in social networks connecting them to the job market, to social relationships and as a way to access influential political actors. We are thus in a relational mode where individual strategies override collective strategies. This could greatly reduce the influence and efficiency of the political demonstration based on socio-professional solidarity.

The meaning of demonstrations is in the process of shifting: It is no longer a group of individuals who assemble to appropriate space signifying their will to participate in public life, to announce through their demands the conditions for this participation to be situated within acceptable conditions. In today's Beirut, one demonstrates to affirm; confirm and preserve a sense of political identity and belonging. Nevertheless, we have not yet observed new forms of struggle and pressure tactics at the level of unions and professional organisations who still tend to strike more than to demonstrate.

At present, there is a rising tendency aimed at ending a specific form of militancy: No more single commitment to a single organisation for an unlimited time. We can borrow Jacques Ion's remark: that

> The current period makes for the coexistence of many forms of involvement in a cause. One can be militant without having to commit over the long term, or even adhere to a group. For the militant, participation can no longer be sustained over the long term, nor can it necessarily pass through a hierarchical organisation separating the public from the private.[10]

It is towards this tendency that the forms of political action could evolve in the metropolis known as 'Greater Beirut'.

Bibliography

Ion, Jacques, *La fin des militants*, Paris: L'Atelier, 1997.
——'Le nouveau paysage militant', in *Sciences Humaines*, no. 166, December 2005, pp. 26–8.
Kassir, Samir, *Histoire de Beyrouth*, Paris: Fayard, 2003.
Maatouk, Frederick, 'al-Tazahurat al bayrutiyya bayna al 'ams wa al yawm', in *al-Hadathat*, winter and fall 2005, pp. 95–107.
Mermier, Franck, *Le Livre et la Ville: Beyrouth et l'édition arabe*, Paris: Actes Sud/Sindbad, 2005.
Tartakowski, Danièle, *La manif en éclats*, Paris: La Dispute, 2004.

Notes

1. This chapter focuses on the changes in the public space and political scene in Beirut in 2005 and does not take the events of 2006–7 into account.
2. Kassir, *Histoire de Beyrouth*; Mermier, *Le Livre et la Ville*.
3. Maatouk, 'al-Tazahurat al bayrutiyya bayna al 'ams wa al yawm'.
4. Kassir, a prolific journalist working for the newspaper *An-Nahar*, emerged as one of the leaders of the 14th March movement. He was assassinated by a car bomb on 2 June 2005.
5. See the special issue of the periodical *L'Orient-Express* dedicated to Samir Kassir. *L'Orient-Express* was a monthly publication headed by Kassir from 1995–8, the year its publication ceased.
6. The testimonials to follow are in part taken from Carmen Abou Jaoudé's article, in the above-cited issue of *L'Orient-Express*, pp. 84–97, and also drawn in part from unpublished accounts graciously provided by Mme Abou Jaoudé.
7. This thirty-five-year-old woman, a former expatriate who returned to Lebanon

following her studies in Canada, started her own professional company and was attending more to her business that thinking about politics. The assassination of Rafik Hariri provoked her to involve herself at the heart of the 14 March movement. She was chosen, in October 2005, as one of *Time Magazine*'s 'Heroes of 2005'.

8. See Tartakowski, *La manif en éclats*. Her research has focused on French demonstrations from 1918–68. She suggests that '... putting individuals to death seems to be a very powerful catalyst for collective indignation and anger. There is also the metaphorical death of enterprises or of regions, the social death.'

9. 'We swear by God Almighty,' Tueni said, 'we Christians and Muslims, to remain eternally unified ...'

10. Ion, 'Le nouveau paysage militant'; Ion, *La fin des militants*.

PART THREE

Spaces of Exclusion

Michel Agier[1]

From Refugee Camps to the Invention of Cities

> The nation state, unable to devise a law for those who lost the protection of their national government, placed the problem into the hands of the police.[2]

Today, the United Nations High Commission on Refugees (UNHCR) estimates that fifty million people worldwide are 'victims of forced displacement'. Among these displaced persons, thirteen to eighteen million are *stricto sensu* refugees, meaning they live outside their home countries. Densely concentrated in both Asia (over six million) and Africa (seven to eight million), these refugees add to the three million Palestinian refugees who, since the 1940s and 1960s, have been scattered throughout countries in the Middle East. In addition, just over three million refugees fall under the UNHCR's 'returnee' category as people who are in 'the process of repatriation'. Finally, an estimated twenty-five to thirty million people are considered 'internally displaced persons' (IDPs),[3] people who have been subjected to forced displacement within their home country due to violent conflict or civil war.[4]

All these figures are approximations, open to debate. They do not include the significant yet officially unrecorded number of undeclared refugees who are often mistaken for outlaws. Among these are, for example, the 130,000 'invisible' Afghan refugees displaced during the 2001 US attack on Afghanistan. It was only when the UNHCR pressured the Pakistani government to recognise these Afghans as refugees that the UN was able to place them in camps hastily set up along the border between Pakistan and Afghanistan.

Also unaccounted for are African and Middle Eastern exiles considered to be 'illegal immigrants' in Europe when they are detained at borders, having no status either as refugees, asylum seekers, or even as persons 'without papers'. While there are also Somalian, Ethiopian and Rwandan refugees who installed themselves in border countries, some chose to take their chances in illegality and in the informal economy rather than to be confined to refugee camps; others became drifters because they did not succeed in gaining official refugee status.

Official statistics offer only a partial picture of the concentration of refugees, asylum seekers and displaced persons living in camps. In 2002, of the 4.5 million people documented in UNHCR camps, almost half were in Africa (47 per cent), 38 per cent were in Asia, and 14 per cent were in Europe.⁵ Half of the three million Palestinians recorded by the United Nations Works and Relief Agency live in camps that were opened between the end of the 1940s and the 1960s, primarily in Lebanon, Syria, Jordan and the West Bank (which is to say, in the heart of the Palestinian territories, as we will see further on). In Africa, the majority of refugees under UNHCR protection live in camps. We need to add to this, among others, the camps for IDPs, especially those in Sudan (the camps around Khartoum hold about 1.5 million inhabitants); Liberia (there were 500,000 IDPs in camps during the civil war, with 240,000 still living there in 2004); or the camps that existed in Angola between 1970–2002, which housed over 1 million displaced people.

To gather refugees in camps is a policing measure as much as it is a rescue effort. The camps constitute 'outside-sites', or enclaves hidden within national spaces. If refugees are, according to an expression Michel Foucault used in the early 1980s, the first beings 'confined outside', they are also, for each excluding state, beings 'cast aside within'. This issue is global, but the political responsibility of the states is primordial: The refugees' request for asylum forces us to reflect on the authority capable of responding – rescue, hospitality: the *refuge*.

Thus, faced with an influx of people who are displaced or exiled due to civil war or violent conflict, the camp is the control response of nation-states (separately, or all together in delegating camp management to the UNHRC). There is no 'outside', no physical space separating the 'global' from the sum of all nation-states. Yet there are constant attempts to hold refugee populations outside the political, legal and social spheres of the nation-state. These two opposing forces result in the creation of artificial and never totally empty spaces, interstitial deserts, fluctuating situations synonymous with liminality, undefined-ness, extraterritoriality or exception. They are 'borders', frontiers or thresholds of ordinary life, inhabited by millions of people who never really find their place. They find themselves, as they say in Colombia, being 'normal people in abnormal situations'. This distancing of asylum seekers has been a reiterated and amplified response for the last century, evolving towards the present use of camps, which is the 'solution' proposed by certain European governments.

The Camps-cities

Today, the camps symbolise the human social condition at precisely the moment when war and humanitarianism meet – an encounter sometimes complemented by the police, as we can see at European borders. This brings us to the first consideration elicited by this text about the contemporary makeup of the camps: it is the formation of a global humanitarian management zone for the most unimaginable and least desirable populations on the planet. The separate treatment of refugees and displaced persons (treated quantitatively as 'populations') goes hand-in-hand with their segregation. Is it a coincidence that the people to whom the humanitarian language refers as 'vulnerable' are the undesirables of the global system? Camps are the place and the ultimate symbol of the double-ascription that occurs in this context: a social ascription by creating rigid categories that stigmatise personal identity on a global as well as national level (refugees, displaced persons, disaster victims, asylum seekers, etc); and a spatial ascription, through their confinement to outside-sites.

The second topic for reflection is that of the 'camps-cities'. The camp is always a precarious place, but it is also a place where a relatively stable situation emerges. Created out of urgency to ensure a minimum level of 'care, cure and control' (as it is called among the UNHCR personnel) for all types of war survivors, the refugee camps agglomerate thousands or even tens of thousands of inhabitants for lengths of time that generally far exceed that of an emergency. The precise duration of an emergency is hard to determine anyway, even from the point of view of humanitarian organisations.

It is also evident that once camps are set up in a more or less fast manner, a certain permanence sets in, for internal as much as external reasons. The continuation of war prevents refugees from returning home, and the humanitarian aid apparatus also generates its own effects in terms of population density, job markets, local integration and even precarious urbanisation. Later on, the closure of a camp becomes problematic. The camps form paradoxical configurations, hybrids that I name, for lack of a specific term, 'camps-cities'.

On one hand, the individuals assembled into these spaces are there solely because they share the recognised status of 'victim'. Far from the 'sounds of war',[6] they must remain separated from ordinary social spheres, the normal (and national) order of things. On the other hand, the camp being a survival system, plus the way it is organised and above all the fact that it represents a relatively important establishment with a continuous density of socially heterogeneous people,[7] creates exchange situations (eventually in the form of conflict) and contexts of cultural and social change. It is therefore appropriate to describe and measure the consequences of the re-socialisation phenomena, of forms of 'urbanisation' where materiality is very real despite being perceived as temporary, and to pay attention to possible re-elaborations of identity among all those who live there, once a few years have passed.

In this sense the configuration of the camps produces the city, if we consider the city from the point of view of its essential complexity. It is because of its 'extraordinary complication', noted urban historian Bernard Lepetit,[8] that the city was able to become a subject of history. A camp that has existed for five years is no longer a row of tents. It can resemble a shantytown, and it can also remind us of an ethnographic museum where people try, with the materials they find in the camp, to reconstruct their native habitat, for better or worse. The result is sometimes a motley landscape of hybrid formation, the coarse blue and white canvas of the UNHCR covering the precarious constructions of wood or dirt, the cloth from bags stamped 'European Union' or 'USA' serving as drapes for the dwellings' entrances. It can become a peripheral neighbourhood, as happened with the Palestinian camps or with the displaced people's camps on the periphery of Khartoum.

In a certain way, an *urban* ethnography of humanitarian sites allows us to go further than what a philosophy of the camps can express, which is a critical philosophy, certainly, but *without subject*. In this way, Giorgio Agamben's analyses concluded that the ending of the city and the beginning of the camp is the 'paradigm of political space at the moment when politics becomes biopolitics'.[9] In this approach, politics confounds itself entirely with the exercise of 'biopower'. Furthermore, the socialisation of the camps can turn them into 'spaces of subjectivity' where, simultaneously, the subject exists and 'politics begins'. In a form more situational than structural, the 'humanitarian scene' administered on the model of exception could then cede its place to a 'democratic scene'.[10]

What political model can we expect from this situation? Not that of the camp that substitutes for the city but, on the contrary, the camp that, in its material and social form, transforms and ultimately *comes undone* in the city at the moment when the action (whether visible or invisible) of those who reside there, their response or resistance to confinement, their endeavouring and wangling, expresses a 'right to life'.

Recovering Refuges, Founding the Hospitable City

Identification with others and with places occurs in the context of a transformation of the camps, of generally confined and confining spaces, into a social and political *world*. This proposition does not coincide with the one that associates the socio-demographic category of 'refugee' with an identity, and this identity to an 'origin', the place from where the displaced arrive and to which they must return. This conception eliminates locality constructed on the space of the camp and organises a new displacement corresponding to a new category, that of the 'returnees'. The return can turn into a new forced displacement, all the while preventing the social and material mutation of the camp into a 'city'. The displaced and the refugees do not correspond anymore to their assigned categories of identity, not at the moment when they return 'home', but rather when they cease to be the victims that a humanitarian qualification implies, and become subjects.

The city in the making and the transformation of precarious spaces – today still largely unpredictable in terms of their future materiality, their economy or their sociability – are like territories that we create and where we forge or found a local identity. To be transmittable from one generation to another, the local identity is not less displaceable. The very idea of founding, of a city, a village or a house, contradicts all belief in autochtony as a local identity, naturally 'coming out of the ground'. In his research on certain ancient and current myths of autochtony, Marcel Détienne substantively notes that 'founding a city' means to create ties *in* and *to* a place, to create roots, without this root having to pre-exist. A fragment of ecology, certain odours, markings for the intention of neighbours, rituals of foundation or settlement … 'Nothing is more trivial for a living being than to make its burrow, its immediate territory. The rest follows.'[11] This 'rest' is everything that flows, technically and administratively, from the necessary anthropological foundation of areas as sites of identification.

This logical order of the production of local space is also that of the *invention of the city* starting from the illegal occupations of camps and other empty and precarious spaces.[12] There, refugees change after two or three years into inhabitants, and subsequently become the dwellers of a naked city.

The inductive, process-based conception of spaces and of urban theory that we have just evoked creates ambivalence, even ideological tension, in the case of the Palestinian camps. Their existence, we know, dates back to the late 1940s for the first camps, the mid-1950s for their more permanent installation and the years 1970–80 for the growth in the number of camps, their stabilisation and material consolidation.

In early 2003, an architecture student received permission from the Palestinian Authority to conduct research on the 'urbanisation of the Kalandia camp'. This camp is located in the West Bank, 3 km from Ramallah and 8 km from Jerusalem; it has existed since 1948 and has a population of approximately 10,000 refugee-inhabitants.[13] The current programme[14] in the city-camps in the West Bank would have been unimaginable only a few years ago. The subject was completely taboo. To understand, we must keep in mind that current Palestinian political identity was born of conflict and ceasefire, and to this day rests on a double foundation: the memory of lost land, kept alive by the reiterated recollections of elders, and the confinement of refugees to the outside-sites of the camps. The camps need to keep the symbol intact of expected return, and therefore form the appropriate framework to express suffering, paralysis and non-existence. Foreign visitors will notice that the information session about the suffering experienced since the war and exile of 1948 until the present is an integral part of the tour of the camps.

All this points to the fact that the actual maintenance of the camps as institutionally distinct and politically enclosed spaces has no basis other than being a sacrifice to the Palestinian cause. They represent the 'knot' or living symbol of the Israeli-Palestinian conflict. The existence of the camps as figures of the Camp – and thus of confinement, of distancing and of waiting – is politically sustained by the two warring parties as long as they have been at war. However, the camps are transforming. For years they have undergone an urbanisation that is at the level of social organisation comparable to the economic practices and material dimension of what we know of urban peripheries around the world. The distinction between the city dweller and the refugee hangs by a thread.

In a speech given at the inauguration of the 'Cities of Refuge' programme, an initiative of the International Parliament of Writers in Strasbourg, 21–2 March 1996, Jacques Derrida recalled, following Hannah Arendt, the 'medieval principle' with the right to asylum as its last modern vestige: *Quid est in territorio est de territorio.* He then pointed out the larger implications, both critical and reflexive, of the battle for the creation of refuge cities:

> If we refer to the city, rather than the State, it is because we expect of a new figure of the city what we have almost given up expecting from the State … If we use the name of our wishes we call it the city-refuge. It is no longer simply a configuration of new attributes

or of new powers added to a classic and unchanged concept of the city. It is no longer simply a question of new predicates to enrich the old subject named 'city'. No, we dream of another concept, of another right, of other politics of the city.[15]

Similarly, the theorising of refugee camps develops within the utopia of the foundation of cities on the basis of refuges. Of the refugee camp, we propose to maintain only the principle of asylum and leave the camps to come undone, to break up and finally to make a city establishing a hybrid social and political world, born of and in war, certainly, yet equally having emerged from war.

Bibliography

Agamben, Giorgio, *Homo sacer: Le pouvoir souverain et la vie nue*, Paris: Seuil, 1997.

Agier, Michel, 'Faire ville aujourd'hui, demain: Réflexions sur le désert, le monde et les espaces précaires', in Guénola Capron, Geneviève Cortes, Hélène Guetat-Bernard, eds, *Liens et lieux de la mobilité*, Paris: Belin, 2005, pp. 167–78.

——*L'invention de la ville: Banlieues, townships, invasions et favelas*, Paris: Éditions des archives contemporaines, 1999.

——'Le son de la guerre. Expériences africaines de l'errance, des frontières et des camps', in *Politix, Revue des sciences sociales du politique*, no. 69, 2005, pp. 83–99.

Arendt, Hannah, *Les origines du totalitarisme: L'impérialisme*, Paris: Fayard, 1951.

Derrida, Jacques, *Cosmopolites de tous les pays, encore un effort*, Paris: Galilée, 1997.

Détienne, Marcel, *Comment être autochtone: Du pur athénien au français raciné*, Paris: Seuil ('Librairie du XXIe siècle'), 2003.

Lepetit, Bernard, 'La ville: cadre, objet, sujet', in *Enquête (La ville des sciences sociales)*, 4, 1996, pp. 11–34.

Meron, Nava, *Proposition d'urbanisation pour Kalandia, camp de réfugiés en Cisjordanie*, Paris: Ecole d'Architecture de Paris-la-Villette, 2003.

Rancière, Jacques, *La mésentente: Politique et philosophie*, Paris: Galilée, 1995.

UNHCR, *Les réfugiés dans le monde: Cinquante ans d'action humanitaire*, Paris: Autrement, 2000.

——*Les réfugiés dans le monde. Les personnes déplacées: L'urgence humanitaire*, Paris: La Découverte, 1997.

Notes

1. Institut de Recherche pour le Développement (IRD, Paris) and École des Hautes Études en Sciences Sociales (EHESS, Paris).
2. Arendt, *Les origines du totalitarisme*, p. 266.
3. The UN category for IDPs describes persons with rights who have left their region of origin but stayed inside the borders of their country.
4. United Nations High Commission on Refugees, *Les réfugiés dans le monde*, 1997 and 2000.
5. UNHCR, *Statistical Yearbook 2002*; see www.unhcr.ch.
6. 'The sound of the war' is an expression among Liberian refugees, used by those who do not have a very precise notion of the political identity of the fighters who invaded their villages. It points at the feeling of fear that dominates the narratives of the refugees. In these narratives, other expressions of the same kind refer to the war as a subject: 'the war entered in Monrovia', 'the war met me in Kono', etc. See Agier, 'Le son de la guerre'.
7. These are notions Louis Wirth used in the 1930s to define the city.
8. Lepetit, 'La ville: cadre, objet, sujet'.
9. Agamben, *Homo sacer*, p. 184.
10. I have borrowed these notions from Rancière, *La mésentente*, p. 172.
11. Détienne, *Comment être autochtone*.
12. Agier, *L'invention de la ville* and 'Faire ville aujourd'hui, demain'.
13. Meron, *Proposition d'urbanisation pour Kalandia, camp de réfugiés en Cisjordanie*.
14. The current project in the West Bank is a Research Project coordinated by Sylvie Bulle (EHESS – Paris) and focuses on urbanism in Palestine. It is a collaboration between Shaml (the Palestinian Refugee and Diasopara Centre) and the French Ministry of Research.
15. Derrida, *Cosmopolites de tous les pays, encore un effort*, p. 17, 22.

ENGIN F. ISIN AND KIM RYGIEL

Of Other Global Cities: Frontiers, Zones, Camps[1]

There are new kinds of spaces emerging across the world. We do not yet recognise them as 'urban' spaces; we do not yet name them. These unnamed spaces are patchworks of arrangements nestled within existing and recognisable spaces yet forming interstitial territories that are literally neither here nor there. These spaces are non-existent insofar as they aim to create spaces of exception that become regular, routine and invisible. It is impossible to estimate how many people are caught in such spaces, nor how extensive they are. It is also very difficult to investigate these spaces, precisely because they are neither here nor there.

Yet they are everywhere. That these spaces emerged in the late twentieth and early twenty-first centuries tells us more about the movement and flow of peoples, commodities and capital across the world than does the literature growing up around the same period on global cities, which has relentlessly focused on describing, analysing and constituting the global city as an object of analysis, which – caught in these movements and flows – has developed various policies and agencies for dealing with them.[2]

We would like to approach the subject of global cities from an entirely different perspective, that of another kind of space emerging across the world which we call 'other global cities'. The otherness of other global cities here cannot be captured by the already-known and understood categories such as the numbered worlds (first, second, third) or geographic descriptions such as North and the South. These other spaces are abject spaces: they aim to render their inhabitants and occupants neither subjects nor objects, but abjects.

These spaces can be found nestled within existing territories and boundaries that constitute cities and states; they are immanent within these known spaces but constitute their otherness insofar as they render other subjects as abjects. We wish to call these spaces 'other global cities' not only because they make global cities (as commonly understood) possible and, hence, are internally connected to them, but also because these spaces internalise certain aspects and characteristics of global cities. What are these spaces? These abject spaces, as other global cities, conglomerate and accumulate in three different forms: frontiers, zones and camps.

1. Frontiers

Frontiers are spaces designed to regulate the mobility of people, where national and international laws are temporarily suspended; they are buffer zones, through which people can be processed, created. This section discusses the emerging frontiers in which various subjects are not only stripped of their citizenship rights, but also given ostensibly differentiated citizenship rights. Such spaces are created with the intent of 'housing' the abject in extraterritorial spaces.

These extraterritorial spaces keep the abject from accessing state and city spaces – in which they would have the opportunity to exercise social, political and economic rights – recognising that the ability to do so is a first step towards becoming political and claiming legal citizenship status. Paradoxically, however, this is done by appealing to a governmental logic of human rights, and more specifically that of protection. The claim is that by creating such abject spaces, new rights are being extended to those who would otherwise remain rightless.

How can such spaces be viewed as other global cities? Closer examination below of some specific examples of these frontier spaces reveals that, while the idea behind them may be to create temporary living spaces, they increasingly come to take on a certain permanence, providing the conditions for people to live increasingly more 'settled' lives such that these supposedly temporary spaces become permanent spaces of transience.[3]

More than this though, such spaces come to take on a certain permanence as increasing numbers of abjects (refugees, non-status peoples, 'illegal' and economic migrants) are forced to reside in them. Rather than being isolated exceptions, however, they perform as part of a network of spaces that are also well-integrated with other, more cosmopolitan spaces like the global city, with which we are more familiar. For it is only by creating spaces through which to regulate the abject that the current regime of global mobility and capital can be maintained. In other words, the experience for some of living in the cosmopolitan global city is increasingly dependent on the creation of what we are calling here other global cities – spaces in which the abject increasingly find themselves forced to live.

1.1 'Zones of Protection': 'Regional Protection Areas' and 'Transit Processing Centres'

Most recent governmental thought has focused on the idea of creating 'zones of protection'. Former UK Home Secretary David Blunkett introduced the idea of zones of protection as part of a new vision for a global asylum system 'fit for the 21st century', claiming that 'we need a radically new approach to delivering the reduction of asylum numbers that we need'.[4] Although plans were put on hold after the proposal received much public criticism, different articulations of this same vision continue to appear. For example, in 2004, German Interior Minister Otto Schily, in agreement with Italian Interior Minister Giuseppe Pisanu, attempted to push forward a proposal very similar to the UK's to create transit or holding centres in North Africa to prevent asylum seekers from travelling and making claims within the EU.[5] In other words, despite being put on hold for the moment, the vision put forth here on zones of protection is of interest, for it reflects current rationalities about how to devise new ways of using extraterritorial forms of detention to govern asylum seekers.

In a report titled 'A New Vision for Refugees', the UK government outlined its proposal for creating a new system of asylum management in coordination with other EU partners and international organisations like the UNHCR and the International Organization for Migration (IOM).[6] Funding for the initiative would come from a coalition of participating Western nations, including 'fellow English speaking nations such as the US, Canada and Australia'.[7] The proposal suggests the creation of two types of zones: 'Regional Protection Areas' (RPAs) and 'Off-territory Transit Processing Centres'.[8]

RPAs are areas to be set up near conflict zones producing major flows of people, and are to be under UNHCR responsibility. They are supposed to provide protection or safe haven to those fleeing conflict or persecution in their home countries and to help them resettle in their home countries or in nearby countries, rather than seeking asylum and resettlement in EU countries. These buffer areas would also be used as areas to which those claiming asylum in the UK or other participating countries could be returned. The proposal notes:

> Returning asylum seekers that spontaneously arrive in the UK to a Regional Protection Area for protection is a key part of the vision. It works on a principle similar to that of safe third countries. We would be saying that asylum seekers do not need protection in the

UK because there is another safe third area where they can access adequate protection.[9]

RPAs would be located in such countries as Turkey, Iran, northern Somalia and Morocco that are part of migration routes and near major refugee-producing areas.[10]

While the description of RPAs suggests that these spaces are temporary arrangements, in fact just the opposite is the case. The proposal differentiates RPAs from refugee camps by claiming that they should offer long-term settlement with 'the opportunity for refugees to live as normal lives as possible'.[11]

In contrast, Transit Processing Centres are to be located along the external borders of the EU in countries such as Romania, Croatia, Albania and Ukraine.[12] The idea of transit centres is to create extraterritorial processing areas where people's asylum claims can be processed without having to travel to the countries in which they are seeking asylum. In other words, it prevents asylum seekers from relocating to certain EU countries by keeping them in buffer zones while they await news of their claims.[13] These zones would be used primarily for the return of economic migrants seeking refuge in the UK while waiting for the processing of their asylum claims.[14]

What is the governmental logic behind these RPAs and Transit Processing Centres? Critics of the UK's proposal, like Amnesty International, have argued:

> The real goal behind the UK proposal appears to be to reduce the number of spontaneous arrivals to the UK and other EU states by denying access to territory, and shifting asylum-seekers to processing zones outside the EU where responsibility, enforceability and accountability for refugee protection would be weak and unclear.[15]

This can be seen as part of a larger strategy of preventing people from claiming citizenship rights by keeping them away from state and city spaces. By virtue of belonging to a state and city, a person becomes entitled to certain citizenship rights (civil, political, and social) or at least the right to claim such rights. By creating these extraterritorial spaces, states are making it impossible to claim such rights. What is denied to the people kept there is the right to have rights. The idea, then, is to create parallel spaces, like zones of protection, in which abjects live in a permanent state of transition for extended periods of time until they are possibly resettled. More than this, these spaces perform the regulatory function of managing who has access to the rights and resources within EU countries; thus they are integral to the existence of the more cosmopolitan global cities.

1.2 'Excised Offshore Places' and 'Offshore Processing Centres': Australia's 'Pacific Solution'

Another example of frontier spaces can be found in Australia's proposal to create excised offshore places and processing centres. Like the UK proposal, Australia's plans are founded upon a similar logic of creating extraterritorial spaces in which to settle asylum seekers and other migrants in spaces of social isolation, away from the rest of Australian society and off its territory where they might more easily be able to exercise certain social, political and civil citizenship rights.

On 26 September 2001 the Australian government passed legislation designed to deter refugees, especially those without valid documents or smuggled in, from reaching its shores. The same logic of creating buffer zones is also at work here. As part of this legislation, Australia removed certain territories from its 'migration zone' as a way of circumventing international refugee law and its own national immigration law and responsibility to process asylum seekers. These territories, called 'excised offshore places', include Christmas Island and the Cocos (Keeling) Islands in the Indian Ocean; Ashmore and Cartier Island in the Timor Sea; and 'any Australian sea installation' or 'offshore resource' (such as an oil rig).[16]

These territories act as spaces where indefinite detention is permitted and provided with limited judicial review as a way of bypassing normal judicial procedures that would normally apply on the Australian mainland. Detention centres such as the one on Christmas Island have been constructed to hold recognised refugees as well as asylum seekers and rejected asylum seekers in mandatory detention, without the right to appeal and prohibited from access to legal counsel.[17]

In addition to 'excised offshore places', the Australian government has also made arrangements with several Pacific islands to establish 'offshore processing centres', essentially amounting to the 'subcontracting of detention to poorer neighbouring states (the so-called 'Pacific Solution').[18] Here asylum seekers, especially those who enter 'illegally' (such as those who arrive by boat) or who are expelled by the Australian government may be turned away to these places and held in facilities similar to detention centres and refugee camps to await the processing of their asylum claims.

Australia's Department of Immigration and Multicultural and

Indigenous Affairs notes that the turning away of an 'offshore entry person' depends upon his or her 'declaring a country for this purpose'.[19] For example, the island of Nauru and Papua New Guinea (Manus Island) have made arrangements with the Australian government to establish processing centres, and have thus each been deemed a 'declared country'.[20] As of August 2002, at least 1,800 asylum seekers had been transferred to these islands.[21] Such arrangements often involve Australia paying these nearby Pacific nations to accept and 'house' its unwanted migrants in offshore processing centres or camps. For example, it paid AU$10 million in August 2001 to Nauru to accept and house refused asylum seekers in makeshift camps.[22] It has also made similar deals with Papua New Guinea, Kiribati and, in November 2001, with Tuvalu. In November 2001 Australia also took some 300 Vietnamese and Middle Eastern refugees to Christmas Island as well as to Ashmore Reef.[23] Critics note that this policy of 'diverting boats to other countries in exchange for aid and money amounts to a trade in human misery'.[24]

Like zones of protection, these offshore places interrupt the process of citizenship and rights-making by removing abjects like asylum seekers into social isolation in detention centres, where they are less likely to be able to exercise citizenship rights like the right to legal council, speech, and access to social services and community networks. Human Rights Watch has documented how persons detained in these camps are denied what we consider civil and political rights, such as contact with the outside world, freedom of movement and due process guarantees like independent legal counsel.[25]

Yet, despite the denial of such basic rights, these spaces increasingly provide alternative living arrangements for asylum seekers and other abjects, some for several years, as they await decisions to be made about their asylum claims. Despite the fact that such offshore arrangements may have been introduced as a short-term method of deterrence and a temporary solution to reducing the numbers of asylum claimants arriving on Australia's shores, it is clear, almost five years later, that these alternative arrangements are becoming more permanent. In a recent announcement on 13 April 2006, the Australian government reaffirmed its commitment to its 2001 policy and noted its intentions to make the policy stricter, mandating that all asylum claimants arriving to Australia by ship, regardless of whether or not that boat makes it to the mainland, must now have their asylum claims assessed and processed at an offshore location.[26]

Moreover, the Australian government has removed itself from the daily governing of these spaces, making the IOM, instead, responsible for the processing of claims and the administration of the centres. The fact that an international organisation is running these offshore places and providing basic services such as counselling also suggests a certain permanence in the operation of these centres.[27] Whereas zones of protection operate by creating extraterritorial spaces that function as buffer zones, offshore places work through a redefinition of state territory. Territory is redefined as either no longer falling under state jurisdiction (e.g., excised offshore places) or as extraterritorial space purchased on a second territory and under the responsibility of a third party such as an international organisation like the IOM. This redefinition thus makes it harder for abjects to make claims to citizenship rights as they would if they were 'housed' within spaces in the city. As such, these offshore arrangements keep asylum seekers in abject spaces away from state and city spaces where they might have a chance of participating in social and economic networks and Australian society.

1.3 Border Zones: the US-Mexico Border

A third example of a buffer zone-type of abject space are the border zones created between certain countries, such as between the US and Mexico. Border zones regulate the movement of millions of people, with one recent IOM study estimating that globally there may be as many as 15–30 million 'irregular migrants'.[28] It is in this context that border zones can be understood as abject spaces.

The US-Mexico border, running about 3,300 km long from San Diego, California to Brownsville, Texas, provides one of the most poignant cases of such abject spaces.[29] Here, the border is enforced through 'border control strategies' like the 1994 Southwest Border Strategy, consisting of four programmes: 'Operation Hold the Line' in El Paso, Texas; 'Operation Gatekeeper' in San Diego; 'Operation Safeguard' in Arizona; and 'Operation Rio Grande' in South Texas.[30] Such border strategies are designed to 'funnel northbound migration through open areas, such as mountains and deserts where migrants can be more easily apprehended by the US Border Patrol'.[31]

But such border strategies also make crossing the border much more dangerous. Since their implementation in 1994, about 2,000 people have died crossing the border, with 2001 figures in California estimating an average 140 deaths per year compared to the twenty-three to twenty-four deaths per year before the implementation of Operation Gatekeeper.[32] Moreover, as border enforcement is tightened, people increasingly turn to other mechanisms, including using so-called *coyotes*, or 'people smugglers', in order to cross. Other methods have included building underground tunnels like the mile-long Otay Mesa tunnel to San Diego.[33]

Different border strategies have also been adopted to deal with varying terrain. For example, Operation Gatekeeper in San Diego is designed to deal with migrant crossings through valleys and canyons. The strategy uses 'three tiers of agents at the border' with 'a row of agents along the border fence, another one a few hundred yards behind, and another several hundred yards behind'.[34]

In addition to using border agents, border strategies depend on the building of a physical wall between the US and Mexico. Since 11 September 2001, for example, the US government has proposed to build a 260-mile-long fence along the Arizona state borders. This follows other fence-building projects along the border that intensified with the Southwest Border Strategy. Operation Gatekeeper proposed plans for the construction of a triple fence, now near completion, which consists of a first wall made of steel, a second fifteen ft high wall and a third ten ft chain link fence.[35] Most border fences, like the Operation Gatekeeper fence, are also increasingly militarised with 'stadium-style lighting that keeps the fence lit twenty-four hours a day and surveillance cameras to monitor activity around the fence'.[36]

The US Citizenship and Immigration Services (USCIS) reports that, as of 1998, Operation Gatekeeper had installed 'six miles of permanent high-intensity lighting', fifty-nine infrared scopes and 1,214 underground sensors, and installed computer systems like IDENT and ICAD to track migrants.[37] Moreover, approximately 9,150 border patrol agents enforced the US-Mexican border as of 2002, a number that contrasts with the mere 334 agents that police the 4,000-mile US-Canada border.[38]

Border areas are thus highly militarised and policed zones. The logic is to render these spaces 'secure' by discouraging travel and settlement and essentially ridding these spaces of people. Yet if border zones have become places that invite dangerous crossings through inhospitable terrain like deserts, as well as militarised zones with border guards, light sensors and motion detectors, they have despite all of these strategies nevertheless become spaces of settlement – but in abject conditions.

The Migration Policy Institute (MPI) notes that about ten million people live along the border area, and that a significant proportion of the populations on both sides live at or below the poverty line.[39] Unemployment rates along the border are also 200–300 per cent higher than in the rest of the US.[40] On the Mexican side, MPI notes that the border areas have become Export Processing Zones (EPZs) where some 1,700 *maquiladoras* employ over 730,000 workers.[41] *Maquiladoras* have encouraged the migration of more than one million Mexicans to the border areas to work for as little as US$0.50 per hour.[42]

In addition to below minimum wage salaries, *maqiladoras* are also notorious for infringing on other labour rights, including forced pregnancy testing for women, harassment and exposure to toxic chemicals without proper warning or protection. In addition, EPZs have also given rise to cities like Ciudad Juárez, made up of shantytowns and lacking basic infrastructure and services, where as many as over 400 women have been murdered since 1993, often on their way to or from work in the *maqiladoras*.[43] Irregular early morning and late night shifts leave women vulnerable as they are forced to make their way home without public transportation and community networks, in a city where the message has now been sent, due to the failure to seriously prosecute the murders, that violence against women is acceptable whether it be drug- or police-related, or domestic.[44] As Esther Chávez, founder of the only battered-women and rape crisis centre in Juárez, explains:

> This city has become a place to murder and dump women ... [Authorities] are not interested in solving these cases because these women are young and poor and dispensable. A woman goes to work so she can support her family. She works hard, but when she is killed, people say she was a prostitute that isn't worth anything.[45]

In other words, border zones give rise to abject places of settlement like EPZs and makeshift cities like Juárez that emerge around the notion of disposable bodies of (often female) cheap labour. It should not surprise us, then, that such spaces grow up alongside wealthier towns and cities across the border, as both are intimately connected as part of the same network of global production.

As abject spaces, border zones operate like buffer zones, but unlike zones of protection the logic is not to protect people but the opposite: to render these spaces inhospitable and treacherous to people to deter mobility or a sense of belonging along the border. They are thus spaces of extreme militarisation, violence and poverty, spaces designed to encourage permanent transience by making community living extremely difficult. However, despite this, these spaces inevitably become places of settlement for the millions of migrants attempting to cross borders like the US-Mexico border. It is these abject spaces – the other global cities like Juárez – that become integral to the migration of cheap labour and the functioning of a global regime of capital accumulation that depends on such expendable labour.

As such, these border zone frontier spaces must be seen as part of a larger network of abject spaces that are integral to the functioning of cosmopolitan spaces like the global city. They serve as reserve areas to which abjects migrate in order to eke out an existence, hoping eventually to one day access the resources and rights across the border in the wealthier cities of the US and Canada.

What, then, is the logic behind all these zones of protection, regional protection areas, excised offshore places, offshore protection areas and protection borderlands that we call frontiers? It is not that there is an inexorable logic enacted through these diverse forms of population control and regulation, but that they are assembled together to create frontiers in and through which subjects are denied possibilities of constituting themselves as political subjects. As we have seen, these frontiers have become spaces with their own logic: they attempt to render abjects with a non-existent status that is without voice, without speech, without presence, without reason – in effect, without the capacity of becoming political – by preventing access to state and city spaces to which abject subjects can make claims to rights.

At the same time, it is through these abject spaces that the dominant regime of a global regulation of movement of peoples and capital by democratic states is made visible for what it is, and rendered so by the very same abjects they have tried to constitute. For the abjects begin to act as political subjects through various forms of resistance, whether it be in acts like suturing mouths to protest detention, setting boats on fire in order to be picked up and brought to the Australian shores, or attempting dangerous border crossings. It is through these acts that abjects render themselves existent and present while simultaneously exposing the web of strategies and technologies of otherness enacted in these abject spaces – these other global cities – that attempt to render them non-existent.

2. Zones

The logic that assembles frontiers can also be found in various zones. These zones of exception are spaces where subjects live under suspended rules of freedom. Unlike frontiers, the logic of which is to keep out and away via extraterritorial arrangements, these zones are spaces nestled within state and city territories. These include zones within global cities to which various subjects are dispersed, but then live under some form of conditional freedom and surveillance. These are zones of exception insofar as subjects who inhabit them are constituted as exceptions and kept from fully making claims to the city by being 'housed' in these abject spaces.

2.1 Detention centres

Over the past decade, democratic states have introduced increasingly restrictive means to deal with refugees and migrants, including the growing use of detention centres. In a November 2002 statement to the UN General Assembly, the UN High Commissioner for Refugees, Ruud Lubbers, noted that there was a 'worrying more general trend towards increased use of detention – often on a discriminatory basis'.[46] The US Committee for Refugees noted that in 1996, with changes to its immigration laws, detention of certain immigrants and refugees became mandatory in the US such that the 'INS [Immigration and Naturalization Service] now detains more than 200,000 people annually at more than 900 sites, the majority of which are county and local jails'.[47] Furthermore: 'Immigration detainees have become the fastest growing segment of the incarcerated population in the United States.'[48]

Like the US, Australia has also implemented laws imposing mandatory detention ranging from months to years for all refugees and migrants who arrive without proper identification,[49] while there has been a similar growing trend in the use of detention centres across Europe.[50] There are different forms of detention centres ranging from 'asylum hotels' or 'induction centres' to 'accommodation centres' and 'removal centres'. There are also detention camps, such as the infamous Woomera camp in Australia or Sangatte in France, but this form of detention facility will be discussed in the section on camps. We are interested here in discussing those abject spaces that are nestled within cities and regions.

2.2 Asylum hotels as induction or reception centres

In its 2002 Nationality, Immigration and Asylum (NIA) Act, the UK government announced plans to build new reception or induction centres to house asylum seekers for the first week, giving them physical examinations and providing information on asylum procedures before moving them to large-scale accommodation centres where they would be housed while waiting for their claims to be processed.[51] The plan was to use various hotels (popularly referred to in the press as 'asylum hotels') as induction centres. One such example was the Coniston Hotel in Sittingbourne, Kent. However, protest from neighbourhood residents led to the eventual government decision to abandon the project because of a lack of proper public consultation.[52]

2.3 Accommodation centres

The NIA Act also proposed to build a network of accommodation centres to house incoming asylum seekers waiting for their claims to be processed. The act proposed to build these centres in rural communities such as South Glamorgan, near Edinburgh, and in Lincolnshire and Bicester, Oxfordshire. Former Home Office Minister Des Browne explained: 'At present, inner city dispersal areas take on virtually all responsibility for asylum seekers and it is only fair that all parts of the country share responsibility.'[53]

While it was expressed as sharing responsibility, the act was clearly designed to mitigate against protests by inner city neighbourhoods regarding the location of such centres. The Home Office stated that such centres would be an improvement to current practice, where the government 'accommodates most asylum seekers around the country in houses, flats or hostels provided by Local Authorities or private landlords', because they will enable the government to process cases faster, have less impact on social services and 'make it easier to stay in close contact with asylum seekers'.[54] The centres are designed with the idea of providing all the basic services to asylum seekers in one spot so that they 'will not be dependent on local services', including education, health, 'purposeful activities and voluntary work', transport, interpretation and legal services.[55]

Rather than having access to such services within the city proper, new spaces of 'accommodation' are created in which to provide the services required for daily living, but in a controlled space removed from the social networks of the city. These euphemisms are designed to mask the fact that the authorities want to control asylum seekers and make it impossible for them to become subjects by becoming part of the daily hustle and bustle of city life. The detention centres are a new form of a ghetto dating back to medieval cities: a segregation technology whereby subjects are constituted as strangers and outsiders rather than people who can claim 'a right to have rights'.[56] Interestingly, plans for the creation of such centres have still met with resistance from local residents. For example, a scheme to convert a formal naval base into a centre to house 400 asylum seekers was recently dropped, in part, because of local protest that the centre would lead to increased crime in the area and concerns about incoming numbers of foreigners to rural communities.[57]

2.4 Removal centres

'Closed centres' are removal centres that are often privately run. They are prison-like holding centres where people are kept behind barbed wire and denied rights of movement, with limited access to legal rights and limited access to time spent outdoors, as in a penitentiary. In the UK, as of June 2003, there were 1,355 people being held in removal centres.[58]

One well-known example is Scotland's Dungavel Immigration and Asylum Centre in Lanarkshire, a removal centre that holds failed asylum seekers until they are deported. Formerly a prison, Dungavel is surrounded by a 20-ft wall, guards and barbed wire.[59] Dungavel has been referred by some as a 'Scottish Guantánamo Bay'.[60]

Critics argue that 'those held have less rights than suspected criminals because they cannot rely on an automatic review of their detention by the courts', and that 'the centres unfairly restrict an individual's right to fight a case because of limited access to legal advice'.[61] Moreover, people are held often for lengthy periods of time. Out of 150 people kept there, government statistics in 2002 showed that fifty-five were held for over a year.[62]

On the other hand, unlike in closed removal centres, asylum seekers housed in so-called 'open centres' are permitted freedom of movement, to come and go as they please. Open centres house both 'illegal' immigrants as well as asylum seekers waiting for either deportation or for their claims to be processed. One well-known example is Belgium's Le Petit Château in Brussels, which houses up to 850 immigrants and refugees, many for more than a year.[63] Le Petit Château makes arrangements for children there to receive an education in nearby schools. Families live in limbo, however, awaiting news of their claims, and those considered 'illegal' or whose claims have been rejected are periodically visited by the police and removed to closed centres until they are deported.[64]

2.5 'Departure and closed expulsion centres'

On 16 February 2004, the Dutch government passed a law to deport over the following three years 26,000 asylum seekers whose claims had been rejected. It also proposed to build departure and expulsion centres to hold those to be deported.[65] This represents a shift in policy, as rejected applicants were not normally forcibly removed in the past, and thus often remained illegally.[66] Critics have referred to this process as creating an 'expulsion factory'.[67] Failed asylum seekers would initially be sent to open departure centres, but if their deportation could not be arranged within a certain time (due to their home countries being unable or unwilling to provide travel documents, for example) then they would be sent to closed expulsion centres.[68] Finally, in cases where people could not be deported within the allowable time limit set, they would then be released and effectively made homeless, as they would be without status or the right to claim social services and housing.[69] The law has been criticised by international organisations like Human Rights Watch for violating international refugee law and has been met with mass protests and hunger strikes; one Iranian asylum seeker even sewed his eyes and mouth shut as a statement of protest.[70]

Detention centres represent a continuum of holding spaces for asylum claimants where the logic is initially one of protection and welcoming by the state. It then shifts to one of transition, where claimants' lives are put on hold in accommodation centres that 'accommodate' refugees by providing basic services all in one spot as they wait for a decision to be rendered on their status. Finally, at the other end of the continuum are the removal and expulsion centres, where the logic is one of incarceration with the state now seeking to punish the 'bad' failed claimants, no longer deserving state protection and human rights.

Detention centres reveal that if the creation of abject spaces is justified through a logic of human rights, that is, to give rights to asylum seekers by granting them protection, then the flip side of this logic is to withdraw these rights through removal and expulsion centres. In both situations, however, these centres are supposed to be temporary spaces of detention designed to facilitate the transition of status of asylum seekers into one of either integration into the larger host society and city life or one of expediting their removal. Yet the very fact that many asylum claimants are held for extended periods of time, and that the centres are capable as a result of providing all of amenities and social services necessary for day-to-day living, belies a different reality. Such 'accommodation' speaks more to the permanent character of such detention centres as alternative city spaces in which asylum claimants increasingly find themselves forced to live.

2.6 Other Abject Spaces within Cities

While refugees living in many cities of the world have been called 'an invisible population' whose needs are often overlooked even under UNHCR programmes, we shall focus here on the plight of refugees in European and American cities.[71] As with detention centres, other abject spaces nestled within cities such as 'informal transit camps' and 'drop houses' essentially 'disappear' failed asylum claimants and 'illegal' migrants into the streets, rendering them invisible, inaudible and, in effect, non-existent. This happens by rendering abjects with an insecure status, turning them out into the streets and then making it difficult for them to access, from their clandestine positions as 'illegals', many of the citizenship rights (such as access to various social services like health care, education and employment) that become available by virtue of being in and of the city.

2.7 Informal transit camps

In Paris, squatter camps have emerged at downtown centres like Alban-Satragne and near the Channel ports. These 'unofficial open-air transit camps' are referred to as 'mini-Sangattes' after the infamous (and now closed) Sangatte detention centre.[72] Young men gather around these sites by day and disperse to nearby building sites to sleep at night.[73] As one refugee aid worker explained:

> There are hundreds of asylum seekers who have been forced to fall back on the Paris region after being told to leave Calais and other ports and are now living rough.[74]

These growing transit camps are, in part, the response of migrants to the crackdown by France and Britain on refugees crossing the Channel to seek asylum in Britain. The asylum seekers find an occasional meal through the Salvation Army, but avoid staying overnight in hostels for fear of police harassment.[75]

In Britain, rejected asylum seekers find themselves in similar situations, suddenly turned out into the streets and left to sleep there, without access to social services. The UK government provides housing to some asylum seekers awaiting claims processing. Once a negative decision has been reached, however, they may find themselves suddenly released without a place to sleep, benefits or even the right to work.[76] In these cases, asylum seekers are turned into literally homeless people without rights.[77] Growing numbers of asylum seekers are rendered 'illegal' by state policies. They find themselves residing in various abject city spaces, living in the city yet not being of the city.

2.8 Drop houses

In the US, private homes leased by *coyotes* are increasingly being turned into 'drop houses', spaces where migrants smuggled into the US can be 'warehoused' while they wait further transportation or for trafficking fees to be paid by relatives. Migrants frequently spend months living in these houses under very poor and cramped living conditions, with very little besides a sleeping bag. There has been a proliferation of drop houses in the last few years, especially in Arizona in the vicinity of Phoenix. In February 2004, twenty-five drop houses holding over 500 people were found in Phoenix. It has been estimated that in early 2001 over 100 drop houses holding some 1,800 people had been discovered by police.[78]

As border controls between Mexico and the US become increasingly policed, migrants turn towards people smugglers to help navigate the dangerous desert crossings. Given this, it is not surprising to see drop houses also on the rise. While drop houses were traditionally found in lower-income and Latino neighbourhoods, they are now also increasingly found in wealthier neighbourhoods as suggested, for example, by the arrests made in a country-club area in northeast Phoenix on 11 February 2004.[79] These types of spaces are essentially abject spaces hidden in residential areas where abjects are held at the mercy of smugglers and state policies that render them illegal.

Again, as with other abject spaces of the city, while drop houses might spring up as temporary living arrangements, the fact is that they have become a more permanent alternative living situation for those who are forced to live clandestine lives. Furthermore, just as in the case of border zones as abject spaces, drop houses exist as part of a larger network of regulatory spaces that are integral to the functioning of what can be seen as a growing global mobility regime, which enables cosmopolitan citizens of the global city greater access to resources while at the same time restricting the access of others to these same rights and resources by forcing them to live lives in hiding.

Like frontiers, zones also restrict the ability of people to enact certain citizenship rights that they might access by making claims on the city, despite not having formal citizenship status and rights. Unlike frontiers, however, which work through the creation of extraterritorial spaces, zones are nestled within cities. What is particular to these spaces and their city locations is that cities are spaces where abjects have been more successfully able to make claims on the city (as compared to the state) by virtue of being able to practise many citizenship rights despite not having formal citizenship status.

Thus the logic of zones is to act as filters in the citizenship-making process, 'weeding out' the 'bad' or illegitimate (i.e. 'illegal') asylum claimants by segregating them in enclosed spaces where their rights and access to social networks can be severely curtailed. Failing deportation, abjects experience a transition to subjecthood in these spaces, from a claimant deserving of being given human rights under the protection of the state, to a criminal with limited rights, to finally being rendered invisible by being made homeless.

3. Camps

Here we illustrate different kinds of camps than those Agamben[80] considered paradigmatic: rather than focusing on camps that reduce subjects to bare life, we consider camps that function as reserves in which subjects and their rights are suspended temporarily, in transition from one subjecthood to another. As examples of other global cities, camps are always established, as Agamben has noted,[81] with the argument that they are exceptional and temporary spaces; but in reality, they become the normal order of things and permanent spaces of transience.[82] As Bülent Diken explains:

> The camp is officially a transitory, so to say, 'exceptional' space, in which the refugee is supposed to spend only a limited amount of time. Yet, everywhere the refugee camp has today become a 'permanent' location and the transient condition of the refugee extends indefinitely, becoming an irrevocable and permanent situation, freezing into non-negotiable, rigid structures'.[83]

Moreover, it is by creating these exceptional abject spaces like the camp that the impending crisis is hidden in a system in which increasingly more and more people are without a state and its protection.

3.1 Refugee camps

One particular example of a camp that has become a permanent feature of life in the twentieth and twenty-first centuries is the refugee camp. The number of people kept in such reservation zones is staggering. As many as thirty-nine million people may now be living in some form of refugee camp, according to Médecins Sans Frontières (MSF).[84] The UNHCR, the international organisation largely responsible for overseeing refugees, notes that approximately twenty million of the world's refugees currently receive its assistance with approximately twelve million living in UNHCR-run camps.[85] The UNHCR operates camps ranging in size from 3,000 to 800,000 people, in approximately 115 countries.[86]

Camps set up along the borders of conflict zones are particularly precarious spaces. As UNHCR spokesperson Joung-Ah Ghedini notes:

> So many borders are porous, and it makes it that much easier for undesirable elements to come in either to hide, to use civilian populations as a human shield, or to recruit soldiers, often forcibly. Camps close to the border are also extremely vulnerable to attack.[87]

For example, in Guinea, those living in border camps set up to deal with the influx of refugees from Sierra Leone and Liberia in 2000–01 found themselves under attack, their camps burned down and refugees killed and abducted by rebels from the Revolutionary United Front of Sierra Leone and by Liberian forces.[88] In Afghanistan, in response to an estimated four million out of a population of twenty-seven million turned refugees, camps were set up along the Iran-Afghanistan border but inside Afghanistan. These camps included the Mile 46 camp in the Northern Alliance-run area that held 1,000 displaced Afghans, the Makai camp in the Taliban area that held another 6,000 and the Spin Boldak camp near the Pakistan border, where 3,000 displaced Afghans resided.[89] Because these camps were set up in a war zone, relief agencies had limited access, and workers and civilians were placed in precarious situations. Some 150,000 refugees ended up crossing through the mountains into Pakistan, often paying large smuggling fees.[90]

In contrast to these more temporary camps, more than half of Palestinians today are registered as refugees under the responsibility of the UN Relief and Works Agency for Palestine Refugees in the Near East (UNRWA); many live in UNRWA-run refugee camps. Although UNRWA was established in 1949 after the first Arab-Israeli conflict as a temporary organisation, after decades of war the refugee life has now become permanent for many Palestinian refugees, with UNRWA providing basic services ranging from education and vocational training to health and sanitation services.

While some two-thirds of the registered refugees 'live in and around the cities and towns of the host countries, and in the West Bank and Gaza Strip, often in the environs of official camps', a third of registered Palestinian refugees (1.3 million) live in fifty-nine recognised refugee camps in Jordan, Lebanon, Syria, the West Bank and the Gaza Strip.[91] UNRWA figures for 2003 indicate that there are ten camps in Jordan with some 307,785 registered refugees; twelve camps in Lebanon with 223,956 registered refugees; ten camps in Syria with 120,865 refugees; nineteen camps in the West Bank with 179,541 refugees; and, in the Gaza Strip, eight camps holding 484,563 registered refugees.[92]

As UNRWA notes, camp land is usually leased such that refugees cannot 'own' land but rather only have the right to 'use' it. Moreover, '[s]ocio-economic conditions in the camps are generally poor with a high population density, cramped living conditions and inadequate basic infrastructure such as roads and sewers'.[93] In contrast to the more makeshift camps set up in response to the recent conflict in Afghanistan, these Palestinian refugee camps show how camps set up during times of war as temporary solutions can evolve into permanent settlements, with these camps now being permanent homes to many Palestinian refugees.

Yet even in the case of more temporary camps, refugee camps routinely display various facets of daily living required for longer-term settlement similar to those that exist in city spaces. For example, MSF notes that in creating camp spaces 'short-term site planning should be avoided, as so-called temporary camps may well have to remain much longer than expected (e.g. some Palestinian refugee camps have been in existence since 1947).'[94] As part of this longer-term planning, MSF emphasises that, in establishing a camp, site planning is crucial and 'must ensure the most rational organisation of space, shelters and the facilities required for the provision of essential goods and services'.[95] Such goods and services include the provision of food and water, sanitation and latrines, health and clinical services. Other factors in creating camp space include security and protection, environmental conditions, readily available energy sources and accessibility (for trucks, for example).

In an in-depth profile by the Canadian Broadcasting Corporation (CBC) titled 'Anatomy of a Refugee Camp', the resemblance of refugee camps to city spaces becomes even more apparent; the CBC website provides a navigable Flash version of the elements that make up a camp, including various characteristics in common with cities like a vehicle entrance, reception centre, food storage warehouse and food distribution point, feeding centre, health centre, hospital, meeting place, school, market and cemetery.[96] The very ability to outline this anatomy of a camp reveals a similar rationality to city planning, with the Flash presentation also indicative of the increasing normalcy with which the refugee camp is regarded as a permanent feature of alternative living arrangements for millions of people in the twenty-first century.

3.2 Detention Camps

A - Australia's Woomera camp

Perhaps one of the more infamous examples of abject camp spaces is that of the Woomera detention camp. As part of the Australian government's 1994 policy of mandatory detention of asylum seekers, the country opened several large-scale detention centres run by the Australian Correctional Management company, a subsidiary of the private US prison company Wackenhut Corrections Corporation. One of the better-known centres was the desert asylum camp, Woomera Detention Centre in the South Australian outback, which ran from 1999 until its closure in April 2003. Built to hold only around 400 people, at some point Woomera held as many as 1,400 asylum seekers,[97] with many detainees being held for over a year and some for as many as three years.[98]

The UN severely criticised camp conditions, and an Australian parliamentary committee in 2001 declared it the worst of the country's seven detention centres.[99] Conditions in the camp were so desperate that 370 asylum seekers went on hunger strikes, with forty of them stitching closed their lips while others cut themselves or attempted suicide by throwing themselves onto the barbed wire surrounding the camp or by swallowing shampoo and sleeping pills.[100] One Iraqi man described how they were only identified in the camp by number, exclaiming:

> I came here with nothing. Now I am taking four tablets, one of them for depression. I am a civil engineer and I don't know where all the information has gone from my mind. They are dealing with us as animals, not as human beings.[101]

Camps like Woomera hold asylum seekers in extremely inhospitable conditions, with the idea of turning refugee claimants into abjects unable to properly access the rights that should be theirs by virtue of being a refugee.

In a 2002 report called 'By Invitation Only', Human Rights Watch criticised the use of 'remote, desert locations' for several of the centres like Woomera, because the isolated location was used as a way of hindering access to lawyers, family and community support networks that would be more easily accessed were the asylum seekers to be housed in city centres rather than the desert.[102] Human Rights Watch also criticised the 'prison-like' conditions of Woomera and other centres like it. A description of a similar facility still in operation, Baxter Immigration Detention Facility in Port Augusta, was described as having 'a 1,200-volt outer electric fence';

'movement detectors between the fences'; 'a perimeter fence and steel gates'; and 'no windows, so detainees can only see the sky from the central courtyard'.[103] In addition, the report observes that detainees 'are locked in their rooms every night from 9:00 PM to 8:00 AM'.[104]

These prison-like conditions reveal that, like border zones, detention camps are often extremely militarised and heavily policed spaces, sending the message that asylum seekers are like criminals and should be treated as such – or worse. In detention camps like Woomera, refugee claimants are not even considered deserving of the rights afforded to criminals, as the point of creating alternative detention facilities in remote locations is precisely to prevent asylum claimants from accessing many of the rights, like legal counsel, that would be made readily available to criminals.

B - France's Sangatte camp

France's Sangatte asylum camp near the port of Calais was opened in 1999, in a warehouse that was used during the Eurotunnel construction, and turned over to the French Red Cross. Sangatte was opened as an emergency camp to house growing numbers of asylum seekers found sleeping on the streets in Calais before trying to cross to Britain through the Channel to seek asylum.[105] The camp was designed to hold around 800 people, but often held between 1,300 and 1,900 people. As with Woomera, such abject spaces often generate overcrowded conditions with minimal facilities.

As many as 67,000 asylum seekers passed through Sangatte before the French government closed it in December 2002[106], after receiving significant pressure from the UK government, which saw the camp as a base for illegal immigration into the UK. Critics have noted, however, that closing the camp simply forced people back onto the streets. Sangatte, in other words, is part of a larger problem of the disparity between how countries in the EU provide protection to refugees and of the type of living situation that results as increasing numbers of people find themselves living in a state of 'temporary permanence' that is becoming a prevalent feature of the global system.[107]

3.3 The other Dubai: desert labour camps

Dubai, in the UAE, is one of the fastest-growing cities in the region and has recently become one of the top tourist destinations, with some 700,000 British tourists visiting annually and other foreigners now investing in real estate there.[108] In keeping with its new status as a globalising city, Dubai is also fast becoming home to the largest hotels and shopping malls.[109] Yet its emerging status as a global city is dependent upon another type of global city – that of desert labour camps where migrants provide some 90 per cent of the private workforce and necessary cheap labour for Dubai's construction boom.[110] As critics like Human Rights Watch note: 'One of the world's largest construction booms is feeding off of workers in Dubai, but they are treated as less than human.'[111]

Conditions in these camps are harsh, with labourers 'crammed into tiny pre-fabricated huts, twelve men to a room, forced to wash themselves in filthy brown water and cook in kitchens next to overflowing toilets'.[112] Working conditions are also extremely poor, with workers denied basic human rights such as the right to voice their opinions, freedom of association and the right to unionise; they are forced to work long hours (sometimes as much as seventy hours a week, seven days a week) at very low pay.[113]

Moreover, workers often come to the UAE by taking a loan from recruiting agencies in their home countries, but then find themselves in a condition of 'virtual debt bondage', constantly needing to work in order to repay the loan.[114] Also commonly reported is the fact that employers often withhold wages. Some 20,000 workers filed complaints with the UAE government in 2005 alone.[115] Under such abject conditions, many migrants are now engaging in various forms of resistance, including filing complaints to government officials; frequent 'illegal' strikes; unionising; and holding protests. In April 2006, one of Dubai's largest protests took place at the construction site for the Burj Dubai Tower (the world's tallest building, to be completed by 2008), involving some 2,500 workers. Causing over one million US dollars in damages as a result of their protest, workers raised awareness about their poor working conditions and even generated sympathy strikes, such as the one that took place at the same time by workers at Dubai's international airport.[116]

Labour camps like Dubai's desert camps are other forms of abject spaces where abjects find themselves in what was originally supposed to be a temporary living arrangement for temporary work in order to be able to send some money to their families back home. These camps, however, have become permanent transient spaces for many as they find themselves working for years under these conditions in order to pay back their debt and make enough money for their families. The labour camps highlight the fact of other global cities, abject spaces in which to maintain reserves of cheap labour needed for globalising cities like Dubai that cater to 'other' cosmopolitan citizens like tourists and investors from wealthier countries in the North.

3.4 Guantánamo Bay

We could not end this chapter without briefly discussing that most infamous, if not paradigmatic, abject space – Guantánamo Bay. Since 2002, this US naval base leased from Cuba has been used for military detention camps like Camp X-Ray, Camp Delta and Camp Echo, which imprison suspected al-Qaʻida and Taliban 'terrorists'. The US government claims that those being held are beyond US law and the constitutional rights they would be afforded as prisoners on US soil.

Guantánamo is currently holding some 650 foreign nationals from over forty different countries, many arrested in Afghanistan in 2002. These men (and some children) are being held without charge or trial, denied the right to legal counsel and subject to degrading and cruel conditions like solitary confinement and intensive interrogation without the presence of a lawyer.[117] In an autobiographical account of his ordeal being falsely detained as an 'enemy combatant', Moazzam Begg describes being kept in virtual isolation in an 8 ft by 6 ft steel cage with mesh sides and steel roof, floor, bed and toilet, only to be let out twice a week for 'shower and rec', meaning a fifteen-minute walk around a caged-in yard.[118]

Yet, at the same time he describes his abjection, Begg also reveals how a certain normalcy consisting of daily routines becomes necessary even amidst such abject conditions of the camp. He describes, for example, how his daily conversations (and even occasional sharing of poetry) with his guards, along with daily prayer, the reading of 'brain-numbing suspense novels [and] courtroom dramas' and frequent letter-writing were all part of his fight against 'the dreary monotony of daily existence'.[119]

Like Begg, most of the men there have also not been charged. Yet the US refuses to clarify the legal status of these inmates, referring to them only as 'enemy combatants' – a designation that, as Amnesty International notes, 'has been used to justify detention without any recourse to the courts, on the decision of the executive, for an apparently indefinite period'.[120] The US has refused to grant the detainees prisoner-of-war status as required under Article Four of the Third Geneva Convention, nor clarify their legal status in front of a tribune as they are obligated to do under Article Five.[121]

Failing to clarify their status, the US is trying these men by military commissions. Amnesty International has argued, however, that these commissions 'do not meet international standards for a fair trial' as they are 'not independent and impartial courts', 'curtail the right of appeal' and 'allow a lower standard of evidence than ordinary civilian courts in the USA'.[122] Moreover, the military commissions are capable of handing down the death sentence. Given the lack of legal rights and due legal process, a few countries such as the UK, Denmark and Spain have negotiated for the rights of their nationals to be repatriated to their respective countries for trial. However, in some cases, repatriation might not be an option, as it would put individuals at risk of torture and execution in the cases of China, Yemen, Saudi Arabia and Russia.[123]

As in other cases of abject detention, detainees have continued to resist their conditions. On 20 April 2004, the US Supreme Court heard *Rasul v. Bush*, a case brought forth by the Centre for Constitutional Rights on behalf of detainees at Guantánamo Bay. The case was based on the principle of *habeas corpus*, or the idea that no one may be imprisoned without clear basis in the law.[124] The case argued that Guantánamo detainees have the right to know the charges against them, and to a fair trial to defend themselves against those charges.[125] In June 2004, the US Supreme Court ruled in favour of the detainees that Guantánamo falls under US civilian court jurisdiction, and as such detainees now have the right to challenge the lawfulness of their detention in a US court of law.

In sum, camps function as reservations where the rights of people can be suspended as a first step towards stripping away their status as political subjects in order to render them abjects. In contrast with both frontiers and zones, camps intervene in the process of rights-making especially by revoking status, that is, by changing the political subjecthood of people rather than focusing on ways to hinder the practice of claims-making (although this too is obviously restricted in such spaces).

The logic of refugee camps is one of giving human rights and protection to those who have lost their rights. Yet, this logic condemns refugees to living in various degrees of impermanence, in inhospitable conditions. Camps halt the subjectivisation of refugees as a political identity with certain rights attached to it (like the right to protection and resettlement), by transforming this group's status to one of not-quite-refugees or refugees-in-waiting. Similarly, detention camps like Guantánamo are used to remove individuals from their political communities into holding areas, where they are kept in legal limbo without recourse to appeal either as citizens or on the grounds of human rights, except in exceptional circumstances where their own countries intervene on their behalf.

Despite the different types and functions of camps, their numbers continue to grow as ever more people find themselves living for extended periods from months to years in these abject spaces, which now act as substitutes to state and city spaces – as other global city spaces.

4 Conclusion

We have wanted to illustrate the kinds of politics and the kinds of new political subjects that are emerging in these other global cities that condemn humans to non-existent states of 'transient permanency' in which they are made inaudible and invisible.[126] Yet abject spaces also expose and render visible and audible various strategies and technologies of otherness that attempt to produce such states of non-existence.

The exposure of this logic by abjects becomes a significant act of resistance. For example, various initiatives are currently being undertaken to make global cities more hospitable to non-status peoples. These include 'don't ask don't tell' campaigns that forbid city workers to ask about a person's status or reveal it to government officials, to ensure that all residents of the city, regardless of status, are able to access essential services without fear of arrest and/or deportation.[127] Residents of these other global cities now include more than 10.4 million refugees, one million asylum seekers, nine million stateless peoples and twenty to twenty-five million internally displaced people worldwide.

As we have shown, the increasing number and novelty of frontiers, zones and camps as abject spaces certainly suggests that it may be time to investigate global cities from the vantage point of the abject as more appropriately offering a much more complex picture than we have so far recognised. Many such spaces come into existence as temporary holding spaces for those whose status is also supposed to be temporary, yet acquire permanent characteristics that for all intents and purposes make them function as cities: agglomerations with associations, sociability and differentiation. The inability or unwillingness to recognise these spaces condemns those caught in them to an abject status that can be described as 'transient citizens' – transient because temporary, citizen because permanent.[128] We are witnessing the emergence of a patchwork of overlapping spaces nestled within each other, of greater and lesser degrees of rights and rightlessness, abject spaces and spaces of citizenship.

We would like to thank Heiko Wimmen for his immense work and very helpful comments on this chapter. We would also like to thank Elizabeth Dauphinee and Cristina Masters, as well as Peter Nyers, Simon Dalby, William Walters, Agnes Czajka and an anonymous reader for their extremely useful critical comments on the original paper from which this chapter was developed. Finally, we would like to thank Agnes Czajka for sharing with us her insights on the 'transient citizen'.

Bibliography

Agence France-Presse, 'Now Abandoned French Refugee Centre to Formally Close,' 27 December 2002.

Agamben, Giorgio, *Homo Sacer: Sovereign Power and Bare Life*, Stanford, CA: Stanford University Press, 1998.

—— *Means without End: Notes on Politics*, Minneapolis: University of Minnesota Press, 2000.

Amnesty International, 'Australia: Asylum-Seekers – Where to Now?', 5 December 2001.

—— 'Australia-Pacific: Offending Human Dignity – the Pacific Solution' [AI Index: ASA 12/009/2002], 26 August 2002.

—— 'Crossing the Line: Human Rights Abuses on the US-Mexico Border'; see www.amnesty.ca/usa/border.php.

—— 'Guantánamo Bay: A Human Rights Scandal', 2004; see http://web. amnesty.org/web/web.nsf/print/guantanamobay-index-eng.

—— 'Mexico: Intolerable Killings. Ten Years of Abductions and Murders in Ciudad Juárez and Chihuahua' [AI Index: AMR 41/027/2003], New York, 2003.

—— 'Strengthening Fortress Europe in Times of War', commentary on UK proposals for external processing and responsibility-sharing arrangements with third countries, JHA Informal Council, Veria 28–9 March 2003, Brussels: Amnesty International EU.

—— 'UK: Britain's Refugee "Regional Protection Zones" Proposals Deeply Flawed', 27 March, 2003; see www.amnesty.org.uk/news_details. asp?NewsID=14427.

—— 'UK/EU/UNHCR Unlawful and Unworkable – Extra-Territorial Processing of Asylum Claims', London: Amnesty International Secretariat [AI Index IOR 61/004/2003], 18 June 2002, pp. 1–38.

—— 'United States of America: Amnesty International's Concerns Regarding the Post 11 September Investigations in the United States' [AI Index: AMR 51/044/2002], 14 March, 2002.

—— 'United States of America: Beyond the Law: Update to Amnesty International's April Memorandum to the US Government on the Rights of the Detainees Held in US Custody in Guantánamo Bay and Other Locations', 13 December 2002.

Arendt, Hannah, *The Origins of Totalitarianism*, New York: Harcourt Brace Jovanovich, 1951.

Asthana, Anushka, 'Living in fear: my week with the hidden asylum seekers', *The Observer*, 28 March, 2004.

Asylum Rights Campaign EU Working Group, 'Sangatte', September 2002; see http://www.refugeecouncil.org.uk/policy/responses/2002/asylum_rights.htm.

Barkham, P., 'No waltzing in Woomera', *The Guardian*, 25 May 2002; see www.guardian.co.uk/australia/story/0,,727855,00.html.

British Broadcasting Corporation (BBC), 'Anger At "Asylum Hotel" Meeting', *BBC News*, 14 February 2003; see http://news.bbc.co.uk/1/hi/england/2760585.stm.

——'Asylum Hotel Scheme May Be Dropped', *BBC News*, 20 January 2003; see http://news.bbc.co.uk/1/hi/england/2675443.stm.

——'Australia's Offshore Camps Are "Hellish"', *BBC News*, 6 December 2001; see http://news.bbc.co.uk/1/hi/world/asia-pacific/1695930.stm.

——'Australia Shuts Asylum Camp', *BBC News*, 17 April 2003; see http://news.bbc.co.uk/go/pr/fr/-/1/hi/world/asia-pacific/2955953.stm.

——'EU Split Over Migrant Camp Plan', *BBC News*; see http://news.bbc.co.uk/2/hi/europe/3750420.stm, 18 October 2004.

——'Politicians Unite Against "Asylum Hotel"', *BBC News*, 19 February 2003; see http://news.bbc.co.uk/go/pr/fr/-/1/hi/england/2779289.stm.

——'Sinking Island Urged to Accept Migrants', *BBC News*, 13 November 2001; see http://news.bbc.co.uk/1/hi/world/asia-pacific/1653472.stm.

Australian Government, Department of Immigration and Multicultural and Indigenous Affairs, 'Fact Sheet 76: Offshore Processing Arrangements', 2005; see www.immi.gov.au/media/fact-sheets/76offshore.htm.

——'Fact Sheet 81: Australia's Excised Offshore Places', 2006; see www.immi.gov.au/media/fact-sheets/81excised.htm, 2006.

Begg, Moazzam, and Brittain, Victoria, *Enemy Combatant: A British Muslim's Journey to Guantanamo and Back,* London: Free Press, 2006.

Biemann, Ursula, 'Performing the Border', in *Been There and Back to Nowhere: Gender in Transnational Spaces*, Ursula Biemann, ed., Berlin: b.books and New York: Autonomedia, 2000.

Black, I., 'Dutch pass law to expel failed asylum seekers', *The Guardian*, 18 February 2004; see www.guardian.co.uk/international/story/0,3604,1150370,00.html.

Bowcott, O., 'UK: asylum processing centre plan abandoned', *The Guardian*, 4 February 2004; see http://politics.guardian.co.uk/homeaffairs/story/0,11026,1140540,00.html.

Cable News Network (CNN), 'UNHCR Attacks Australian Immigration Policy', 1 February 2002; see http://archives.cnn.com/2002/WORLD/europe/02/01/unhcr.australia/?related.

Canadian Broadcasting Corporation (CBC), 'Anatomy of a Refugee Camp', *CBC News*, 2 April 2003; see www.cbc.ca/news/background/refugeecamp/.

Casciani, D., 'Dungavel: Target of Asylum Campaign', *BBC News*, 5 September 2003; see http://news.bbc.co.uk/1/hi/uk/3082164.stm.

Centre for Constitutional Rights, 'Optimistic on Guantánamo After Vigorous

Supreme Court Argument', 20 April 2004; see www.ccr-ny.org/v2/reports/report.asp?ObjID=rg1zf8P8It&Content=350.

Czajka, Agnes, 'Transient Citizens: The Paradox of Permanent Refugees', unpublished paper, presented at the conference 'Mediating Acts of Citizenship', Montreal: Concordia University, 12–14 October 2005.

Denber, Rachel, 'Netherlands: Safety of Failed Asylum Seekers At Risk', letter to the Dutch Minister for Integration and Immigration by the Acting Executive Director, Europe and Central Asia Division, Human Rights Watch, 2004.

Diken, Bülent, 'From Refugee Camps to Gated Communities: Biopolitics and the End of the City', *Citizenship Studies*, vol. 8, no. 1, 2004, pp. 83–106.

Gibson, Sarah, 'Accommodating Strangers: British Hospitality and the Asylum Hotel Debate', *Journal for Cultural Research*, vol. 7, no. 4, 2003, pp. 367–86.

González, D., 'Feds Aid Drop-House Crackdowns', *The Arizona Republic*, 4 March 2004; see www.azcentral.com/specials/special03/articles/0304drophouses04.html.

Government of the United Kingdom – Cabinet Office and Home Office, 'A New Vision for Refugees', 2003, pp. 1–31, London; see www.proasyl.info/texte/europe/union/2003/UK_NewVision.pdf.

Government of the United Kingdom – Home Office, 'Accommodation Centres for Asylum Seekers – Your Questions Answered', 6 April 2004.

Government of the United Kingdom – Home Office, 'Bicester Accommodation Centre Gets the Green Light', 6 April 2004.

——'Home Secretary's Statement on Zones of Protection, 29 March 2003; see www.asylumaid.org.uk/Press%20statements/home_secretary_statement_on_zone.htm.

Human Rights Watch, '"By Invitation Only": Australian Asylum Policy, New York, December 2002.

—— 'Hidden in Plain View: Refugees Living Without Protection in Nairobi and Kampala', New York, 2002; see www.hrw.org/reports/2002/kenyugan/kenyugan.pdf.

—— 'Not for Export: Why the International Community Should Reject Australia's Refugee Policies', New York, 2002; see www.hrw.org/press/2002/09/ausbrfo926.htm.

—— 'Refugees, Asylum Seekers, Migrants and Internally Displaced Persons', New York, 2006; see www.hrw.org/campaigns/race/refugeepresskit.html.

—— 'Special Issues and Campaigns: Refugees, Asylum Seekers, Migrants and Internally Displaced Persons', in *World Report 2002*, New York, 2002; see www.hrw.org/wr2k2/.

—— 'UAE: Address Abuse of Migrant Workers: No Free Trade Pacts without Reform', New York, 30 March 2006; see http://hrw.org/english/docs/2006/03/28/uae13090.htm.

——*World Report 2002: Special Issues and Campaigns: Refugees, Asylum Seekers, Migrants and Internally Displaced Persons*, New York, 2002.

——*World Report 2003*, New York, 2003.

International Organization for Migration, 'Counter-Trafficking'; see www.iom. int.vn/iom_counter_trafficking.html.

Jesuit Refugee Services, 'Detention in Europe', in *JRS-Europe Observation and Position Paper*, pp. 1–17; see www.migreurop.org/IMG/pdf/jrs-detention2004.pdf#search=%22JRS-Europe%20Observation%20and%20 Position%20Paper%222004.

Latin America Working Group, 'Fencing off America', Washington, DC, 2004; see www.lawg.org/countries/Mexico/mexfence.htm.

Light, J., '*La Linea*: Gender, Labour and Environmental Justice on the US-Mexico Border', in *CorpWatch*, 30 June 1999; see www.corpwatch.org/article. php?id=690.

Lubbers, Ruud, 'Statement to the Third Committee of the General Assembly', 7 November 2002; see www.unhcr.org/cgi-bin/texis/vtx/admin/opendoc. htm?tbl=ADMIN&id=3dcf8e0f4.

Martinez, R. L., 'Immigration, Migration, and Human Rights on the US/Mexico Border', *Motion Magazine*, 28 August 2001; see www.inmotionmagazine. com/rmcol1.html.

——'US Border Patrol in Southern California Developing Deadly But Ineffective Operation Gatekeeper: Interview With Roberto Martinez', *Motion Magazine*, 12 December 1999; see www.inmotionmagazine.com/ rm99.html.

Mayell, H., 'World Refugees Number 35 Million', *National Geographic*, 16 June 2003; see http://news.nationalgeographic.com/news/2003/06/ 0616_030616_refugee1.html.

McDougall, D., 'Tourists become targets as Dubai's workers take revolt to the beaches', *The Observer*, 9 April 2006; see http://observer.guardian.co.uk/ world/story/0,,1750003,00.html.

McGuirk, R. 'Australia to send asylum seekers to camps', *The Guardian*, 13 April 2006.

Migration Policy Institute, 'US In Focus: The US-Mexico Border', 1 June, 2006; see www.migrationinformation.org/Feature/display.cfm?ID=32.

Médecins Sans Frontières, 'Visit a Refugee Camp'; see www.msf.ca/ refugeecamp/.

Nathan, Debbie, 'The Juárez Murders: Sexism, Corporate Greed, and Drug Trafficking Make Juarez a Deadly Town for Mexico's Women. Hundreds Are Dead, but the Killers Remain Free', *Amnesty Magazine*, spring 2003; see www.amnestyusa.org/amnestynow/juarez.html.

Newell, A., 'Drop House Not Likely a Trend, Officials Say', *The Arizona Daily Star*, 3 March 2004.

Nyers, Peter, 'Abject Cosmopolitanism: The Politics of Protection in the Anti-Deportation Movement', *Third World Quarterly*, vol. 24, no. 6, 2003, pp. 1069–93.

Pritchard, L. G., 'The INS Issues Detention Standards Governing the Treatment of Detained Immigrants and Asylum Seekers', *Immigration Daily*, 2001; see www.ilw.com/lawyers/articles/2001,0403-Pritchard.shtm.

Roxburgh, A., 'Belgium's Asylum "Lottery"', *BBC News*, 27 October 2003; see http://news.bbc.co.uk/1/hi/world/europe/3208539.stm.

Scott, Allen John, ed., *Global City-Regions: Trends, Theory, Policy*, Oxford: Oxford University Press, 2001.

Travis, A., 'Shifting a problem back to its source: Would-be refugees may be sent to protected zones near homeland', *The Guardian*, 5 February 2003; see http://www.guardian.co.uk/uk_news/story/0,3604,888990,00.html.

'Dungavel Alternative is Turned Down', *The Sunday Herald*, 22 March 2004.

UN Relief and Works Agency for Palestinian Refugees, 'Refugee Camp Profiles'; see www.un.org/unrwa/refugees/camp-profiles.html.

——'Where Do the Refugees Live?'; see www.un.org/unrwa/refugees/wheredo. html.

US Citizenship and Immigration Services, 'Fact Sheet: Operation Gatekeeper: New Resources, Enhanced Results'; see www.rapidimmigration.com/www/ news/news_70.html, 1998.

US Committee for Refugees and Immigrants, 'Country Report: United Kingdom', *World Refugee Survey*, 2003, pp. 231–5; see www.refugees.org/ data/wrs/03/country_reports/EU5SpainToYugoslavia.pdf.

Webster, P., 'Would-be refugees make a mini-Sangatte in the heart of Paris', *The Guardian*, 29 April 2003; see www.guardian.co.uk/international/ story/0,3604,945470,00.html.

Willis, Paul, 'UK: Asylum Seekers Face Life on Leeds Streets', *Yorkshire Evening Post*, 2 March 2004.

Worldstream (Associated Press), 'Tough Dutch Measures Bring a New Dimension to Europe's Clampdown on Immigration', 25 March 2004.

Notes

1. This chapter builds upon another chapter we published as 'Abject Spaces: Frontiers, Zones, Camps', in Elizabeth Dauphinee and Cristina Masters, eds, *Living, Dying, Surviving: The Logics of Biopower and the War on Terror*, Houndmills, Basingstoke, Hampshire: Palgrave, 2006. There we developed the concept of 'abject spaces' with reference to a body of work that emerged in relation to Hannah Arendt's critique of human rights. Here we employ the concept to reflect upon these spaces as 'other global cities' and expand on various such spaces as border zones, drop houses, labour camps in Dubai and refugee camps, and with other examples such as the Woomera camp in Australia and the Sangatte camp in France.
2. Scott, *Global City-Regions*.
3. Diken, 'From Refugee Camps to Gated Communities', pp. 93–4.
4. Home Office, UK, 'Home Secretary's Statement on Zones of Protection'.

5. BBC News, 'EU Split over Migrant Camp Plan'.
6. Cabinet Office and Home Office (UK), 'A New Vision for Refugees'.
7. Ibid.
8. Amnesty International, 'Britain's Refugee "Regional Protection" Zones Proposals Deeply Flawed'.
9. Cabinet Office and Home Office (UK), 'A New Vision for Refugees', p. 14.
10. Ibid., p. 26.
11. Ibid., p. 12.
12. Amnesty International, 'Strengthening Fortress Europe in Times of War'.
13. Amnesty International, 'UK/EU/UNHCR Unlawful and Unworkable – Extra-Territorial Processing of Asylum Claims'.
14. Travis, 'Shifting a problem back to its source: would-be refugees may be sent to protected zones near homeland'.
15. Amnesty International, 'Strengthening Fortress Europe in Times of War'.
16. Department of Immigration and Multicultural and Indigenous Affairs (Australia), 'Fact Sheet 81: Australia's Excised Offshore Places'.
17. Human Rights Watch, 'Not for Export: Why the International Community Should Reject Australia's Refugee Policies', p. 4.
18. Ibid.
19. Department of Immigration and Multicultural and Indigenous Affairs (Australia), 'Fact Sheet 76: Offshore Processing Arrangements'.
20. Ibid.
21. Amnesty International, 'Australia-Pacific: Offending Human Dignity – the Pacific Solution', p. 5.
22. BBC News, 'Sinking Island Urged to Accept Migrants'.
23. BBC News, 'Australia's Offshore Camps Are "Hellish"'.
24. Amnesty International, 'Australia: Asylum-Seekers – Where to Now?'
25. Human Rights Watch, 'Special Issues and Campaigns: Refugees, Asylum Seekers, Migrants and Internally Displaced Persons', pp. 16–17.
26. McGuirk, 'Australia to send asylum seekers to camps'.
27. Department of Immigration and Multicultural and Indigenous Affairs (Australia), 'Fact Sheet 81: Australia's Excised Offshore Places'.
28. International Organization for Migration, 'Counter-Trafficking'.
29. Amnesty International, 'Crossing the Line: Human Rights Abuses on the US-Mexico Border'.
30. Martinez, 'Immigration, Migration, and Human Rights on the US/Mexico Border'.
31. Ibid.
32. Ibid.
33. Martinez, 'US Border Patrol in Southern California Developing Deadly but Ineffective Operation Gatekeeper'.
34. Ibid.
35. Ibid.
36. Latin America Working Group, 'Fencing Off America'.
37. USCIS, 'Fact Sheet: Operation Gatekeeper: New Resources, Enhanced Results'.
38. Migration Policy Institute, 'US in Focus: the US-Mexico Border'.
39. Ibid.
40. Ibid.
41. Ibid.
42. Light, '*La Linea*: Gender, Labour and Environmental Justice on the US-Mexico Border'.

43. Biemann, 'Performing the Border'; Amnesty International, 'Mexico: Intolerable Killings. Ten Years of Abductions and Murders in Ciudad Juarez and Chihuahua'.

44. Nathan, 'The Juarez Murders'.

45. Ibid.

46. Lubbers, 'Statement to the Third Committee of the General Assembly'.

47. Pritchard, 'The INS Issues Detention Standards Governing the Treatment of Detained Immigrants and Asylum Seekers'.

48. Ibid.

49. Human Rights Watch, 'Refugees, Asylum Seekers, Migrants and Internally Displaced Persons'.

50. Jesuit Refugee Services, 'Detention in Europe'.

51. USCRI, 'Country Report: United Kingdom', pp. 1–6.

52. BBC News, 'Asylum Hotel Scheme May be Dropped'; 'Anger At "Asylum Hotel" Meeting'; and 'Politicians Unite Against "Asylum Hotel"'; Gibson, 'Accommodating Strangers'.

53. Home Office (UK), 'Bicester Accommodation Centre Gets the Green Light'.

54. Home Office (UK), 'Accommodation Centres for Asylum Seekers – Your Questions Answered'.

55. Ibid.

56. Arendt, *The Origins of Totalitarianism*, p. 296.

57. Bowcott, 'UK: asylum processing centre plan abandoned'.

58. Casciani, 'Dungavel: Target of Asylum Campaign'.

59. *The Sunday Herald*, 'UK: Dungavel Alternative is Turned Down'.

60. Casciani, 'Dungavel: Target of Asylum Campaign'.

61. Ibid.

62. Ibid.

63. Roxburgh, 'Belgium's Asylum "Lottery"'.

64. Ibid.

65. Worldstream (Associated Press), 'Tough Dutch Measures Bring a New Dimension to Europe's Clampdown on Immigration'.

66. Ibid.

67. Ibid.

68. Denber, 'Netherlands: Safety of Failed Asylum Seekers at Risk'.

69. Ibid.

70. Black, 'Dutch pass law to expel failed asylum seekers'.

71. Human Rights Watch, *Human Rights Watch World Report 2003*, p. 526.

72. Webster, 'Would-be refugees make a mini-Sangatte in the heart of Paris'.

73. Ibid.

74. Ibid.

75. Ibid.

76. Asthana, 'Living in fear'.

77. Willis, 'UK: Asylum Seekers Face Life on Leeds Streets'.

78. Newell, 'Drop House Not Likely a Trend, Officials Say'.

79. González, 'Feds Aid Drop-House Crackdowns'.

80. Agamben, *Homo Sacer* and *Means without End*.

81. Agamben, *Homo Sacer*.

82. Diken, 'From Refugee Camps to Gated Communities', pp. 93–4.

83. Ibid., p. 93.

84. Médecins Sans Frontières, 'Visit a Refugee Camp'.

85. Mayell, 'World Refugees Number 35 Million'.

86. Ibid.

87. Ibid.
88. Human Rights Watch, *World Report 2002*, p. 11.
89. Ibid., p. 4.
90. Ibid., p. 5.
91. UNWRA, 'Where Do the Refugees Live?'.
92. UNRWA, 'Refugee Camp Profiles'.
93. UNWRA, 'Where Do the Refugees Live?'
94. Médecins Sans Frontières, 'Visit a Refugee Camp'.
95. Ibid.
96. CBC News, 'Anatomy of a Refugee Camp'.
97. BBC News, 'Australia Shuts Asylum Camp'.
98. CNN, 'UNHCR Attacks Australian Immigration Policy'.
99. BBC News, 'Australia Shuts Asylum Camp'.
100. Barkham, 'No waltzing in Woomera'.
101. Ibid.
102. Human Rights Watch, 'By Invitation Only: Australian Asylum Policy'.
103. Ibid.
104. Ibid.
105. Asylum Rights Campaign, EU Working Group, 'Sangatte'.
106. Agence France-Presse, 'Now Abandoned French Refugee Centre to Formally Close'.
107. Asylum Rights Campaign, EU Working Group, 'Sangatte'.
108. McDougall, 'Tourists become targets as Dubai's workers take revolt to the beaches'.
109. Ibid.
110. Human Rights Watch, 'UAE: Address Abuse of Migrant Workers'.
111. Ibid.
112. McDougall, 'Tourists become targets as Dubai's workers take revolt to the beaches'.
113. Ibid.
114. Human Rights Watch, 'UAE: Address Abuse of Migrant Workers'.
115. Ibid.
116. McDougall, 'Tourists become targets as Dubai's workers take revolt to the beaches'.
117. Amnesty International, 'United States of America: Amnesty International's Concerns Regarding the Post 11 September Investigations in the United States'.
118. Begg and Brittain, *Enemy Combatant*, pp. 194–205.
119. Ibid., pp. 18–19.
120. Amnesty International, 'United States of America: Beyond the Law: Update to Amnesty International's April Memorandum to the US Government on the Rights of the Detainees Held in US Custody in Guantánamo Bay and Other Locations', p. 1.
121. Ibid., p. 2.
122. Ibid., p. 5.
123. Amnesty International, 'Guantánamo Bay: A Human Rights Scandal'.
124. Centre for Constitutional Rights, 'Optimistic on Guantánamo after Vigorous Supreme Court Argument'.
125. Ibid.
126. Diken, 'From Refugee Camps to Gated Communities', p. 94.
127. Nyers, 'Abject Cosmopolitanism'.
128. Czajka, 'Transient Citizens'.

Mariana Cavalcanti[1]

Redefining (Il)legal Boundaries

Space and Citizenship in Rio de Janeiro's Favelas

Rio de Janeiro is a city of roughly six million inhabitants where, for safety reasons, it is legal to run through red traffic lights between 10 PM and 6 AM. Sporadically, major thoroughfares, tunnel accesses and expressways are closed due to shootouts in their adjacencies; sometimes these thoroughfares are blocked by criminal checkpoints (often impersonating police operations), set up for the purpose of ambushing and robbing random drivers. Here a notoriously corrupt police force – which, according to a recent UN study, is responsible for at least 10 per cent of all homicides in the city[2] – roams the streets with machine guns sticking out the windows of their patrol cars, even in broad daylight. Since the early 1990s, the army has been deployed on several occasions[3] to patrol the city, in futile but highly publicised attempts to repress violent crime; the possibility of further army intervention is unfailingly discussed in the public sphere following highly visible criminal incidents.

The enduring 'public security crisis' has been, since the mid-1980s, the main – if not the only – political issue in a city where every citizen has come to perceive her/himself as a potential victim of violent crime. Or, to use the 'native category', Rio residents have come to act as virtual victims of 'violence'.[4] 'Violence', not crime, is the key term for the current urban (dis)order. The emergence of 'violence' as a collective social representation is a relatively recent phenomenon that names the quotidian sense of insecurity shared by citizens of all social classes. In so doing, it bundles together phenomena of different orders, comprising a plethora of modes of real or virtual victimisation that range from stray bullets to hijackings and carjackings, armed robberies to mundane muggings, but also encompassing police ineptitude and corruption and a defunct criminal justice system.

However, the spatial distribution of violent crime is not as evenly spread as the sense of potential victimisation. As in so many other metropolises worldwide where high crime rates have become a 'normal social fact',[5] the incidence of crime follows historically constituted patterns of social segregation: low-income areas concentrate the bulk of violent crime, particularly homicides. Hence in the more than 600 shantytowns in the city – Rio's *favelas,* home to roughly one million residents – homicide rates are six times higher than in the so-called 'formal city'. (This figure is certainly underestimated, as is it based on data provided by the Brazilian Civil Police.) The overwhelming majority of these deaths are connected to the city's retail sale of cocaine that has, since the late 1970s, constituted the *favelas* as the final node of complex global networks of illegal flows of weapons and drugs.

But differently from other cities where patterns of socio-spatial segregation tend to maintain the poor (and, with them, high crime rates) at the urban periphery or in clearly demarcated ghettos, segregation in Rio is highly fragmented in space, generating an overall pattern of sharp social contrasts. In several of Rio's elite neighbourhoods, middle- and upper middle-class streets deaden in the steep stairways and alleys leading up to the *favelas*, many of which are located on the city's numerous hill slopes. As a result of this spatial configuration, the frequent armed confrontations between rival drug factions or between the drug trade and the police literally reverberate into middle-class homes, reinforcing the sense of insecurity and the representation of the *favelas* as the source of all 'violence' in the city.

This chapter seeks to examine the politicisation of violent crime from the standpoint of its social effects on the *favelas*. It develops the thesis that notions and practices of citizenship in the *favelas* are being woven simultaneously by their progressive legalisation and incorporation into the city and by the emergence of a violent political economy that thrives on reinforcing the *favelas'* boundaries as 'territories' of the drug trade. I will suggest that these two processes, incorporation into the city and territorialisation by the drug trade, which at first glance seem contradictory, have in fact become entwined in the (re)production of the *favelas* as social and physical spaces over the past two decades.

In order to render this claim more concrete, I will begin to unpack my argument with a brief description of a rather banal scene I witnessed during my field research in the *favela* of Bela Vista in 2004–05.[6] Bela Vista is a rather typical *favela*, in that it is located on an extremely steep hill slope just off one of the main streets of the declining middle-class neighbourhood of Carioca.

On the afternoon in question, I parked my car in a paid parking lot accessed through Carioca's main street and joined the steady traffic of people through the overpass leading to an alley that acts as an extremely effective shortcut uphill. Most people walking up take this path, for it saves the pedestrian from having to climb up the narrow, windy and congested sole main street of the *favela*; getting around a *favela* by foot is made much easier by knowing such routes. This particular alley leads directly to the juncture where the *favela's* main *boca* (drug sale points are referred to as *bocas de fumo*, or just *bocas*) is located. As I approached the *boca*, I nodded my usual respectful but distant greeting to the six or seven young men bearing M-15s and AK-47s while passing around a marijuana joint. They looked rather bored, as is usual this early in the afternoon; sales only really get going after 5 PM or 6 PM.

Today, however, they had company. Parked a mere 3 m away from the *boca* was a car from the city electricity company. Its driver straddled the electricity pole located right by the *boca*, fixing the damage I found out later had been caused by a shootout with police the night before. Although he dangled a scarce 2 m over the heavily armed young men, he seemed as indifferent to his surroundings as the drug dealers themselves.

Only twenty-five years ago, this incongruous scene would have been inconceivable. The drug dealers might have been there, though their weaponry would have been less destructive and most likely concealed; they would not have been smoking marijuana in public and their general demeanour would have been more low-profile. But the technician would certainly not have been there, for the post he was fixing simply would not have existed; the incorporation of the *favelas'* electricity network into the city's material infrastructure only dates back to the mid-1980s.[7]

Each of these social actors, the drug dealers and the technician, owed their presence there to different and new dynamics of appropriation of *favela* space: the technician here represents the state's recent recognition of the *favelas* as a legitimate form of housing, which underwrites the new paradigm of *favela* 'integration into the city'. This new mode of intervention has replaced removal programmes that were, up until the 1970s, primary state policy *vis-à-vis* what were then perceived as illegal settlements. This constitutive illegality, over decades, engendered other illegalities such as the informal/illegal markets of weapons and drugs produced by the encroachment of the drug trade within *favela* boundaries, represented in the scene I describe by the young men at the *boca*.

Yet this scene is not a mere sum of the presence of two contradictory modes of appropriation or production of urban space; the indifference of each of these social actors to each other is, analytically, its most relevant aspect. It indicates that the *favelas* are not the mere result of two contradictory social dynamics, but that this contradiction is itself naturalised and productive of new forms of sociability. Hence the 'contradiction' lies in the outsider's gaze.

Through an analysis of 'native' perceptions, I shall suggest that these two processes are, or have become, in fact, interconnected. More concretely, I will argue that as the neo-liberal order consolidated itself in the 1990s, the *favelas*' progressive legalisation by the state and their constitution as territories of the drug trade dovetailed as they became fixed as a social and political category in the context of Rio's 'public security crisis'.

This chapter is organised in three parts, woven together in a trajectory common to many residents of Rio's so-called 'consolidated' *favelas*: the transition from shack (*barraco*) to house (*casa*) to fortress (*fortaleza*). Two underlying assumptions shape my outline of the problem: first, that a historical perspective is necessary in order to assess the metamorphosis of illegality as the defining feature of the *favelas* as a particular type of urban formation; second, that an examination of the transformations in the built environment of the *favelas* over the past two decades will capture the seemingly contradictory social dynamics through which the politicisation of violent crime has recast the *favelas* as a social category, and the effects of this politicisation for the constitution of *favela* residents as political subjects.

From Shack to House

The *favelas* have been perceived as the site of the most extreme poverty in the city since their emergence in the late nineteenth century. Vacant lots mainly on the hill slopes of the city centre were (often illegally) appropriated by individuals who constructed shacks to be rented out or fraudulently sold.[8] By the 1930s these minor illegalities, on a citywide scale, constituted a considerable informal housing market constantly fed by the inflow of migrants to the city.

Official prohibition of such settlements came in 1937 with the passing of a city building code, which labelled the *favelas* as 'anti-hygienic' temporary dwellings, thereby making them subject to removal. Legal, bureaucratic proscription, however, did not prevent the *favelas*' expansion, particularly during the industrialisation surges in the city that drew migrants first from the hinterlands of the state of Rio, the neighbouring states of Minas Gerais and Espirito Santo and later from the northeast of Brazil. The *favela* settlement pattern followed the expansion and urbanisation of the so-called formal city along two main axes: the beachfront in Rio's elite southern zone, where removal threats were more frequently enforced but employment – though informal and often temporary – was easily found; and in its northern zone, in the vicinity of industries where blue-collar jobs were also available.

Throughout the twentieth century, a pattern emerged in governmental policies *vis-à-vis* the *favelas* whereby in periods of authoritarianism removal projects were implemented, particularly for the *favelas* located in the elite southern zone of the city; whereas in democratic bursts, partial urbanisation became the norm in the form of clientelist arrangements between local politicians and particular *favelas*. These arrangements, informally known as the 'politics of the water well' (*política da bica d'agua*) characterised an unstable tolerance towards the *favelas* that translated into palliative and isolated material improvements in their collective infrastructure. From the 1940s onwards, the Catholic Church provided some assistance to such improvements as part of a wider project of 'moral education' of the poor, with the aim of containing the infiltration of communist militants within the *favelas*: 'It is necessary to climb the hills before the communists descend from them' was the Church's motto.[9]

By the 1950s and in spite of its prohibition, the occupation of hill slopes had become fairly institutionalised, and house construction had become a carefully orchestrated task: newcomers attained clearance of emerging but not yet fully recognised residents' associations through referrals by current residents; a plot of land was 'marked' and the house was collectively built in the middle of the night to avoid police surveillance. Residents attribute the emergence of a political consciousness and identities based on locality to the threat of removal and to collective efforts to order and improve the common spaces of the *favelas*. However, as an emerging neighbourhood movement concerning the rights of residents of unrecognised settlements to the city, their political bargaining powers and visibility remained extremely limited.[10]

Prohibition and the ever-present spectre of removal therefore made the *favelas* transitory places, marked by a precarious architecture that was often washed away during the rainy season. Several of my older informants recall having to rebuild their homes a number of times, after 'losing everything' to floods and landslides. These residents were relatively lucky; between 1962 and 1973, nearly 140,000 *favela* residents were displaced in the largest-scale *favela* removal programme to date. Most of those affected by removal programmes came from *favelas* in the southern zone, and were often forcibly relocated to housing projects in remote areas on the periphery where urban services and public transportation were extremely deficient.[11]

The transition from 'shack' to 'house' *per se* would only take place in the early to mid-1980s, in the context of democratic opening after nearly twenty years of military rule. During Leonel Brizola's first tenure as State Governor (1983–6), large-scale programmes for the installation of water, electricity and sewage systems in the *favelas* connected them to the citywide infrastructural networks. Public schools, small medical centres and day-care centres were set up in both the adjacencies and within the perimeter of several *favelas*, benefiting a quarter of a million residents.[12] Just as significant was the implementation of the programme '*Cada Familia, um Lote*' ('Each Family, One Plot'), aimed at granting land tenure to one million families. Its huge failure notwithstanding – only 32,000 titles were granted – the programme initiated a paradigm shift from *favela* removal to *favela* incorporation into the city. This shift was further consolidated in the early 1990s, beginning with the passing of legislation such as the Statute of the City and the City Planning Charter (*Plano Diretor*), both of which prescribe the granting of land titles as the main aspect of future planning policies.

In the *favelas* that survived the 'removal era', the social and spatial effects of such legislation and infrastructural investment surpassed the physical interventions themselves. Official recognition, and hence the assurance of permanence, allowed for an accumulation of capital in the form of home ownership. Easier vehicle access decreased the cost of delivery of construction materials and other durable goods like household appliances. This, in turn, led to a private construction boom on the part of residents that radically changed the physical landscape of the *favelas*, with permanent masonry houses infrastructurally connected to the city replacing the archetypical clandestine wooden shacks.

The transition from 'shack' to 'house', therefore, encompasses more than a shift in the material aspects of *favela* dwellings. It comprises massive transformations in the infrastructural linkages between the *favelas* and the so-called formal city; improvements in their physical access and the availability of city services to *favela* residents. It is not surprising that older residents share a perception of upward social mobility, couched in the material improvements of the *favela* environment over the past decades and particularly in home ownership.

The trend of *favela* 'integration' into the city finally became the norm in 1994, with the launching of the *Favela-Bairro* programme, a US$600 million project partially funded by the Inter-American Bank for Development. Its extremely ambitious blueprints aimed at transforming both the physical space of the *favelas* and their perception in the public view by their full incorporation into the city, and encompassed environmental, sanitary, housing, social, income generation and land tenure components.

Seen in isolation, the shift in governmental policy from *favela* removal to 'integration' into the city would appear to be a happy tale of *favela* residents' decades-old demands for recognition of their rights to the city being met. However, if one takes into account the conditions of the transition from removal policy to integration programmes, this tale of empowerment and recognition emerges as a new predicament that recasts old prejudices and modes of subjugation, and reconfigures the constitutive illegality of the *favelas*. I will briefly examine two instances of this reconfiguration.

First, the progressive legalisation of land occupancy in the *favelas* coincided with the intensification of illegal and extremely violent practices within their boundaries. The ultimate aim of the trade is to ensure the continuity of its illegal business of drug sales, and it does so through the instilling of a political economy of fear, grounded in exemplary punishment through the use of force. I shall discuss this in further detail in the next section; for now, I wish to highlight that the process of territorialisation is not only the result of the exercise of power of the trade itself, but also of the recognition of the *favelas* as territories of the trade by other powers, such as the repressive apparatus of the state.

Territorialisation as a social fact takes place also on the level of discourse and practice of instances that are external to the *favelas*. Hence the *favelas* are produced as territories of the trade both from within – through the trade's enforcement of a set of rules that regulate the conduct of those who live or transit through them – and from outside, through the differentiated actions of the police and private and public social interventions that recognise the *favelas* as areas of 'social risk' as opposed to the so-called formal city. Though the latter manifestly and ultimately aim to transform the very regime of illegitimate domination their actions denounce and seek to subvert, they are nonetheless agents in the reproduction of the social and spatial boundaries their actions aim at eradicating.

Second, because current legislation drafted in the paradigm of *favela* 'integration' into the city distinguishes 'consolidated *favelas*' as the object of their intervention from recent squats, it produces a new regime of (il)legal occupation of land. On one hand, on the outskirts of legally defined *favela* boundaries the auto-construction of houses and commercial establishments continuously extends the perimeter of the *favelas*, reproducing the illegal patterns of settlement that constituted them in the first place. 'Consolidated *favelas*' also grow vertically: new generations of long-established families tend to construct houses on the roofs of their parents' homes, taking advantage of the existing legalised infrastructure and social networks developed over the years. On the other hand, partly due to the precedent set by the *Favela-Bairro* programme whereby displaced residents received financial compensation,[13] there has been a significant rise in the number of *favela* settlements themselves through new invasions of private and public areas and squats of abandoned buildings, usually in the vicinity of older, more established *favelas*.

Another set of observations regarding the *Favela-Bairro* programme relates to its unintended but inevitable consequences. First, the juxtaposition of *favela* 'integration' policies with the International Monetary Fund debt crisis of the 1980s gave rise to a new pattern of socio-spatial segregation in the city. In the 1980s, Rio de Janeiro became the city with the highest absolute number of poor people in Brazil (3.65 million), while the proportion of families living under the poverty line increased from 27.2 per cent to 32.5 per cent.[14] Migration to the city was considerably staved off by its declining importance in the regional economy.

Meanwhile, the population of the *favelas* increased at a greater rate than that of the so-called 'formal city', though this influx came not from other states but by impoverished former residents of the 'formal city' itself.[15] As a result, the most extreme levels of poverty and deficient urban services are no longer found in the 'consolidated' *favelas* of the central, southern and northern zones of the city, but in more recent settlements, particularly in the western zone of Rio and on the periphery.[16] Therefore the idea that the *favelas* contained the most extreme poverty in the city and that their population largely comprised migrants illegally settled in these areas has been severely undermined in the past twenty years.

These social and spatial dynamics are increasingly blurring both substantive and conceptual notions of '*favela*'. As a result, a certain image constructed by planners, social scientists and *favela* residents themselves in opposition to the 'formal city' throughout the twentieth century today fails to account for the diversity of the 600-plus urban formations we call *favelas*. This blurring takes place just as '*favela* residents' have come to be constituted as political actors who symbolically and strategically embody the greatest contemporary predicament of Rio de Janeiro, namely the 'social risk' posed to all 'citizens' by the drug trade.

From House to Fortress

The mere existence of the drug trade pervades every aspect of the phenomenology of daily life in the *favelas*. Here I wish to explore two aspects of the trade: first, how it constructs, performs and negotiates material and immaterial boundaries; secondly, I shall discuss how their constitution itself produces new boundaries within the *favelas*, through an examination of the transition from 'house' to what my informant Helena calls her 'fortress' (*fortaleza*).

In order to understand the different sorts of boundaries and spatialities produced by the drug trade, it is necessary to have some basic knowledge about how the retail sale of cocaine is organised in the city.[17] The key term here is 'retail': the drug trade of the *favelas* is but a loose end of the global trade that, in the late 1970s, established routes from Bolivia, Peru and Colombia with a stopover in Rio de Janeiro on its way to Europe, the US and South Africa. According to the Brazilian Federal Police, about 20 per cent of the cocaine routed through Rio on such global circuits is reserved for this internal market.[18]

The local distribution of cocaine as we know it today established itself according to existing illegal networks. The sale of marijuana in the *favelas*, for instance, has been a constant for decades, as early reports from the 1940s bear witness.[19] Its distribution initially organised the *bocas de fumo*, forming an organisational structure entwined with that of the *jogo do bicho*, an illegal lottery very similar to the racket described in Drake and Cayton's classic work on Chicago's Bronzeville in the mid-1940s.[20]

Like today's drug trade, the *jogo do bicho*, though organised from within the *favelas* and peripheries, extended into the 'formal city'. Its structure was highly decentralised, though hierarchical, and involved localised corruption schemes with the police.[21] Such networks were transformed in scale and profitability with the availability of large quantities of cheap Colombian cocaine, which in the 1980s became the merchandise around which criminality organised itself on a citywide level. The first such organisation was initially known as the *Falange Vermelha*, today called *Comando Vermelho*, or CV, constituted initially inside the maximum-security prison in the island of Ilha Grande off the shore of the state of Rio de Janeiro. The *Comando Vermelho* has since then fractured several times, giving rise to new organisations, the most important of which are the *Terceiro Comando*, or TC, and the *Amigos dos Amigos*, ADA, which resulted from a split inside the TC in the mid-1990s.

Territorial conflicts between the factions pit neighbouring communities against each other, often making it impossible even for people not involved in the drug trade to cross the physical boundaries between two *favelas*. The *favela* of Bela Vista, for instance, is one of three communities that from the ground appear to be one large *favela*. But these three *favelas* – and a fourth one facing them – have been 'at war' for some twenty years, with alliances among them shifting over this period. This pattern repeats itself citywide, though the CV tends to have a greater hold on the more lucrative territories of the southern zone of the city. These ongoing disputes translate into nightly shootouts, occasional 'invasions' and a strict enforcement of the boundaries of each community, even for those who have no involvement whatsoever in the trade.[22] Such boundaries, furthermore, extend into the 'formal' city and impose themselves upon public institutions; public schools in 'conflict zones' are attended by residents of *favelas* under the domination of either one faction or the other, and the same goes for medical centres and other city services – and especially for prisons, where inmates are separated according to their drug factions. Unauthorised crossing of such borders is often – and exemplarily – punished with the death of the trespasser.

Faction disputes are not the sole source of conflict in the city. As any *favela* resident will tell you, the police remain the greatest source of insecurity. In fact, nothing is as consensual in any *favela* as a collective and very intense – for the lack of a more conceptually accurate term – hatred of the police. Over the course of the eighteen months of my field research the police killed at least eight traffickers from Bela Vista. Perhaps four of these deaths made it into official statistics; a few more made it to the media.

As I have argued at length elsewhere,[23] the sort of violent practices applied by the police within the *favelas*, is very much in continuity with those institutionalised under the military regime, to the extent that re-democratisation does not figure as a significant marker in the collective memory of the *favelas* particularly in relation to police behaviour; the break is only perceived with regard to the infrastructural investments discussed earlier. Hatred of the police does not stem only from their trigger-happiness, but most of all from their systematic disrespect of *favela* residents' civil rights, in the form of illegal entry into people's homes, brutal rounding-up of suspects and outright stealing (usually of electronic goods) – not to mention their habit of conducting 'incursions' into the *favelas* at times when the traffic of children back and forth from school is at its peak.

Because the trade is run as a hybrid of business and paramilitary organisation, the boundaries it establishes cannot afford to be as hard-edged as they seem. On any given day there is a significant flow of deliveries, NGO workers, schoolteachers, visitors, government technicians and, of course, drug consumers, whose every move is monitored but not hindered. The paramilitary component of the trade is basically comprised of lower-level employees known as *olheiros*, *vapores* and *soldados*.

Olheiros are usually the most recent and youngest recruits; they are not necessarily armed (save for the fireworks they use to warn the entire *favela* of possible invasions), and they earn a fixed salary. The *vapores* execute the same function, but also work at the *bocas*, distributing drugs, and their earnings are based on the sales they make. Next up in the hierarchy are the *soldados* – soldiers – who are entitled to bear weapons. *Soldados* guard the *bocas* and all entries at night, earn more than *vapores* and *olheiros* and may be summoned to take part in invasions of enemy territories.

All these lower-ranking 'employees' answer to the *gerente* (literally, 'manager') of each *boca*, who in turn, reports to the *dono do morro* ('owner of the hill'). This basic hierarchical diagram repeats itself in all *favelas*, with a few variations according to the complexity of the trade and physical layout of each *favela*.[24] The paramilitary powers of the trade also constitute a composite of local judiciary system and police force in which rapes, assaults and robberies within the boundaries of the community are strictly forbidden and punishable by death, beating or banishment from the *favela*. As a business, the trade is a generous employer: it pays pensions to families of 'employees' who have been arrested or killed, as well as other benefits, such as health insurance and a thirteenth wage at Christmas, that is an important aspect of Brazilian labour rights.

The embeddedness of the trade in the social fabric of the *favela* brings each and every episode of violence close to residents, if only in the form of a sense of heightened insecurity and a constant fear of possible victimisation by the police, the trade or stray bullets. Such a context of uncertainty has had significant effects on the spatialities of the *favela*, particularly in the proliferation of gates, bars on windows and fortified walls to offer multiple layers of protection. All these measures make evident residents' attempts to keep violent conflict outside the private spaces of their homes. Such efforts are furthered by investments in videogames for children, television sets, personal computers and DVD players to keep as much activity as possible indoors and therefore minimise the chances of being caught in the frequent shootouts.

Figures One through Four illustrate the progressive construction of one such fortified space: the home of Helena, a thirty-five-year-old assistant nurse and mother of three raised in Bela Vista. In Figure One, taken in 1985,

Helena is a newlywed, and she and her husband Pedro are posing in front of the first version of their house in Bela Vista. The house stands on the very spot where Pedro grew up in a wooden shack, but on a recently constructed second storey, as Pedro's sister lives in the masonry version of his childhood home. The house is located on a family *vila*, as such family plots are referred to, and shares a courtyard of sorts with six other houses.

This first version of Helena and Pedro's home was a two-room house. When the picture was taken, she was unaware that she was already pregnant with her eldest daughter, who appears in her lap in Figure Two. That photo was taken on the occasion of the first expansion of her house, when two other rooms were constructed, circa 1987. On that occasion, they moved the kitchen to the east side of the house, so as to reduce the vulnerability of the interior to shootouts from the neighbouring *favela*. They also took a chance keeping their bedroom next to the kitchen, so as to keep the kids on the 'safe' side of the house; the outside wall already bore the marks of the decade-old conflict with the neighbouring *favela*.

By the time her third daughter was born in 1996 – she appears in Figure Three – Pedro and Helena had already built an enclosed balcony for the house with an ever-locked gate to enhance the security of their home, even though by then the family *vila* had an external door that was kept closed most of the time. Figure Four was taken by Helena's youngest daughter. It depicts the bricklayer responsible for the last expansion of their home. This last measure was as unplanned as it was urgent and unwanted, and took place in the middle of a crisis in the *vila* brought about by their neighbour on the lower east side, Carlos, who had recently joined the trade.

The news of Carlos' recruitment by the trade spread quietly but swiftly through the *vila*. Less than two weeks later, a wall went up blocking access to Helena's roof to avoid police invasions. Very soon after I heard the news, the police began a new offensive in Bela Vista, and major shootouts were breaking out at odd hours, daily: I was prevented from conducting field research for two weeks. By the time I came back, Helena's wall was nearly finished. As I caught up with her on everything that had happened, she told me for the first time that she was considering moving out of Bela Vista.

'But,' she said, 'where could I go?' Helena knew full well that she would encounter similar dilemmas anywhere she could possibly afford; that she would never sell her house for the amount of money she had already invested in it; that their house's location allowed her to keep two jobs, because it was close enough to two hospitals; and that she already had a hard enough time

Newly-weds Helena and Pedro pose in front of their recently built one-room brick house, circa 1985

Helena with her daughter Luiza, 1987. The picture was taken in order to document the couple's first home expansion effort

Helena and Pedro's youngest daughter Clara, posing to document the construction of the house's enclosed balcony, 1999

Fortress building: a hired bricklayer builds a wall around Helena's roof, February 2005

getting her kids to and from one of the last good public schools in the city. She sighed and said: 'While I can't move out, I'll just build my fortress here.'

Conclusion

Helena's sense of being trapped in her own relative prosperity is not uncommon in Rio's so-called consolidated *favelas*; it is a result of the politicisation of crime and fear in contemporary Rio. The frequent shootouts in the *favelas* reverberate in elite apartment buildings, sometimes very concretely in the form of stray bullets. While this frequency of armed confrontations and violent crime might apply to other cities worldwide that are not going through wars or ethnic conflicts, it is unlikely that such events are anywhere as visible – or in this case, as audible – to the middle and upper classes as in Rio de Janeiro.

The sense of insecurity is furthered by the proliferation of holdups and hijackings that often have no relation to the trade but are fostered by its territorialisation of the city. It is therefore not surprising that over the past decade or so journalists, citizens of every social class and even social scientists have often resorted to using the metaphor of war to describe the city's predicament. Newspaper headlines comparing the city to Bogotá, Kabul, Gaza and, more recently, Baghdad, are a daily staple in sensationalist and mainstream media alike.

The metaphor of war produces, however, insidious political effects. Its repetition in the media, reinforced by headlines that compare Rio to war zones throughout the world, decontextualises the social field in which violent crime unfolds; it effaces the linkages of violent crime to the effects of global economic restructuring, to the decline of the welfare state as a normative ideal and hence of its at least aspired network of social protections, all of which translate into an amplification of the social vulnerability of the poor.

The metaphor of war disregards how transnational flows of weapons and drugs on an unprecedented scale offer a livelihood to the socially vulnerable, and that this process repeats itself where the effects of state retrenchment are more dramatic: ghettos, slums, working-class neighbourhoods and *favelas* in their multiple denominations in Latin America. Finally, the metaphor of war reduces the *favelas* and their residents to 'conflict zones' where institutionalised violent police practices become acceptable to the general public as the clamour for tough measures increases. This decontextualisation underpins a global tendency to criminalisation of the poor. While only an estimated 1 per cent of *favela* residents partake in such illegal activities and not all violent crime in the city can be attributed to the drug trade, in the public view '*favela*', 'drug traffic' and 'violence' remain inextricably connected.[25]

Indeed, the politicisation of violent crime, or simply 'violence', in Rio de Janeiro takes place in a world in which politics have been 'depoliticised'. As Jean and John Comaroff have argued, the lack of ideological alternatives to global capitalism produces a naturalisation of the existing social order:

> The social is dissolved into the natural, be it in the guise of economic efficiency, the fetish of the free market, the needs of capital growth or science and technology.[26]

Hence, the *Favela-Bairro* programme consolidated the neo-liberal order in the agenda of urban politics. On one hand, the horizon of granting land tenure to *favela* residents is viewed in terms of a 'social' measure to incorporate the disenfranchised masses into the capitalist order. As the Brazilian Minister of Justice, Márcio Thomaz Bastos, proclaimed on the occasion of the launching of a similar land tenure programme on a nationwide scale:

> Land regularisation is the social measure that will make the machine of capitalism spin. It is unacceptable that thousands of people remain unable to access bank credit just because they do not have a property title to offer as a guarantee for loans.[27]

On the other hand, one of the *Favela-Bairro*'s manifest goals is the 'reduction of violence through the establishment of the urban order', as one of the programme's coordinators put it.[28] As such, it channels investment into areas that concentrate a series of risk factors – such as poverty and a young population in the context of rampant unemployment and glaring social contrasts – to the established social order.

Therefore, recent state investment in so-called consolidated *favelas* constitutes certain *favelas* as strategic sites, both for residents and for the state. For residents, 'consolidated *favelas*' figure as strategic sites because in addition to the proximity to schools, health services and job markets, the concentration of public and private investment further improves residents' (still limited) chances of upward social mobility. However, because 'consolidated *favelas*' are also strategic sites for the state, the bulk of these investments tend to privilege those in the southern, central and near-northern zones of the city, i.e. the *favelas* located in the midst of upper- and middle-class neighbourhoods. So the politicisation of fear and 'violence' feeds back into the *favelas*, but unevenly, tending to reinforce inequality among the poor through the unequal distribution of these new social actors (and funding to them) among low-income areas in the city.

My point is that the contemporary political visibility of the *favelas* hinges on their fixation as spaces of risk that are to be accordingly appraised, managed and controlled. Hence the astounding number of governmental, NGO and privately funded social projects in the *favelas*, which include urbanist projects, complementary education programmes, encouraging entrepreneurship and development programmes aimed at encouraging youth participation in sports and the arts – all of which are underwritten by a pedagogical notion of 'citizenship' that hinges on notions of personal 'empowerment' and 'self-esteem'. Such notions, as Wendy Brown has argued, 'signal an oddly adaptive and harmonious relationship with domination insofar as they locate an individual's sense of worth and capacity in the register of individual feelings, a register implicitly located on something of an otherworldly plane *vis-à-vis* social and political power'.[29]

This fixation produces a paradoxical situation that traps *favela* residents in a double bind: the conditions for their political visibility and leverage rest on their constitution as a threat to the city. It is this very perception that has brought them unprecedented levels of political recognition and material improvement. That is, the conditions of the politicisation of the *favelas* fixes their residents as risk-bearing subjects, in a movement that binds them to an externally produced identity that itself comes to constitute the site of contentions. The double bind is not lost on residents. As my informant Samanta, a fifty-four-year-old mother of three who works for the *Favela-Bairro* programme, puts it:

> It's no use to say that the *Favela-Bairro* is bad. Yes, but there were people living in the middle of sewage! I know them! I know [people] from many communities ... People who had sewage running through their houses. Real sewage ... People who lived in basements that didn't even ... I don't know how they survived. And now at least they live in a decent house. So are you going to tell these people it's bad? They're happy because they don't live in filth like they did. And there is one more thing: people talk about youths. Talk about the community, about youngsters, about the [drug] traffic. Right, all the time. It's all people talk about. We're already marginalised, stigmatised ... all that ... Why is it that everyone that comes here with their [social] projects say that it is for risky youths? No – [they say it is] to get youths out of risk ... Let's stop that, because my kids are not risky! My kids! – I raised

three sons inside the community, right ... I brought them up all on my own! ... And they never joined the [drug] traffic. Why do they say that? The majority, the majority are people who study, who work. So I say: most youths inside the community study and work. Right? Study *and* work! And those who don't work, they go to school, because they can't get a job, they do odd jobs, they do something! Right? And the minority that is in the traffic is 1, 2 per cent! The majority of the community is struggling! So stop saying that the community, that the children, that the young are risky!

Hence the politicisation of fear and of violence in contemporary Rio de Janeiro fixes *favela* residents as risk-bearing subjects, second-rate citizens, and traps them in their newly built fortresses.

Bibliography

Brown, Wendy, *States of Injury: Power and Freedom in Late Modernity*, Princeton, NJ: Princeton University Press, 1995.

Burgos, Marcelo. B., 'Dos Parques Proletários ao Favela-Bairro: As políticas públicas nas favelas do Rio de Janeiro', in A. Zaluar and M. Alvito, eds, *Um século de favela*, Rio de Janeiro: Fundação Getulio Vargas Editora, 1998, pp. 25–60.

Cavalcanti, Mariana, 'Memoria y Cotidianidad de la Represión en el Morro do Borel', in E. Jelin and P. Del Pino, eds, *Luchas Locales, Comunidades e Identidades*, Madrid y Buenos Aires: Siglo XXI, 2003, pp. 175–207.

Comaroff, Jean and Comaroff, John L., 'Figuring Crime: Quantifacts and the Production of the Unreal', *Public Culture*, vol. 18, no. 1, 2006, pp. 209–46.

—— 'Naturing the Nation: Aliens, Apocalypse, and the Postcolonial State', *HAGAR: International Social Science Review*, no. 1, 2000, pp. 7–40.

Dowdney, Luke, *Crianças do Tráfico: Um estudo de caso de crianças em violência armada organizada*, Rio de Janeiro: 7 Letras, 2003.

Drake, St. Clair and Cayton, Horace R., *Black Metropolis: A Study of Negro Life in a Northern City*, Chicago: University of Chicago Press, 1993.

Fiori, Jose L., Riley, Elizabeth and Ramirez, Ronaldo, 'Physical Upgrading and Social Integration in Rio de Janeiro: The Case of *Favela Bairro*', *DISP*, no. 147, 2001, pp. 48–60.

Garland, David, *The Culture of Control: Crime and Social Order in Contemporary Society*, Chicago: University of Chicago Press, 2001.

Gomes, Manoel, *As Lutas do Povo do Borel*, Rio de Janeiro: Ilha, 1980.

Holston, James and Caldeira, Teresa. P. R., 'Democracy, Law, and Violence:

Disjunctions of Brazilian Citizenship', in F. Agèuero and J. Stark, eds, *Fault Lines of Democracy in Post-Transition Latin America*, Boulder, CO and Coral Gables, FL: North-South Centre Press/University of Miami, 1998, pp. 263–96.

Lago, Luciana C., *Desigualdades e Segregação na Metrópole: O Rio de Janeiro em tempo de crise*, Rio de Janeiro: Revan, Fase, 2000.

Lima, Nisia V. T., *O Movimento de Favelados do Rio de Janeiro – políticas do Estado e lutas sociais (1954–1973)*, Rio de Janeiro: Instituto Universitário de Pesquisas do Rio de Janeiro, 1989.

Misse, Michel, 'As Ligações Perigosas: Mercado informal ilegal, narcotráfico e violência no Rio de Janeiro', *Educação e Contemporaneidade*, no. 2, 1997, pp. 93–116.

O Globo, 'Lula decide regularizar propriedade nas favelas', in *O Globo Online*, 5 January 2003, Rio de Janeiro.

Preteceille, Edmond and Valladares, Licia, 'A Desigualdade entre os pobres – favela, favelas', in R. Henriques, ed., *Desigualdade e Pobreza no Brasil*, Rio de Janeiro e Brasilia: Instituto de Pesquisa Econômica Aplicada, 2000, pp. 459–86.

Rios, Rute M. M. M., 'Amando de Modo Especial os menos favorecidos, 1945–1954', in V. V. Valla, ed., *Educação e Favela*, Petrópolis, Rio de Janeiro: Editora Vozes, 1992, pp. 43–60.

Rose, Nikolas, 'Government and Control', *British Journal of Criminology*, no. 40, 2000, pp. 321–39.

Valladares, Licia, *Passa-se Uma Casa: Análise do programa de remoções de favelas do Rio de Janeiro*, Rio de Janeiro: Editora Zahar, 1978.

Vaz, Paulo, Cavalcanti, Mariana and Sá-Carvalho, Carolina, 'Vítima Virtual e Medo do Crime no Rio de Janeiro', *Trajectos: Revista de Comunicação, Cultura e Educação*, no. 7, 2005, pp. 95–106.

Vaz, Paulo, Cavalcanti, Mariana, Sá-Carvalho, Carolina and Oliveira, Luciana J., 'Pobreza e Risco: a imagem da favela no noticiário de crime', *Fronteiras – Estudos Midiáticos* VII, 2005, pp. 95–103.

Notes

1. The author would like to acknowledge the generous support of the CAPES Foundation/Brazilian Ministry of Education for the PhD fellowship that made the research for this article possible, and is grateful to the Foundation for Urban and Regional Studies for granting her a studentship for the period of the write-up.

2. The report, by Leonarda Mesumeci, is titled 'Relatório de Desenvolvimento Humano do Rio de Janeiro'; see www.ucamcesec.com.br/pb_txt_dwn.php. A special feature was also published in the newspaper *O Globo* on the major findings of the report. See *O Globo*, 24 April 2001, 'Retratos do Rio'.

3. The exact number of army deployments is nine, one of which is taking place as I conclude this article.

4. On the concept of 'virtual victims' see Garland, *The Culture of Control*; Vaz, Cavalcanti and Sá-Carvalho, 'Vítima Virtual e Medo do Crime no Rio de Janeiro'; Vaz, Cavalcanti, Sá-Carvalho and Oliveira, 'Pobreza e Risco: a imagem da favela no noticiário de crime'; Comaroff and Comaroff, 'Figuring Crime: Quantifacts and the Production of the Unreal'.

5. Garland, *The Culture of Control*, p. 140.

6. The names of the *favela*, the neighbourhood in which it is located and all the *favela* residents quoted here have been changed to protect the anonymity of my informants.

7. Before the 1980s there was electricity in the *favela*s, connected through precarious and often illegal local distribution systems; the significant transformation of the 1980s occurred when the same company that managed the electricity connections in the city at large began installing meters for individual houses. In fact, electricity bills are usually the sole documents that *favela* residents have to prove home ownership.

8. Gomes, *As Lutas do Povo do Borel*.

9. Rios, 'Amando de Modo Especial os menos favorecidos, 1945–1954'. The progressive wing of the Catholic Church, through the establishment of the Cruzada São Sebastião in 1955, advocated *favela* urbanisation as opposed to removal. In part due to the Cruzada's militancy, a pilot program for *favela* urbanisation in the *favela* of Bras de Pina was implemented side by side with the large-scale removals of the 1960s and 1970s.

10. Cavalcanti, 'Memoria y Cotidianidad de la Represión en el Morro do Borel'.

11. Valladares, *Passa-se Uma Casa*, p. 39.

12. Burgos, 'Dos Parques Proletários ao Favela-Bairro'; Fiori, Riley and Ramirez, 'Physical Upgrading and Social Integration in Rio de Janeiro'.

13. As a rule, the *Favela-Bairro* programme only resettled residents whose houses were either located in areas subject to landslides, or buildings whose structures were themselves compromised. Those displaced were eligible for financial compensation in order to buy houses in the same *favela*. As a result, existing property values rose exponentially as soon as the *Favela-Bairro* intervention was announced. As one resident of the *favela* of Bela Vista, my primary field site, told me: 'People found out that the *Favela-Bairro* was compensating and would pay whatever [people] asked for. So in the beginning houses cost 4,000, 5,000, 6,000 *reais* [between US$2,500–3,500 at today's exchange rates] and they would get it. Then it started from 12,000 *reais* up.'

14. Fiori *et al.*, 'Physical Upgrading and Social Integration in Rio de Janeiro', p. 50.

15. Lago, *Desigualdades e Segregação na Metrópole*, p. 178.

16. Ibid., p. 156; see also Preteceille and Valladares, 'A Desigualdade entre os pobres – favela, favelas'.

17. I am working here with a mixture of second-hand information on the drug trade in scholarly work and residents' reports to me (including former members of the trade). In the eight years I have worked in *favela*s, I have never had 'professional' contact with members of the drug trade; that is, I never approached them as an anthropologist, though they knew about my business there. The closest contact I had with them was a message conveyed to me through the president of the Residents' Association saying that they were watching over me, and that I had nothing to worry about. My contact with them was reduced to respectful greetings on both sides as I walked past the *bocas*. I attribute such 'protection' to my previous work in Bela Vista as supervisor for an NGO project aimed at reconstructing the memories of Rio's *favela*s.

18. Dowdney, *Crianças do Tráfico*, p. 26.
19. Lima, *O Movimento de Favelados do Rio de Janeiro*, p. 99.
20. Drake and Cayton, *Black Metropolis*.
21. Dowdney, *Crianças do Tráfico*; Misse, 'As Ligações Perigosas'.
22. This includes the anthropologist; soon into my fieldwork, I found I had incorporated the territorial logic despite my better judgment. One day I came home visibly shaken after a major shootout had occurred with a neighbouring *favela*. My husband asked me what the problem was and without flinching (or thinking), I replied: 'Those sons of bitches from the TC! Shooting at us in the middle of the afternoon!' I offer no excuse for my behaviour, but it *is* indicative of how such dynamics are easily and unconsciously incorporated.
23. Cavalcanti, 'Memoria y Cotidianidad'.
24. Dowdney, *Crianças do Tráfico*; Misse, 'As Ligações Perigosas'.
25. A recent study on the image of the *favela*s in the press, in which I had the opportunity to participate, yielded extremely significant results. We analysed the 'Metro' section of Rio's leading newspaper, *O Globo,* for six weeks each in 2001–02, comprising a total of twelve weeks' coverage. Out of the 744 news items that made up our sample, the term *tráfico* ['traffic', shorthand in Rio for drug traffic, or the drug trade] appeared in 368 pieces (49.4 per cent). The word *favela* was present in 250 articles, or 33.5 per cent of the sample; thus one-third of all crimes portrayed in the media were linked to the *favela*s (Vaz et al., 'Pobreza e Risco').
26. Comaroff and Comaroff, 'Naturing the Nation'.
27. 'Lula decide regularizar propriedade nas favelas', *O Globo* (online version), 5 January 2003.
28. Fiori *et al.*, 'Physical Upgrading and Social Integration in Rio de Janeiro', p. 56.
29. Brown, *States of Injury*, p. 22.

PART FOUR

Imagining the City

AYŞE ÖNCÜ

The Politics of Istanbul's Ottoman Heritage in the Era of Globalism

Refractions through the Prism of a Theme Park

The current resurgence of interest in Istanbul's Ottoman past, and its transformation into a key site of political struggles, cannot be divorced from transnational trends. In the world of late capitalism that we experience today, large metropolises figure prominently as core settings for the display and promotion of 'cultural heritage' as a marketable commodity. The symbolic and economic comodification of 'history' for display and consumption can be theoretically located in what Sharon Zukin has called 'the new symbolic economy' of cities,[1] or what Allen Scott has referred to as the 'culture generating capabilities of cities' in transnational markets.[2]

Invoking continuities with a legendary past, however ambiguous, enhances a city's attractiveness in the new global game and gives it cultural cachet in the competition for foreign investments and tourist trade. In many parts of the world, ranging from Southeast Asia to Europe, transformations of metropolitan space and urban culture are currently driven by the deliberate creation of cultural-historical packages and marketable pastiches that offer 'entertainment value'. There is now an extensive literature on how this process both reinforces prevailing inclusions and exclusions in the social fabric of cities, and also produces new ones.

The segmentation of tourist enclaves in urban space is perhaps the most immediately recognisable and widespread imprint of mass tourism on a global scale. Susan Fainstein and Dennis Judd[3] use the term 'tourist spaces' to encompass both the historic/cultural attractions designed for tourist consumption and also the related constellation of services (hotels, convention facilities, restaurants, etc) that accompany them. They argue that the functioning of such tourist spaces is usually designed to cosset travellers from their local contexts, to heighten the sense of theatrical reality they anticipate. But where income inequalities and cultural distance between affluent tourists and local inhabitants are very sharp, they also serve as 'fortified enclaves', designed to 'keep undesirable natives out'.[4] This is obviously the case in the large and densely settled cities of the global South. In many instances, the promise of tourism as the engine of miracle growth has spurred deliberate state intervention – literally, through bulldozers – to create secure and protected environments for tourist consumption.[5]

In the context of the Middle East, the recent histories of Cairo and Istanbul illustrate how the imprint of tourism is mediated through direct state intervention in the region. In the case of Cairo, Farha Ghannam has described how the ambitions of the Sadat regime, with its political discourse of *Infitah* (economic opening to the outside) were translated into visions of a 'modern' Cairo fit to be gazed upon by foreign visitors and upper-class Egyptians.[6] She describes how some of the oldest neighbourhoods of Cairo were demolished to make room for highways and 'tourist spaces' segregated from urban poverty and decay, a very similar process to that undergone by Istanbul in the political conjuncture of the 1980s, when the city was remade as the 'showcase' of Turkey's economic opening to global markets.

Thus, in both Cairo and Istanbul, 'history' has now been transformed into a prized collection of architectural fragments to be preserved in bits and pieces and protected from the sights, sounds and smells of local populations. City authorities constantly battle with the creeping tendency of the city's inhabitants to take over 'tourist sites'. The cleanliness and order of 'tourist spaces' – the glittering convention centres, hotels, restaurants, cafés, galleries – stand in stark contrast to the dirty streets, perpetually snarled traffic and crowded daily existence of most urban inhabitants. The cases of Cairo and Istanbul, as the two largest and most complex metropolises of the region, also highlight the difficulty of distinguishing the imprint of the transnational tourism industry from the series of interlocking changes we have come to describe as 'globalisation'.

Diane Singerman and Paul Amar's recent volume of collected essays on Cairo,[7] for instance, highlights how protected spaces of affluence ranging from shopping malls to gated communities are rapidly proliferating across the cityscape. The contrasts between the cosmopolitan lifestyles of the increasingly 'globalised' bourgeoisie and the 'localised' inhabitants of Cairo and Istanbul are no less stark than the differences between 'foreign' tourists and 'native' populations. It is also worth noting that in both Cairo and Istanbul, downtown districts associated with 'foreigners' at the turn of the twentieth century are currently undergoing gentrification.[8]

Many of the contradictions and cleavages engendered by the conversion of Istanbul's '2,000 years of history' into commercial revenues remain familiar in their generalities. A series of urban restoration projects, supported by coalitions of government- and corporate-run interests, have obliterated from memory some of the most densely populated areas of the city, to selectively recreate them as historical sites for aesthetic preservation. No published statistics inform us how many poor households and small establishments were displaced during these massive clearance operations. Numerous old neighbourhoods have simply vanished, their streets and lanes erased from the map. Others have become progressively gentrified and taken over by restaurants, boutique hotels or souvenir shops selling Oriental kitsch, marginalising their old inhabitants and driving out the urban poor from the urban core.

All of this – amidst a building boom and real estate speculation on an unprecedented scale – has ushered in a dizzying proliferation of developer-led malls and multiplex clusters, five-star hotels, luxury apartment colonies and gated communities across the landscape of the city. Thus, within a decade, a new order of polarities and segregation has been mapped onto the physical and social topography of Istanbul. Throughout, spectacles and events celebrating Istanbul's unique historical heritage and cultural attractions have invaded the public spaces of the city, bringing along with them a profusion of commercialised images that defy segregation in physical and social space. So for the majority of the city's ten million inhabitants, nearly half of whom are recent immigrants, the glorification of Istanbul's ancient history along with its aesthetic preservation and display in segregated 'tourist spaces' has become the 'new' exclusionary rhetoric of the moment. It has served to highlight the diverse cultural pasts and multiplicity of ethno-religious heritages in the living present of Istanbul. In short, the mass marketing of Istanbul's history has proceeded in tandem with growing visibility and *politicisation* of cultural differences among the city's inhabitants.

The historical specificity of Istanbul's heritage struggles resides elsewhere, in how the city's multilayered past(s) have become the political site of unfolding conflicts in the *national* arena. Most immediately, the appropriation of the city's imperial past inevitably breached national historiography, to underscore its ruptures and silences. Many of the ancient monuments and heritage sites that symbolise the unique attractions of Istanbul in transnational markets refer back to layers of contested memories, dislocations and serial destructions that have been a part of nation-making. The designation of particular sites in the material fabric of the city (and not others) as 'historical treasures' has been accompanied by intense political debate, calling forth competing interpretations of different epochs in the city's history. More broadly, the mobilisation of Istanbul's imperial legacy to articulate future aspirations for a 'global' future have challenged modernist imagination of the Republican past.

In the cosmology of Turkish nationalism, Istanbul's name had been debased as emblematic of Ottoman decadence, pollution, miscegenation, against which the purity of a new national culture – located in Ankara – could be imagined. The polarity between these two cities, both as a set of images and the power relations implied in them, has been one of the central axes of modern Turkish history. Their names have been continuously valorised in modern Turkish literature, music and cinema as well as architecture as a way of articulating such binary oppositions as East and West, progress and backwardness, modernity and Islam. Hence Istanbul's self-promotion as a City of Culture in transnational markets has undermined the very categories upon which the cosmology of Turkish nationalism and modernity has been based. It has opened the multiple layers of 'Ottoman past' to opposing political claims and projects, not only for the city, but also for the *nation*.

Pitched at a more abstract level, the complexity of Istanbul's heritage struggles must be situated in the theoretical terrain, which Andreas Huyssen has famously described as 'a world-wide turn to history as the site of memory struggles'.[9] In seeking answers to the current 'obsession with memory and the past' in Europe and the US, Huyssen traces the complexity of global processes that have ruptured and transformed older forms of historical consciousness. But he argues that 'the *political* site of memory practices is still the national, not post-national or global'.[10] The backdrop to Huyssen's work is, of course, the significance of Berlin in the political and cultural terrain of European history and German national identity. The layers of contested memories associated with Istanbul's name evoke parallels with such 'world-cities' as Shanghai[11] or St Petersburg,[12] where historical trajectories have been dramatically reshaped by the dissolution of empires – classical or colonial – and the consolidation of modern nation-states in the twentieth century.

Huyssen's general point of argument is relevant, in the sense that growing uncertainties and ambivalences about Turkey's role in the global arena and its future in Europe have been accompanied by a paradigmatic shift towards

Ottoman history as the political site of reworkings of *national* memory. Istanbul, as the prominent symbol and bearer of Ottoman legacy, has become a major point of reference in the emergent power struggles.

To recapitulate, the intensity and complexity of Istanbul's heritage struggles can be located at the intersection of two analytically distinct processes, namely:

1. A new order of class polarisation that has sharpened the existing hiatus between the city's culturally dominant elite and its disenfranchised immigrant majorities;
2. A 'memory turn' to Ottoman history as battleground of what 'national culture' might mean, and who owns it in the global era.

It goes without saying that these processes are part and parcel of the same world-historical conjuncture – blowing winds of neo-liberalism, explosive growth of commercial markets, declining cultural hegemony of the state, and so forth.

My aim in this article is not to rehearse these generalities, but to explore how competing visions of Istanbul's Ottoman past and political claims to its heterogeneous present are intertwined in ongoing 'heritage struggles'. The centrepiece of my discussion will be a brand new 'heritage park' in Istanbul, designed and executed by the city government as a flagship project in its millennial civic consciousness campaign called 'Our Istanbul'. To be able to contextualise the city government's millennial vision of 'bringing together Istanbul and the Istanbulites', however, I would like to introduce a brief caveat on competing political narratives of Istanbul's 'multicultural past'.

Competing Narratives of Istanbul's 'Multicultural' Heritage

The catchword 'multicultural' (*çok kültürlü*) circulates in an endless variety of commodity forms across Istanbul's fragmented public spaces, along with such associated phrases as 'cradle of civilisations' (*uygarlıkların beşiği*); 'treasury of culture' (*kültür hazinesi*); 'cultural inheritance' (*kültür mirası*); 'cultural diversity' (*kültürel çeşitlilik*); 'city of culture' (*kültür kenti*); and 'world city' (*dünya kenti*). Such phrases are obvious 'adaptations' from the global lexicon of city marketing that has swept across the world over the past two decades to become variously 'naturalised' in different languages. As they currently circulate in Istanbul's cultural markets – both high and low – they seem to make immediate common sense, and sound so familiar as to be beyond questioning. They are often used interchangeably, to invoke the remembered past and lived present of Istanbul simultaneously, suggesting a seamless unity between them. They also convey a sense of belonging and connection with Istanbul, which is, as *we* all know, 'a world city'. In short, they mark the parameters of a new urban imaginary – devoid of ethno-racial conflicts, dilemmas of urban hierarchy or poverty – which connects *us* together as Istanbulites.

But the very familiarity of these catchwords also means they are picked up and strategically deployed by various political actors and power groups to narrate alternative political versions of the city's present/pasts. So their dizzying proliferation across various commodity, consumer and media markets is the product of a double dynamic, both politically informed and interactive. They are strategically mobilised, reframed and challenged by political actors (both dominant and subordinate) to articulate their own political visions and agendas. As such they constitute a 'popular idiom', or repertoire if you will, which allows for multiple, divergent interpretations of what 'multiculturalism' was/is all about – which is another way of saying that the term 'multiculturalism' acquires referential solidity in the context of competing political scripts or public narratives.

In Istanbul's cultural markets, there are currently two such competing narratives that ebb and flow in cross-reference to one another. These are public narratives in the sense that they inform and knit together an enormous range of ongoing 'cultural' events in the cityscape, to lend them coherence as part of alternative political scripts.[13] They also 'suck the past into the orbit of the present' (to invoke Huyssen)[14] by furnishing ready-made scenarios for a series of performances, displays and exhibits as well as spatial practices and interventions.

The Multiculturalism of Istanbul's Nineteenth-Century Heritage

For Istanbul's corporate elite, affluent upper and upper middle classes as well as public intellectuals, it is the 'spirit' of Istanbul's *Belle Epoque* towards the end of the nineteenth century that captures something akin to its future promise in the global era. As it is currently framed and configured, turn-of-the-century Istanbul is not so much a historically specific conjuncture saturated with politically charged events, but a timeless moment bringing together a constellation of elements (a mixture of intellectual freedoms, political emancipation, economic vitality and cultural creativity) and tying them to the present through the idea of 'multiculturalism'. It also suggests that after decades of provincialism, decay and dreary nationalism mandated by Ankara governments, Istanbul is now experiencing a rebirth of its identity as a world-class metropolis.

Of course, contemporary reinventions of *fin-de-siècle* Istanbul as a 'golden moment' are not necessarily counter-factual. As many historians have pointed out, the Ottoman capital was swept by unprecedented changes towards the latter half of the nineteenth century, as it became increasingly separated from the rest of the imperial realm by special fiscal and political privileges. The relentless efforts of Ottoman bureaucrats to modernise the city fabric through a series of ambitious physical and social engineering projects paved the way to a renaissance in 'blended' public architecture.[15] Rival European powers competed with one another in the grandeur of their embassy buildings, and the glittering lifestyle of the settler-bourgeoisie affiliated with them. The wealthy and educated Greek and Armenian bourgeoisie of the city began to actively carve out an urban public space of associations, confessional schools, clubs and publications. They were at the forefront of a municipal movement that introduced a new style of urban life – paved avenues, street cars, gas lighting, European-style hotels, department stores and cafés.[16]

These new spaces of urban anonymity, with their 'modern' forms of contact and interaction, allowed the upper crust of Ottoman elite to intermingle with the city's native and foreign bourgeoisie outside the nexus of commerce and trade. They also fostered a heightened sense of political engagement, and of imminent change towards an unknown future, which meant that Istanbul became the crossroads of diverse ideological currents ranging from advocates of constitutional Ottomanism or Pan-Islamism to Young Turks of all hues, along with Christian missionaries of every denomination and nationality dispensing education, alms and sermons.

'This was a time and place when cosmopolitanism could be born,' suggests Çağlar Keyder,[17] one that offered 'the possibility of different material and cultural life-styles to co-exist' and held 'the promise of a liberal framework which could accommodate diverse political platforms'.[18]

But *fin-de-siècle* Istanbul also had a much more troubled and troubling visage marred by shameless racism, social schisms and religious conflicts. This is perhaps best illustrated by the following 'tourist accounts' from European guidebooks from the late nineteenth century, intended to prepare travellers for the unfamiliar topography of Istanbul as well as offering practical advice. Such guidebooks offer fragmentary glimpses of a city in motion, with a changing and fluid population of nearly a million souls:

> Constantinople is a city not of one nation but of many, and hardly
> more of one than of another ... There is no people who can be
> described as being *par excellence* the people of the city, with a
> common character or habits of language ... Among the 943.575
> inhabitants there are representatives of nearly every nation of the
> globe.[19]

The plethora of human types described in these accounts – permeated by the
racial stereotypes of the moment – conjure all the curiosities and dangers
awaiting European travellers who would venture onto the busy streets of the
city:

> Moslems are mostly poor people and lazy ... Greeks, Armenians
> and Bulgarians have little in common, for each cherishes its
> own form of faith, and they hate one another as they hate the
> Turks. Many of their members are wealthy, highly educated and
> admirable men ... There is a motley crowd of strangers from the
> rest of Europe. Eight or nine languages are constantly spoken
> in the streets ... These races have nothing to unite them; no
> relations, except those of trade, with one another; everybody lives
> in a perpetual vague dread of everybody else; there is no common
> civic feeling and no common patriotism.[20]

Interspersed with romantic descriptions of the city's natural beauties, these
guides provide easily comprehensible maps of Istanbul's social schisms:

> Constantinople is made up of three cities. North of the Golden
> Horn lies the European city, with its two suburbs of Galata and
> Pera playing host to ambassadors, bankers, European merchants.
> It is the outpost of the West, its ideas, activities and culture. In
> the south, facing both as a go-between, Stamboul is slowly and
> sadly losing out to the continual penetration of European ideas
> and innovations ... The third city, Skoutari, on the Asian side, is
> the Turkish city *par excellence*, inhabited by old Muslims.[21]

It is not difficult to surmise that most European travellers saw the nineteenth-
century changes in the Ottoman capital as little more than a thin 'veneer
of the West', imposed upon spectacles of horror associated with the Orient,
which they consumed so avidly. But the racial hatreds, ethnic divisions
and religious tensions that seem so palpable in these accounts cannot be
dismissed as a figment of the Orientalist imagination. They presage the

violence of events that were to seal the fate of Istanbul in the subsequent decades.

As Keyder summarises starkly: 'In 1913, one out of five persons in the geographical area that is now Turkey was Christian; by the end of 1923, the proportion had declined to one in forty.'[22] During these ten devastating years, an estimated two-thirds of the Armenian population perished in massacres, or from deprivation and disease during forced marches, and those who escaped death left for other parts of the world. The majority of the Greek Orthodox population fled under the most adverse conditions, or became subject to forced population exchanges. Istanbul's population declined from an all-time high of an estimated 1.1 million just before the First World War to around 600,000 by 1922. Bereft of its native bourgeoisie, its foreign residents and its imperial household and bureaucracy, Istanbul 'died'.[23]

The Aesthetics and Spaces of 'Multiculturalism' in Contemporary Istanbul

In contemporary Istanbul, visions of the city's global future and the multiculturalism of its nineteenth-century history have become inextricably bound in public, popular and scholarly discourses. In the emergent power configurations of this new order, the celebration of Istanbul's unique 'historical heritage' and distinctive 'cultural legacy' has become an imaginative point of consensus among segments of the urban elite. The monumental objects of this history are the mosques and churches that 'naturally' grace the landscape of the city and comprise gratifying testimony to a harmonious multi-religious past. Infused with the spirit of globalism, Istanbul's 'multicultural' heritage becomes a general term to designate an imagined past of harmonious cultural coexistence, one that offers the potential of 'openness' to cultural flows from across the world without fear of contamination. It also creates a space, in Istanbul's contemporary corporate circles, to appropriate and display a distinctive 'high culture' that is different from its 'Western' counterparts. As Sakıp Sabancı, one of Turkey's most prominent corporate tycoons, explained in an impromptu press interview:

> Outside Turkey, when talking to my partners, I ask, 'How much is your capital? How many people do you employ?' The man talks about culture. I ask, 'How many subsidiaries?' They tell about their art collections. So it is not enough to have money in transnational markets, money is banal. Business life cannot be one-sided. It must be combined with culture, education and art.

> My Japanese partner invested what he earned [in] art, established museums. I saw them. I said I must also begin.[24]

The occasion that prompted these comments was the opening of an exhibit featuring Sabancı's collection of Ottoman headgear. In Istanbul's increasingly transnational corporate culture, sponsoring innumerable exhibits, concerts, performances by artists of 'world stature' is something more complex than promoting a corporate image. It is an implicit assertion of involvement and contribution to the (re)creation of a 'world-class' Istanbul – one that celebrates its Ottoman heritage of 'multiculturalism' as its distinctive mark of identity in transnational space.

In its more consumable and popular versions, as told in a multitude of photography books, novels and autobiographies, or performed by whirling dervishes and classical musicians, this is a narrative which condenses the entire chronological expanse of Ottoman history to highlight what is referred to as the 'multiculturalism of nineteenth-century Istanbul'. In the ethnographic present of Istanbul, multiple valences of the word 'multicultural' seem to encompass all that is 'blended' – from Sufi electronica (cutting-edge beats laced with Sufi Islamic mysticism) to trendy nightclubs where the young and beautiful rise spontaneously from their tables and perform a *horon* (a Black sea line dance).

Needless to say, the above rendering glosses over the complicated nuances of political standing and social distinction embedded in narratives of Ottoman multiculturalism, which circulate in contemporary Istanbul. What is of immediate import is the way this narrative transgresses the canons of official historiography without, however, threatening to expose its silences. The 'multiculturalism' of nineteenth-century Istanbul is no longer to be understood as cultural domination by the foreign, but a rich blending of cultures that lends credence to utopian visions of 'globalism' for the city and for the nation. At the same time, of course, the traumas of massive population displacement, ethnic cleansing and forced deportations that separates the 'real' from the 'mythical' past are deleted from memory. Narratives of Istanbul's multiculturalism, as mobilised by different groups to underwrite claims to a 'global' present and future, remain tied to nationalism in its core.

In the Realm of Municipal Politics: From 'Conquest' to Narratives of 'Tolerance' in Islam

In 1994, when Istanbul's first metropolitan mayor with 'Islamic' credentials came to power in the aftermath of an astounding electoral victory, a sense of radical change swept across nearly all strata of the city's population. Within the circles of the victorious Refah Party (RP), this was a prophetic event, referred to as the 'second conquest' of Istanbul, 500 years after victorious Ottoman armies entered Constantinople in the sixteenth century.[25] The Party had nominated a young and dynamic new candidate for the mayoralty of Istanbul, who pledged a 're-conquest of Istanbul, in the sense of bringing light to darkness', during the election campaign.[26] He was now catapulted into the national limelight as the new *fatih* (conqueror) of the city.

For the secular and leftist political forces, already in disarray, the local elections of 1994 spelled disaster. The RP had succeeded in capturing the majority vote in nearly all major urban centres in Turkey. The loss of Istanbul, however, where the left had been entrenched in the city administration for more than a decade, was especially significant. After years of corruption scandals and failed reforms, it had lost its grassroots support among the overwhelming majority of the urban poor and lower middle classes, and along with it its institutionalised power base in metropolitan government. It is not possible to over-exaggerate the political, economic and cultural resources at the disposal of Istanbul's metropolitan mayoralty. These resources have grown in tandem with the city's mounting significance as the growth pole of Turkey's neo-liberal economy, so that Istanbul has become increasingly autonomous from the central administration in Ankara. The mayor of Istanbul himself, with more popular votes behind him than any single politician, has been transformed into a key figure in national arena. In this sense, the 'conquest' or 'seizure' (*fetih etmek, ele geçirmek*) of Istanbul was both a symbolic quest and a very astute political strategy on the part of the RP.

For Istanbul's secular elite and middle classes, the militant and mobilising language of a 'second conquest' amounted to a nightmare scenario of an 'Islamic takeover'. Overwhelmed by a sense of fear and alarm, segments of the leftist intelligentsia, the bourgeois elite, a host of women's associations and the leading media institutions mobilised to fight against this 'Islamic takeover' in the cultural spaces of Istanbul.[27] Political analysts rushed in to analyse the political affinity between neo-liberal policies, growing poverty in Istanbul's peripheral neighbourhoods and the populist appeal of political Islam. The mainstream media turned its spotlights on the 'Islamic' practices of the new city administration, uncovering yet another example of 'Islamisation' on a daily basis, from the headcoverings of female employees to the banning of alcohol in public spaces owned and operated by the municipality.

In the intervening ten years, the governance of Istanbul by 'Islamic' mayors has become something taken for granted. In local elections, the suspense, if any, centres on individual candidates for mayor. The metaphor of 'conquest' has lost its relevance, in part because the Islamic movement itself has been transformed into a neo-liberal, religious-nationalist establishment. The 'religious' bourgeois are major investors in Istanbul's expanding world of malls, multiplexes, five-star hotels, gated neighbourhoods and luxury apartment colonies.

Also, in the dominant spaces of Istanbul's increasingly transnational corporate culture, 'Islam' has been opened to consumption, continuously performed and displayed as part of the city's 'multicultural' past and present. In the constant round of conferences, summits and visits by foreign dignitaries, events such as the recent 'Islamic Nations Culture Week' sponsored by the Metropolitan Municipality come and go without attracting attention. The 'alcohol-free' public facilities owned and operated by the city administration (parks, restaurants, wedding halls) have now been defined as offering relatively inexpensive consumer-cum-entertainment alternatives for lower-middle-class families.[28]

The issue is how Istanbul can be imagined and represented as a 'Muslim City' now that the religious spaces and landmarks that might be defined as intrinsically 'Islamic' are in continuous circulation as icons in the transnationalised spaces of the city. In the context of Istanbul's local politics, this has become an increasingly crucial issue, as the support base among the low-income populations of the city – fragmented along regional, ethnic and sectarian lines – is contingent on promoting 'unity and harmony in Islam'.

Of Tulips and Magnificent Gardens

The following local news item was tucked away in the back pages of mainstream dailies, not meriting more than passing attention, if at all:

> The Tulip Era in Istanbul
> The campaign for 'three million Tulips for Istanbul' was launched today by Mayor Topbaş at a ceremony on Taksim Square ...
> The mayor explained that tulips, which were part of daily life in Istanbul, will be returning home again. What Westerners described as 'Ottomans raise a flower, which cannot be eaten', he reminded, has today become a major source of revenue for

Holland. He indicated that efforts were underway to encourage the cultivation of tulips and flowers in villages within the boundaries of the greater Istanbul municipality. 'Tulips are very important in our lives. We name our children after them. They exist in our textiles, our ceramics, our literature, our poems, our life. The tulip is returning home', he said ...

Of the three million bulbs, one million will be distributed to citizens to plant in their own gardens and homes. The mayor noted that when they flower in April, anyone who sends a photograph will be eligible to enter the competition for 'the best tulips grown in Istanbul'. The most beautiful 100 tulips will be selected and awarded a prize of 300 YTL [approximately US$200] ... After the ceremony, packages containing five bulbs, a flowerpot and planting instructions were distributed to citizens.[29]

The 'city pages' of major national newspapers in Istanbul are devoted to 'problems' of immediate concern to readers, such as traffic congestion, water shortages or intimations of corruption at city hall, which journalists so diligently try to expose. Favourable reporting of activities sponsored by the mayor's office is rare as they are simply non-news, unless they border on the humorous – as was the case with the 'tulips returning home'.

For the metropolitan mayoralty of Istanbul, however, the tulip campaign was part of a persistent institutional effort to objectify, in the territorialised space of ongoing events and landmarks in Istanbul, an alternative 'golden moment' in history when the ethos of Ottoman-Islamic civilisation was at its peak. The explicit use of tulips as a trope for Ottoman-Islamic high culture dates back to the early eighteenth century, evoking a moment referred to as the Tulip Era in history textbooks. Framed as part of Turkish national history, and committed to memory by successive generations of children to this day, the Tulip Era epitomises the glories – and excesses – of Ottoman rule, as revealed by the following textbook paragraph:

The Tulip Era: In Turkish history, the name given to the years between 1718 and 1730 corresponding to the second half of the reign of Sultan Ahmet III (1703–1730). Since tulips became the rage among the state elite who began to cultivate them in their gardens, and tulip designs and motifs became widespread in embroidery, carpets, tiles and miniatures as well as poetry and literature, this period was subsequently named the Tulip Era by poets and historians. The prominent figure of this period was Grand Vizier Damat Ibrahim Paşa (1718–1730), who encouraged poetry, scholarship and the arts. Beginning with Istanbul, many artworks were built throughout the land, including parks, gardens, fountains, educational endowments, mosques, libraries and palaces. A tile factory was established in Istanbul to decorate the newly built or repaired buildings. Among the scholarly achievements of this period was the establishment of the first Ottoman printing house by Ibrahim Müteferrika. The Tulip Era came to an end in 1730, when the pleasure-loving excesses of the state elite led to the rebellion of Patrona Halil, resulting in the dethroning of Ahmet III.[30]

Of course, it is never entirely clear what adults remember from textbooks, but the defining images of the Tulip Era offer such exciting visions of magnificent gardens and sumptuous palaces, saturated with pleasures of poetry and art, that the drama of its ending in a violent rebellion is transformed into a compelling episode that resonates with abiding themes of injustice and retribution. It also constitutes a core event in historical narratives of Ottoman decline, signalling the moment when the ruling dynasty began to degenerate. So through a mixture of popular mythology and historical narrative, the story of the Tulip Era has mutated into 'common knowledge', as a timeless moment when the poor people of Istanbul went hungry while the Ottoman rulers were engaged in 'pleasure-seeking activities'. This makes its ending immanently plausible and memorable, so that most adults can summon (or embellish or invent) a series of 'historical facts', such as the 'beheading' of the Grand Vizier and his associates (in front of the palace gates), the installation of a 'figurehead' Sultan (amidst palace rivalries and intrigues) and so forth, in a way that prefigures and explains the entire progression of events during the 'long' nineteenth century of Ottoman decline.

Not surprisingly then, trying to reinvent the Tulip Era as an imaginative point of reference when the Muslim populations of Istanbul occupied a privileged status and Islam was the locus of authority merging both religious and political power raises the troublesome issue of its ending. It is only by resuscitating its mythical location in territorial spaces along the shores of the Golden Horn that it becomes possible to highlight its significance as a moment of equilibrium, when the tolerance of Islam reigned supreme.

A Miniaturised Heritage Park on the Shores of the Golden Horn

The idea of building a heritage park displaying miniaturised models of architectural monuments was born during the Metropolitan Municipality's millennium campaign. In search of a 'global vision' for Istanbul in the new millennium, Mayor Gürtuna (1998–2004) commissioned a large survey to measure 'civic consciousness' among the city's population. The findings of the survey were widely publicised in the media, and gave birth to the campaign theme '*Kentim Istanbul*' (My City Istanbul). As highlighted in a campaign pamphlet:

> Only 33 per cent of the city's inhabitants define themselves as Istanbulites [*Istanbullu*]. We must analyse this well. A person lives in Istanbul for years and thinks of others as Istanbulites, but not himself.
>
> 17 per cent say they do not like anything about Istanbul ... They do not love the history, culture and natural beauties of Istanbul. We cannot remain indifferent.
>
> 47 per cent say that when they go back to their region [*memleket*], they do not miss Istanbul. They do not miss it because no identity relationship has been established. Istanbul does not deserve this.
>
> Of those who live in Istanbul, 17 per cent have never seen the Princess Islands; 11 per cent have never been to the Bosphorus; 28 per cent have never been to any of the historical and tourist sites of the city. Do you know that we have citizens [*hemşehri*] who have never gone across to the other side [*yaka*] from where they live?
>
> In our beloved Istanbul, which aspires to be a World City of Culture, 64 per cent of inhabitants say that they have never participated in any cultural, artistic or informative [*bilimsel*] activity. This is not something Istanbul can accept.
>
> When we examine the findings as a whole, we observe a serious problem with identity and sense of ownership [*sahiplenme*]. Inhabitants of such cities as New York, Paris or London define themselves as New Yorkers, Parisians and Londoners. Those who live in Istanbul must also become Istanbulites.

To describe the numerous activities that were part of the millennium campaign would be tedious. Most were modelled after similar 'civic consciousness' projects elsewhere: drawing competitions in schools; conferences and panel discussions where academics discussed the findings above; posters of popular stars saying 'I am an Istanbulite'; and so forth. The idea that the immigrant poor, once they *see* the historical monuments and natural beauties of Istanbul, will develop a sense of belonging and identity with the city, is very much in tune with 'middle-class' sensibilities. It is difficult to say what it meant for the immigrant populations it addressed.

But the miniaturised heritage park, which was initiated as part of this campaign (but not completed until 2003) proved to be huge success, with some 900,000 visitors during its first year. It also suggested that the millennium slogan itself, '*Kentim Istanbul*', was embraced and implemented at the grassroots level by the mayors of Istanbul's thirty-two district municipalities, as an empowering theme, in the sense of 'our Istanbul' that connotes a *claim*. In the opening ceremonies of the park, Mayor Gürtuna expressed the significance of Miniaturk as follows:

> As the Metropolitan Municipality, our vision of Istanbul as a star shining among World Cities is synonymous with the cultural synthesis that emerges from its becoming a centre of many civilisations. We are proud and happy to hand over Istanbul's Golden Horn to the coming generations in its identity as a gleaming [*tertemiz*] centre of culture, art and tourism. Miniaturk shoulders a very important mission in this new identity of the Golden Horn. The interest it has generated not only in our own country but also abroad resides in bringing together the richness of all the civilisations that have passed through Anatolia and nourished this land for millennia ... This is the heritage of humanity.

'A delightful journey through the history of civilisations'; 'a fairyland where civilisations meet, not in war but in peace'; 'from Antiquity to Byzantium, from Seljuk to Ottoman and Republican Turkey, all the cultures that have left their imprints in this geography are brought together in a single park': these are the kinds of expressions that have been used to describe Miniaturk in a host of publications ranging from newspaper columns and journal articles to websites.[31] What such descriptive accounts attempt to capture, in words, is the experience of an entirely new order of historical time, within the enclosed boundaries of Miniaturk. In the tangible reality of the park itself, close to 100 'major works of architecture' from different historical epochs have been lifted out of time and place and reduced in scale with extraordinary detail, such that they can be experienced simultaneously. These miniaturised models not only 'represent' different civilisations, but also transform them into a new whole, by bringing them together in the enclosed spatial order of the park itself.

The miniaturised models of 'architectural monuments' displayed together in Miniaturk 'bring together three millennia of history over an area of forty thousand square meters', as described in its brochure. These were selected from an original list of all possible works with the help of an advisory committee of historians, to ensure that they are representative of different historical epochs; but only those that could be miniaturised were included. The originals of more than half of these 'architectural works' are from Istanbul, and include buildings such as the Galata Tower, the Haghia Irini Church and the Blue Mosque (which are popularly recognised as having 'tourist value', as their photographs constantly circulate in postcards, on television screens, etc) as well as contemporary works (*eser*) such as the Istanbul Bridge and Atatürk Airport (with miniature airplanes). Completing the list from Istanbul are models donated by sponsors such as the Profilo Shopping Mall and the Yapı Kredi Bank. These have all been reduced and miniaturised in exactly the same proportion to their original size, so that they are graspable in fascinating detail, and placed along the walking paths of the park. There is a card-operated machine next to each of these, which 'speaks' in several languages (Turkish, English, German) to provide brief, 'encyclopaedic' information.

The remaining 'architectural works' (*eserler*) are neatly classified as 'Anatolia' and 'Ottoman Heritage Abroad' in sections of the printed catalogue. Those from Anatolia (forty-five models) range from the 'Rock Houses of Mardin' and the 'Ruins of Mt Nemrud' to the 'Sumela Monastery', the 'Temple of Augustus', 'Atatürk's Mausoleum' and the 'Izmir Clock Tower'. In addition to representing different civilisations and historical epochs (as explained by the catalogue and the machines next to them) the geographical location of these 'works' has been taken into account so as to include all the regions of Anatolia.

There are only twelve models representing 'Ottoman Heritage Abroad'. Still, these are crucial in providing closure to the times and spaces invoked in the microcosmos of the park. Miniature models of the 'al-Aqsa Mosque' and 'Damascus Gate' (both in Jerusalem), the 'Mehmed Ali Paşa Mosque' (in Cairo), the 'Gül Ali Baba Tomb' (in Budapest) and the 'Mostar Bridge' (in Bosnia), continuing with 'Atatürk's House' (in Thessaloniki), mark the geographical boundaries of the Ottoman Empire at the peak of its glory, at the beginning of seventeenth century. They also frame the symbolic boundaries of an Ottoman/Islamic/Turkish civilisation whose achievements (and heritage) extend from Jerusalem to Bosnia.

The politics and semiotics of how 'three millennia of history' are represented and recast in the spatial and temporal order of Miniaturk merits a much more detailed interpretative analysis than the cursory description I have offered above. What is flagrantly obvious is that the choice of individual historical monuments to claim particular epochs (as expressively articulated), as well as the conception of their imaginary totality (as articulated through their symbolic ordering in the park) have been orchestrated so as to convey a new 'golden age' for Istanbul. It is also evident that in the political choreography of the park, commonly recognised symbols of nationalist historiography have been selectively mobilised and realigned in ways that resonate with the religious symbolism of Islam.

A semiotic reading of how the symbolic communities of Islam and Turkish nationalism are simultaneously invoked and brought into dialogue with one another in the representational world of Miniaturk would exceed the boundaries of this paper. It would also fall short of conveying how the 'political design' embedded in the iconography of the park actually operates in the experiences of visitors to the park. So I will turn below to the 'lived' reality of the park itself, to talk about how it is (re)choreographed through the routines and practices of the visitors themselves.

On a Hot August Day in Miniaturk

In the sweltering August heat, trying to reach Miniaturk through the congested traffic of Istanbul takes close to two hours by public transportation. Upon approaching Miniaturk, one's first encounter is a huge parking lot, mostly empty apart from municipal buses lined on one side. The park is walled off from the street, with uniformed guards at the gate. Moving through the imposing gates, one steps onto a vast platform of gleaming granite, with a glass-walled ticket office on one side and a souvenir shop/bookstore on the other. The platform leads up to a panoramic view of the park below. Hanging over the parapet, shoving each other, are some thirty giggling young boys waiting for their teacher to buy tickets. I join them on the lookout, anticipating the childlike spell of an artificial city with miniaturised models of buildings.

Spread out before me, as though conjured by magic, is a magnificent carpet of lush green grass and manicured flowerbeds that seem to extend as far as the eye can see. So overwhelming is the contrast with the congested city streets and the harshness of grey concrete that one's gaze compulsively falls upon the profusion of colours, and the senses surrender to the chimera of a cool breeze drifting across the open air. Who could possibly imagine the existence such a wondrous park in the city centre of Istanbul, with greener-than-green lawns and rows upon rows of flowers in synchronised colours? The whole panorama seems to have leaped out of the pages of a glossy gardening magazine, especially in August when every scraggly patch of grass in Istanbul's public parks turns yellow and a layer of grey dust settles on all the shrubbery and tree leaves. My own first sensation is sheer pleasure, even as I recognise the hyperreality of such brilliant colours and register the existence of people milling about in the park, dwarfed by the distance.

The children lining up to follow their teacher into the park are students from a Qur'an Course (*Kuran Kursu*) in Esenler, one of Istanbul's peripheral municipalities. There are four such student groups in the park that day, all arriving by bus from Esenler. 'We try to keep them off the street, and teach them something without pressuring and boring them too much,' their teacher explains. Like all the other Qur'anic teachers, he is a young man dressed in a somewhat shabby suit and tie, looking very sombre amidst the excited crowd of boys in cheerful T-shirts and clean sports shoes. Trailing behind the group are two older municipal employees, who help keep track of the children and keep them in order.

At ground level, the park, which looked almost empty from afar, turns out to be full of boys who had arrived earlier. The teacher chooses one of the empty pathways and stops in front of the first 'miniaturised monument' he comes across. He inserts the magnetic card into the machine, as the children early crowd around him. But the metallic voice spouting from the machine cannot be heard, unless you stand right next to the teacher; so most of the children become restless and began to drift off from the group. By the time we reach the third 'monument' along the pathway, the teacher himself has become bored with the lengthy stream of information coming from the machines. He roams ahead, reading aloud the names of buildings from the placards, then gives up the effort altogether and simply gazes around. The rest of us scatter in different directions.

The children end up, inevitably, at the Istanbul Bridge (which one can walk across) and Atatürk Airport. The municipal employees congregate in a corner to chat with one another. After some desultory conversation with the other Qur'anic teachers (who have all lost their charges and seemed to be equally bored with gazing at miniaturised buildings), I spot a lively group of women at the far end of the park and decide to join them.

The women's group – they are of all ages, including children – are on a daily tour, having arrived by bus from the outskirts of Istanbul early in the morning. They are affiliated with one of the numerous immigrant associations (*Biga, Çanakkaleliler Derneği*) within the boundaries of the Kartal municipality, which sponsors such daily bus tours on a regular basis throughout the summer months. The young man who accompanies them turns out to be a former tourist guide, currently employed by the Kartal municipality. He purposefully leads the group to particular monuments, to talk about them enthusiastically, holding the interest of everyone, including myself. So I spend the next two hours with them, enjoying the leisurely pace and free-floating chatter of the women. Their tour of the park ends in front of the largest model (Cappadocia) to allow for a last photo opportunity for the entire group.

At around 1 PM, all the municipal tours end, and the buses begin to leave one after another. As the sun becomes unbearably hot, the army of park employees (who had been picking invisible weeds from the flowerbeds all morning and warning visitors to stay off the grass) also disappear from the scene. Thus the park becomes deserted, apart from a small group of foreign tourists with backpacks and a couple of families with children. By this time I am too exhausted myself to continue further, and decide to come back on another day, in the late afternoon. On my subsequent visits to the park, I discover that the late-afternoon visitors are overwhelmingly composed of middle- or lower-middle-class families, arriving by car.

I have told the story of my first morning in Miniaturk to emphasise a particular paradox, a puzzle if you will, which kept repeating itself in each of my later visits. Of course, all of my visits led to different kinds of encounters and conversations. They also opened the door to a host of questions and avenues of inquiry that extended beyond the microcosm of the park itself, such as the world of Qur'anic schooling in Istanbul or the complexity of differences among district municipalities on the periphery of the city.

So on every visit, the 'blindness' of my own earlier observations became apparent; but they also brought me back to the same question, namely: if visitors (regardless of age, gender, education, etc.) become so rapidly bored with 'miniaturised monuments', then what is the 'wonder' of experiencing Miniaturk all about? This question came up because all my encounters and conversations in the park on different visits revealed that visitors had in one way or another learned about the park as 'absolutely worth seeing' ('*mutlaka görülmesi gerek*'). Afterwards, they raved about it as a 'wondrous' ('*büyülü*', '*sihirli*') and 'wonderful' ('*şahane*') experience. But what was so 'wondrous' and 'wonderful' about this experience, if not the miniatures?

A Detour by Way of Nineteenth-Century Panoramas and Miniaturised Cities

In her discussion on the newly emergent world of public spaces and pleasure grounds in European capitals of the nineteenth century, Susan Buck-Morss dwells on the popularity of 'panoramas' as favourite attractions.[32] In the arcades of mid-nineteenth century Paris for instance, they were among the pleasures on offer, vying with the spectacle of goods on display behind the glass windows of shops. People who paid to look at 'panoramas' (through viewing holes) were enthralled by sweeping views of cities, battling armies, historic events that seemed to unfold before their eyes, as lighting dissolved from one scene to another in rapid succession to create the illusion of seamless movement. Buck-Morss emphasises how this 'magical' experience of movement across time and space, at an accelerated pace, corresponded to that of moving along the passages of the arcades. Strolling along the galleries replicated a panoramic 'tour' of an entirely new world of urban spectacle – including crowds. So wondrous was the combination of commodity displays and pleasures they offered (from gastronomic perfections and intoxicating drinks to gambling halls, vaudevilles and sexual delights) that they seemed 'like fairy grottoes'.

The principle of panoramic representation – the creation of environments that transport people from one time or place to another – was replicated in many of the new public spaces of European capitals throughout the 1800s. Public parks, ornamental gardens, railroad stations, sports palaces, exhibition halls, wax museums were all designed to transform the material world into a new reality. There is little doubt, however, that it was the world expositions, each more spectacular than the rest, which surpassed the imagination in creating 'incomparably fairylike' environments.[33] As dramas of visibility for imperial power, the fantastical quality of such environments demonstrated the ability to fashion 'objective' reality, appropriating and transforming the whole world into a dazzling exhibit.

For visitors, they offered the experience of being transported to fully realised 'unreal' worlds, so extraordinary (i.e. monumental, exotic, miniaturised) and at the same time realistic (made concrete through realistic representations and real objects), that how they were accomplished seemed incomprehensible. The 'amazing' quality of this experience is perhaps best conveyed in Tim Mitchell's seminal account of the members of an Egyptian delegation that travelled all the way to the Paris Exposition in 1889, and found themselves walking on a Cairo street so realistically recreated, with the façades of the buildings made to look dirty, and with donkeys from Cairo; even the Egyptian pastries on sale claimed to taste like the real thing.[34]

What 'shocked' the Egyptians, as Mitchell describes it, was not only extraordinary scale and realism of the representation itself, but the mystery of how it was made possible. It is this element of mystery, or inexplicability, that makes visual spectacles a distinctive mode of displaying power. On one hand there is the wonder of the simulated-yet-real experience itself. On the other, there is wonder at the incomprehensible (hidden, inexplicable) machinery of power that makes it happen.[35] In this sense, visual spectacles do more than represent or symbolise power, they inspire belief in its amazing (fantastical or magical) abilities to control and shape the world.

More often than not, visual spectacles are calculated to astound by their sheer extravagance or excessiveness. They are 'spectacular' in the everyday sense of the word, remarkable for their larger-than-life qualities. Worlds in miniature, by contrast, are designed to astound visitors by the exactitude with which they duplicate reality, both in detail and solidity. They are 'spectacular' in the sense of demonstrating the power to make *anything* happen – such as duplicating entire cities in mimetic accuracy and detail, so that they can be comfortably inhabited and pleasurably explored in representational space – as if by *magic*.

Indeed, some of the most elaborately detailed miniaturised worlds created for world expositions of the nineteenth century were models or panoramas of the imperial capital in which they were held. These were often mounted and illuminated in such a way that visitors felt as through they were standing in the middle of the city, which lay outside the grounds of the exhibition itself. In his classic account, Mitchell emphasises how the 'astonishing realism' of such models or panoramas served to mark 'the common centre shared by the exhibition, the city and the world'.[36] As visitors were drawn into and encircled by the exhibits, they found themselves positioned at the centre of the imperial capital (in object form), surrounded by 'national' pavilions whose majesty was commensurate with their colonies-on-display. The mythic imaginary of historical progress implied in this spatial configuration, conflating colonial domination with capitalism's achievements, needs little elaboration. It was a common theme of successive world expositions organised throughout the nineteenth century, along with the utopian promise of technology to revolutionise the future of humankind. Cities hosting successive international exhibitions were expected to celebrate technology's unlimited possibilities, each by staging more spectacular exhibits than ever attempted before, to affirm its continuous advancement.

Whatever the spectacles on offer in previous expositions, the 1888 Paris Exposition eclipsed them all with the Eiffel Tower, a triumph of engineering and a spectacular city panorama wrapped in one. By all accounts, the tower was intended to demonstrate the unlimited possibilities of iron by making its strength resemble the 'lightness of lace'. Its vertical aspirations were abhorred and deplored by critics of its time, who described it as a 'monstrous erection' and a 'barbarous mass' at the very heart of the city, 'humiliating' and 'diminishing' all the cultural monuments and architectural works of Paris. It was also a huge popular success, recouping its entire cost in less than a year from the sale of tickets.[37] The crowds that thronged to climb its height could explore the whole city of Paris laid out below them, with its avenues, parks, railroads, etc 'miniaturised' and made accessible to the gaze, in its totality. In 1889, visitors standing on top of the Eiffel Tower must have 'felt as though they were standing at the centre of the exhibition, the city, and the world'[38] – an illusion so 'real' that it can only be described in the language of 'magic'.

In contemporary metropolitan life, panoramas of cities, viewed from high on top, remain a compelling experience. This is so despite, or perhaps because, our imagination of the city as a totality is increasingly constituted through a profusion of visual representations that remain outside the realm of mundane existence. Rolling cameras and beaming satellites sweep across entire cities and whole continents, linking them together across space and time to remind us that there is more to experiencing the city than what meets the 'eye'. But since such images are *a priori* merged with what the 'eye' absorbs, they can no longer be separated from the 'reality' we engage with. Everyday experiences are registered through dominant representations of space/vision, which precede and overlay them in complex ways.

In actual life, with its predictable routines, the possibility of rethinking such dominant representations is often foreclosed before it even occurs. The majority of the time we occupy the physical city by 'habit', navigating streets, billboards and traffic signs as the eye skips over the familiar and fills in the missing links. Only as a stranger, a lost newcomer, do we pay attention to our surroundings. So our memories of the city do not show dramatic confrontations but rather scenes from its habitual topography, which co-exist in the mind together with a host of dominant representations of the cityscape as a totality – without necessarily contradicting each other.

When viewed from high, on top, the city reveals itself as a totality as though to a stranger on first encounter. As the 'naked' eye touches and absorbs that which it observes, images in the mind overlay physical space, creating an entirely novel experience. This is neither the city of representational images, nor the city we navigate in habitual existence. The panorama transforms the 'remembered' city of images and habituation into an experience of 'wholeness'. Looking below, we seem to comprehend the entire city in its totality, and experience the *self* as part of that totality – the ultimate inclusion. In contemporary metropolitan life, the panoramic experience encapsulates a *feeling* we can never retrospectively imagine, a sense of wholeness with the city.

The Privilege of Panoramas and Labyrinths of Impoverishment in Contemporary Istanbul

The notion of panoramic perspectives is more than a metaphor in contemporary Istanbul. The physical topography of the city, famously described as being situated on seven hills and surrounded by sea on all three sides, offers panoramas of breathtaking beauty that have historically been the crucial marker of its acclaimed glory. Views of the city's 'natural beauty' have always been closely interlinked with residential hierarchies of wealth and privilege. In present-day Istanbul, the boom in property and land markets is increasingly driven by the proliferation of gated communities and shopping malls outside the built-up core areas of the city. But for the upper crust of the city's wealthy elite, 'a panorama of the sea' remains the *sine qua non* of urban residence – secured by hidden cameras and high-tech surveillance. Perhaps the easiest way of conveying the sense of privilege associated with panoramas of the sea in Istanbul is to borrow a quote from an interview with the Nobel Prize-winning Turkish novelist Orhan Pamuk, whose work has been closely associated with the city:

> Nobody until now has seen the entirety of Istanbul as I have, horizontally and perpendicularly, that is in depth, in a manner which penetrates its history and its soul, and which comprehends its positioning, the way it settles on the seas, the way it extends. The view from my office has such a privilege that it suits a novelist. Sometimes I think I deserve everything that I see from here.[39]

Pamuk's image of himself looking out from his office window and taking in all of Istanbul, locating himself at 'the heart of the city', conveys the sense of privilege and inclusion associated with city panoramas in Istanbul in more ways than one. In many of his novels, Pamuk mobilises panoramic perspectives of Istanbul to intimate how the past and present of the city are fused, constantly investing the sights of the city with meaning. For him, the inhabitants of Istanbul have always remained 'strangers' to the city, unable to comprehend its repository of secrets – the Ottoman elite because they came from different countries, and 90 per cent of its population because they migrated to the city over the last fifty years. How Pamuk sets up the city as a mystery that conceals its secrets from its inhabitants, and defines himself as a 'novelist of Istanbul' by appropriating its signs as a text to be illuminated, remains beyond the scope of this paper.[40] My purpose in borrowing a quote from this interview is to emphasise how 'possessing' a panoramic overview of the Bosphorus constitutes a 'privilege' in contemporary Istanbul, making the owner an insider within the city's hierarchies of wealth and power, symbolically and literally.

The inhabitants of Istanbul whom Pamuk refers to as 'strangers' to the city (or as people who have arrived from Anatolia) are subsumed in a diversity of groups in terms of their history and experiences in the physical/social topography of the city, which makes generalisations meaningless. Below I want to offer some excerpts from a set of interviews with workers who clean the windows of skyscrapers in Istanbul, i.e. men who 'see' the city from on high on a daily basis. Hasan, in his late twenties, was born in the Eastern Anatolian town of Maraş, worked in cotton fields and vegetable gardens and ended up cleaning the windows of a corporate tower in Istanbul. He narrates his arrival in Istanbul as follows:

> I came to Istanbul by bus. First I came to Göztepe, to my uncle. I came to Istanbul to earn money and go back. I found a job in a furniture workshop at Göztepe industrial zone. I used to go with my uncle's son. I worked for a week. Then the employer told me to bring six cups of tea. I went out, but see, I did not know my way to anywhere. I found a teashop near the corner ... two or three streets, they all look alike. I went in and out of streets, but could not find my way back. So what I knew was going up to the Göztepe Bridge and taking the minibus back home ... and so I did.[41]

When questioned about what the city looks like from above, Hasan did not have much to say, explaining that he had been cleaning windows for a long time. Metin, his co-worker (born in the village of Amasra on the Black Sea), was more forthcoming:

> It is different, above is better, and down below makes you feel like suffocating. But when you go up it is like you are free. Istanbul is underneath. Now when you are walking down there, everything is concrete, you suffocate, as if you were jammed in it.[42]

Celil used to work in a teashop in the bazaar of Erzurum in northeastern

Anatolia. Migration to Istanbul was tough for him, and he worked in various jobs before he began to clean windows. He tells the story of how he accidentally got the wrong minibus and ended up in one of Istanbul's affluent neighbourhoods:

> I got on the wrong minibus. I got off in Etiler, everything changes there, because it is full of women in furs and men with ties. Even within the district, things differ. I have been in Istanbul for twenty-eight years, and I could not once take my aunt to the place I like most, Beşiktaş. If I take my wife there, we have to sit down, drink something. No way. How is it possible, on 420 *lira*?[43]

Although Hasan, Metin and Celil were co-workers (hired by a subcontracting firm), they arrived in Istanbul from different provinces and resided in different neighbourhoods in its sprawling periphery, among their own kin and relatives. But their stories follow a similar pattern; their topography of Istanbul was mapped by a series of low-paying, often temporary jobs they have held. They give the names of districts where their work was located, but the district itself rarely appears in their stories. The city of Istanbul they inhabit evokes a labyrinth, with identical streets, minibus routes, different yet equally low-paying jobs – a suffocating drudgery that seems to offer no exits. Although they work on skyscrapers, they do not register or absorb Istanbul's panorama.

Ending with Miniaturk

Anatolia is described as the 'cradle' of civilisations in the promotional literature of Miniaturk and represented as such by the choice of models on exhibit. The idea of ancient Anatolia as the 'cradle' of modern civilisation dates back to the latter half of the 1930s in Turkey, when a new generation of cultural theorists sought to revise official historiography. This was an attempt to replace earlier theories of the origins of 'Turkish race' with a 'humanist culture', by establishing continuities between ancient and modern inhabitants of Anatolia. In art as well as literature, a new wave of Turkish humanism emerged, elaborating the similarities between the culture narrated in the Homeric legends and a highly selective, often anecdotal account of Turkish folklore. Thus Hellenism was embraced as a 'universal' ideal and conflated with Anatolia's 'native' identity, as the 'cradle' of civilisation.[44] Since then, the rhetoric of Anatolia as the 'cradle' of civilisations has been transformed into common knowledge – something taken for granted, without questioning. In the context of Miniaturk, the forty-five monuments representing Anatolia as the 'cradle' of civilisations have been very carefully chosen by the committee of historians to locate the origins of Hellenic civilisation in the present territory of Anatolia, along with its native 'treasures'. But the majority of visitors to Miniaturk already *know* that 'Anatolia is the cradle of civilisations', and do not reflect on the choice of monuments on display. When asked to do so (by me), they search their memory for omissions and try to come up with suggestions on what else might have been included.

The *people* who have migrated from Anatolia, however, are a 'problem' in Istanbul; or, perhaps more accurately, the Anatolian origins of people who live in the city's sprawling low-income peripheral neighbourhoods (the *gecekondu*) are part of the problem they constitute. In the listing of Istanbul's major problems, which demand urgent solutions, what is referred to as *gecekondu sorunu* ('the problem of *gecekondu*') heads the list, next to none other than the traffic problem and the crime problem, with the corruption problem following close behind. Given the spatial connotations of the term *gecekondu*, many of the urgent problems identified on the pages of daily newspapers, or on the evening television news, become mapped onto city space as a part of the *gecekondu* problem – i.e. associated with the inhabitants of Istanbul's low-income neighbourhoods (with the exception of the traffic problem).

The 'causes' of the *gecekondu* problem as well as the 'solutions', as identified and elaborated by planners, journalists, politicians and intellectuals, have shifted over time. In the early 1950s and 1960s, for instance, the *gecekondu* problem was predominantly defined as a temporary matter that would be resolved as the peasants coming from Anatolia became 'integrated' into the city. In the latter half of the 1970s, when the political left in Turkey became prominent on the national scene, the *gecekondu* problem was formulated as one of unemployment and exploitation. But now, in the 'global' Istanbul of Turkey's future ambitions, the '*gecekondu* problem' has assumed greater urgency than ever before, as it is 'polluting' the city aesthetically and culturally. So the clearance of *gecekondu* neighbourhoods, by relocating property owners to municipally financed apartment blocks (and letting renters take care of themselves), has become the official policy of the metropolitan city government as well as the district municipalities. The metropolitan government's millennium project of promoting urban citizenship and identification with the city is fraught with contradictions.

For visitors of Miniaturk, however, the Anatolia on display is fused with the ancient past and global future not only of Istanbul but the whole nation. Roaming its paths offers the experience of a totality, with the *self* at its very centre – the ultimate inclusion. It is this sense of inclusion I want to suggest, which makes Miniaturk a 'magical' experience, difficult to recapture retrospectively but 'absolutely worth visiting'.

In Lieu of a Conclusion

Over the past two decades, the idea of a 'global' Istanbul has become the site and symbol of Turkey's aspirations in the twenty-first century. Future visions of the city and of the nation have become inextricably bound up in public, popular and scholarly discourses. Claims to a global future for Istanbul have breached the canons of official historiography, calling forth new interpretations of its Ottoman legacy. In the process, Istanbul's multiple and multilayered pasts have come under intense debate as the negotiating ground for alternative political projects, not only for the city but for the nation as well.

In the Istanbul of the 1990s, 'history' is produced, reconfigured and disseminated in a host of commercialised forms, from tourist brochures and auction houses to news broadcasts and political summits. This is obviously very different from 'history' as written and disseminated by the Turkish state. Hence my emphasis is on a number of competing public narratives that circulate in commodity forms to mediate between the past and the ethnographic present of the city. These are 'political' narratives in the sense that they mobilise alternative versions of the past, from different socio-cultural locations, and address different constituencies. What they have in common is the way they accentuate forms of belonging, or yearning to belong, to a wider cultural configuration than the territorially bounded nation state. At the same time, of course, they reveal how yearnings for collective identities beyond the nation-state are shot through with the kinds of essentialisms we tend to associate with nationalist rhetoric.

Bibliography

Abbas, Ackbar, 'Cosmopolitan De-scriptions: Shanghai and Hong Kong', *Public Culture*, vol. 12, no. 3, 2000, pp. 769–86.

Bartu, Ayfer, 'Rethinking Heritage Politics in a Global Context: A View from Istanbul', in Nezar AlSayyad, *Hybrid Urbanism: On Identity Discourse and the Built Environment*, Westport, CT: Praeger Publishers, 2001.

—— 'Who Owns the Old Quarters? Rewriting Histories in a Global Era', in Çağlar Keyder, ed., *Istanbul: Between the Global and the Local*, Lanham, MD: Rowman & Littlefield, 1999, pp. 31–46.

Bilsel, Can, 'Our Anatolia: the Making of the "Humanist Culture" in Turkey', paper presented at the symposium 'Historiography and Ideology: Architectural Heritage of the 'Lands of Rum', Cambridge, MA: Harvard University, 11–12 May 2006.

Bora, Tanil, 'Istanbul of the Conqueror: The "Alternative Global City" Dreams of Political Islam', in Çağlar Keyder, ed., *Istanbul: Between the Global and the Local*, Lanham, MD: Rowman & Littlefield, 1999, pp. 47–58.

Boym, Svetlana, *The Future of Nostalgia*, New York: Basic Books, 2001.

Bozdoğan, Sibel, *Modernism and Nation Building: Turkish Architectural Culture in the Early Republic*, Seattle: University of Washington Press, 2001.

Buck-Morss, Susan, *The Dialectics of Seeing: Walter Benjamin and the Arcades Project*, Cambridge, MA: MIT Press, 1991.

Çelik, Zeynep, *The Remaking of Istanbul*, Berkeley: University of California Press, 1993.

—— 'Urban Preservation as Theme Park: The Case of Soğukçeşme Street', in Zeynep Çelik, Diane Favro and Richard Ingersol, eds, *Streets: Critical Perspectives on Public Space*, Berkeley: University of California Press, 1994.

Çinar, Alev, 'National History as a Contested Site: The Conquest of Istanbul and Islamist Negotiations of the Nation', *Comparative Studies in Society and History*, vol. 43, no. 2, 2001, pp. 363–91.

—— 'Refah Party and the City Administration in Istanbul: Liberal Islam, Localism and Hybridity', in *New Perspectives on Turkey*, no. 16, spring 1997, pp. 1–22.

Eldem, Ethem, 'Istanbul: from Imperial to Peripheral Capital', in Ethem Eldem, Daniel Goffman and Bruce Masters, eds, *The Ottoman City between the East and the West*, Cambridge: Cambridge University Press, 1999, pp. 139–206.

Fainstein, Susan and Judd, Dennis, 'Global Forces, Local Strategies, and Urban Tourism', in S. Fainstein and D. Judd, eds, *The Tourist City*, New Haven: Yale University Press, 1999, pp. 1–34.

Ghannam, Farha, *Remaking the Modern: Space, Relocation and the Politics of Identity in a Global Cairo*, Los Angeles: University of California Press, 2002.

Hastaoğlou-Martinidis, Vilma, 'Visions of Constantinople/Istanbul from Nineteenth Century Guidebooks', *Proceedings, ACSA International Congress*, New York: ACSA Press, 2001, pp. 8–13.

Houston, Christopher, 'Brewing of Islamist Modernity: Tea Gardens and Public Space in Istanbul', in *Theory, Culture and Society*, vol. 18, no. 6, 2001, pp. 77–97.

Huyssen, Andreas, 'Present Pasts: Media, Politics, Amnesia', in *Public Culture*, vol. 12, no. 1, 2000, pp. 21–38.

——*Present Pasts: Urban Palimpsests and the Politics of Memory in the Present*, Stanford, CA: Stanford University Press, 2003.

Irzik, Sibel, 'How to be a Novelist of Istanbul: The Black Book', in Franco Moretti, ed., *Il romanzo* (*The Novel*), Torino: Einaudi, 2003, pp. 555–62 (to be reprinted in *The Novel*, Princeton University Press, forthcoming).

El Kadi, Galila and ElKerdany, Dalila, 'Belle-Époque Cairo: The Politics of Refurbishing the Downtown Business District', in Diane Singerman and Paul Amar, eds, *Cairo Cosmopolitan: Politics, Culture, and Urban Space in the New Globalized Middle East*, Cairo: The American University in Cairo Press, 2006, pp. 345–76.

Keyder, Çağlar, 'The Consequences of the Exchange of Populations for Turkey', in Reneé Hirschon, ed., *Crossing the Aegean: An Appraisal of the 1923 Compulsory Population Exchange between Greece and Turkey*, London: Berghahn Books, 2003.

—— *Istanbul: Between the Local and the Global*, Oxford: Rowman and Littlefield, 1999.

Lee, Leo Ou-fan, *Shanghai Modern: The Flowering of New Urban Culture in China, 1930–1945*, Cambridge, MA: Harvard University Press, 2000.

——'Shanghai Modern: Reflections on Urban Culture in China in the 1930s', *Public Culture*, vol. 11, no. 1, pp. 75–107.

Mansel, Philip, *Constantinople: The City of the World's Desire, 1453–1924*, New York: St. Martin's Press, 1996.

Miniaturk Minyatür Türkiye Parki, http://www.miniaturk.com.tr.

Mitchell, Timothy, *Colonising Egypt*, Cairo: Cairo University Press, 1988.

Öncü, Ayşe and Weyland, Petra, 'Introduction', in Ayşe Öncü and Petra Weyland, eds, *Space, Culture and Power: New Identities in Globalising Cities*, London: Zed Books, 1997, pp. 1–20.

Rosenthal, Steven, 'Foreigners and Municipal Reform in Istanbul: 1855–1865', in *International Journal of Middle East Studies*, vol. 11, no. 2, 1980, pp. 227–245.

Saktanber, A., 'Indoor/Outdoor? Urban Woman Goes to Socialize: Local Governments, Gender and the Reformulation of Islamic Neo-Liberalism through Leisurescapes', paper presented at the 'Workshop on the Comparative Urban Landscapes and their Subaltern Citizen-Subjects in the Middle East and South Asia', Istanbul: 29–30 January 2004.

Scott, Allen, 'The Cultural Economy of Cities', in *International Journal of Urban and Regional Research*, vol. 21, no. 2, 1997, pp. 323–40.

Shadid, Y. and Weiping, W., 'Pathways to a World-city: Shanghai Rising in an Era of Globalisation', in *Urban Studies*, vol. 39, no. 7, 2002, pp. 1213–40.

Slater, Don, 'Photography and Modern Vision: The Spectacle of "Natural Magic"', in Chris Jenks, *Visual Culture*, New York: Routledge, 1995, pp. 218–37.

Stewart, Susan, *On Longing*, Durham: Duke University Press, 1999.

White, Jenny B., *Islamist Mobilization in Turkey*, Seattle: University of Washington Press, 2002.

Zukin, Sharon, *The Cultures of Cities*, Cambridge: Blackwell Publishers, 1995.

Notes

1. Zukin, *The Cultures of Cities*.
2. Scott, *The Cultural Economy of Cities*.
3. Fainstein and Judd, 'Global Forces, Local Strategies, and Urban Tourism'.
4. Ibid., pp. 26–7.
5. Öncü and Weyland, 'Introduction', *Space, Culture and Power*.
6. Ghannam, *Remaking the Modern*.
7. Singerman and Amar, *Cairo Cosmopolitan*.
8. El Kadi and ElKerdany, 'Belle-Epoque Cairo'.
9. Huyssen, 'Present Pasts: Media, Politics, Amnesia' and *Present Pasts: Urban Palimpsests and the Politics of Memory in the Present*.
10. Huyssen, 'Present Pasts: Media, Politics, Amnesia', p. 26.
11. Lee, 'Shanghai Modern'; Shadid and Weiping, 'Pathways to a World-City'.
12. Boym, *The Future of Nostalgia*.
13. Somers, 'The Narrative Construction of Identity'.
14. Huyssen, 'Present Pasts: Media, Politics, Amnesia', p. 33.
15. Çelik, *The Remaking of Istanbul*; Bozdoğan, *Modernism and Nation Building*.
16. Rosenthal, 'Foreigners and Municipal Reform in Istanbul: 1855–1865'.
17. Keyder, *Istanbul: Between the Local and the Global*, p. 35.
18. Ibid.
19. Quoted from an 1892 guide from Baedeker of Leipzig, a publisher of guidebooks for German travellers, in Hastaoğlou-Martinidis, 'Visions of Constantinople/Istanbul from Nineteenth Century Guidebooks'.
20. Quoted from a 1900 guide from John Murray of London, a chief publishing house for guidebooks, in ibid., p. 10.
21. Quoted from a 1912 *Guide Joanne*, published by Hachette, in ibid., p.10.
22. Keyder, 'The Consequences of the Exchange of Populations for Turkey'.
23. Mansel, *Constantinople*.
24. *Hürriyet*, 30 March 1999.
25. Bora, 'Istanbul of the Conqueror'; Çınar, 'National History as a Contested Site'.
26. *Hürriyet*, 26 December 1993.
27. Bartu, 'Who Owns the Old Quarters?'.
28. Houston, 'Brewing of Islamist Modernity'; Saktanber, 'Outdoor/Indoor?'.
29. *Hürriyet*, 3 December 2005, (abridged).
30. This paragraph is from one of numerous 'preparatory' history books available on the market, designed for high school students taking the national university examinations. Since university entrance examinations are centrally administered, and highly competitive, there is a lucrative market for such 'preparatory' books, with new ones appearing each year. They all replicate the same high school curriculum, but with a different set of sample test questions based on the previous year's examination, and at different prices depending on quality of print and paper.
31. A cultural management firm, Istanbul Kültür A.Ş., which was initially established to run the millennium campaign, has since become the main operational arm of

Istanbul's metropolitan administration in 'cultural affairs'. In addition to organising and publicising a host of 'cultural activities' financed by the metro administration, Kültür A.Ş. publishes a glossy bi-annual magazine titled *Gezinti*, devoted to 'enhancing knowledge of Istanbul's cultural heritage'. The first issue, published in the summer of 2003, was almost entirely devoted to Miniaturk, with extensive excerpts from Mayor Gürtuna's inaugural speech (including the paragraph translated here), as well as an in-depth interview with him on the regeneration of the Golden Horn. The broad publicity campaign that coincided with the opening ceremonies generated a burst of journalistic commentary in the daily press and news reports on television. For the sake of brevity, I have picked out a few of the most frequently used phrases used in numerous superlative accounts of the park.

32. Buck-Morss, *The Dialectics of Seeing*, pp. 82–3.
33. Daily life in Istanbul of the 1990s was marked by a dizzying proliferation of commodities and images. This experience of mundane life through a new object-world – through the circulation of new forms of media, mobile phones, music CDs, large-scale spectacles – evoked nineteenth-century European cities, when daily life suddenly took on new meaning. Thus I have heavily borrowed from Susan Buck-Morrs, whose book captures the 'phantasmagoric' quality of this urban experience so well. The vast literature on the 'hyperreality' of contemporary theme parks does not seem particularly relevant or illuminating in the context of Miniaturk.
34. Mitchell, *Colonising Egypt*, p. 10.
35. Slater, 'Photography and Modern Vision', pp. 219–27.
36. Mitchell, *Colonising Egypt*, p. 9.
37. Buck-Morss, *The Dialectics of Seeing*, p. 399.
38. Ibid.
39. Interview published in *Istanbul*, 1999; see Irzik, 'How to be a Novelist of Istanbul'.
40. Irzik, 'How to be a Novelist of Istanbul'.
41. Interview, December 2005, courtesy of Eda Çakmakçı.
42. Ibid.
43. Ibid.
44. For an extended discussion of the construction of Anatolia in the works of several novelists during this period, see Bilsel, 'Our Anatolia'.

VYJAYANTHI RAO

Post-Industrial Transitions

Citizenship and Historicity in Mumbai's 'World Class' Makeover

Transitions

Over the last fifteen years, the city formerly known as Bombay has undergone numerous transformations and transitions. Most notably, in 1996, the city's name was changed to Mumbai – the name commonly used for Bombay by native speakers of Marathi, the official language of Maharashtra (the state of which Mumbai is the capital). This nomenclatural change is a symptom of other shifts, and at least three books use this shift as a point of departure for understanding aspects of urbanism unique to Bombay. These include two edited volumes, *Bombay to Mumbai: Changing Perspectives*[1] and *Bombay and Mumbai: A City in Transition*[2] as well as anthropologist Thomas Blom Hansen's *The Wages of Violence: Naming and Violence in Postcolonial Bombay*.[3] The first two assume quite explicitly that 'Bombay' stands for a different city than the one named 'Mumbai'. Hansen, too, associates a specific bundle of practices with the name 'Mumbai'. These have to do with a certain proletarian and masculine culture of violence associated with the militant Hindu nationalist party, the Shiv Sena, which was responsible for introducing the name change and whose undertow now pervades the atmosphere of the city.

For others, this rise in a culture of violence – against persons, things and property – coincides with profound transformations in the cosmopolitan ethos and modernity of the city. But the content of this cosmopolitanism has certainly not been stable. Arjun Appadurai identifies it as a tolerance of diversity that rested upon commercial relations. He describes Bombay as a 'cosmopolis of commerce'.[4] A new geography and economy of violence

Inside India United Mills, 2002 (Photo: Rajesh Vora)

have been evident since December 1992, when the city witnessed the first of a series of cataclysmic incidents of violence.

First, a series of riots between Hindus and Muslims in several neighbourhoods across the city broke out immediately after the destruction of a sixteenth-century mosque in the northern Indian city of Ayodhya by hundreds of young men mobilised by militant Hindu nationalist politicians. Following the riots, the coordinated serial bombing of the city on 12 March 1993 took it entirely by surprise; there was, particularly, the realisation that the city's underworld had been polarised along communal lines[5], and had been used to execute the bombings. In the years since, the liberalisation of the Indian economy weighed heavily on Bombay as it struggled to reconstitute its place as *urbs prima in Indis* against this violence from within and without that had turned the city into a stage for all sorts of claims made through the medium of violence. It was also struggling against its own image as the region's 'city of gold', a place where untold fortunes could be made.

As a city of industrial capital – known in the colonial period as the 'Manchester of the East' for its huge textile base, with more than 500 mills – the city was also attempting to make the transition from the increasingly obsolete textile economy and the increasing technological obsolescence of its port, for which it had been renowned throughout colonial history. The importance of making space for the 'new economy' of IT-enabled industries, for financial and other services and for the people who came along with these new industries was increasingly evident as smaller Indian cities like Bangalore became investment sites for international capital. Bombay's attempt to become a 'global city' in Sassen's terms[6] thus involved a struggle not only against its own atmosphere of decaying and degrading social relations but also against its already bloated demographic state.

But the most visually evident forms of violence are those exemplified in the very built forms of Mumbai. In this essay, following Achille Mbembe's argument in his recent essay on Johannesburg, 'The Aesthetics of Superfluity',[7] I shall try to unpack the relationship between surfaces, citizens, violence and the temporal experiences of change in Mumbai's post-industrial aspirations to becoming a 'world-class' city.

Space: The Final Frontier

I begin with the surface of the city as a site, and not the more commonly posed problem of housing *per se* that takes us into a more functional realm of how to achieve dignified living. Here I want to think about the legibility of what is happening in the city and to the city by making built space the object of my reading – that is, to position these surfaces as the 'projective extension' of the city's transitions. I also want to highlight the relationship between architectural forms and *spatial imagination* – in a city like Mumbai, the phenomenology of density, the juxtaposition and crowding that assaults the senses, is the ground upon which social interactions take place. Not surprisingly, forms of the imagination are dominated and oriented by this density, and beneath the mask of architecture one is confronted constantly by the need to calibrate the archaeology of spatial imaginaries. Daniel Libeskind, who recently visited Mumbai for the first time remarked:

> Mumbai is clearly a city that eludes architects who see the city
> as a material object. It's a city where human beings are far more
> important than brick and mortar, concrete, glass and steel.[8]

In the logic of such remarks, Mumbai becomes a place where architecture itself disappears as a material fact, and is substituted by a sheer demographic density that constitutes its visual overlay, even taking the more traditional place of infrastructure as its underneath. How does one read these signs?

For a theorist like Mike Davis, the architectural expression and arrangement of these densities in vast slum settlements exemplifies the creation of a 'surplus humanity' by a system of neo-liberal governance.[9] But there are also some paradoxes to consider. According to a recent World

Bombay Development Department (BDD) Chawls, Central Mumbai: Tenement housing for workers, constructed in the early 20th century, 2006 (Photo: Colleen Macklin)

Bank document, Mumbai has the world's largest slum population sitting on some of the world's most expensive real estate. It is the globe's most densely populated city and the most 'topographically challenged' of the world's largest cities. At the same time that Davis was writing his essay, 'Planet of Slums' (now a book), several Mumbai-based urbanists noted that the city's problems of density and degraded built forms had less to do with poverty and more to do with policy – that, in fact, the city continued to attract migrants because of its ability to generate jobs, but because the mechanisms for a fair housing market simply did not exist, even those who might be considered middle-class in terms of income had to end up living in slum colonies.

While the job-creation ability of Mumbai's economy is a point of some contention, it is also clear that even without new migration from the rural areas, Mumbai has a huge crisis on its hands. But this crisis is not merely a crisis in housing. The idea of a 'surplus humanity', of a superfluous population, is very much a key issue if one examines Mumbai's present economic situation.

The connection of this class of workers to the built forms of the city is vital because a logic of 'productive sacrifice' of this 'superfluous population' appears to be one of the key underpinnings of the forms, policies and

Dharavi District, North Mumbai, 2005 (Photo: Soumik Kar)

institutions of private property in the city.[10] This might account for the very complex game of the calibration of private property to housing and other needs of the city that has been going on since independence, but suddenly accelerated and intensified after the liberalisation of the Indian economy. Even if jobs are available in the city, the working class is better defined, as Sandeep Pendse[11] has put it, as 'toilers' – those whose existence in the city is underwritten by forms of degraded and destructive labour, 'predetermined by a logic of productive sacrifice'.[12] The post-industrial economy in Mumbai, in fact, is characterised by a whole subterranean world involving such sacrifices in terms of the sorts of industries that are occupying the interstitial, transitional economy (for example, recycling industries of various kinds), from the sacrifice of migrant children in the sweatshops of the gold and diamond processing industries and embroidery shops and countless other examples of small-scale, hazardous kinds of work, to that of the faceless toilers in the new economy, those 'knowledge workers' who are treated as night-shift fodder by an industry prepared for high attrition rates.

These sites of production are themselves situated within and at the edges of post-industrial space: spaces abandoned by industry or contaminated by their very adjacency: the abandoned textile mills and other large infrastructure, the slums, the crumbling housing stock, the marshes, mangroves, creeks, salt pans, rivers and hills. To complete the circle, the appetite for space, created by the dense concentration of populations, turns to these very sites to conjugate or tie together the visible needs of this population with the motive for profit.

These sites are being revisited apparently because of the lack of space for building in the city. Here we encounter a significant paradox. As several studies have pointed out, there is not so much a lack of space as 'frozen space': as much as 2,600 acres of land in the centre of the city are occupied by derelict mills and declining port functions; building heights are severely restricted by a universal limit on floorspace on all plots throughout the city (with zoned exceptions); growth in rental stock was practically non-existent because rents were frozen at 1940s levels (and continue to be so); the state and its various agents – the railways, the municipality and so on – own over a thousand acres of land themselves, much of it lying idle or occupied by slums (and this does not include the slum settlements on 'encroached infrastructure' or encroached public works). All this space and potential space is frozen from development, suspended in time. This perception of frozen space is also just that at one level – a perception, and in particular a perception that is promoted by the reform-minded private sector, eager to bring about a market in space.

In the absence of comprehensive reforms of these policies (I shall end by looking a bit more at the implications of this reform), an interim city has been quietly developing on the ruins of the industrial city. The sites I mentioned earlier are 'post-industrial' landscapes not merely in the sense of supporting new economies that no longer depend on factory-based production, but they are such in the temporal sense as well – terrain that becomes available to an archaeological imagination *because* their toxic ecologies are deliberately re-engineered by the market and turned into palatable real estate products.

In comparison to post-industrial sites elsewhere in the world, and especially in Euro-American cities where industrial decline has arguably been taking place over a longer period of time, the cultural fate of post-industrial sites in places like Mumbai have been much less predictable. This is specifically the case because these places have begun to serve as a 'back-office' for the more toxic functions associated with worldwide industrial decline, including industries such as toxic waste recycling, shipbreaking and so on. Mumbai's own industrial infrastructure, now deployed in these activities, is thus in a state of suspension between its obsolescence in the new world economy and its continued usefulness to this very world as a recycling site. It is therefore difficult to imagine, for the city, the sorts of gentrification projects that refurbish, renovate and reuse industrial spaces that have

Worker in the ship-breaking yard (Darukhana), Mumbai Port Trust, Mumbai, 2004 (Photo: Vyjayanthi Rao)

become commonplace in the European and American cities like Manchester and New York. In Mumbai, gentrification itself is a newly emergent project, visible in the language of a nascent heritage movement.

Outside the ambit of any kind of protection or public debate, a new city, an experimental city – what one might call an 'ex-city' – is being born. The pursuit of short-term changes has created a new landscape within which these questions must now be raised. This landscape is both dramatic and mundane, an ecology of new spatial forms that have created new layers of obsolescence, decay, vacancy and a sense of temporariness underneath the skin of the existing built fabric. This sense of temporariness is created both by acts of destruction as well as acts of construction whose simultaneous presence characterises Mumbai's peculiar territorial and visual condition today. The haunting silence of the cloth-making machines in the textile mills of central Mumbai, presently on the block awaiting auction and conversion into real estate products, now meets its audacious counterpart in strange new reclamation projects that create contiguous space stitching together a dramatic ecology of salt pans, paddy fields and chemical factories. But to understand what is happening, we need to probe a bit further beyond the visage of these experiments.

The Mumbai Makeover Project

A lively debate is raging these days in Mumbai about how to 'make the city over' – the project, which newspapers have been referring to as the Mumbai Makeover project, began when a group of elite citizens formed an NGO called Bombay First and hired the international consultancy group McKinsey & Co. to prepare a report on how to transform Mumbai into a 'world-class city'.[13] This was an unprecedented move, and signals a real investment of the elite in making claims to the city for practically the first time in the city's post-colonial history. Earlier investments amounted to philanthropic actions, which were largely disconnected from the arena of politics, governance and other matters of the state.

In exchange for being left alone to pursue their goals of profit and their largely discrete lifestyles, the first citizens of the city were content to leave the political sphere in the hands of politicians and bureaucrats. With liberalisation and the decline of the industrial economy and the tightening control of the state in industrial policy plus its conscious decision to de-industrialise the city in favour of developing the rural hinterlands, it became clear that more investment would be needed to kickstart the city's shift to becoming a service provider. The growing tensions within Mumbai between ethno-religious groups, and the contest over space between rich and poor, only served to exacerbate these views, and sometimes translated into a feeble concern on the part of elite groups over the degraded environment of the city and the declining quality of life.

This project has not only successfully mobilised public opinion within the city, including the emergence of serious and lively opposition and the cultivation of knowledge about the arcane planning policies that have driven the city's spatial development, but it has also managed to mobilise the World Bank's special interest in supporting the project. Interested actors within and outside the city take McKinsey's 'Vision Mumbai' report document and its recommendations as a point of departure. In fact, the World Bank, in recent consultations with the state government, has been urging land use reforms to improve urban efficiency, because the city's size and scale mean that the its functioning has an economy-wide effect. Land use reforms are the Holy Grail, the key that might have an effect equivalent to the economic reforms that India adopted as the price for opening up its economy to international capital.

What is interesting is that, for the first time, a range of citizens are being exposed to technocratic solutions as an answer to counteract the damage done by populist political reforms that the state has been attempting to enact over the course of the 1990s and in this decade. In a sense, this debate has succeeded in 'fomenting a crisis' for a range of actors, bringing the problems and issues into public view. An even more urgent reason came to light when the northern parts of the city were flooded on 26 July 2005 by a downpour that deposited nearly 1 metre of rainfall in a single afternoon, completely overwhelming Mumbai's already fragile infrastructure and resulting in a huge loss of life and property. By this time, the makeover project was already well underway, at least in a series of highly visible measures.

Shortly after assuming power, the new prime minister had promised, in October 2004, to put the weight of the central government behind turning Mumbai into Shanghai. Dreams of a shining future for the nation were being pinned on the future of the city. One of the first acts of the new Maharashtra state government elected in October 2006 was to demolish 90,000 huts with great brutality, rendering 400,000 people homeless; they were cast out from their makeshift shelters for not being able to prove that they had been in the city prior to 1995, the 'cut-off' date for the legalisation of residencies. The logic of the 'cut-off' date was central because it had become a crucial instrument in classifying and categorising people, in deciding who could stay in the city and who could not.

In 1995, the Shiv Sena government had also launched a 'free housing' scheme to rehouse those who could prove that their residency in the city predated 1995. This scheme was to be supported by providing incentives for private developers to rehouse the eligible poor using market instruments, specifically tradable development rights (TDR), to mobilise the resources to address the needs of the poor. In exchange for rehabilitating slum dwellers into an agreed-upon, barracks-like SRA (Slum Rehabilitation Authority) development, developers would be allowed to build on the plot, now freed of 'encroachments', or on another plot, and sell the built space to a starving market of middle- and upper-class consumers.

The pragmatics of frozen space discussed earlier is crucial to the distorted market values of land in Mumbai. This distortion has had the effect of making Mumbai one of the most expensive real estate markets in the world. Thus private developers have benefited enormously from this situation, while the poor became currency for releasing locked space. In practical terms, slum dwellers consenting to the agreement would first be dislocated into 'transit camps' and then resettled into SRA housing, to which they were assigned by a consultative process involving the government and the developer. The same scheme was applied for the redevelopment of the frozen-rent buildings. These buildings, in the centre of the island city – which is to say, historically among the oldest developments – have been in a state of disrepair and dilapidation, rendered obsolete from the point of view of the market, unable to realise their potential exchange value through rent harvesting or through the sale of the extremely valuable real estate plots upon which they sit.

Developers therefore view the individuals eligible for resettlement and relocation as equivalent units of space. Thus, to obtain the rights to a certain amount of saleable square footage, developers calculate the equivalent number of tenants or slum dwellers who need to be resettled and fabricate the numbers accordingly if they happen to fall short of the figure required. These schemes create equivalencies between various categories of people affected – through ideas of space or infrastructure deprivation – to yield an overarching category of the urban poor.

As a route to the mass reconstruction of the city, the establishment of such notional rights actively connects this technocratic form to mass displacement and to the destruction of a complex ecology of built and social forms that have developed over time. Translating these 'obsolete' chunks of inhabited space and time into an updated experience of the city involves a complex experience of displacement and suspension for these residents. The assertion of the state's sovereignty in creating rights to 'free' housing is thus a process in which an effective abolition of the reality of space takes place in favour of a dematerialised image of that space which can be retailed on the market. Urban subjectivity takes on qualities of exile and transience.

All these 'reformative' acts, which are also acts of reformatting with the intended effect of creating a market in real estate, have in fact aided speculative investing based on insider knowledge and connections, and the creation of a peculiar form of right – the right to free housing, which is, in effect, the enabling mechanism for the creation of the market. The speculative, profit-driven temporality of the market is linked to the dreams and aspirations of those who are effectively cut off from participating in it. These displaceable people are also, broadly speaking, the class of 'toilers' who are at once indispensable and expendable in terms of their labour for the new city.

In the last part of this essay I want to turn to the real effects of this experimental stage upon the culture and phenomenology of citizenship in the contemporary city. I am not interested in doing this in order to predict what might happen to the city in the future as a reading of a conspiracy between various actors: politicians, bureaucrats, developers and international real estate capital. But I am interested in reading the intersections between the creation and circulation of real estate capital as a particular form of global capital, and the delirium of poverty in the city. This delirium has unleashed a peculiar state of speculation that exploits the current freezes and impasses in the market for space, creating transition and transience, suspending residents into states of expectation and waiting for indefinite periods.

Time in Crisis

The foundational logic of the city of the future is thus a certain assumption that the rights of the urban poor, created within the broader functional framework of citizenship as a consequence of claims and needs, are a kind of wealth that can be lavishly spent in the process of creating the market for space. The wasted lives of the poor, their expendability and debasement, constitutes this foundational logic of the future. But this is not, as I said earlier, a functionalist argument about the conspiracies that thwart the development of the 'good city' and propertied citizens. I am interested in the phenomenological state unleashed in the present as it appears to brush against the future, in the juxtaposition of new forms against old ones.

As various planning instruments – like Floor Space Index (or Floor Area Ratio), TDR and so on – have become weapons enabling construction, we see bizarre mutations of the built landscape. Defying all possible logic in terms of infrastructure and therefore of sustainable living, these buildings have instead become a new symbol of the 'politics of verticality' that makes legible changes in the nature of urban citizenship resulting from being merely adjacent to mutations of the built fabric. The verticalisation of the island city has added a three-dimensional twist to the drama of hierarchy, exclusion and dispossession. Juxtaposed against the built fabric, these structures transform not only the social and cultural life of the city but also, equally, the representational order within which space is conceived.

From the point of view of the market, they render existing built and yet-to-be built space – the space of slums, of the rent-controlled buildings, the factories, warehouses, the salt pans, the mangroves, urban villages, and industrial housing stock – 'inefficient' and 'obsolete' in their present state. These spaces, in other words, are turned into spaces of severely diminished exchange value by this process. This emerging vertical city thus renders these landscapes obsolete by the sheer force of juxtaposition against this fabric, now perceived as one of dereliction.

Navigating a precarious territory between populist mobilisation and corporate profits, these changes are significant as acts of speculation and also for serving as the speculum, or mirror, in which the future can be viewed. The city of the future is a floating world; it is being built, not on space *per se*, which has to be created and unlocked from a labyrinth of regulations. This floating world goes with a floating population of persons subject to displacement – categories of persons who could be moved in order to make urban space more 'efficient'. The most evident of these categories is the urban poor, who serve as an instrument, the counterfeit currency for urban improvement. They stand both as signs of the failure of the current development process as well as the vehicle, a resource to be deployed in the reconstruction of the city. By contrast a whole world of others, who are barely keeping their heads above this slum situation, are rendered invisible as their struggles to secure rights of residence have only resulted in the outward expansion of the city turning them into a travelling population of commuters spending increasing amounts of time in motion from the distant peripheries to the centre. They are cut off from the current logic of space creation because the space they occupy is not yet within the ambit of 'exchangeable' or tradable space.

The right to shelter in the city is thus not, by any stretch, a right to propertied citizenship. It is rather a right that reduces residence to remaining, as remainders, as an effectively mobile population. The nature of space inherent in property can be read as a relationship to various forms of transitoriness and obsolescence. The ideology of flexible planning takes time to be a purely *temporal* fact, not a *social* one, implying a static and homogenous notion of future time. However, the sort of flexible and 'speeded'-up landscapes that I have been describing are suffused with a sense of time in suspension, with the sense of suspension that is the social prelude to displacement, relocation and transience in general. Indeed, in defending the rights-based development schemes such as those offering 'free' housing and rehabilitation to slum dwellers able to prove the occupation of their shanties from a certain date in the past (which itself keeps shifting) in exchange for development rights to private developers, a prominent housing rights activist declared publicly that the scheme was agreed to in order to protect slum dwellers from the threat of demolition. Where demolition is a constant and imminent threat, the SRA scheme suspends the slum dweller in a space of constant anticipation, sometimes lasting an entire lifetime.

The conjugation of landscapes crafted by the sort of flexible planning process being pursued at present hesitates between the market and senses of place. The presence of the state, even through its absence in terms of provisioning, produces strange new worlds of subjects whose experience of time and space are caught within a series of manipulations and transformations performed on the preserved conditions of dysfunctionality, which are, in turn, transmuted into increasingly transient physical conditions. They are, in other words, caught within the space of a fundamentally speculative temporality. Within this speculative space, the temporality of planning, of modernisation, of cycles of construction and destruction and the *longue durée* of ecological time are headed for an inevitable, head-on collision.

A distinct rhetoric about built space seems to underwrite visions of the city of the future. This vision builds on normative ideas about the built environment – the city must resemble Shanghai or Singapore, and must therefore be reassembled. The non-modern and the not-yet-modern – both classified in the inimical zones of the 'temporary' by the high priests of modernist planning – are slated either for preservation as signs of a completed past or for erasure as abhorrent signs of dysfunction, disorder and even disease. In their place, the city of the future is sought, to be endowed with homogenous, 'modern' built forms by a slew of experts. These solutions, however, must tailor ingenious legal formats together with a particular set of forms, premised on the impossibility of the coexistence of diverse experiences of city-making and inhabitation as well as a diverse built formats, apparently preferring the rise of vertical forms as neutral and desired solutions to the housing crisis. On the other hand, while liberal notions of citizenship were underwritten by the permanence of property, the only constant in the transient space of the city is an imminent sense of dispossession, which is beginning to underwrite a new form of citizenship, as it were: a form of transient citizenship premised on an impermanent, speculative future.

Bibliography

Appadurai, Arjun, 'Deep Democracy', *Public Culture*, vol. 14, no. 1, 2002, pp. 21–47.

——'The Illusion of Permanence: Interview with Arjun Appadurai by Perspecta 34', *Perspecta 34: The Yale Architectural Journal*, June 2003, pp. 44–52.

——*Modernity at Large: Cultural Dimensions of Globalization*, Minneapolis: University of Minnesota Press, 1996.

—— 'Spectral Housing and Urban Cleansing in Millenial Mumbai', *Public Culture*, vol. 12, no. 3, 2000, pp. 627–51.

Bertaud, Alain, 'Mumbai FSI Conundrum', July 2004; see http://alain-bertaud.com/AB_Files/AB_Mumbai_FSI_conundrum.pdf.

Davis, Mike, 'Planet of Slums: Urban Involution and the Informal Proletariat', in *New Left Review*, no. 26, March–April 2004, pp. 5–34.

Dubin, Nina, 'Robert des Ruines: Speculating in the market for ruins', *Cabinet*, no. 20, Winter 2005/06.

Hansen, Thomas Blom, *The Wages of Violence: Naming and Identity in Post-Colonial Bombay*, Princeton, NJ: Princeton University Press, 2002.

Lipuma, Edward and Lee, Benjamin, *Financial Derivatives and the Globalization of Risk*, Durham, NC: Duke University Press, 2004.

Mbembe, Achille, 'The Aesthetics of Superfluity', *Public Culture*, vol. 16, no. 3, 2004, pp. 373–405.

McKinsey & Company, Inc. and Bombay First, 'Vision Mumbai: Transforming Mumbai into a World Class City', September 2003; see www.bombayfirst.org/McKinseyReport.pdf.

Mehta, Suketu, *Maximum City: Bombay Lost and Found*, New York: Alfred A. Knopf, 2004.

Patel, Sirish, 'Housing Policies for Mumbai', *Economic and Political Weekly*, 13 August 2005.

Patel, Sujata and Masselos, Jim, *Bombay and Mumbai: The City in Transition*, Oxford: Oxford University Press, 2003.

Patel, Sujata and Thorner, Alice, *Bombay: Metaphor for Modern India*, New Delhi: Oxford University Press, 1995.

Pendse, Sandeep, 'Toil, Sweat, and the City', in Sujata Patel and Alice Thorner, eds, *Bombay: Metaphor for Modern India*, New Delhi: Oxford University Press, 1995, pp. 3–25.

Rohatgi, Pauline, Godrej, Pheroza and Mehrotra, Rahul, eds, *Bombay and Mumbai: Changing Perspectives*, Mumbai: Marg Publications, 1997.

Sassen, Saskia, *The Global City: New York, London, Tokyo*, Princeton, NJ: Princeton University Press, 2001.

Varma, Rashmi, 'Provincializing the Global City: From Bombay to Mumbai', *Social Text* 22(4), 2004, pp. 65–89.

Notes

1. Rohatgi, Godrej and Mehrotra, *Bombay and Mumbai: Changing Perspectives*.
2. Patel and Masselos, *Bombay and Mumbai: The City in Transition*.
3. Hansen, *The Wages of Violence*.
4. Appadurai, 'Spectral Housing and Urban Cleansing in Millenial Mumbai'.
5. 'Communalism' is a term of colonial origin, used by the British to describe what they perceived as pathological forms of social and political relations between religious groups in colonial India, based on what they perceived as primordial and essentialist forms of attachment to religious identity. The term continues to be used in scholarly and popular discourse to mark pathological forms of political relations in contemporary India.
6. Sassen, *The Global City*.
7. Mbembe, 'The Aesthetics of Superfluity'.

8. Quoted in *The Times of India* (Mumbai Edition), 15 October 2004.
9. Davis, 'Planet of Slums'.
10. Mbembe, 'The Aesthetics of Superfluity'.
11. Pendse, 'Toil, Sweat, and the City'.
12. Mbembe, 'The Aesthetics of Superfluity'.
13. McKinsey & Company, Inc. and Bombay First, *Vision Mumbai: Transforming Mumbai into a World Class City*.

FRANCK MERMIER

Beirut: Public Sphere of the Arab World?

The Role of the Publishing Sector[1]

.

The connection between the spread of the printed word and the formation of the public sphere was noted by Jürgen Habermas[2] and later by Robert Muchembled, who sees in the literary field of seventeenth-century France a true public sphere that 'precisely constitutes itself as the locus of a symbolic dialogue between the different actors of the social, religious and political game'. It forms 'a space of cultural experimentation that allows for the coalescing of ideas, which are preliminaries necessary to new forms of political functioning.'[3]

The function of the publisher that involves 'giving a text and an author access to public existence'[4] makes of the publishing milieu a source of public information that is in turn a vector for ideological and cultural entrepreneurship. This double figure of the publisher, as an intermediary as well as an actor on the intellectual scene, turns him into a protagonist in a public sphere.

The Lebanese publishing industry contributed to the formation of a pan-Arab public sphere by giving necessary publicity to numerous authors who would have failed to gain access to the Arab market at large had they been published only in their own countries, and who would not have gained pan-Arab recognition. These authors were able to find in Beirut a unique space for expression.

Its function as a public sphere is, to a large extent, due to the weakness of the Lebanese state, torn as it is by centrifugal currents. The trust of Arab readers is granted to Lebanese publications; the Lebanese publishing industry attracts a public interested in contemporary debates and suspicious of the state censorship that has infiltrated publication in other Arab countries. In contrast to other Arab states, the minor role played by the Lebanese state in the cultural domain, in addition to the liberalism of its political regime, has thus allowed the emergence of a pan-Arab public sphere at the heart of Beirut, the most extroverted city in the region.

A Safe Haven

Even during the worst moments of the civil war, Beirut never ceased to play the role of cultural intermediary, at least in the field of book publishing. Indeed, the continuity or even the increase of book publishing during those dark years remains a significant witness to the importance of Beirut as a cultural metropolis in the Arab world. In 1962, the number of officially registered publishing houses was ninety-five, while the number of registered printing houses was 251. Among the former, only some twenty houses boasted a regular output.[5] In 1985, there were 493 publishing houses and 500 printing houses,[6] but the actual number of publishers probably did not exceed 150.[7] Finally, in 2004, 639 publishing houses were affiliated with the Union of Lebanese Publishers, and 700 printing houses were active.[8]

Nevertheless, in various sectors, Lebanon's pre-eminent role in the Arab publishing industry is diminishing. Lebanon must deal presently with increasing competition of the Arab Gulf states that took over a large portion of the publicity market and gained control over the main Arab newspapers,[9] fields in which Lebanon previously played the leading role. However, to this day, no other Arab centre, with the notable exception of Cairo, Beirut's perpetual rival, can claim to compete with the Lebanese capital in the domain of book publishing. Thus Beirut, where the near-totality of Lebanon's publishing houses are confined, can rightly be viewed as the capital of the Arab book. This is due not only to the vast number of printing professionals and publishers there, but these printers and publishers also actually reflect and even sometimes lead the different trends of the Arab book market through multiple networks of distribution and exchange based in the Lebanese capital.

The singularity of both Beirut's cultural role and Lebanon's Arab publishing industry cannot be explained without referring to the history of the city and to the way in which it became a cultural crossroads for the Arab world. One must also take into account the simultaneous emergence in Beirut of a professional environment and of a publishing milieu subject to the risks of fluctuations in the Arab book market and of the regional political situation.

The remarkable development of the silk trade in the middle of the nineteenth century progressively and firmly connected Beirut to European ports, in particular Marseille, where the bales of Lebanese-grown silkworm cocoons transited before reaching the silk factories of Lyons. During that same period, Beirut became a pole of attraction drawing immigrants from all over the region as well as foreign and Lebanese tradesmen, so that by the end of the nineteenth century, the population of the city multiplied more than tenfold.

Little by little, Beirut succeeded in marginalising its rivals on the Lebanese coastline, Sidon, Tyre and Tripoli. It became the main port of the Levant for trade between Europe, Lebanon and the rest of the Middle East. The creation and the development of steamship navigation that began in 1835, as well as the construction of a new Beirut-Damascus road (1859–63), the building of a railway connecting the two cities (in 1895) and finally the modernisation of Beirut's port (1890–5) were factors that contributed to the rapid economic expansion of the city.

This growth was linked to the fact that Beirut became a political capital of the Levant due to the various powers that forged the shape and the limits of its influence. It became the capital of a whole province during the Egyptian occupation of the city by the troops of Muhammad Ali Pasha (1831–40). The city recovered this prominent status in 1888 when the Ottomans chose it as the administrative capital of the province (*vilayet*) of Beirut. Finally, it became the capital of the new Lebanese state in 1920 under the French Mandate and then, after independence, of Lebanon, in 1943.[10] Moreover, to its administrative and political roles we could add educational functions that helped consolidate Beirut's relations with its hinterland. The Syrian Protestant College created in 1866 later became known as the American University of Beirut, while the Jesuit College, founded in 1875, was subsequently named Université Saint-Joseph. Both institutions can be considered as the oldest and the first truly modern universities in the Arab World.

The year 1956 marked the demise of the 'cosmopolitan' intellectual centres of Alexandria and Cairo with the departure of important segments of their population of foreign origin, mainly Europeans and Levantines, following Gamal Abdel Nasser's economic reprisals to the Anglo-French attempt of recovering the Suez Canal by military force. The renowned Egyptian writer Taha Husayn declared in the 1950s that Beirut had superseded Cairo as the cultural capital of the Arab world,[11] even though the presumed pre-eminence of Beirut was much more manifest on the economic level than in the cultural sphere.

The development of Beirut since Lebanon's independence in 1943 is, to a large extent, due to the Arab refugees fleeing Palestine in 1948, and exiles from Syria in 1957–8 following the economic and political radicalisation of the Baath regime. Beirut likewise welcomed Egyptian resources after Nasser's nationalisation policies, as well as Arab Gulf capital.[12] New commercial opportunities compensated for the decline of the Lebanese silk industry during the period between the two world wars. In the 1950s, Beirut captured more than a third of the world's gold market. More importantly, it became the first financial market in the Middle East draining Arab resources from oil-rich countries and playing the role of a privileged intermediary for foreign companies in the region.

In contrast to the other capitals of the region, Beirut – described as 'the last cosmopolitan city of the Arab World after the decline of Alexandria'[13] – was the home, at the end of the 1950s, of the only liberal Arab parliamentary political system. Much of this appealed to the business bourgeoisie participating in its economic liberalism, which turned the city into a nodal point on the regional scale until 1975, while Arab intellectuals were seduced by Beirut's higher level of political freedom that prevailed at the time. Elias Khoury sums up very well the particular status acquired by Beirut during this period when he highlights its role as a safe haven and a 'strange' place of encounter between two types of 'fugitives':

> The Arabs running away from oppression and the Lebanese fleeing confessional communities, tribes and clans ... [met] in a city which was bordered on the West side by the American University and on the East side by the Saint-Joseph University. Both institutions were complementary since the former was a gate for the Arab space and its tumultuous political currents, while the latter was a centre for the formation of the Lebanese ruling and conservative class.[14]

An Ideological and Literary Laboratory

The concentration of the book market in Beirut's downtown led to the creation of a real publishers' centre. Between the two world wars, several bookstores, and in particular school bookshops, chose the area of the old markets; but in the beginning of the 1950s, many publishing houses moved their headquarters into newly constructed office buildings. Thus Beirut's principal publishing houses were found in four buildings located on Syria Street (al-Azariyah, al-Binayah al-Markaziyah, Salihah wa-Samadi and

Darwish), which became the real centre of the Lebanese publishing industry until the destruction of Beirut's downtown starting in 1975.

The publishing milieu in Lebanon formed an important vector for the ideological debates of the Arab world, with Beirut as the melting pot of Arab intellectual production. As of the 1950s, the Lebanese capital became the scene for inter-Arab dissension as well as a sounding board for the different Arab political currents – Baathists, Nasserists and Marxists – that competed for regional supremacy and dominated the Arab ideological scene until the late 1970s. Whether they represented the official ideologies of some Arab states or were radically opposed to the Arab regimes, they competed ideologically by creating or funding publishing houses, taking advantage of Lebanese political and linguistic pluralism and flexible censorship. After the Arab defeat of 1967, the rhythm with which these publishing ventures were launched rapidly increased, especially with the arrival of Palestinian organisations (1969) and radical Arab leftist movements.[15]

In addition to the Institute for Palestine Studies, created in Beirut in 1963 by a group of Palestinian, Lebanese and Syrian intellectuals and academics, the Centre for Palestinian Research, tied to the Palestine Liberation Organisation (PLO), was an important publishing centre until the Israeli army destroyed it in 1982. Furthermore, different Palestinian organisations funded, directly or indirectly, several publishing houses, such as Dar al-Kalimah, headed by the Syrian Arab nationalist Husayn Hallaq and sponsored by Abu Jihad (Khalil al-Wazir), a high-ranking PLO official. Dar al-Awdah, which was headed by Muhammad Saʿid Muhammadiyah and specialised in the publication of leading Arab poets such as the Palestinians Samih al-Qasim and Mahmud Darwish, received for its part indirect support from the PLO, which regularly purchased its books. Dar al-Quds, which nowadays publishes a single periodical called *al-Jil*, was directed by the Palestinian Mazin al-Bandaq. Moreover, Nabil Shaath, who later became the Palestinian Authority's Minister of Foreign Affairs, founded Dar al-Fata al-Arabi (The Arab Youth Publishing House) in Beirut, specialising in children's books – a pioneer in that field. After the Israeli invasion of Lebanon, it moved its headquarters to Cairo before ceasing all activities.[16]

Another Palestinian political leader, Abd al-Wahhab al-Kayyali,[17] established an important publishing house, al-Muassasah al-Arabiyah lil-Dirasat wal-Nashr (the Arab Institute for Studies and Publishing), in 1969, and published during its first years the complete works of the main thinkers of the Nahdah period (the Arab Renaissance) of the late nineteenth and early twentieth century, as well as military, political, arts and philosophical encyclopaedias. Following the assassination of its founder in 1981, his brother Mahir al-Kayyali, who had worked there since 1970, took over. When the situation deteriorated during the last phase of the Lebanese civil war in 1989, he moved to Amman. However, the headquarters of his publishing house, registered as a Lebanese company, is still located in Beirut.[18] This generalist publishing house releases some 150 titles each year, of which only a few deal with Islamic heritage while the rest are essentially devoted to contemporary literature and social science books. Moreover, its pan-Arab dimension, which the extent of its distribution and the diverse origins of its authors reflect, was lately reinforced through coediting projects with several Arab cultural institutes.[19]

The constellation of competing politicised publishing houses was a new and unique phenomenon in the Arab world. Its convergence in Beirut was a gradual process. The first signs of this process appeared in the establishment in 1956 of Dar al-Adab (The House of Literature) by Suhayl Idris, a Nasser sympathiser, followed in 1959 by the creation of Dar al-Taliah (Avant-garde Publishing House) by Bashir al-Dauq, who had an Iraqi Baath orientation. The former grew out of the literary magazine *al-Adab* (*Literatures*), created in 1953, whereas the latter produced a socio-political periodical called *Dirasat Arabiyah* in 1964, which was an equally important publication. Dar al-Adab gathered in its publication catalogue the best works of modern Arab literature, and is considered today as one of the most prestigious publishing houses in the Arab world. Its acting director Rana Idris, the founder's daughter, took charge in 1986 after finishing her studies in anthropology in the US. She created a reading committee and succeeded in increasing the number of publications from fewer than a dozen books annually during the civil war to eighty titles a year, focusing on new trends in Arab and foreign literature. Often compared to the French publishing house Gallimard, Dar al-Adab is one of the rare examples of literary production independent from official cultural sectors.

Ideological debates and confrontations went far beyond political quarrels and rivalries between the Arab regimes that financed their local representatives. 'Beirut was not only a safe haven, but was also a laboratory for Lebanese and Arab writers, many of whom sought to obtain the Lebanese nationality, such as the three great poets of Syrian origin, Adonis, Yusuf al-Khal and Nizar Qabbani.'[20] This is how Arab publishing in Beirut became the scene of a confrontation between ideological battles and aesthetic issues, shown in the example of a rivalry between the two literary magazines *al-Adab* and *Shi'r*. *Al-Adab* continues to be published to this day, while *Shi'r*, created in 1957 by Yusuf al-Khal and influenced by Antun Sa'adah's pan-Syrian ideology, ceased publication in 1962.[21]

In contrast to *al-Adab*, which at the instigation of its founder Suhayl Idris promoted Arab Nationalism and the struggle against imperialism, *Shi'r* advocated for a clear demarcation between poetry and politics.[22] Different conceptions of poetical modernity superposed these ideological divergences with conflicts on the use of free verse and poetic prose. Such arguments reflected contrasting visions of the Arab cultural past and of the influence of Western literature. Suhayl Idris's testimony helps to clarify some of the political stakes underlying this literary battlefield:

> *Al-Adab* magazine carried an Arab nationalist vision and it opposed the National Social Syrian party whose ideology affected *Shi'r* magazine. *Al-Adab* adopted free verse poetry 'with metrical foots'[23] [*al-qasidah al-tafilah, al-shir al-hurr*]. In contrast, *Shi'r* was in favour of 'poetical prose' [*qasidat al-nathr*], and more particularly translated prose poetry. We were, and still are, opposed to prose poetry because it is a foreign imitation. It did not spring naturally from the evolution of the Arabic *qasida*, while the free verse constitutes a poetical renewal that has its roots in the Arabic *qasida*.
>
> *Shi'r* was not interested in the literary heritage [*turath*], but wanted to destroy it, to surpass it or attack it as Yusuf al-Khal declared. In 1962, *Shi'r* stopped publication. None of the advocates of prose succeeded in affirming himself as a poet, whereas the prosodic poetry adopted by the review *al-Adab* introduced a great number of poets. Muhammad al-Maghut, who took part in *Shi'r*, abandoned prose that corrupted Arabic poetry. For that reason, there was a violent struggle between the two magazines, *al-Adab* and *Shi'r*. At one point, we even accused *Shi'r* of having ties with the American secret service![24]

If some publishing houses were nothing but auxiliaries for political parties that propagated their political projects under the guise of cultural enterprises, others played a major cultural role that surpassed the simple function of propaganda, even though they often kept organisational or ideological ties with political parties. In addition to their role as 'mediators of European culture'[25] through translations into Arabic – a role shared by other segments of the Lebanese (or Egyptian) publishing milieu – some militant publishing houses constituted new cognitive references that broke with traditional and modern educational institutions, be they sectarian or state-sponsored.

They left a deep imprint on the Arab intellectual scene with, on one hand, oppositional and subversive ideas formed outside the Arab world and, on the other hand, a hybridisation of these ideas with new forms of endogenous thought and discourse. These were new 'Arab languages for the present'[26] tied up with the problems of underdevelopment, issues of political power, secularism and nation-building, as well as the Palestinian cause.

Far from being reduced to the Lebanese political arena, ideological confrontations and intellectual debates contained a pan-Arab dimension, all the stronger since the majority of the works published were written by non-Lebanese authors. The 1975 establishment in Beirut of the Centre for Arab Unity Studies,[27] a non-governmental organisation and dynamic publishing house for intellectuals coming from all Arab countries, is symbolic. Moreover, the Centre for National Development (Markaz al-Inma al-Qawmi) was established in 1980, and also belonged to the Arab Nationalist ideology. Directed by Muta al-Safadi, it published two periodicals and many translations, notably in the field of philosophy.[28]

The spheres of influence and the distribution networks of publishing houses such as Dar al-Farabi, tied to the Lebanese Communist Party, Dar al-Taliah, affiliated with the Baath Party, al-Markaz al-Thaqafi al-Arabi (the Arab Cultural Centre),[29] connected to Arab Nationalists and Dar Ibn Khaldun, created by Muhammad Kishli, a former leader of the Organisation for Communist Action in Lebanon (OCAL), had strong connections within some 'progressive' Arab regimes (South Yemen, Iraq, Syria, Algeria, Libya). These regimes helped these publishing houses by placing book orders, sometimes including schoolbooks, or by directly purchasing significant quantities of their stock, especially during book fairs. For example, Dar Ibn Khaldun had important ties with South Yemen, where the leading members of the regime were directly influenced by OCAL, and subsequently profited from their orders of schoolbooks.

The same applied to Dar al-Farabi, which drew, however, more substantial benefits from printing Soviet books in Arabic, in addition to its militant and economic links to counterparts such as the Brazilian Communist Party (it published translations of Jorge Amado) and Algeria through the Société Nationale d'Edition et de Diffusion. Dar al-Taliah, well implanted in Iraq, found an important source of funding in translating the works of the Korean ruler Kim Il-Sung into Arabic.[30] Dar al-Arabiyah lil-Mawsuat (Arab Encyclopaedia Publishers) received subsidies from the Iraqi regime until 2003, and displayed its propaganda books at Arab book fairs. There was even a Maoist publishing house, Dar Ibn Sina (Avicenna Publications), which published translations of Chinese books; it was set up by Jamal Shatila, head of the short-lived Party of the Socialist Revolution.[31]

On the other hand, the American Franklin Foundation financed, between 1956 and 1964, and during the years of the Cold War, translations of at least 500 books published by Lebanese publishers (such as Dar al-'Ilm lil-Malayin), under the cover of transmitting knowledge and disseminating American culture. The hidden objective was to counter the Communist influence in the region and to diffuse Anglo-Saxon culture. This is how al-Muassasah al-Ahliyah, directed by Angèle Abboud, published many Arabic translations of English literature. She was probably the only Lebanese woman to head a publishing house in the 1960s.[32] However, the censorship of Marxist books in Iraq, starting in 1977–8, and in Libya and in Sudan under the Numayri regime, as well as problems with exchange rates and money transfers, made these markets quite risky. It was in Syria that book importation policies were most tolerant with regard to publishing houses that belonged to the 'progressive' line.

More and more, the publishing line of these 'progressive' publishers in Lebanon surpassed propaganda to include literary works and criticism, as well as essays that had, in their heyday, quite an impact. Among these publishing houses were the Arab Institute for Studies and Publishing and Dar al-Taliah. The latter's initial Baathist inclinations were steadily supplanted by Marxism after the Arab defeat of 1967. This publisher did not hesitate to publish works critical of religious thought and inspired by Marxism, such as the works of the Syrians Yasin al-Hafiz, Ilyas Murqus and Sadiq Jalal al-Azm, whose book *Critique of Religious Thought* (1969) was republished over ten times. The publication of this book gave a counter-example to Beirut's reputation for liberalism, as the author was imprisoned in 1969 for about ten days, then set free as a result of the mobilisation of the liberal and intellectual milieu and leftist professional and political organisations. Intervention by Kamal Jumblatt, then Minister of the Interior, allowed for a rapid release and the rejection of legal prosecution of the author and his publisher, Bashir al-Dauq.[33] Al-Azm's account of this censorship illustrates, even in a paradoxical way, the relationship of numerous Syrian intellectuals with Beirut and Damascus:

> Before the beginning of the Lebanese civil war, it may have seemed that problems, as well as their perception, were more important in Syria than in Lebanon. But the margin left to public expression in Syria was narrower, and thus more oppressive and more dangerous than in Beirut. Evidently, Beirut possesses spaces of freedom, and

the safety valves there are greater and numerous. When the row over my book *Critique of Religious Thought* broke out, I think that I was the first writer or intellectual who had to flee Lebanon and take refuge in Syria. In those days, people fled from Damascus to Beirut and not the other way.[34]

From Damascus to Beirut

For several Syrian publishers, Beirut played and still plays the role of 'safety valve' for their publishing activities, through the establishment of their enterprises (such as al-Maktab al-Islami, Dar Ibn Rushd, Dar al-Haqiqah, Dar al-Tanwir, Dar al-Kitab al-Hadith, Dar al-Qalam ...), and through the opening of a local branch of Damascus's main houses (Dar al-Fikr al-Muasir, Dar Qadmus, Dar al-Mada, Dar Ibn Kathir ...). For some this was an escape from Syrian censorship, while taking advantage of the Lebanese economic liberalism and the role played by Beirut as a platform to other Arab markets. Furthermore, several Syrian publishers found technical skills and tools more developed in Lebanon than in their own country, notably in the fields of book stitching and binding.[35] The political orientation of many of these publishers encompassed the whole Middle Eastern ideological spectrum. The dates of their establishment in Lebanon reflect the different phases of the Baath regime's history and the evolution of its relationship with the opposition.

Among the publishing houses that belonged to the Marxist sphere, one can mention Dar al-Haqiqah headed by Yasin al-Hafiz, Ahmad Mansur's Dar al-Haqaiq and Muhammad al-Zanabili's Dar al-Tanwir (all of which did not survive for long), as well as Dar Ibn Rushd, which belonged to the Syrian Sulayman Subh,[36] who died in Tunis in the early 1990s, putting an end to its activities. These publishing houses profited, in particular during the civil war, from the sporadic support of some Palestinian organisations or, at least, from protection from the arbitrary repression of the Syrian regime. After the end of the Syro-Egyptian union (1958–61), the Nasserist Tammam Armush sought refuge in Beirut, where he established Dar al-Nafais in 1970. In 1994, he obtained the authorisation of the Syrian Ministry of Culture to create a publishing house in Syria under the same name.

The Lebanese capital also hosted several publishing houses specialising in Islamic works that were founded by Syrians. Some were established there for political reasons, such as Tammam Armush's Dar al-Nafais, Ridwan Dabul's al-Sharikah al-Muttahidah (Ridwan Dabul also heads the Mu'ssasat al-Risalah) or Zuhayr Qusaybati's Dar Ibn Hazm, the last two being connected to the Muslim Brotherhood. One could also mention the Maktab Islami (the Islamic Bureau) of Sheikh Zuhayr al-Shawish, a leader of the International Organisation of Muslim Brothers and a former member of the Syrian parliament as well as a scholar of the Hanbali school of Islam. Dar Ibn Hazm was created in Beirut to spread works of the Muslim Brotherhood, and it even published works by Abdallah Azzam, one of the most radical ideologists of the Islamic Jihad movement. It is noteworthy that many of its books, including those by Azzam himself, were co-published with the al-Jil al-Jadid bookstore in Sanaa, an old landmark of the Muslim Brotherhood in Yemen.[37]

Al-Maktab al-Islami was founded in Damascus in 1957 and transferred to Beirut in 1963. Bilal al-Shawish, son and associate of the founder, presents this publishing house as having a paramount religious mission, different from other houses specialising in Islamic heritage books because of its Salafist orientation (*al-minhaj al-salafi*), and its exclusively religious production. This contrasts with the more enterprising style of Dar al-Fikr, founded by Safwan al-Jabri and Mahmud Salim in Beirut in 1967, which also specialised in Islamic heritage publications. Al-Jabri's partner is the brother of Adnan Salim, the manager of Dar al-Fikr in Damascus, which is considered the largest publishing house in Syria. When the Baath Party gained power in Syria, its owners were impelled to move their warehouse to Beirut, where they started a branch that soon became independent. The initial stock of the Lebanese Dar al-Fikr was bought from the Egyptian publisher Mustafa Muhammad, whose al-Maktabah al-Tijariyah specialised in publishing religious 'yellow books' translated into African languages. He was forced to move to Beirut after Nasser's nationalisation law in the 1960s. The publication policy of Dar al-Fikr may seem similar to that of its Syrian homonym, but the former's choice of publishing Islamic heritage books is purely commercial, with no cultural or ideological considerations.

Were it not for this choice, it would be difficult to discern any other religious signs in the large building where the publishing house, its printing press and its bookbinding workshop have been located since 1979. In a beehive atmosphere, about 200 employees work to produce books that are marketed in all parts of the Islamic world, but mainly in Africa and notably in Nigeria. An important source of its income lies in sales of the Qur'an, translated into several African languages.

Several Syrian publishers also take recourse in Beirut's printing houses in order to publish works that are banned in Syria, without necessarily opening branches in the Lebanese capital. The marketing of the book is done in Lebanon but also in Syria, if the books are smuggled successfully into Syria. Lebanon, often viewed as Syria's economic lungs because of all the licit and illicit trade tying the two countries, is thus a vital relay for the Syrian publishing industry, for it allows it existence beyond the constraining girdle of censorship.

Towards the Southern Suburbs

The departure of Palestinian organisations from Beirut in 1982 had negative repercussions on some publishing houses that they directly or indirectly financed. The occupation of Beirut by the Israeli army that same year marked the end of Beirut's role as a safe haven for exiled writers and as a centre for the defiant Arab left. The decline in the 1980s of leftist publishing houses coincided with the development of Islamic publishing. The latter manifested itself throughout the Lebanese publishing industry, either through the creation of new Islamic publishing enterprises or through the increase in the production of works from the Islamic heritage.

Another result of the Lebanese civil war was the disappearance of downtown Beirut as a centre for publishing and selling books.[38] During the 1980s, the publishing houses scattered all over the city, often distributed along ideological and confessional rifts that demarcated both publishers and neighbourhoods. Only the Hamra district preserved a greater communitarian mixture of publishers from all confessions.

In the Southern suburbs of Beirut, several Shi'i publishing houses with Islamist tendencies are now concentrated, as well as the educational, social, religious and political institutions of different Shi'i movements.[39] The majority of these publishing houses were created after 1979 in the wake of the Iranian Revolution and the rise of Shi'i political parties such as Amal and Hizbullah. Several of these publishing houses were founded by Iranians who, after having lived in Iraq, settled in Lebanon in the 1970s (Dar al-Qari, Dar al-Mufid, Dar al-Taaruf, Dar al-Irshad), or by Iraqis (Dar al-Zahra, Dar al-Adwa). Thus Beirut became, along with London, a refuge and a centre of cultural and political investment for many Shi'is. These publishing houses played an important role for the dissemination of different trends of religious and political Shi'i thought:

> Dozens of publishing houses have been founded since the 1970s which specialise in editing theological source material and Islamist treatises. Beside Iran, Lebanon has become the second important centre for this kind of religious Shiite literature. The numerous

traditions and new schools of thought are brought together in Lebanon where they are debated, compared and intermingled. From here they are redistributed to other Shiite regions in Iraq, Iran, the Gulf States and Syria – and spread all over world. The Lebanese publishing houses form an important link in this process.[40]

Among the most important houses are Dar al-Hadi and Dar al-Mahajjah al-Bayda, which benefited from close relationships with Hizbullah and the Iranian regime. Dar al-Andalus publishes the works of Imam Musa al-Sadr, who disappeared in Libya in 1978, and whose leadership is claimed by the Amal movement headed by Nabih Berri, Speaker of the Lebanese Parliament. Incidentally, Berri happens to be the brother-in-law of Samirah Asi, the director of Dar al-Andalus. Dar al-Malak publishes the works of Muhammad Husayn Fadlallah, one of the highest Shi'i religious authorities in Lebanon.

Some restrictions imposed on the distribution of Shi'i books in countries such as Iraq or Saudi Arabia were recently lifted. In Egypt, where a small Shi'i community exists, censorship of Shi'i books lessened at the end of the Iran-Iraq war and the death of Ayatollah Khomeini, even though some books are still on al-Azhar's blacklist. Since the 1990s, several Lebanese Shi'i publishing houses have participated in the Cairo Book Fair,[41] although Egyptian Shi'i publications have practically disappeared after being banned in the 1980s.

In Saudi Arabia, negotiations between the Saudi authorities and Sheikh Hasan al-Saffar, a Saudi Shi'i leader,[42] led to a decrease in discriminatory measures imposed on the Shi'i community and the partial lifting of the ban on Shi'i books. Access to these types of publications remain very difficult in that country, whereas some Gulf states have allowed the distribution of the works of the two most important Lebanese Shi'i religious figures, Fadlallah and Muhammad Mahdi Shams al-Din.[43] The book fair in Bahrain, a country where the Shi'i population is in the majority, is considered a unique centre for the dissemination of Shi'i books, and Lebanese publishing houses are present there in great numbers.

The fall of Saddam Hussein's regime in 2003 and the subsequent lifting of the embargo marked the return of what has for a long time been considered the most important book market in the Arab world. Iraq has the greatest potential for the distribution of Shi'i books, a great number of which, and especially the most recent publications, have been banned for political reasons. Nowadays the Shi'i publishing houses located in Beirut's Southern

Suburbs send thousands of books to Iraq, and some houses have already opened offices in Baghdad and Najaf.

Post-War Lebanon

Despite the ideological ebb of secular, nationalist and socialist thought during the 1980s and the absence of stable educational institutions and autonomous intellectual spaces, multilingual publishing houses such as Dar an-Nahar and Naufal Publications, which were oriented since their creation towards the Lebanese market, and were less ideologically marked, were able to keep their publishing goals.

Dar an-Nahar is supported by an institution that is firmly established on the Lebanese cultural and media scene. It emanates from the newspaper with the same name (*an-Nahar*) and which remains a regional reference in the field of journalism. It was founded in 1933 by Gebran Tueni, who had also occasionally published books until the Mandate authorities closed his newspaper. He established an ephemeral political party, the Ghassanids, which was supposed to recruit members from within the Greek Orthodox community, and in 1942 he founded the Movement of Orthodox Youth.

When he died in 1947, his son Ghassan Tueni interrupted his studies at Harvard University and replaced him. The latter established, in 1967, Dar an-Nahar, publishing in both Arabic and French. The first of the publishing directors of Dar an-Nahar was Yusuf al-Khal, who worked there from 1967–71 while simultaneously editing *Shi'r* (which was republished by Dar an-Nahar in 1967).[44] Riad El-Rayyes, a journalist and future publisher, worked there for some time, starting in 1969, while Charles Raad succeeded al-Khal before resigning in 1973 to set up his own publishing house, Dar al-Ahliyah, one year later.

Although Dar an-Nahar mainly publishes some of the best-known Lebanese writers, it also gives an important place to other Arab writers. Its power to establish an author is similar to that of Dar al-Adab, and it receives hundreds of manuscripts from all over the Arab world each year. Its highest sales are, however, of books on Lebanon for the Lebanese market, which is rare enough that it deserves to be mentioned.[45] Dar an-Nahar can depend on the newspaper's photographic and documentary support for both its publishing projects and publicity.

Since the end of the war, Dar an-Nahar has undertaken the great enterprise of the reconstruction of memory through the publication of books on old downtown Beirut, which was partially destroyed during the war and even more so during the period of reconstruction. According to

Ghassan Tueni: 'Dar an-Nahar represents what it means to be Lebanese in all its diversity, and with the political and cultural expressions it entails.'[46]

Created in 1985 by Georges and Kamal Feghali, Mukhtarat Publications is oriented primarily towards the local market, and has only published Lebanese authors in the fields of literature and social sciences, with the exception of a few translations. Its collections of poetry are financed, to a great extent, through successful publications such as Ziyad Rahbani's theatrical works, Kamal Feghali's books on the Lebanese legislative elections and books on such figures as Nabih Berri and Elie Hobaika, a former warlord and minister assassinated in 2002. Its acquisition of Dar al-Makshuf's stock in 2005 highlights its attachment to Lebanese subject matters as well as a certain audacity.

Dar al-Adab's engagement in the field of Arab literature, to which it has added new voices, has not prevented it from pursuing its mission in the ideological domain. Its choice of translations of non-fiction into Arabic shows its ideological stand, concerned mainly with anti-imperialism and anti-Zionism, and it features the books of Edward Said, Noam Chomsky and Norman Finkelstein.[47] Thus the militant commitment of its early days is maintained, and also reflected in the editorial choices of the magazine *al-Adab*, which remains one the most prominent in the Arab world. Under the impetus of Samah Idris, it even opened up to free verse poetry, thus breaking away from the founder's aversion.[48]

Since Beirut became, during the 1960s and the 1970s, a 'public sphere' for the Arab world and a space for the formation and dissemination of networks of political and cultural influences, what is its present role as can be gleaned from its publishing industry? In the post- civil war period, the establishment of new publishing houses with autonomous cultural projects suggests that Arab publishing in Lebanon still remains a field of cultural experimentation, as well as a sounding board for ideological debates across Arab space. This is confirmed by the establishment of two large publishing houses founded in London, Dar al-Saqi (Saqi Books) and Dar Riad El-Rayyes, as well as the creation of several publishing houses that enriched the modernist orientation of the Lebanese and Arab publishing sectors, such as Dar al-Jadid (1990), Dar al-Masar (1993) and Dar al-Intishar al-'Arabi (1997).

These 'newcomers',[49] whose publications include essays, novels and modern Arab and Lebanese poetry, are not far from the field of ideological confrontation, even though they are far from being homogeneous and place themselves at different degrees of the spectrum of commercial and intellectual investment.

Saqi Books started publishing in Arabic in 1987, and founded an independent company in Lebanon in 1992 under the name of Dar al-Saqi. Willing to enrich the Arabic library with innovative works, but also concerned with quality, its choice of authors and translations comprises the most eminent Arab and Western specialists of the Arab world and of Islam. The editorial committee meets in London, which continues to be a hub for Arab culture. The pan-Arab dimension of this publishing house can be gleaned from the pages of its catalogue, where one finds such names as the Franco-Algerian Mohammed Arkoun, the Syrian Georges Tarabishi, the Saudi Turki al-Hamad and the Lebanese Fuad Khuri, along with the Kuwaitis Khaldun al-Naqib and Muhammad al-Rumayhi, the Syro-Lebanese Adonis and the Moroccan Mohamed Choukri.

Some of these authors were also published in Dar al-Saqi's cultural monthly *Abwab*, which ceased publication in 2003 because of the censorship it faced in many Arab countries, particularly in Saudi Arabia. The relative immunity conferred by its London address has allowed Dar al-Saqi to publish many works critical of Saudi Arabia, and more recently it has published the books of Sheikh Hasan al-Saffar, a leader of Saudi Shi'is. Moreover, it also has a desire to take an active part in the Arab cultural scene, even to influence it, which has determined its publishing choices to a great extent, according to publisher André Gaspard. He asserts his conviction or 'assumption' of having a role to play through his publishing house, the role of a cultural intermediary concerned with politics in the general sense and acting at the same time as a substitute for political action.

The Riad El-Rayyes publishing house, like Dar al-Saqi, had its beginnings in London. Although they differ on some publishing choices, they are in close competition for the same Arab book market that concerns modern and critical thought. Both Dar Riad El-Rayyes and Dar al-Saqi are important contemporary publishing houses that attract authors from all Arab countries by giving an important place to contemporary literature as well as political and sociological studies. They have become unavoidable actors both on the Arab literary scene and on the terrain of ideological confrontation.

A journalist of Syrian origin, Riad El-Rayyes left Lebanon in 1976 to settle in London where, two years later, he created the weekly *al-Manar al-Usbu'i*.[50] In 1986, he established the publishing house bearing his name, followed by the literary monthly *al-Naqid* (1989–95) and the al-Khashkul bookstore. In contrast to Dar al-Saqi, Riad El-Rayyes adopted the principle of never publishing translations, but only works written in Arabic by Arab writers.[51] Since its foundation, it has published more than 800 titles and is considered one of the most active publishing houses in the Arab world.

In 1991, El-Rayyes transferred all his publishing activities to Beirut, where he created a cultural and political weekly, called *al-Nuqqad*. His decision to base the company in Lebanon was dictated, according to him, by patriotism and by nostalgia. It has certainly brought him closer to the Arab market, but also made him lose that British 'immunity' that allowed him, like Dar al-Saqi, to reach various readers, notably from the Arab Gulf, without confronting censorship.[52]

The publishing guidelines of Dar Riad El-Rayyes are closely connected to the journalistic and political line adopted by its founder. His 'adventurous' character, according to his own description, is reflected in the choice of controversial topics. He is himself the author of several books devoted to the Arabian Peninsula, some of which have been banned in Saudi Arabia. The path taken by this publishing house is arduous, not only because it faces censorship, but also must confront a scattered public that often needs to be attracted by eye-catching titles. In the 1990s, in Lebanon, it faced several court trials over its publication of authors such as the Libyan Sadiq al-Nayhum and a fourteenth-century book of erotica by Sheikh al-Nifzawi. Riad El-Rayyes has attempted to encourage young Arab literature by creating two prizes, one for poetry and the other for fiction, and publishes the winners.

The end of the civil war in 1990 gave rise to much hope in Lebanon. Reconciliation was supposed to proceed through reconstruction of the zones devastated by the war, such as downtown Beirut, but also through the restoration of national consciousness. A new Lebanese identity had to be rebuilt, and lessons had to be drawn from the madness of war that had overrun the country for fifteen years; Lebanon had to find its way back to the Arab environment without losing its own 'specificities'. Culture could play the role of a centripetal force that could overcome confessional and political fragmentation within Lebanese society, reinforced by the new political system established by the Ta'if Agreement. Culture was seen as an instrument to propagate a political message and a counterforce for the monopolisation of the political arena by the new powers that emerged during the war and with the Syrian order. The aim was a mobilising intellectual investment for a new generation of Lebanese and Arab thinkers and creators.

By creating Dar al-Jadid (New Publications) in 1990, Lokman Slim and Rasha al-Amir launched into a publishing venture to which they attached a political and cultural project linked, at the same time, to the Arabic language and to literary creation, as well as to the reshaping of Lebanese identity and to the renewal of Arab cultural sources. In its publishing guidelines, an important space is accorded to poetry, one of the least lucrative genres, and notably the publication of debut collections of poems. Their ambition 'to experiment with new horizons for the Arabic language'[53] also guides their choice of translations, which they regard as literary creations in their own right, seen even as linguistic laboratories.

With a publishing policy oriented towards works of critical thought, Dar al-Jadid intervenes in debates connected to society and the post-Ta'if Lebanese political system, in addition to the fields of religion and Islamic politics. Thus, by publishing Arabic translations of the works of Iranian President Mohammad Khatami or Sudanese Islamic ideologist Hasan al-Turabi, Dar al-Jadid aims at introducing the public to various points of views concerning Islam and its relationship to politics. Similarly, by re-editing the works of the 'red *sheikh*', al-Alayli,[54] it aims at extricating from the *turath* (heritage) what could constitute a modernist and 'alternative' Islamic heritage.

It is also in the fields of literature and critical thought, whether inspired by secularism or focused on the renewal of Islam, that publishing houses such as al-Markaz al-Thaqafi al-Arabi (Arab Cultural Centre) and Dar al-Intishar al-Arabi (Publications of Arab Diffusion), have succeeded in imposing their presence as foremost among protagonists of Arab publishing and the Arab intellectual sphere. The first has two branches, the older one located in Casablanca (founded in 1978) and the second in Beirut (set up in the 1980s). It stands out because it publishes North African and Middle Eastern authors who critically explore aspects of modernity in literature, philosophy, sociology and religion. Its original focus was on North African thinkers such as Said Yaqtan, Muhammad Khattabi and Salim Yaqut, but it progressively enlarged its spectrum to include Egyptians (Hasan Hanafi, Jabir Asfur, Nasr Hamid Abu Zayd), Lebanese (Ali Harb, Ahmad Baydoun, Waddah Shararah), as well as Saudis such as Abdallah al-Ghadhdhami, who is very controversial in his country because of his stance in favour of social and cultural change. In the domain of translation, this publishing house has pursued its mandate advocating modernity by publishing the most innovative French thinkers in the fields of the human and social sciences such as Gilles Deleuze and Michel Foucault.

More recently established, Dar al-Intishar al-Arabi was launched by two brothers from the Muruwweh family of South Lebanon. Dar al-Intishar al-Arabi also encompasses a pan-Arab dimension, and its publishing guidelines are directed towards critical thought, as attested by its slogan: 'To swim against the tide' (*al-sibahah aks al-tayyar*). Furthermore, its distinct anti-Islamist predilection is confirmed by its choice of publications, as well as the content of its monthly magazine *al-Kashkul*, launched in 2000, which publishes 'selections from contemporary texts for the modern family'. It thus promotes dissident voices in the face of religious conservatism and political Islam, ranging from the reformist Libyan thinker Sadiq al-Nayhum to the Saudi modernist Abdallah al-Qasimi.

Urban Space and Public Sphere

The Beirut publishing milieu, with its diversity, force of attraction and potential for diffusion, succeeded in making its own public sphere coincide with that of the whole of the Arab world.

The Beirut publishing milieu acted as the vector for this movement when numerous publishing companies were created to answer the needs of the Arab market. Although a large portion of this production is devoted to the educational sector, one must not neglect the existence of a cultural demand concerned with questions of identity, society and politics that agitate Arab societies, all of which are well-reflected in the catalogues of publishers established in Lebanon. The latter represent the point of convergence of an intellectual production where the different public spheres of the Arab world are crystallised.[58] In Beirut, these public spheres are evident in their plurality, which is surely the '*sine qua non* premise of the public domain'.

Hannah Arendt speaks of a sphere of appearances and insists more on its 'stage quality'[59] than on its 'communicational nature', as defined by Habermas.[60] This supposes that action and speech can be deployed in places of assembly and of co-presence, the city being the perfect example for both.[61] The distinctive characteristics that are supposed to define urban public spheres would then become the criteria for urbanity if placed on the scale of a whole city, in this case Beirut. These are accessibility; threshold; hospitality; visibility; and anonymity, i.e. criteria that underlie non-appropriated spaces of encounter.

One could indeed question the autonomy of the different Arab intellectual spheres *vis-à-vis* their states. Nevertheless, the fact remains that the Beirut sphere has benefited from a relative independence, where the different state constraints neutralised each other in order to prevent the predominance of a single influence. Thus the political hegemony of the Syrian regime in Lebanon was never able to confine both politics and the media completely, even though it managed to reinforce the practice of self-censorship. The conjunction of this relative autonomy with the development of a publishing capitalism presented necessary factors for the formation of a modern public sphere, which has always been Beirut's privilege. The question can be raised of how much longer it will last, considering the recent rise of new publishing centres in the rest of the Arab world.

Bibliography

Abboud, Angèle, *Shahadat fa sirah raidah wa-baqah min athariha* (*Testimonies on the Life of a Pioneer*), Beirut: Dar al-Jadid, 1998.

Abu Fakhr, Saqr, 'al-Muthaqqafun al-arab wa-bayrut ...' ('Arab intellectuals and Beirut'), *Nahar al-Arab wal-alam* (published in the Arabic edition of *Le Monde Diplomatique*), April 1999, pp. 21–2.

Amateis, Jacques, *Yusuf al-Khal wa majallatu-hu shir* (*Yusuf al-Khal and his magazine* Shi'r), Beirut: Dar an-Nahar and Orient-Institut der Deutschen Morgenlädischen Gesellschaft, 2004.

al-Amir, Rasha, 'Abdallah al-Alayli (1914–1996)' in *Liban, figures contemporaines*, Paris: Circé/ Institut du Monde Arabe, 1999, pp. 193–206.

Amoretti, Biancamaria Scarcia, 'La produzione editoriale sciita in Libano negli ultimi quindici anni', *Oriente Moderno*, nos 1–6, January–June 1995, p. 115–51.

Arendt, Hannah, *Condition de l'homme moderne*, Paris: Calmann Lévy, 1983.

al-Azm, Sadiq Jalal, *Hiwar bila difaf* (*Dialogue with No Shores: Interviews with Saqr Abu Fakhr*), Beirut: al-Muassasah al-Arabiyah lil-Dirasat wal-Nashr, 1998.

Berque, Jacques, *Langages arabes du présent*, Paris: Gallimard, 1980.

Bin Hamzah, Husayn 'Suhayl Idris: Kitabat al-sirah wasilah li-"qatl al-ab" wa-tariyat al-mujtama' ('Suhayl Idris: Autobiography as a way to "kill the father" and to denude society'), *Zawaya*, no. 10–11, January 2005, pp. 4–5.

Bourdieu, Pierre, *'Une révolution conservatrice dans l'édition'*, *Actes de la Recherche en Sciences Sociales*, vol. 126, no. 7, March 1999, pp. 3–28.

Calhoun, Craig, 'Introduction: Habermas and the Public Sphere', in Craig Calhoun (ed.), *Habermas and the Public Sphere,* Cambridge, MA: MIT Press, 1992, pp. 1–48.

Casanova, Pascale, *La République Mondiale des Lettres*, Paris: Seuil, 1999.

Daghir, Sharbil. 'Bayrut tabhath an bayrut' ('Beirut looking for Beirut'), *al-Nashirun*, no. 1, winter 1999, pp. 7–16.

El-Rayyes, Riad, *Akhir al-Khawarij: Ashya min sirah sahafiyah* (*The Last Outsider: Parts from a Journalist's Memoirs*), Beirut: Riad El-Rayyes Books, 2004.

Fadil, Jihad, 'Bayrut ayyat asimah thaqafiyah?' ('Beirut, what cultural capital?'), *al-Nashirun*, no. 1, winter 1999, p. 22.

Fandy, Mamoun, *Saudi Arabia and the Politics of Dissent*, New York: St. Martin's Press, 1999.

Favier, Agnès, 'La mobilisation "d'intellectuels" en politique dans la décennie de 1960–1970: Le cas "Liban Socialiste" (1974–1970)', in Joseph Bahout and Chawqi Douayhi, eds, *La vie publique au Liban: Expressions et recomposition du politique, Les Cahiers du CERMOC,* no. 18, 1997, pp. 147–81.

Guide du Livre. Industrie, Edition, Diffusion, Antelias: Antelias Cultural Movement/ Mukhtarat Editions, 1985.

Habermas, Jürgen, *L'espace public: Archéologie de la publicité comme dimension constitutive de la société bourgeoise*, Paris: Payot, 1978.

Hachem, Maud Stephan, 'L'édition du livre au Liban: Etude bibliologique et sociologique', unpublished PhD thesis, Université Saint-Joseph, Beirut, 1988.

Kassir, Samir, *L'Histoire de Beyrouth*, Paris: Fayard, 2003.

Khoury, Elias, 'An Bayrut' ('On Beirut'), *al-Mulhaq*, literary supplement of *an-Nahar*, 21 November 1998, p. 19.

Khubayz, Bilal, 'Bayrut asimat al-kitab al-Arabi, al-riqabah baqiyah wal-kitab ila al-zawal' ('Beirut: capital of the Arab book. Censorship remains and the book disappears'), *al-Kashkul,* September 2002, pp. 15–20.

Ladkany, Gilles, 'A la recherche de la modernité', in Jean-Charles Depaule, ed., *Cent titres à l'usage des bibliothécaires, libraires et amateurs: Poésie de langue arabe*, Marseille: Centre international de poésie, 2002, pp. 91–113.

Mermier, Franck, *Le livre et la ville: Beyrouth et l'édition arabe*, Paris: Actes Sud/ Sindbad, 2005.

Muchembled, Robert, *La société policée: Politique et politesse en France du XVIᵉ au XXᵉ siècle*, Paris: Seuil, 1998.

Naba, René, 'Les médias libanais face aux défis du XXIᵉ siècle', *Les Cahiers de l'Orient, quatrième trimestre*, 52, 1998, pp. 49–59.

Quéré, Louis, 'L'Espace public: de la théorie politique à la métathéorie sociologique', in *Quaderni*, no. 18, Fall 1992, pp. 75–92.

Rosiny, Stephan, *Shia's Publishing in Lebanon: With Special Reference to Islamic and Islamist Publications*, Berlin: Verlag Das Arabische Buch, 2000.

Saghieh, Hazem, 'Marifat (bad) tawaif wa-ailat Lubnan, manatiq wa-ahzab siyasiyah (4)' ('Information on some confessions, families, regions and political parties in Lebanon'), *al-Hayat*, 19 August 1999, p. 14.

Salim, Muhammad Adnan, *al-kitab fil-alfiyah al-thalithah, la-waraq wa-la hudud*, ('The book in the third millennium, no paper and no frontiers'), Damascus, Dar al-Fikr, 2000.

Shararah, Abd al-Latif, *Qadiyat al-kitab al-Lubnani*, Beirut: Jam'iyat Asdiqa' al-Kitab, 1962.

Union of Publishers, *Dur al-nashr fi Lubnan* (*Publishing Houses in Lebanon*), Beirut, 2004.

al-Wardani, Salih, 'al-Kitab al-shii fi Misr' ('The Shi'i book in Egypt'), *Rose el-Youssef*, 13–19 January 2001, pp. 35–6.

Notes

1. This research has benefited from the financial support of the Social Science Research Council (New York).
2. Habermas, *L'espace public*.
3. Muchembled, *La société policée*, p. 84.
4. Bourdieu, 'Une révolution conservatrice dans l'édition', p. 3.
5. Shararah, pp. 16–17.
6. *Guide du Livre*.
7. Hachem, *L'édition du livre au Liban*, p. 34.
8. Union of Publishers, *Dur al-nashr fi lubnan*.
9. Naba, 'Les medias libanais face aux défis du XXIᵉ siècle', p. 52.
10. For a history of Beirut, see Kassir, *L'Histoire de Beyrouth*.
11. Fadil, 'Bayrut ayyat asimah thaqafiyah?', p. 22.
12. Abu Fakhr, 'al-Muthaqqafun al-Arab wa-Bayrut ...', pp. 21–2.
13. Ibid., p. 21.
14. Khoury, 'An bayrut', p. 19.
15. Hachem, *L'édition du livre au Liban*, p. 61–2.
16. Interview with Saqr Abu Fakhr (Institute for Palestine Studies) in Beirut, May 2000.
17. Holder of a PhD in political science from London University in 1966, Abd al-Wahhab al-Kayyali was the Secretary-General of the Arab Liberation Front, a member of the general command of the Iraqi Baath Party and the head of the Cultural Section in the Palestine Liberation Organisation.
18. Interview with Mahir al-Kayyali in Beirut, August 2000.
19. With the Ministry of Information in Bahrain for the publication of Bahraini authors, with Dar Suwaydi, owned by Muhammad al-Suwaydi, also Director of the Abu Dhabi Cultural Foundation (al-Majma al-Thaqafi) for the publication of Arab travellers' accounts, and with the Shuman Foundation in Amman and the Jordanian Ministry of Culture.
20. Daghir, 'Bayrut tabhath an bayrut', p. 14.
21. Many other periodicals should also be mentioned here, such as *al-Thaqafah al-arabiyah* (*Arab Culture*), created by Husayn Muruwweh of the Lebanese Communist Party; *al-Mawaqif*; *al-Hiwar*; *al-Huriyah*; etc. The case of *Shir* and *al-Adab* remains exemplary because of the influence exerted by the people involved, as well as the entanglement of literary and political standpoints.
22. See Amateis, *Yusuf al-khal wa majallatu-hu shi'r*, pp. 148–9.
23. Here I follow Ladkany's translation of the expression '*Shir al-tafilah* in his article 'A la recherche de la modernité'; see Ladkany, 'A la recherche de la modernité'.
24. Interview with Suhayl Idris in Beirut, June 1999.
25. According to the terms used by Agnès Favier, who notes the role played to this effect by Lebanese leftist militants: '... It would be interesting to draw a list of the works translated by the members of Socialist Lebanon (in general published by Dar-al-

Taliah) in order to assess the level and nature of their role as mediators of a European culture.' See Favier, 'La mobilisation "d'intellectuels" en politique dans la décennie de 1960–1970', p. 172.

26. After the title of Berque's *Langages arabes du présent*.

27. The Centre gained its internal statutes and regulations during a constitutive assembly held in Kuwait in January 1976.

28. The Centre has replaced the National Development Institute founded by Libya in Beirut at the beginning of the 1970s. Its two periodicals are *Majallat al fikr al-arabi al–muasir* (*Arab Contemporary Thought*) and *Majallat tarikh al-arab* (*History of the Arabs*). It has published the first Arabic translations of Michel Foucault.

29. The Arab Cultural Centre has been established as a publishing house in Casablanca since 1978, with a branch in Beirut established in 1980. It publishes works written by Moroccan thinkers such as Abdallah Laroui and Muhammad al-Jabiri.

30. Hachem, *L'édition du livre au Liban*, p. 62.

31. Saghie, 'Marifat (bad) tawaif wa-ailat lubnan, manatiq wa-ahzab siyasiyah', p. 14.

32. Abboud, *Shahadat fa sirah raidah wa-baqah min athariha*, p. 9.

33. Interview with Sadiq Jalal al-Azm in Beirut, June 2004.

34. al-Azm, *Hiwar bila Difaf*, pp. 38–9.

35. Salim, *al-kitab fil-alfiyah al- thalithah, la-waraq wa-la hudud*, pp. 142–3.

36. Dar al-Haqiqah was the rallying point of the small Workers' Revolutionary Party, present in both Syria and Lebanon, which assembled several Marxist militants who were former Baathists. Originally from Dayr al-Zurr, Yasin al-Hafiz was a Marxist theoretician who had an important influence on the Syrian Baath Party after the *coup d'état* of 1963. It was a short-lived influence: al-Hafiz sought refuge in Beirut in 1964.

37. It is worth mentioning that titles by Abdallah Azzam were erased from the catalogue of Dar Ibn Hazm after 11 September 2001. Beginning in 1996, the publisher printed a caption on one of his books that 'the ideas expressed in the works published by Dar Ibn Hazm only express the authors' point of view'.

38. Many publishing houses had their offices in the four buildings on Syria St: al-Azariyah, al-Binayah al Markaziyah, Salihah wa-Samadi and Darwish.

39. Stephan Rosiny has estimated the number of these houses to be 136 during research he conducted in Lebanon in 1997. He estimates the number of publishing houses managed by Shi'is at 312, 136 of which have an 'Islamist' orientation. See Rosiny, *Shia's Publishing in Lebanon*. See also Amoretti, 'La produzione editoriale sciita in Libano negli ultimi quindici anni'.

40. Rosiny, *Shia's Publishing in Lebanon*, p. 41.

41. Notably the Muassasat Ahl al-Bayt, a religious institution of Iranian origin whose headquarters is located in Tehran); Dar al-Mufid; Dar al-Rawdah; Dar al-Hadi; Dar al-Amir; Dar al-A'lami; Dar al-Adwa'; and Dar al-Ghadir. On recent developments in the censorship of Shi'i books see al-Wardani, 'al-Kitab al-shii fi misr', pp. 35–6.

42. On Sheikh Hasan al-Saffar see Fandy, *Saudi Arabia and the Politics of Dissent*. Many of his books have been published by Dar al-Jadid, Dar al-Saqi and, more recently, by the Arab Cultural Centre (al-Markaz al-Thaqafi al-Arabi).

43. Rosiny, *Shia's Publishing in Lebanon*, p. 51.

44. Amateis, *Yusuf al-Khal wa-majallatu-hu shi'r*, p. 92.

45. To use one example: a biography of the Druze leader Kamal Jumblatt, translated from Russian into Arabic, sold more than 9,000 copies in 2002 – a success by Lebanese standards for this type of book.

46. Interview with Ghassan Tueni in Beirut, November 1999.

47. See an analysis of this publishing policy in Khubayz, 'Bayrut 'asimat al-kitab al-'arabi, al-riqabah baqiyah wal kitab ila al-zawal'.

48. See the interview with Suhayl Idris published in the review *Zawaya*, no. 10–11, January 2005, pp. 4–5.

49. According to Pierre Bourdieu's expression; see Bourdieu, 'Une révolution conservatrice dans l'édition', p. 16.

50. His father Najib El-Rayyes (1898–1952) was one of the great names in Syrian press and politics.

51. Riad Najib El-Rayyes, *Akhir al-khawarij: Ashya min sirah sahafiyah* (*The Last Outsider: Parts from a Journalist's Memoirs*), Beirut, 2004, pp. 256–7.

52. Interview with Riad El-Rayyes in Beirut, February 1999.

53. Interview with Rasha al-Amir and Lokman Slim in Beirut, November 1998.

54. Notably his famous *Introduction to the Study of the Language of the Arabs*, published in Cairo in 1938. See al Amir, 'Abdallah al-Alayli (1914–1996)'.

55. Habermas, *L'espace public*.

56. Muchembled, *La société policée*, p. 84.

57. Bourdieu, 'Une révolution conservatrice dans l'édition', p. 3.

58. Calhoun, 'Introduction: Habermas and the Public Sphere', p. 37.

59. Arendt, *Condition de l'homme moderne*, p. 283.

60. Quéré, 'L'Espace public: de la théorie politique à la métathéorie sociologique'.

61. Hannah Arendt, *Condition de l'homme moderne*, pp. 259–62.

JEAN-FRANÇOIS BAYART

Conclusion: 21st Century Cities of the South

The political scientist for whom 'the city was never his actual research subject but who has attempted a historical sociology of globalisation' certainly learned a lot about the city in the context of globalisation, thanks to the richness of the contributions in this book and the debates they generated during the conference that preceded this publication. However, precisely because of their profuse character, it becomes impossible for him to synthesise them in a way that would do justice to the work of the different authors. Rather than aiming at a vain exercise of academic politesse citing all the authors in a somewhat artificial way, we propose here five points of reflection:

I

First of all, we have treated the city in a precise historical context: the neo-liberal moment of globalisation starting in the 1980s with Margaret Thatcher and Ronald Reagan coming into power, the discarding of Keynesianism by the World Bank, the generalisation of structural adjustment programmes and the establishment of a new engineering of urban power in the name of 'good governance'. Its results were not the disappearance but rather the recomposition of public policies of the city framed within the 'privatisation of the state'.[1] The application of these policies has been consigned, on the one hand, to local authorities following the categorical principle of 'decentralisation' and, on the other hand, to private operators, either enterprises or non-governmental organisations. This systematic 'discharging'[2] of public powers onto private sector actors resembles somehow the re-establishment of the old colonial regime of Indirect Rule, but also to the mercantile or neo-mercantile consolidation of the European monarchies and empires.[3]

One feature of the neo-liberal moment that we have considered is that there is a massive intervention of multilateral donors in the urban domain, shown by the numerous programmes of the World Bank. These are mainly private Western operators in favour of privatisation measures for public services such as water, electricity, telephone, rubbish collection, public housing and even of part of the road, rail and water networks plus urban planning and security. They are in favour of the promotion of an 'international civil society', omnipresent in the 'struggle against poverty' or AIDS, of micro-credits, of humanitarian action and political mobilisations. The collateral effects of this new urban 'governance', largely globalised in its ideological inspiration, its financing and its *modus operandi*, have often been paradoxical. They have frequently resulted in an increase of poverty and social exclusion detrimental for the popular classes. At least part of these have been excluded from access to water, electricity, schools and transportation because of the privatisation of these public services. They have been prevented from access to the city centre, due to its gentrification and 'museification' under the pretext of the patrimonial rehabilitation and historical restoration or, on the contrary, from certain fashionable suburbs, the 'edges of the city' of Joel Garreau,[4] when downtown was abandoned – as happened in Los Angeles.

Of course, it would be dishonest to generalise this presentation. In a good number of cases the public services were *de facto* non-existent except on paper. Liberalisation permitted the improvement of the management of public enterprises that were badly failing. Private actors – sometimes non-governmental organisations, sometimes political movements or also simply individual initiatives by leading persons – have been able to conduct real beneficial strategies in the field with more or less the participation of the population.[5] But the many and loud songs of praise announcing the advent of 'the Millennium Development Goals' shouldn't cover the murmurs of the losers of neo-liberalism. Thus most African countries have passed during the last thirty years from the city of light to the city of darkness: electricity cuts do not spare large cities such as Dakar, without even mentioning Kigali, plunged in darkness during the long weeks preceding the genocide of Tutsis in April–June 1994.

Furthermore, neo-liberal politics have contributed to the de-industrialisation of many cities, and to their dismantling in the literary sense of the word, as superbly shown in Wang Bing's documentary *West of the Rails* (1992), about the steel zone of Shenyang in China. Here also, we must be careful in our analysis. Apparently liberalisation or the destruction of the public sector doesn't put an end to social redistribution by the state to the working class, even though internal migrants are largely excluded. It is less a triumph of the private sector then an emergence of multiple ways of straddling the positions of Communist or bureaucratic power and the private positions of economic accumulation, in the shade of *guanxi* ('connections'/ networking).[6] The de-industrialisation of old workers' cities goes side by side with the rise of new productive poles giving birth to impressive conurbations and totally new urban fabrics, such as in the hinterlands of Shanghai, Hong Kong and Guangzhou, or also on the Mexican-American border. Its price is a terrible exploitation of labour in sweatshops and particularly coercive, even predatory forms of putting workers to work and disciplining them.[7]

On this level, the analysis of the city caught within globalisation should surpass its administrative and geographic borders. 'The city is anything but a well-circumscribed entity in space or time',[8] existing historically only since about thirty years. Internal or international migrants submerge the city with their endless comings and goings between it and their places of origin and, with their travelling projects towards different cities. The city is a knot of global commercial, economic and other exchanges: 'flux cities', therefore; we still need to better understand their political and moral economy. They often claim to be economic and financial 'virtuous' poles, archetypes of growth and 'good governance', at least for their industry, banking and security systems.

Meanwhile, they only persist because of their environments, which are much less presentable and which provide them with their substance. The prosperity of Hong Kong, Singapore or Bangkok owes a lot to the crime and misery of their hinterlands and to the diaspora from China, to Myanmar, Cambodia and Indonesia. Dubai's prosperity is tributary to South Asia, Afghanistan, Iran, Central Asia and even a part of Southeast Asia. And what would the dynamism of Johannesburg, Durban or Cape Town be without the backing of African and, more and more, Chinese migrants? For several centuries already – London, Paris, Amsterdam, New York, Istanbul and Mumbai are there to remind us of this fact – there is no metropolis that isn't global and cosmopolitan, except maybe Tokyo or Beijing, but can they still be considered exceptions today? Increasingly, global cities are centres of transgression of the morality of the market in terms of violence and mafia 'protection',[9] of fraud, counterfeiting, falsification, mutation of values. The social scene is doubled in the dimension of the invisible, be it the realm of witchcraft or the cultural underground, of informal work or international financial activity.[10]

II

The historicity of the neo-liberal moment that we consider, its complexity and social pluri-vocality, has to forbid us from any meta-discourse about the 'global city', something that hasn't been always avoided in social sciences these past years. There is no other solution than to concentrate on the practices that constitute the global city and mainly on what Michel de Certeau calls the 'practices of space'. Contemplating New York from the top of the World Trade Center, this Jesuit historian escaped from the panoptical fascination inspired by this '*tableau* that was possible only on condition that one forgets or disregards the practices':

> The ordinary practitioners of the city live 'down below', below the thresholds at which visibility begins. They walk – an elementary form of this experience of the city; they are walkers, *Wandersmänner*, whose bodies follow the fullness and gaps of an urban 'text' they write without being able to read. These practitioners make use of the spaces that cannot be seen; their knowledge is as blind as that of lovers in each other's arms. The paths that correspond in these intertwining, unrecognized poems in which each body is an element signed by many others, elude legibility. It is as though the practices organizing a bustling city were characterized by their blindness. The networks of these moving, intersecting writings compose a manifold story that has neither author nor spectator, and is shaped out of fragments of trajectories and alternations of spaces: in relation to representations, it remains daily and indefinitely other.[11]

This is an important observation in these times of ideological and phantasmic elaboration of the 'global city', as used by city authorities, the media, public relations, enterprises and, last but not least, the architects and urbanists, even the urban dwellers themselves when they are but a little bit fashionable, or the migrants fascinated by the lights of Los Angeles, New York, London or Paris. This leads us to the issue of the speech acts of the city:

> The act of walking is to the urban system what the speech act is to language or to the statements uttered. At the most elementary level, it has a triple "enunciative" function: it is a process of appropriation of the topographical system on the part of the pedestrian (just as the speaker appropriates and takes on the language); it is a spatial acting-out of the place (just as the speech act is an acoustic acting-

out of language); and it implies relations among differentiated positions, that is, among pragmatic "contracts" in the form of movements (...) It thus seems possible to give a preliminary definition of walking as a space of enunciation.[12]

This argument permits us to understand theoretically why and how the 'global city' that is supposed to be a centre of 'Westernisation' or 'Americanisation', of alienation and anomie, if only through mass consumption, is in fact the epicentre of the 'reinvention of the difference'[13] that characterises globalisation. By definition imitation, even for trade, is appropriation, and therefore creation.[14] *De facto*, the city in the process of globalisation becomes the matrix of new cultural, religious, political and financial or economic actions, despite the immense pressure of the neo-liberal 'governance' in favour of the universal 'market'.

We understand better today that this does not dispel the historicity of the societies. What is out of laziness classified under 'culture' is larger than the space that capitalism consents to beliefs and irrationality. World economy rests on this *bric-a-brac* of practices and representations and merges with it. The city remains the favourite site for these organic compromises between trade transactions that are supposed to be universal and historical trajectories in the form of a series of commercial and financial 'performances', as is masterfully shown by Jane I. Guyer for the Yoruba cities of Nigeria.[15]

Definitely, there is no other sociology of urban change than a 'paradoxical' one. Even the idea of intentionality or causality has to be removed from the reasoning, and the attention has to be directed towards social practices as modes of appropriation, i.e. of the creation of the city even in its cruelty. Pillaging, riots, suicide attacks contribute to shape the public space and, barbaric though they may be, they are acts of citizenship, carriers of a certain conception of social justice and political freedom, of collective claims, of an imaginary of the city.[16] The blind and unbearable violence that they use is generally a sign of huge inadequacy, the discrepancy between the political offer and effective urban practices – illustrated, for example, by the vain attempts at repressing migratory fluxes, the spatial politics of relegating the poor to the suburbs or programmes of ethnic cleansing and expropriation in situations of armed conflict. The interaction between these practices has deeply marked the city over the last twenty years, and the way terrorism became a commonplace as a mode of political action, becoming a 'natural' category for its actors and critics, suggests that this process is far from complete. From control to surveillance, the city has become a security space of which Eugène Zamiatine foresaw its totalitarian virtuality.[17]

III

Our debates have confirmed that the contemporary city is also substantiated through practices of consumption. Merchandise, the material culture of the city, is the necessary but not sufficient requirement for citizenship. Moreover, we have tried to show how merchandise is a vector of subjectivation, also political, in a context of globalisation.[18] The city is a place of choice of this 'constitution of the moral subject'.[19] In particular, cities house the main social institutions that are its supports: shopping malls, enterprises, cult places – starting with the mosques, tombs of saints visited by pilgrims/tradesmen, or the Pentecostal temples where the gospel of Prosperity is celebrated.[20] The urban practices of consumption that create civilisation and progress in the hinterland, also create social relations between classes, gender, age. They also mark the boundaries of public space and the modalities of its access, i.e. the civic capacity.

From this perspective, wearing the *hijab*, using bicycles and driving behaviour have been, for women in Muslim societies, arenas of social struggle that were already highlighted very early by the pioneering studies of Fariba Adelkhah in Iran. The multiple new forms of the veil that have been generalised with the establishment of the Islamic Republic have even been an emblem of urbanity, especially in intermediary cities or in the main big cities among the new Iranian or Afghan immigrants.[21] These types of practices of material culture might take a political turn and play a role even in elections, as happened in Tehran and Isfahan during the elections of 1996. These conflicts of political subjectivation around merchandise are, in fact, very common, even if they haven't interested political scientists until now.[22]

Contemporary globalisation has seriously transformed the material culture of the city. Indeed, it is now less walking than driving behaviour that constitutes its 'space of enunciation'. De facto, the car is an instrument of exclusion, of promotion or social classification. It is also a technique to occupy the public space in the form of autocades for marriages, sports manifestations, even political gatherings. On its limit car and city confound as is wanted in the urbanism of Los Angeles and dreamed of by Georges Pompidou in Paris or Mohammed Reza Shah in Teheran. And for those who know Bangkok, Cairo or Teheran there is no doubt that the use of the car (and of the city) belongs to the order of the speech acts of performances. In the same way the mobile phone changed the borders between the private and the public sphere in daily life because it permits everyone to share in the intimacy and professional activity of his fellow man, but also allows for the organisation of public demonstrations or the control of elections right under the nose of the authorities as in Dakar 2000 or Beirut 2005.

IV

In its materiality, the city in the situation of globalisation remains all in all cultural, like the city in Greco-Roman Antiquity or during the Italian Renaissance.[23] Under the cover of neo-traditionalism, the procession remains a way to invent it, as shown in the popular marches of Saint Anthony of Padua in Lisbon, introduced by the Estado Novo in 1932, putting the most 'typical' quarters of the city in competition. This procession even coopted certain suburbs like Alcântara[24] and, seventy years after their creation, they are still very fashionable in the democratic context of 'Europeanisation' and of the accelerated 'mercantilisation' of the city. Clearly Alcântara, now with a lot of restaurants and dancing in the shade of the Salazar suspension bridge, was not undone when it had to become up-to-date.

The political demonstration is the natural reincarnation of the civic procession. During the conference we observed this; it was through demonstrations that the inhabitants of Beirut re-appropriated their city and partly, at least for a few months, their independence. The suicide attack is another ritual, a murderous one, through which citizens take their destiny in their own hands, less out of despair, as is too often written with an air of condescension, than out of political, not inefficient, calculation. After all, they are performative acts that, much more than the ballots, have caused defeat for the US in Baghdad and made its failure in the imaginary global fight evident. It is also these acts that keep the tragic flame of Palestinian resistance alive against Israeli occupation, despite the compromises of the PLO and its impotence to make the Jewish state see a minimum of reason. The height of cynicism lies undoubtedly in the fact that we are still exasperated, while everything has been done to push the actors to similar radical positions.

The city is also a place of different liturgies, more pleasant ones, such as cinema. This contributes to its imaginary production; what would New York, San Francisco, Paris, Hong Kong be without the eye of the camera that has in some way 'branded' them? The cinema can provide publicity for the democratic imaginary as in Madras, where the stars of the Seventh Art appear on the electoral scene. It nurtures the political, criminal economy of a city like Mumbai.[25]

Furthermore, the city in the context of globalisation has been characterised by a religious recovery, about which a lot has been said. It is now clear that the Islamism of 1970–80, and especially of the Iranian Revolution, far from a cultural regression or a return to the 'Middle Ages', was a way to enter into urban culture and 'being-in-society' at the other extreme of what is called traditional ethos.[26] To the great displeasure of the original inhabitants of Istanbul, the same occurs today on the shores of the Bosphorus, and the individualisation of the youth of Dakar happens through the space of the Muride brotherhood.[27] Strangely enough, the boom of Pentecostal churches in Latin America and Africa – not to speak of Lisbon and Porto, or the sub-Saharan immigrant communities in Europe[28] – doesn't incite the same worry. It is, nevertheless, one of the most impressive social phenomena of the neo-liberal moment of the city that certainly participates intrinsically in cult activity.

V

Simultaneously, the city in the context of globalisation, as tributary as it may be to international markets – those of beliefs, goods, capital, cultural and media flux – remains a place of power and coercion on a local or national level, in a very classical manner. It is a place of expulsions and of left-behinds, *déguerpissements* as they call them in Africa: witnesses of massive operations that have displaced thousands of people in Mumbai or Harare recently. It is a place of police control and of 'bravery' that sometimes enflames whole quarters with responding riots, as happened in the French suburbs in autumn 2005 and in Los Angeles in 1992. It is a place for the implementation of capital punishment as in China or the US – extra-judiciary executions also, as is the case in Brazil, Cameroon or the Ivory Coast. It is a place where one whips, as in most of the sub-Saharan capitals, but also in an official and judiciary way in Kuala Lumpur and Singapore. A place where one attacks, steals, rapes, a place roamed by gangs, militias, armed movements, regular troops, with often irregular behaviour, and where ethnic cleansing or, as in certain US cities, a 'racial war on low-intensity' wages.[29] It is a place that is the target of bombs, even when they are with 'zero casualties', and the preferred theatre of suicide attacks.

The harshest forms of violence dominate the city in the situation of globalisation, which raises the question of its ideological and political construction through the intermediary of the media. In France, the same journalists who drew an apocalyptic image of the suburbs in flames in the autumn of 2005 were much less talkative when describing the destruction of public buildings by enraged farmers. The English-language media questioning seriously the risks of a civil war in Paris or the failure of the French model of social integration were quite oblivious to the events of Los Angeles and Brighton. Similarly, the Lebanese are convinced that the international press neglected their suffering during the war in the summer of 2006, while the Israelis were indignant that their suffering was silenced or at least perceived as deserved.

The globalisation of the mediascape[30] has probably amplified this type of distortion and made it more frequent. Simultaneously, it has contributed to crystallising the feeling and the discursive type of 'insecurity', which we too often forget is largely the result of the ideology of the Cold War, like the anti-subversive thought of the Brazilian army before its 'vulgarisation' turned it into a trivial source of legitimisation for the conservative and neo-liberal right wings from the 1970s on.[31] The 'ecology of fear'[32] imposed itself and turned into a hegemonic discourse.

The result is a double particularity of the city in a process of globalisation. It is neo-liberal economic politics that produce poverty and the politics of the city aim at managing this poverty through imprisonment, thanks to the adoption of an ad hoc ultra repressive legislation, type 'zero-tolerance' as it is commonly expressed in New York.[33] Furthermore, this relates to the practices of spatial segregation of a coercive type, with at least partial colonial inspiration, whose application is delegated to private operators, such as the security forces guarding companies.

Against the background of apartheid, and in a context of impending civil war at the time of the political transition, South Africa was the pioneer for this type of urbanism. The extent and the violence of crime justify the more wealthy individuals transforming their houses into fortresses, and shopping malls presenting themselves as garrison-*entrepôts*, to adopt the term of colonial conquest. The protection of the wealthy from the less fortunate – and even of police stations! – was consigned to numerous private security companies that bloomed at the initiative of ancient officers or fighters from the army of the ancient regime.[34] The riots of Los Angeles in 1992 also contributed to a 'militarisation of the social landscape in South California' already pointed out by Mike Davis in 1990.[35] The spatial apartheid developed with the systematic 'zoning' of the habitat through the multiplication of almost fortified 'edge cities', by confining the poor to subsidised lodgings. These were put under high police surveillance comparable to emergency villages, real "strategic niches" placed under a state of exception that isn't declared, and through the generalisation of the practice of 'neighbourhood watch.'[36] Numerous big cities in Latin America, Africa and Asia follow this evolution, towards which Europe seems hesitant – even a city as secure as Istanbul cedes to the temptation of 'secured residential complexes', foreign as they may be to the sociability of the banks of the Bosphorus.[37]

To this extent, the new urban century will probably be one of walls. One single edition of *Le Monde* of 17 August 2006 announces, on p. 5, that the US army in Baghdad builds cement barriers around the neighbourhood of al-Dora to separate Sunnis and Shi'is and – on p. 6 – that the municipality of Padua has constructed a metal wall of 84 m long and 3 m high to isolate the Anelli quarter, victim of the drug trade. The wall that separates Israelis and Palestinians is now famous, as the one of Melilla is becoming, as an outpost of Fortress Europe and Bush's wall between Mexico and the USA. In short, the fall of the Berlin Wall in 1989, in which many theoreticians of international relations and globalisation pretentiously saw the dawn of new hope, was only a pretence; this disappearing of a historical enclosure that was, in fact, quite exceptional, left space for the proliferation of ordinary enclosures. In the cities, in the context of globalisation, walls are from now on written without capitals ...

Bibliography

Adelkhah Fariba, 'Les Afghans iraniens', *Les Etudes du CERI*, no. 125, April 2006.

——'Economie morale du pèlerinage et société civile en Iran', in Jean-François Bayart and J. Lonsdale, eds, *Moral Economies and State-Formation in the Non-European World*, forthcoming.

——*Etre moderne en Iran*, Paris: Karthala, 1998 (new extended edn, 2006).

——*La Révolution sous le voile. Femmes islamiques d'Iran*, Paris: Karthala, 1991.

Appadurai, Arjun, 'Disjuncture and difference in the global cultural economy', *Public Culture*, vol. 2, no. 2, spring 1990, pp. 1–24.

Ashforth, Adam, *Madumo: A Man Bewitched*, Chicago: University of Chicago Press, 2000.

Bayart, Jean-François, *Le Gouvernement du monde: Une critique politique de la globalisation*, Paris: Fayard, 2004.

Brown, Peter, *Le Culte des saints: Son essor et sa fonction dans la chrétienté latine*, Paris: Le Cerf, 1996.

Clifford, James, *The Predicament of Culture: Twentieth Century Ethnography, Literature and Art*, Cambridge, MA: Harvard University Press, 1988.

Davis, Mike, *Au-delà de* Blade Runner. *Los Angeles et l'imagination du désastre*, Paris: Editions Allia, 2006.

——*City of Quartz: Excavating the Future in Los Angeles*, London: Verso, 1990.

De Boeck, Filip and Plissart, Marie-Françoise, *Kinshasa: Tales of the Invisible City*, Belgium: Ludion, 2006.

de Certeau, Michel, *L'Invention du quotidien, Volume I: Arts de faire*, Paris: U.G.E., 1980.

Deleuze, Gilles, *Différence et répétition*, Paris: PUF, 1968.

Dessert, Daniel, *Argent, pouvoir et société au Grand Siècle*, Paris: Fayard, 1984.

Dickey, Sara, *Cinema and the Urban Poor in South India*, Cambridge: Cambridge University Press, 1993.

Ellis, Stephen, 'Africa and international corruption: the strange case of South Africa and Seychelles', *African Affairs*, no. 95, April 1996, pp. 165–96.

Elyachar, Julia, 'Finance internationale, micro-crédit et religion de la société civile en Egypte', *Critique internationale*, no. 13, October 2001, pp. 139–52.

Farges, Joël, 'Le cinéma en Inde: rasa cinematografica', in Christophe Jaffrelot, ed., *L'Inde contemporaine de 1950 à nos jours*, Paris: Fayard, 1996.

Foucault, Michel, *L'Usage des plaisirs*, Paris: Gallimard, 1984.

Garreau, Joel, *Edge City: Life on the New Frontier*, New York: Doubleday, 1991.

Guyer, Jane I., *Marginal Gains: Monetary Transactions in Atlantic Africa*, Chicago: University of Chicago Press, 2004.

ter Haar, Gerrie, *Halfway to Paradise: African Christians in Europe*, Cardiff: Cardiff Academic Press, 1998.

Haenni, Patrick, *L'Ordre des caïds: Conjurer la dissidence urbaine au Caire*, Paris and Cairo: Karthala/ CEDEJ, 2005.

Harding, Jeremy, 'The historical significance of South Africa's Third Force', *Journal of Southern African Studies*, vol. 24, no. 2, June 1998, pp. 261–99.

——'The Mercenary Business', *London Review of Books*, 1 August 1996.

Havard, Jean-François, *Bul Faale! Processus d'individualisation de la jeunesse et conditions d'émergence d'une 'génération politique' au Sénégal*, Lille: Université de Lille-II, 2005.

Hibou, Béatrice, 'L'Etat en voie de privatisation', *Politique africaine*, no. 73, March 1999, pp. 6–121.

——'La privatisation de l'Etat', *Critique internationale*, no. 1, autumn 1998, pp. 128–94.

——ed., *La Privatisation des Etats*, Paris: Karthala, 1999.

——'The "social capital" of the State as an agent of deception, or the ruses of economic intelligence', in Jean-François Bayart, S. Ellis, Béatrice Hibou, *The Criminalization of the State in Africa*, Oxford: James Currey, 1999, pp. 69–114.

Kandiyoti, Deniz and Ayse Saktanber, eds, *Fragments of Culture: The Everyday of Modern Turkey*, London: I. B. Tauris, 2002.

Kernen, Antoine, *La Chine vers l'économie de marché: Les privatisations à Shenyang*, Paris: Karthala, 2004.

Mamdani, Mahmood, *Citizen and Subject: Contemporary Africa and the Legacy of Late Colonialism*, Princeton: Princeton University Press, 1996.

Malaquais, Dominique, 'Arts de feyre au Cameroun', *Politique africaine*, no. 82, June 2001, pp. 101–18.

—— 'Villes flux. Imaginaires de l'urbain en Afrique aujourd'hui', *Politique africaine*, no. 100, December 2005–January 2006, pp. 17–37.

Marshall-Fratani, R., 'Prospérité miraculeuse: Les pasteurs pentecôtistes et l'argent de Dieu au Nigeria', *Politique africaine*, no. 82, June 2001, pp. 24–44.

Mary, André, 'Prophètes pasteurs: La politique de la délivrance en Côte d'Ivoire', *Politique africaine*, no. 87, October 2002, pp. 69–94.

Meyer, Birgit, 'Commodities and the Power of Prayer: Pentecostalist Attitudes towards Consumption in Contemporary Ghana', in Birgit Meyer and Peter Geschiere, eds, *Globalization and Identity: Dialectics of Flow and Closure*, Oxford: Blackwell, 1999.

Navaro-Yashin, Yael, *Faces of the State: Secularism and Public Life in Turkey*, Princeton: Princeton University Press, 2002.

Ong, Aihwa, *Flexible Citizenship: The Cultural Logics of Transnationality*, Durham: Duke University Press, 1999.

Parenti, Christian, *Lockdown America: Police and Prisons in the Age of Crisis*, London: Verso, 1999.

Pérouse, Jean-François, *La Turquie en marche: Les grandes mutations depuis 1980*, Paris: Editions de la Martinière, 2004.

de Polignac François, *La Naissance de la cité grecque*, Paris: La Découverte, 1984.

Rocca, Jean-Louis, *La Condition chinoise: La mise au travail capitaliste à l'âge des réformes*, Paris: Karthala, 2006.

Rodrigues, Donizete, 'Pentecôtisme et identité tsigane: Le cas de l'Eglise évangélique de Philadelphie du Portugal', *Revue Lusotopie*, vol. XIII, no. 1, 2006, pp. 85–93.

Roitman Janet, 'The garrison-*entrepôt*: a mode of governing in the Chad Basin', in Aihwa Ong and Stephen J. Collier, eds, *Global Assemblages. Technology, Politics, and Ethics as Anthropological Problems*, Oxford: Blackwell, 2005.

Ros, Reeve and Ellis, Stephen, 'An insider's account of the South African Security Forces' role in the ivory trade', *Journal of Contemporary African Studies*, vol. 13, no. 2, 1995, pp. 227–44.

Schooyans, Michel, *Destin du Brésil: la technocratie militaire et son idéologie*, Gembloux: J. Duculot, 1973.

Trexler, Richard C., *Public Life in Renaissance Florence*, Ithaca: Cornell University Press, 1991.

Vidal, Frédéric, 'Images urbaines. Alcântara à Lisbonne, du faubourg à la ville', *Revue Lusotopie*, vol. XIII, no. 1, 2006.

Volkov, Vadim, *Violent Entrepreneurs: The Use of Force in the Making of Russian Capitalism*, Ithaca: Cornell University Press, 2002.

Weber, Max, *Histoire économique: Esquisse d'une histoire universelle de l'économie et de la société*, Paris: Gallimard, 1991, pp. 79–92.

Zamiatine, Eugène, *Nous autres*, Paris: Gallimard, 1971.

Notes

1. Hibou, *La Privatisation des Etats*; 'La privatisation de l'Etat'; L'Etat en voie de privatisation'.

2. Weber: *Verpachtung* or *Überweisung*; see Weber, *Histoire économique*.

3. Elyachar, 'Finance internationale, micro-crédit et religion de la société civile en Egypte', especially pp. 141, 148, 151). The author uses the notion of *indirect rule* in the sense that has been given to it by Mahmood Mamdani; see Mamdani, *Citizen and Subject*. Béatrice Hibou, on his part, relates the 'privatisation of the States' to the mercantilist (Hibou, *La Privatisation des Etats*) and cites, among others, the works of Daniel Dessert (see Dessert, *Argent, pouvoir et société au Grand Siècle*).

4. Garreau, *Edge City*.

5. See, for example, Patrick Haenni on the dignitaries of Cairo: Haenni, *L'Ordre des caïds*.

6. Kernen, *La Chine vers l'économie de marché*; Rocca, *La Condition chinoise*.

7. Ong, *Flexible Citizenship*. See among others the case – not elaborated – of the disappearance of young women in Ciudad Juárez.

8. Malaquais, 'Villes flux', p. 26.

9. Volkov, *Violent Entrepreneurs*.

10. See for example, for Africa: De Boeck and Plissart, *Kinshasa: Tales of the Invisible City*; Guyer, *Marginal Gains*; Malaquais, 'Arts de feyre au Cameroun'; Hibou, 'The 'social capital' of the State as an agent of deception, Chapter 4.

11. de Certeau, *L'Invention du quotidien*, pp. 173–4.

12. Ibid., pp. 180–1. Cited in the translation of Rendall Steven, 1984, California University Press.

13. Clifford, *The Predicament of Culture*, p. 15.

14. Deleuze, *Différence et répétition*, pp. 269, 273.

15. Guyer, *Marginal Gains*.

16. Davis, *Au-delà de* Blade Runner, pp. 28–44. The recurrent practice of pillaging in certain countries suffering from social misery such as Zaire/Congo or Argentina would be particularly interesting to study from this perspective.

17. Zamiatine, *Nous autres* (written in 1920, and never published in the USSR).

18. Bayart, *Le Gouvernement du monde*, Chapter VI.

19. Foucault, *L'Usage des plaisirs*, p. 35.

20. Adelkhah, 'Economie morale du pèlerinage et société civile en Iran'; Meyer, 'Commodities and the Power of Prayer', pp. 151–76; Ashforth, *Madumo*; Marshall-Fratani, ' Prospérité miraculeuse'; Mary, 'Prophètes pasteurs', p. 79 ff.

21. Adelkhah, *La Révolution sous le voile* and *Etre moderne en Iran*, as well as 'Les Afghans iraniens'.

22. See, for example, for Istanbul, Navaro-Yashin, *Faces of the State*, p. 79, especially the chapter with the significant title 'The market for identities: buying and selling secularity and Islam'.

23. de Polignac, *La Naissance de la cité grecque*; Trexler, *Public Life in Renaissance Florence*; Brown, *Le Culte des saints*.
24. Vidal, *Images urbaines*, p. 123.
25. Dickey, *Cinema and the Urban Poor in South India*; Farges, 'Le cinéma en Inde', Chapter XXIV.
26. Adelkhah, *Etre moderne en Iran*.
27. Kandiyoti and Saktanber; Navaro-Yashin, *Faces of the State*; Havard, *Bul Faale!*.
28. ter Haar, *Halfways to Paradise*; Rodrigues, 'Pentecôtisme et identitié tsigane'.
29. Davis, *Au-delà de* Blade Runner, p. 107.
30. Appadurai, 'Disjuncture and difference in the global cultural economy'.
31. Schooyans, *Destin du Brésil*.
32. Davis, *Au-delà de* Blade Runner.
33. Parenti, *Lockdown America*.
34. Harding, 'The Mercenary Business'; Ros and Ellis, 'An insider's account of the South African Security Forces' role in the ivory trade'; Ellis, 'Africa and international corruption' and 'The historical significance of South Africa's Third Force'. On the notion of 'garrison-*entrepôt*' in a colonial context, see Roitman, 'The garrison-*entrepôt*', Chapter 22.
35. Davis, *City of Quartz*.
36. Davis, *Au-delà de* Blade Runner, p. 55 ff.
37. Pérouse, *La Turquie en marche*, p. 132: 'La question de la sécurité ne semble pas pour le moment une priorité, mais les promoteurs de complexes résidentiels sécurisés tendent à grossir les risques pour justifier leur existence.'

Contributors

Michel Agier is Anthropologist and Senior Researcher at the Institut de la Recherche pour le Développement. He directs the Center of African Studies at the Ecole des Hautes Etudes en Sciences Sociales (EHESS) in Paris, where he is Research Director. He coordinates the ASILES programme, 'Corps des Victimes, Espaces du Sujet: Réfugiés, Sinistrés et Clandestins', of the Ministère de l'Enseignement Supérieur et de la Recherche. He is member of the directing committee of the *TERRA* programme (Travaux, Études et Recherches sur les Réfugiés et l'Asile). He published several books such as *Aux Bords du Monde, les Réfugiés* (Flammarion, 2002) and *La Sagesse de l'Ethnologue* (L'Œil Neuf Editions, 2004).

Jean-François Bayart is a researcher at the Centre National de la Recherche Scientifique (CNRS) in France and specialises in comparative politics. Former director of the Centre d'Etudes et de Recherches Internationales (Paris, 1994–2000), he has been president of the Fonds d'Analyse des Sociétés Politiques in Paris since 2003. He is the founder of the journals *Politique Africaine* (1980) and *Critique Internationale* (1998), and founder and director of the collection *Recherches Internationales* at Karthala Editions (1998). He teaches historical sociology of the state at the Institut d'Etudes Politiques de Paris, the universities of Lausanne and of Turin, and at EHESS. He is the author of *L'Etat en Afrique: La politique du ventre* (Fayard, 2006), *L'Illusion identitaire* (Fayard, 1996) and *Le gouvernement du monde: Une critique politique de la globalisation* (Fayard, 2004).

Myriam Catusse is a Political Scientist and researcher at CNRS. She is currently affiliated with the Institut Français du Proche-Orient (IFPO-Beirut). Her research focuses on the social and political effects of 'neo-liberal' reforms. She participated in a study on the *Municipalities in the Field of Local Politics: Effects of Imported Models of Decentralisation on the Governance of Cities in Africa and the Middle East* (IRD, Paris, IREMAM, Aix-en-Provence, CREAD, Algiers, CERMOC, Beirut). In this framework she wrote *Municipaliser les Villes au Maroc? Le Gouvernement Urbain à l'Epreuve du Politique et du Territoire* with Raffaele Cattedra and Mohammed Idrissi, and published several articles on this topic.

Mariana Cavalcanti is a Research Fellow at the CPDOC/Getulio Vargas Foundation in Rio de Janeiro. She received her PhD from the University of Chicago's Department of Anthropology for her dissertation *Of Shacks, Houses and Fortresses: An Ethnography of Favela Consolidation in Rio de Janeiro*. She has worked in Rio de Janeiro's *favelas* since 1997 in audiovisual, social and cultural projects and, most recently, has conducted anthropological field research there.

Melhem Chaoul received his PhD from EHESS and is currently Professor of Sociology at the Lebanese University in Beirut. He has published several studies in the field of political sociology, urban studies and communication and is the author of *Association and Division* (Dar an-Nahar, 1996, in Arabic).

Barbara Drieskens is Visiting Assistant Professor at the American University in Beirut. She received her PhD in social and cultural anthropology at the Catholic University of Leuven in Belgium in 2003 and was researcher at IFPO-Beirut. She conducted fieldwork for five years for her PhD on the multiple ways of understanding and dealing with the invisible in everyday life in Cairo and participated in several projects of archeology and architecture. She is the author of the ethnography *Living with Djinns* (Saqi, 2007). Since October 2003 she has been conducting research in Beirut on the increase in female celibacy; social control and individual freedom. In December 2005 she co-organized a conference on 'Cites and Globalization: Challenges for Citizenship' at the French Institute.

Engin F. Isin is Canada Research Chair and Professor in the Division of Social Science at York University, Toronto. His research has focused on the origins and transformations of 'occidental citizenship' as a political and legal institution that enables various ways of being political. He has written numerous journal articles, book chapters, technical reports and public lectures and editorials and is the author of *Cities Without Citizens: Modernity of the City as a Corporation* (Black Rose Books, 1992), *Citizenship and Identity* with Patricia K. Wood (Sage, 1999), *Democracy, Citizenship and the Global City* (Routledge, 2000, co-editor), *Being Political: Genealogies of Citizenship* (University of Minnesota Press, 2002) *Handbook of Citizenship Studies* with Bryan S. Turner (Sage, 2002) and *Handbook of Historical Sociology* with Gerard Delanty (Sage, 2003). More recently, Professor Isin has embarked on investigations concerning 'oriental citizenship and justice' with a focus on Islamic and Ottoman institution, *waqf*.

Marc Lavergne, Geographer and Political Scientist, is a Senior Researcher at CNRS. Presently posted at the Maison de l'Orient et de la Méditerranée, Lyons-II University, he is an expert of the contemporary Arab Middle East. He has been a witness to the changes occurring in the Gulf Countries for the last thirty years. Besides numerous works dealing with the socio-economic changes in the region, he is the author and editor of *Le Soudan Contemporain* (1989), *La*

Jordanie (1996) and with B. Dumortier, *L'Oman Contemporain: Etat, Territoire, Identité* (Karthala Publishing House, 2002).

Franck Mermier received his PhD in anthropology in 1988 after conducting three years of fieldwork in Yemen. From 1991 to 1997, he was Director of the Centre Français d'Etudes Yéménites in San'a', Yemen. In 1998, he was appointed researcher at CNRS and in 2002 he became affiliated with IFPO-Beirut. Franck Mermier is currently Director of Contemporary Studies at IFPO-Beirut where he has launched several research programmes on topics such as the media, cultural production and leadership in the Near East. His research deals principally with urban societies in the Arab world.

Ayce Öncu is Professor of Sociology at Sabanci University. Her main research interests focus on issues of cultural politics in contemporary Turkey. She has published extensively in various international journals and co-edited various volumes, focusing on questions of space, culture and power in globalising cities, with special emphasis on Istanbul. She has also been involved in research networks in the Middle East, such as GURI, MEAwards, and MERC and is engaged in collaborative research with partners in the region. Her work is situated in the intersection of sociology and cultural theory.

Vyjayanthi Rao received her PhD in Anthropology from the University of Chicago and is Assistant Professor of Anthropology and International Affairs at the New School University in New York. She was previously the Research Director of the Center for Cities and Globalization at Yale University. She is working on a book project on Mumbai, tentatively titled, *Infra-City: Space, Violence and Speculation in Post-Industrial Mumbai*. She has taught courses on politics, religion and gender in contemporary South Asia; the impact of globalisation on South Asian cities; globalisation and ethnic violence; and modern social theory. Her interests include globalisation and the production of space; memory and subjectivity; and urbanism, infrastructure and technologies of the city. She is General Secretary of the Interdisciplinary Network on Globalisation, a network of Northern and Southern academic institutions on five continents.

Kim Rygiel is an Assistant Professor at Trent University in the Politics Department. She received a PhD in Political Science from York University and an MA in International Affairs from the Norman Paterson School of International Affairs at Carleton University. Her current research investigates technologies and practices of governing through citizenship in relation to processes of globalisation and securitisation. More specifically, her research focuses on understanding citizenship as a globalising regime of government in relation to surveillance and detention practices, such as biometrics and risk profiling, and the international harmonisation of asylum and detention practices. Her most recent work, *Engendering the War on Terror: War Stories* *and Camouflaged Politics* with Krista Hunt (Ashgate Press, 2006), investigates the gendered impacts of the 'war on terror'.

Diane Singerman is Associate Professor in the Department of Government at the American University. She has published *Cairo Cosmopolitan: Politics, Culture, and Urban Space in the New Globalized Middle East* with Paul Amar (American University in Cairo Press), *Avenues of Participation: Family, Politics, and Networks in Urban Quarters of Cairo* (Princeton University Press, 1995) and *Development, Change, and Gender in Cairo: A View from the Household* with Homa Hoodfar (Indiana University Press, 1996). Her work draws from the fields of comparative politics; Middle East and Egyptian politics; gender and politics in the Middle East; and scholarship on informal politics, political participation and social movements. Her recent research interests include Personal Status Law Reform; the cost of marriage; poverty and the problems faced by young people in the Middle East; and urban politics in the era of globalisation. She received her PhD in 1989 from Princeton University and did graduate work at the American University in Cairo.

Alain Tarrius is Professor of Sociology and Urban Anthropology at the University of Toulouse and has been affiliated with the Centre d'Analyse et d'Intervention Sociologiques at EHESS since 2003. As a Sociologist and Anthropologist with a comprehensive and phenomenological inspiration, he tries to grasp the contemporary expression of the historical layers of movements (of migrant populations in the first place) that are tied in with spaces and territories and continuous tensions between their mobility and their rootedness. He is engaged in the development of new notions that permit the description of these movements (the 'methodological paradigm of mobility' following four different levels of the relation space/time) and in capturing their sense within the processes of globalisation (circular territories').

Leïla Vignal is a French Geographer working on the impacts of globalisation in the Middle East. Her PhD, *Globalisation in the Middle East: Urban Change and the Emergence of a Regional System* (Cairo, Beirut, Damascus), was completed in 2006. She is currently Deakin Fellow at St Antony's College, University of Oxford.

Index